WISDOM IS A WOMAN

WISDOM *is a* WOMAN

The Canonical Metaphor of Lady Wisdom of Proverbs 1–9
Understood in Light of Theological Aesthetics

Lance Rundus

☙PICKWICK *Publications* · Eugene, Oregon

WISDOM IS A WOMAN
The Canonical Metaphor of Lady Wisdom of Proverbs 1–9 Understood in Light of Theological Aesthetics

Copyright © 2019 Lance Rundus. All rights reserved. Except for brief quotations in critical publications or reviews, no part of this book may be reproduced in any manner without prior written permission from the publisher. Write: Permissions, Wipf and Stock Publishers, 199 W. 8th Ave., Suite 3, Eugene, OR 97401.

Pickwick Publications
An Imprint of Wipf and Stock Publishers
199 W. 8th Ave., Suite 3
Eugene, OR 97401

www.wipfandstock.com

PAPERBACK ISBN: 978-1-5326-8270-4
HARDCOVER ISBN: 978-1-5326-8271-1
EBOOK ISBN: 978-1-5326-8272-8

Cataloguing-in-Publication data:

Names: Rundus, Lance, author.

Title: Wisdom is a woman : the canonical metaphor of Lady Wisdom of Proverbs 1–9 understood in light of theological aesthetics / Lance Rundus.

Description: Eugene, OR: Pickwick Publications, 2019 | **Includes bibliographical references and index.**

Identifiers: ISBN 978-1-5326-8270-4 (paperback) | ISBN 978-1-5326-8271-1 (hardcover) | ISBN 978-1-5326-8272-8 (ebook)

Subjects: LCSH: Bible.—Proverbs—Criticism, interpretation, etc. | Wisdom (Biblical personification) | Wisdom—Biblical teaching | Bible.—Proverbs I–IX—Criticism, interpretation, etc. | Women in the Bible

Classification: BS1465.52 R86 2019 (print) | BS1465.52 (ebook)

Manufactured in the U.S.A.　　　　　　　　　　　　　　DECEMBER 3, 2019

Biblia Hebraica Stuttgartensia, hg. v. Karl Elliger und Wilhelm Rudolph, fünfte, verbesserte Auflage, hg. v. Adrian Schenker, © 1977 und 1997 Deutsche Bibelgesellschaft, Stuttgart

Scripture quotations marked (ESV) are from ESV® Bible (*The Holy Bible, English Standard Version*®, Copyright © 2001 by Crossway, a publishing ministry of Good News Publishers. All rights reserved. ESV Text Edition: 2016

To the LORD and to my family who have been the vehicles of his strength, encouragement, and love

Contents

List of Illustrations / viii

Preface / ix

Acknowledgments / xi

Abbreviations / xiii

1   Introduction / 1

2   Methodological Challenges / 24

3   Hemispheric Balance and Methodological Stability / 53

4   The Diversity and Paradox of Lady Wisdom in Proverbs 1–2 and the Diversity and Paradox of the Triune God / 83

5   Women and the Divine / 118

6   Wise or Strange? / 164

7   Faithful Desire / 222

Appendix A / 237

Appendix B / 239

Appendix C / 243

Appendix D / 245

Appendix E / 250

Bibliography / 253

Author Index | 265

Scripture Index | 267

List of Illustrations

1. Diego Velázquez, *Venus At The Mirror (Rokeby Venus)* / 3
2. Source-Target Mapping / 71
3. Metonymy / 73
4. Hierarchy of Metaphor / 79
5. Virus Integration Network / 80
6. Metaphor and Structure in Proverbs 2 / 104
7. Diego Velázquez, *Christ after the Flagellation Contemplated by the Christian Soul* / 234
8. Simplex Network / 245
9. Mirror Network / 246
10. Double Scope Network / 248

Preface

> "We are all going on an Expedition," said Christopher Robin, as he got up and brushed himself. "Thank you, Pooh."
>
> "Going on an Expotition?" said Pooh eagerly. "I don't think I've ever been on one of those. Where are we going to on this Expotition?"
>
> "Expedition, silly old Bear. It's got an 'x' in it."
>
> "Oh!" said Pooh. "I know." But he didn't really.
>
> "We're going to discover the North Pole."
>
> "Oh!" said Pooh again. "What is the North Pole?" he asked.
>
> "It's just a thing you discover," said Christopher Robin carelessly, not being quite sure himself.
>
> "Oh! I see," said Pooh. "Are bears any good at discovering it?"
>
> "Of course they are. And Rabbit and Kanga and all of you. It's an Expedition. That's what an Expedition means. A long line of everybody."[1]

So it seems with the search for Wisdom. We join "a long line of everybody" but at the same time nobody seems precisely sure what it is that we are looking for. There is an assumption that we will know it when we find it but a great diversity of thoughts about precisely what it might look like. This book sets out to address this simple question by means of the metaphor of *Lady Wisdom* that is found in the first nine chapters of the book of Proverbs and it seeks to do so by examining the canonical presentation of *WOMAN* as she is presented in the book of Proverbs. After much study, my conclusion is that feminine imagery in Proverbs is employed to accent *relational fidelity* as the cornerstone of what we call Wisdom and that

---

1. Milne, *Winnie-the-Pooh Story Book*, 189–90.

this quality is best exemplified in the Triune witness born in the person, life, death, and resurrection of Jesus Christ.

In writing, however, I have been placed in a curious position. Relational fidelity is always figured as faithfulness to someone. Academic writing requires a certain commitment to the scholarly community and academic convention. Simultaneously, I am writing not only for the academic community, but for Christians on several continents. For the first audience I have maintained the literature review, provided the Masoretic text, an extensive treatment of the scholarly discussion of the translation, and a careful discussion of the underlying assumptions and theological ramifications of metaphor. For the second audience I have translated all excerpts into English and tried to the best of my ability to erase the division that sometimes exists between "scholar and saint." Ultimately, the work endeavors to be faithful to the LORD by being faithful to his children.

The methods employed in this work are heavily influenced by theological aesthetics, canonical theology, and theological exegesis (especially as practiced by Dr. Willem VanGemeren). This is in no way intended to dismiss diachronic or higher critical methods. Wisdom is not found in methodology, but in the relational fidelity in which such methods are employed. As such, any silence on higher critical or diachronic questions should not be considered dismissive.

This work proceeds in a given direction determined by a few commitments. First is a commitment not only to determine how previous efforts at discovering *Lady Wisdom* have been educative or damaging, but a consideration of how our cultural theory of knowledge may undercut our ability to *gain wisdom* and provide methods adequate to our expedition. Second, since *beauty* is to guide and clarify our search for Wisdom, I present the Masoretic Text of Proverbs because it is beautiful. The translation of this text, however, is less so. I have maintained a wooden and sometimes awkward translation to preserve, as much as possible, the alien-ness of the text (following from the translation philosophy of Lawrence Venuti and others).

Finally, in discussion of metaphors I have employed the conventions popularized by Lackoff and Turner. When metaphors or components of metaphors are discussed they are presented in italic, all-capital letters (i.e., *WISDOM IS A WOMAN*). *Lady Wisdom* and the *Strange Woman* appear in lower case italic characters because these are personifications frequently drawn from a combination of texts throughout the book of Proverbs. With these preliminary comments, let us begin our "expotition."

Acknowledgments

Words are poor payment for the substance of faith, love, and commitment shown by so many for so long. There are many people who have aided in the process, direction, and writing of this work. The support of these many is beyond the tiny scope of this acknowledgment. Yet I would be remiss not to at least mention the outpouring of support from our little area in North Central Kansas. I have been blessed by the tireless encouragement, assistance, and prayer of some of our local pastors: Bruce Burfield, Fred Mikesell, and Wade Moss as well as a number of churches in our area. Moreover, our little public library went to extreme lengths to request books for me from around the world. I am humbled and honored to be a part of this body of Christ. Know that I have and do praise the LORD for your timely guidance, help, and encouragement. In addition to these many there are a few without whom this work could not have been written. First, numerous professors at Trinity provided encouragement and instruction, but chief among these are: my mentor, Dr. Willem VanGemeren, the program head, Dr. Richard Averbeck, and my second reader, Dr. John Monson. For Dr. VanGemeren in particular, words fall short of my debt of gratitude. I can only pray that the LORD will repay what I cannot. His immense patience, open-mindedness, and guidance, supplemented at times by the wisdom and encouragement of Dr. Averbeck, may be credited for much of the good that can be found in this work. Likewise, as an extension of the Trinity family of scholars I must also offer my gratitude to Dr. Stephen Garrett for his expertise, input, and encouragement specifically in the domain of theological aesthetics. Second, my North American Baptist family were the impetus, substance, and support that enabled this project. NAB churches from Texas to Edmonton supported and sustained us for many years. Drs. Dennis and Nancy Palmer encouraged me to begin the project and supported me emotionally and materially throughout. Dr. Jerry and Monie Fluth kept me accountable and challenged me to stay engaged with the real life of the church. Rev. Tim and Amy Moline prayed for us daily and commended me to be faithful in discharging the task. Finally, those who sacrificed the most for the longest are my parents-in-law, my sons, my daughters, my wife, and my parents. I can only say, "Thank you."

Abbreviations

ANE	Ancient Near East
ANET	Ancient Near Eastern Texts Relating to the Old Testament
AJSL	American Journal of Semitic Languages and Literature
AT	Alten Testament
CBQ	Catholic Biblical Quarterly
CMT	Cognitive Metaphor Theory
ET	English Translation
GKC	Gesenius, Kautsch, Cowley Hebrew Grammar
HALOT	Hebrew and Aramaic Lexicon of the Old Testament
ICC	International Critical Commentary
IJST	International Journal of Systematic Theology
LXX	Septuagint
OLZ	Orientalistische Litteratur-Zeitung
SPAW	Sitzungsberichte der preussischen Akademie der Wissenschaften
SBL	Society of Biblical Literature
SPCK	Society for Promoting Christian Knowledge
SVT	Supplements to Vetus Testamentum
MT	Masoretic Text
TrinJ	Trinity Journal

1

Introduction

A Survey of Difficulties in the Treatment of the Metaphor of Lady Wisdom

IN Proverbs 1–9, the abstract concept of wisdom is personified as a woman; as such this *Lady Wisdom* exists as a metaphor in which some qualities of what we know as *a woman* are intended to teach us something about what we do not know about wisdom. Following a traditional definition of metaphor, the term *woman* may be described as a *vehicle* or *source* because it functions as a source of concepts or *entailments* which then are to be purposefully understood in relation to the *tenor* or *target* of the metaphor (i.e., wisdom). So, in the metaphor, "This room is a pig-sty." The *source* category, *pig sty*, is chosen to provide elements of comparison to the *target* category of *room*. In this case the relative disorder of the room is to be illustrated with regard to the housekeeping habits of swine. Therefore, in light of the discussion of personified wisdom (*Lady Wisdom*), common sense would dictate that something about *woman* is supposed to provide the reader with insight about *wisdom*. However, as will be seen in the literature review, the metaphor of WISDOM IS A WOMAN[1] has been historically problematic, with interpreters substituting a wide range of different source categories in place of that set forth by the text. Therefore, the ultimate aim of this work is to consider what elements of *women* and *womanhood* are

---

1. Turner and Lackoff conventionalized the presentation of metaphors in this manner, italicized and printed in all capitals in either the form TARGET IS SOURCE or *SOURCE AS TARGET*. In this manner, the reader is made aware that we are speaking of both elements of the source-target relationship as well as its metaphorical entailments.

highlighted in Proverbs 1–9, and how these entailments help us to approach and understand wisdom as an abstract entity.

However, this ultimate aim is immediately complicated by reality. First, the historic difficulty in establishing clear entailments for the metaphor of *WISDOM IS A WOMAN* is due in large part to the lack of a clear, consistent and meaningful definition of metaphor. Without an understanding of what metaphor is (i.e., ornamental function of speech or organizing function of mind) and how it works within a poetic text there will be a necessary unraveling of stable conclusions. Second, as will be seen in the review of literature, in too many cases the *target* of the metaphor—that of *acquiring wisdom*—has been lost in the search of the identity of the metaphorical *vehicle* or *source*. As will be illustrated below, many studies end up being so focused upon *Lady Wisdom*, that they lose track of the fact that the *woman* part of the metaphor only exists to provide and understanding of the *wisdom* part. In the following study, the aim of *understanding* and *obtaining* wisdom must remain central. However, this presents yet another subsidiary problem. In the book of Proverbs the experience of wisdom is deeply *inter-subjective* and dependent upon the correct inward disposition of the reader. As such the ambiguous poetic expression that is characteristic of wisdom is adversarial to the scientific empiricism of the modern west. Wisdom challenges our western materialistic and empirical epistemology and therefore our basic assumptions of perception, knowledge, and ontology. As will be discussed at greater length below, wisdom is characteristic of right hemispheric thinking that is essentially relational, empathetic, perceptive, and *aesthetic* in nature. In this it is helpful to consider an illustration from the world of art.

Engaging *Lady Wisdom* in Proverbs 1–9 is akin to approaching Diego Velázquez's, *Venus at her Mirror* (aka *Rokeby Venus*) (fig. 1). Approaching this work as though it were a linear string of propositions, or endeavoring to discover the historical background, would bring us no nearer to understanding the deified personification of love that reclines both openly and obscurely before us. Rather, the aesthetic requires a different sort of perception:

Figure 1. Diego Velázquez, *Venus at the Mirror (Rokeby Venus)*, (1648–51, oil on canvas, 122.5 x 177 cm, National Gallery, London).

It is a double gaze, rather than a fleeting one, that bears in mind both the specific and the ideal, capable of perceiving a synthesis of both. By rendering his almost faceless Venus anonymous, Velázquez has a great deal of leeway because her body lends itself to both these ways of seeing and is thus ideal for the projection of a blend of individual form and standardized construct. Velázquez takes the impossibility of seeing and perceiving precisely and turns it into a key artistic element of his painting. In the unclear contours of the face, he dissolves the identity of this apparently so individualized body and denies the viewer the certainty of seeing the gaze of Venus in the image of this woman.[2]

To really experience this artwork is a complex matrix of careful attention, reflection and openness that transcends a simple true-false propositionalism. Our attention to *Lady Wisdom* within the pages of scripture should be no less enthralling and no less rigorous. In the same way that one

2. Prader, *Venus at Her Mirror*, 50.

might take a seat across from the *Rokeby Venus* in the National Gallery in London, we shall endeavor in what follows to trace the contours *of Lady Wisdom's* face in Proverbs in light of the broader context of the diverse and dichotomous presentation of woman in the book of Proverbs.

As an opening caveat, it is important to note that both *Lady Wisdom* and the *Rokeby Venus* exist in some sense as "dangerous pictures." For the *Rokeby Venus*, it was produced in defiance of the dictates of the Spanish Inquisition regarding nude painting, by a Spaniard at the height of the Inquisition's power.[3] As early as 1640, Spanish artists who painted female nudes were threatened with excommunication, fines and banishment.[4] Despite this fact, Velázquez not only painted a nude but painted a nude from a live model.[5] Moreover, the *Venus* is painted life-size, or *aequalitas*, a mode typically reserved for religious work.

> Velázquez's *Venus* is a "dangerous" picture due to its quality of *aequalitas*. Not only because it portrays the goddess of love in life-size, but also because it presents her body in the foreground of the picture without any perspectival foreshortening of distance. Compositional means are used to emphasize what "life-size" implies: the *similtudo* of appearance with that portrayed, *aequalitas* that transcends the boundary of mere *imago* and raises a claim to direct reality.[6]

In a very similar way, *Lady Wisdom* is a dangerous picture because first of all she is described in terms and metaphors reserved for YHWH himself.

---

3. Prader believes that it is most likely that Velázquez produced the work while in Italy for a number of reasons. First, Spain's severe "anti-nude" laws did not extend to other nations. Second, because of the law finding female models in Spain was very difficult. Artists were reduced to appealing to family members, prostitutes, or using statues or other classical models (Prader, *Venus at Her Mirror*, 54–57). Moreover, the "unfinished" style of the painting points to the likelihood of a later date when Velázquez was endeavoring to break into the nobility. The most likely times are therefore between 1648 and 1651 (Prader, *Venus at Her Mirror*, 25–26).

4. Prader, *Venus at Her Mirror*, 54.

5. "It is generally taken for granted that Velázquez's *Venus at the Mirror* was painted from life. The vitality of her appearance alone precludes the notion that Velázquez might have worked from ancient or paper models.... There is even a possibility, that we do know who she was, if only indirectly. While he was in Rome, Velázquez had a relationship with a woman who bore him a son. The child, according to contemporary legal records, was cared for by a nursemaid when Velázquez returned to Spain. In Rome, artists working with nude models were not threatened with such drastic sanctions as they were in Spain, and so it was perfectly conceivable that, as so often happened, the model became the artist's lover—or vice versa" (Prader, *Venus at Her Mirror*, 58).

6. Prader, *Venus at Her Mirror*, 58.

As such she seems to threaten the very idea of monotheism. Through the history of interpretation, the existence of such a vaunted female depiction becomes a problem to be explained away through various types of allegorical interpretation. On the other side, the terms and images chosen to describe *Lady Wisdom* are also dangerously close to those used to describe her antitype, the *Strange Woman*. However, the poet uses these dichotomous characters to educate desire and highlight the central role of fidelity to divine covenant and human relationships as the central quality for discerning and obtaining wisdom.

In what remains of chapter 1, we will briefly survey the academic framing of the book of Proverbs as a whole and then proceed to examine the categories and methods previous scholarship has employed to make sense of the metaphor of feminine personification of Wisdom in Proverbs 1–9. Then we will briefly restate the main elements of the research project and provide a summary of the remaining chapters and projected significance of the study.

Review of Literature

Pre-critical Approaches

In the earliest vestiges of Jewish interpretation as they are preserved in Ben Sirach and Wisdom of Solomon, *Lady Wisdom* becomes a full-fledged and mystical entity who calls for union with the sage.[7] Meanwhile, in Intertestamental Literature as a whole there is a much stronger negative role for feminine imagery, even as sapiential discourse becomes more theological, devotional, sectarian and esoteric.[8] Over time the notion of the "mystic"

---

7. The Qumran documents preserve an even more spiritually erotic version of Ben Sirach which depicts the mystical union of the sage with Lady Wisdom. "I bestirred my desire for her, and on her heights I could not relax. I spread my 'hand' . . . and perceived her nakedness" (IIQPS 21–22). The LXX subdues the eroticism of the Qumran document by interposing more pious and abstract language, "I directed my soul toward her, and in my deeds I was exact. I stretched my hands on high and perceived her secrets."

8. While this generalization is broadly accepted by scholarship the dichotomous presentation of woman in Ben Sirach is illustrative. In 36:21–26, a wife is depicted as a pillar, a hedge, and valuable possession without which a man is rootless and insecure. Conversely in 42:9–14, the birth of daughters is a hardship and the "courtesy of woman" is depicted as less than the "churlishness of man." On the balance, Sir 26:10–27 explains how the fortunes of a man are wrapped up in the identity of the woman with whom he is paired; the wise with the wise and the foolish with the foolish. These texts suggest a fuller and more balanced understanding of feminine imagery than that reflected by much of modern scholarship.

identity of *Lady Wisdom* is largely abandoned, and instead wisdom in the abstract becomes conflated with Torah.[9] While the rabbis were certainly aware of the superficial meaning of the metaphor, WOMAN as source of concepts illustrating wisdom is changed to a target category to be explained via allusion to other scriptural contexts. The problematic identity of *Lady Wisdom* is resolved by making her equivalent to a personification of Torah.[10]

In most ways, early Christian interpretation mirrors that of the Jews. While many early interpreters spoke of Wisdom precisely as a literary trope, the correspondence between *Lady Wisdom* in Proverbs and of Christ the only-begotten became progressively more problematic. The crux of this interpretative difficulty came with the growth of the Arian controversy, centered in their interpretation of Prov 8:22, wherein the Arians asserted that Christ was equivalent to the first-created *Lady Wisdom* and therefore not a member of the Godhead.[11] In the wake of this theological conflict, parallels between Christ and *Lady Wisdom* became suspect.

Interestingly, there is theological common ground between Jew and Christian for most of a thousand years of interpretation. Whether *Lady Wisdom* is understood as a mystical abstraction, Torah or Christ, she represents an entity that puts the student into correct *relationship* with the created order and God. Creation theology is not primarily descriptive, but merely predicates claims of Torah, Christ, or the church. Depictions of "dangerous women" are understood primarily as literal and immediate dangers to life and purity, even if taken as a symbol for some greater risk. Conversely, the "good women" are not so treated. In all interpretations of Prov 5, sexual imagery is recognized but transcended to attach to theological ideals that are consonant with interpretations of Song of Songs. Despite a greater variance in establishing the referent of Prov 31, the method is typically allegorical and textual connections to the book of Ruth are ignored. Ruth remains merely historical while the poetry is urged on to what are deemed deeper spiritual and relational ideals. Finally, any overarching understanding of an opposed dichotomy of the *Strange Woman* vs. *Lady Wisdom* is absent in the interpretation of this era.

In short, for most pre-critical interpreters womanhood stopped being a source category that illuminated wisdom. Rather, she became an embodiment of Torah, the church, the righteous, the soul or any number of other allegorical target categories. The depth of the imagery was maintained, but

---

9. For a complete consideration of the development and fusion of Law and Wisdom in intertestamental literature, see Schnabel, *Law and Wisdom*.

10. Cf. Vistotzky, *Midrash on Proverbs*, 26–28.

11. Wright, *Proverbs, Ecclesiastes, Song of Songs*, 59–67.

the locus and control of that meaning was frequently unhinged. Instead of looking into the face of woman to find wisdom, the interpreters found ways of using *other* metaphorical sources in place of feminine metaphor via *allegoresis*.

Critical Approaches

By the late-eighteenth and early-nineteenth centuries there was disagreement as to *when* the book of Proverbs was written and who wrote it but nearly unanimous agreement on the book's nature and function. Whybray notes, "A number of commentaries on the book were published during the latter half of the nineteenth century but these offered little assessment of its theology; the Old Testament theologies of the period also showed little interest in it . . . Proverbs seems in fact to have been generally regarded as a rather commonplace and pedestrian moral handbook with little theological content."[12]

The research focus of many studies at the turn of the twentieth century was upon the personification of Wisdom as a woman in chapters 8 and 9 with attention being divided between finds in Mesopotamia and Egypt. However, with the publication of *Second Series of Facsimiles of Egyptian Hieratic Papyri in the British Museum, London, Plates I–XIV*, by E.W. Budge in 1923, comparative studies of Proverbs took a new turn.[13] Critical scholarship shifted to determining the relationship between these documents. For the next 60 years Amenemope dominated critical discussions of Proverbs. If a direct material dependence could be shown this dependence would resolve more general interpretive arguments.[14]

---

12. Whybray, *Book of Proverbs*, 115.

13. These papyrus documents had actually been brought to the London Museum by E. W. Budge in 1888 but had remained unpublished. In the following years, "The Instruction of Amenemope," replaced the archival title. In 1924, A. Erman and H. Gressman argued that Proverbs was a substandard imitation of "The Instruction of Amenemope." In response, E. W. Budge produced his own translation and commentary of Amenemope wherein he argued that the Egyptian document had been influenced by Semitic ideas during the Middle Kingdom. This translation of *The Instruction* remains the most frequently referenced English translation to this day.

14. R.N. Whybray writes: "It is perhaps surprising that the controversy still appears to flourish more than sixty years after the publication of Amenemope. Although Prov 22:17–24:22 constitute only a very small part of the book of Proverbs and these chapters are somewhat different in character from the major parts of the book, and although most of the discussions of the international affinities of Proverbs have moved on to more general grounds, this continued preoccupation is no doubt due to the fact that direct dependence of even a single text on another, if proven, may be supposed to carry

From the very beginning of the comparative study of Proverbs certain scholars pointed out non-Egyptian parallels, mainly from Aramaic (i.e., *Ahiqar*) but also Assyrian, Akkadian and Ugaritic. It was not, however, until the 1960's when the wealth of comparative literature caused a loosening of the grip of *Amenemope* on the scholarly imagination.[15] As more and more examples of Egyptian and Mesopotamian sapiential literature have become available, scholarly interest has grown both more general in scope and more interested in the particular communicative agenda of Proverbs.[16] In the late 1960s scholarship began to embrace the dawning realization that the provenance and redactional history of Proverbs might be beyond reconstruction.[17] At the same time a renewed interest in Hebrew poetry, parallelism and form turned the methodological tide away from questions of provenance and redaction and toward the content and structure of the book.[18]

Whybray notes a broad consensus in modern critical scholarship at the turn of the twenty-first century on ten basic points. First, scholars agreed that Proverbs says nothing about Israel's historical or theological particulars. Second, it was universally acknowledged that there is some relationship between Israel's wisdom literature and that of her neighbors. The nature and extent of that relationship is debatable but the existence of some relationship is assumed. Third, most scholars agreed that Proverbs is concerned with practical advice for the individual living in community. Fourth, Proverbs was understood as a basically optimistic book untroubled with the doubts of reflective theology. Fifth, Proverbs is unsystematic. Sixth,

---

more weight than a host of more general arguments" (Whybray, *Book of Proverbs*, 12).

15. In particular, during the early ascendancy of Amenemope, W. Baumgartner pointed to the likelihood of Aramaic and Mesopotamian influence on the book of Proverbs. Even earlier W. O. E. Oesterly had not only cast doubt on the primacy of Amenemope as an interpretive model, but also noted clear parallels with *Ahiqar* and suggested that there was a "common stock" of sapiential thought in the ANE.

16. "During recent years a number of Egyptologists have questioned the previously universal opinion that Amenemope and Prov 22:17 are directly connected. This new tendency is largely the consequence of a greatly increased knowledge of Egyptian literature and a vast increase in the number of comparable Egyptian texts now available: the recent collection of translations of ancient Egyptian *Lehren* or Instruction by H. Brunner includes no less than seventeen texts belonging to the genre together with more than twenty other relevant texts whose dates range from the Old Kingdom to the Greek period (from c. 2530 to c. 300 BC)—in fact, a whole literature which was probably even more extensive than the extant examples" (Whybray, *Book of Proverb*, 13).

17. Cf. Murphy, "Assumptions and Problems," 101–12.

18. While comparative treatments of wisdom literature continue unabated, the 1970s witnessed a renewed concern in form and purpose of the Proverbs (e.g., Hermisson, *Studien zur israelitischen Spruchweisheit*) and a renewed interest in the theological function of the book (e.g., Rad and Martin, *Wisdom in Israel*).

Proverbs was deemed to be concerned with the relationship between deeds and consequences.[19] Seventh, while much of Proverb's advice was understood as "practical" and seemingly secular in nature, at least some of the material was deemed ethically or religiously motivated. Eighth, Proverbs is monotheistic throughout. There is no mention, nor assumption of polytheism. Ninth, most recognized that Proverbs teaches wisdom as the key to life and that this is available to all but the most incorrigible. Tenth, in Prov 1–9 Wisdom is portrayed as a woman and is characterized as a gift of God.[20]

Conversely, Whybray notes ten areas of research where the field has been divided.[21] First, is Proverbs a literary unity?[22] Second, there remain significant dissension as to whether the portrayal of God within the book of Proverbs is consistent with or divergent from that in the rest of the Old Testament.[23] Third, should Proverbs be deemed as divine revelation or merely the product of human experience?[24] Fourth, though the "secular versus religious" argument of former days had been mostly settled, there was still an open question as to how Proverbs relates to the religion of the

---

19. This relationship may be figured as "retribution theology" in the classical sense or as with Koch and others as a "Deed-Consequence nexus" where the outcome of the action is inherent in the deed itself. See Koch, "Gibt es ein Vergeltungsdogma?," 1–42; Crenshaw, *Theodicy in the Old Testament*, 57–87.

20. Whybray, *Book of Proverbs*, 112–13.

21. Whybray, *Book of Proverbs*, 113–14.

22. Throughout the history of Proverbs it seems that the assumption of many scholars was that a lack of uniformity in style and substance automatically required a commensurate lack of unity. Since O. Eissfeldt's "Der Maschal im Alten Testament," there has been an ongoing conversation about the provenance and unity of the book. Eissfeldt and Plöger suggested that Proverbs was loosely organized around *catchwords* (*Stichworte*) wherein one topic was linked to another by loose association (see Wolff, *Probleme biblischer Theologie*, 402–416). One of the best recent entries into the discussion is Meinhold who argues that there is a complex redactional unity that can be demonstrated within the book based upon the placement of Proverbs pertaining to the "Fear of Yahweh" (Meinhold, *Die Sprüche*, 1:1–50).

23. H. D. Preuss argues that not only is the god of Proverbs *not* consistent with the portrayal of Yahweh in the Old Testament, but rather argues that it *is* entirely consistent with the portrayal of pagan deities in Egypt and Mesopotamia (Preuss, "Das Gottesbild," 116–45). At the other end of the spectrum, F. J. Steiert argues that Proverbs is in accordance with the teaching of the Law and the Prophets, and discordant with contemporaneous material in the ANE (see Steiert, *Die Weisheit Israels*, 307–8).

24. Alt's assessment of Proverbs as a poor-quality Hebrew reproduction of Amenemope is among the lowest assessments of the inspiration of Proverbs, wherein the book not only lacks inspiration, but literary artistry as well (see Alt, "Zur literarische Analyse des Amenemope," 16–25). On the other hand, Bruce Waltke surveys a number of different passages outside of wisdom literature that show that Proverbs should be read as inspired and authoritative (see Waltke, "Authority of Proverbs," 65–78).

Old Testament.[25] Fifth, the nature and function of punishment in the book remains disputed. Should the consequences of actions be read as divine retribution for sin or does each action itself bear with it the seed of the outcomes?[26] Sixth, but related to the third, scholars disagreed as to whether Proverbs should be read in agreement with the Law and the Prophets as categorically binding instructions, or whether it should be read merely as exhortation and advice to be heeded only relative to given situations.[27] Seventh, is Proverbs dependent upon creation theology?[28] Eighth, does Proverbs attest to an independent and discoverable world order akin to the Egyptian notion of *ma'at*?[29] Ninth, specifically with regard to sentence lit-

---

25. For example, E. Gerstenberger argued that the admonition form of Proverbs (*Mahnung*) derived from traditional oral wisdom (*Sippenweisheit*) that was the common root of wisdom writings and Torah (see Gerstenberger, *Wesen und Herkunft*). On the other hand, R. D. Moore speaks not of how oral traditions formed wisdom, but rather how the process of canonization shaped the material of Proverbs for theological reasons (see Moore, "Home for the Alien," 96–107). Specifically in regard to the interaction between wisdom and the cult, the only significant treatment has been by L.G. Perdue, *Wisdom and Cult*.

26. Until K. Koch (1955) it was broadly assumed that Proverbs asserted a bare retribution theology, wherein violation of laws and mores resulted in the intentional judgment of YHWH. In "Gibt es ein Vergeltungsdogma im Alten Testament?" Koch argued that in the majority of cases wherein judgment is described, neither YHWH nor punishment is mentioned. Rather, Koch argued for an impersonal machinery in which the action itself contained the seed of the consequence. The notion of this "deed-consequence nexus" generated considerable controversy and no small amount of consensus. See Koch "Gibt es ein Vergeltungsdogma?," 1–42. On the other hand, H. Gese argued that while there was a "fundamental order" to the world, this order was still a direct result of YHWH's agency. YHWH's agency in these actions is not mentioned because it is assumed. See Gese, *Lehre und Wirklichkeit*, 33–34. G. von Rad synthesizes the views of Koch and Gese in Rad, *Theologie des Alten Testaments I*, 436–41.

27. Although much early critical scholarship viewed Proverbs merely as a "practical handbook" with little theological import, the first scholar to argue for a distinction for understanding the imperatives in Proverbs was W. Zimmerli in 1933. He argued that Proverbs was *not* dependent upon divine inspiration, but on human advice and was therefore not categorical in nature but rather hortatory. It was meant only to advise, not to command.

28. W. Zimmerli, G. von Rad, and H. J. Hermisson assert in different ways that wisdom is founded in creation theology. See Zimmerli, "Ort und Grenze der Weisheit" 121–37; "Place and Limit," 146–58; Hermisson, "Observations on Creation Theology." The most direct refutation of the notion of creation theology is that of P. Doll who argues particularly against Hermisson, that his argument is based upon isolated texts, which Doll argues, are later insertions. See Doll, *Menschenschöpfung und Weltschäpfung*.

29. As noted above, Egyptian parallels with Proverbs were noted early in the history of critical research, but it was not until C. Kayatz's *Studien zu Proverbien 1–9* (1966) that scholarly attention was drawn to possible parallels between הכמה and *Ma'at*. G. von Rad accepted and perpetuated this view in his *Old Testament Theology* (1957) and *Weisheit*

erature, is it heterogeneous in appearance but homogenous in provenance or does it constitute a redactional unity?[30] Tenth, what is the origin, nature, and function of personified wisdom in Prov 1–9?

In the last twenty years, scholarly activity has continued unabated, with an exponential proliferation of method and viewpoint, however, scholarship appears to be no nearer a consensus on any of these points. While this work will touch on a number of the areas in which modern scholarship is divided, the area of chief concern is with the origin, nature and function of personified Wisdom in Prov 1–9. It should be noted, however, that a great deal of earlier critical research was concerned primarily with *objective* questions of proposition, provenance and form, while omitting questions of relationship, motivation and ontology.

Modern critical scholarship on Prov 1–9 has generally focused upon the historical source and significance of the *rhetorical* metaphor of *Lady Wisdom* and bypassed the concern for relationship as it is set forth in the canon. The typical approach has been to shift the source category for the metaphor from *WOMAN* to *DEITY* and then pursue a meaningful historical referent in one or a composite of female deities found in the ANE. In the following sections we will survey how different regions and eras are used to explain the metaphor of *Lady Wisdom* in Proverbs 1–9.[31]

Babylonian Deities as a Metaphorical Source

The first major historical and comparative treatment of *Lady Wisdom* came in 1920 when W.F. Albright proposed that the personification of wisdom as a woman was derived from a Mesopotamian deity which was filtered through the Aramaic *Sayings of Ahiqar* which in turn was reimagined in Hebrew.[32] While the connections to Albright's proposed goddess could not be substantiated, the race was on to determine the historical referent which would

---

in Israel (1970), but this view has since come under considerable criticism as will be discussed in greater detail below.

30. Although earlier critical scholarship found attempts at discovering structure within sentence literature dubious, recent years have witnessed a renewal of interest in the canonical form and function of Proverbs. In addition to the previously noted work of A. Meinhold, Van Leeuwen, *Context and Meaning in Proverbs 25–27*; Whybray, *Interpretation*, 83–96; Heim, *Poetic Imagination in Proverbs* argue for a purposeful structure within the sentence literature.

31. This brief review is not intended to be understood in anyway as being exhaustive, but rather to provide a few examples of types of conceptual framing provided by different scholars in the modern period.

32. Albright, "Goddess of Life and Wisdom," 258–94.

make sense of *Lady Wisdom*.³³ Gustav Boström attempted to understand the duality of *Lady Wisdom* opposed to the *Strange Woman* by understanding the *Strange Woman* as a devotee of the worship of Babylonian Ishtar. By analogy, *Lady Wisdom* becomes a figurative reference for orthodox worship of YHWH. Unfortunately, this requires an understanding of the word for "outside woman" (נכריה) that is not necessarily established by the text. Furthermore, this interpretation either forces the metaphor into an allegorical mold not signaled within the text or implies that *Lady Wisdom* should be figured as a consort to YHWH.³⁴

Egyptian Deity as a Metaphorical Source

While connections between Proverbs and Egyptian Instructional Literature had been noted by E.A. Wallis Budge from 1922–1924,³⁵ Egyptian sources were not brought to bear on the discussion of *Lady Wisdom* until 1966. In this year Christa Bauer-Kayatz proposed that the Egyptian goddess *Ma'at* provided a suitable parallel for *Lady Wisdom*. Using a formal methodology that drew elements from first-person speeches, royal and funerary inscriptions, Bauer-Kayatz showed a number of common representations that seemed to draw *Ma'at* and *Lady Wisdom* into parity. Notions of rulership, order, garlands, life and wisdom in the hand: all seemed to suggest a borrowing of one sort or another. Unfortunately, methodological problems undercut most of Bauer-Kayatz's conclusions.³⁶

---

33. The problem of importing a foreign goddess into the pages of Proverbs was addressed by H. Ringgren who proposed that the depiction of wisdom in Proverbs is a *hypostasis* of YHWH's wisdom, wherein that particular attribute was isolated from YHWH himself and given its own will and personality. He asserts that where this process normally produced new gods in polytheistic pantheons, in Israel's case the process was stunted because of orthodox monotheism (Ringgren, *Word and Wisdom*, 23–24). Unfortunately, Ringgren was not able to prove Lady Wisdom's status as a hypostasis, nor to provide any evidence that would substantiate the existence of such a process in Israel.

34. Boström, *Weisheit*, 28–32.

35. Budge, *Teaching of Amen-em-apt*. At around the same time A. Erman produced his influential article that opened the field for comparative treatment of Egyptian and Hebrew documents. See Erman, "Das Weishetsbuch," 241–52.

36. The documents and imagery compared are too greatly removed in genre, time, and function. *Ma'at* is never given personified depiction in any of the Egyptian instructional literature. In the *Book of the Dead*, *Ma'at* is concerned with the attainment of eternal life unlike Lady Wisdom, whose concerns are pragmatic. See Bauer-Kayatz, *Studien zu Proverbien 1–9*, 87–92.

Speculative Israelite Goddess as Metaphorical Source

Bernhard Lang is similar to Bauer-Kayatz in his intention of framing *Lady Wisdom* as a goddess, but instead of a foreign goddess he proposes that she is the residue of a former *Israelite* goddess of Wisdom. He has been most effective in establishing the rhetorical purpose of feminine metaphor as a complex progression wherein the young man is motivated by gendered desire. Lang asserts that there are four reasons for the choice of WOMAN as the metaphorical source category for depicting wisdom. (1) The grammatical gender of *Ḥokmah* is feminine; (2) feminine personification was relatively commonplace in ancient Israel (i.e., Daughter, Maiden of Zion, etc.); (3) this metaphor fit neatly with the ANE notion of royal goddesses who were said to protect the king and his officials; and (4) finally, he asserts that figuring wisdom as woman allowed the abstract value to be described in erotic and relational categories that would appeal to young men. He grants that the speeches of personified wisdom do not themselves employ erotic speech but those of the surrounding lectures *do* employ erotic imagery for just these ends (e.g., Prov 7:4). In this manner the trope of *Lady Wisdom* serves not only to make the curriculum more palatable, but also by means of the warning against illicit relationships exhorts scholarly diligence and faithfulness.[37] "Vom Schüler wird *geistiger Eros* gefordert, und die attraktive Gestalt der Frau Weishet hat gewiß dazu beigetragen, daß dieser Forderung entrsprochen wurde."[38] *Lady Wisdom* becomes an educational centerfold; a spokesmodel for wisdom, so to speak.

In most of these earlier critical treatments the role of gendered metaphor in Proverbs and the surrounding canonical books is assumed but bypassed. First, meaning was predicated upon authorial provenance and setting. Scholarship generally agreed in its assumption that the writings as a whole and Proverbs in particular were the product of disparate authorship through time. Any unity in text, theme, or metaphor were therefore conceived of as secondary accretions and therefore corrupted the human authors' intended meaning. Second, since the purpose of historical and comparative work was to understand the author and audience of the most primitive document; history and extrabiblical exemplars became the criteria for discerning what was original to the text. Canonical transmission and acceptance were not part of attaining theological normativity but rather an obstacle.

---

37. Lang, *Frau Weisheit*, 171.
38. Lang, *Frau Weisheit*, 172.

Moreover, because each of these approaches shift the metaphorical source category for the metaphor from WOMAN to some unmentioned ANE deity there are a number of interpretive ramifications that are unavoidable. First, scholars are forced to reckon with the implication of a secondary deity in the otherwise monotheistic world of scripture and second, the historical process by which the polytheistic elements of this deity were purged from the canon of scripture. Third, shifting the context of Proverbs from the canon to ANE comparative documents makes it seem an "alien body" within scripture and therefore changes its status from "inspired and theologically normative" to some secondary category.[39]

From pre-critical to contemporary scholarship the treatment of *Lady Wisdom* as a metaphor passed from allegorical readings concerned with ontology that misplaced the source and function of metaphor into a reductive methodological drive that placed emphasis upon *disfiguring WOMAN* through a myriad of different and largely alien conceptual contexts. In the last 20 years there has been a more concerted effort to consider WOMAN as the source category for WISDOM.

Comparative Treatments that Maintain Woman as Metaphorical Source for Wisdom

Through the last decade comparative treatments have continued to labor under similar assumptions of disunity and preference for hypothetical reconstructions but with greater methodological precision and growing concern for theological ramifications. Nili Shupak, for example, provides a methodologically precise and independent study of generically similar Egyptian and Hebrew documents. She is able to prove beyond reasonable doubt linguistic parallels, shared and unshared values, and epistemological and educational differences. Shupak believes that, despite the fact that no

---

39. Helmut Gese was the first to articulate the "alien" nature of wisdom literature (Gese, *Lehre und Wirklichkeit*, 2). Von Rad published his *Weisheit in Israel* (1970) in part to explain the theological role and value of Wisdom Literature, but unfortunately further marginalized the value of wisdom literature by popularizing the notion that wisdom served as an alternative to revelation that was partially established by a self-revelatory impulse in creation and partially by man's quest for God. Wisdom Literature is the "unfinished and unfinishable" deposit of that search. See Rad, *Wisdom in Israel*, 318. Framing these essentially imperfect human reflections as canonical teaching, therefore, becomes problematic. The same impulse can still be seen in present scholarship. Notably, Michael V. Fox states in his commentary, "The background question of Wisdom Literature is formulated by Qohelet: 'What is good for man?' . . . The answer is to be discovered by human resources. This is what Wisdom Literature is all about" (Fox, *Proverbs*, 949–50).

personifications of wisdom or folly exist in Egyptian instructional literature, these figures did in fact come to Israel from Egypt and were then balanced with Mesopotamian influences which were retrofitted to Israel's monotheistic worldview. Specifically in regard to the male/female relationship, Shupak understands personified wisdom and folly to "belong to the metaphoric stratum of the Book of Proverbs, although in that book the line between the real and the metaphorical is blurred."[40] The wife of one's youth is figured in binary opposition to the *Strange Woman*, who is deemed her rival. This creates an interesting difficulty for Shupak. The "good and bad women" are real types that are paralleled in Egyptian literature and serve rhetorically to motivate the young man. At the same time however, they are dislocated from the personifications of wisdom and folly which are thought to draw not from the metaphor of woman, but of deity.

Christine Roy Yoder, on the other hand approaches the problem from a different angle and provenance. She begins with linguistic and contextual proofs to establish Proverbs 1–9 and 31 as post-exilic documents.[41] From this point she makes extensive use of Persian era realia to establish a case for the "woman of substance" as a post-exilic and solidly Persian phenomenon which in turn becomes the primary metaphor for understanding wisdom as a woman. Yoder notes the use of spoil (שלל), and gird (הגר), and the framework for the martial metaphor and how this metaphor has been overlooked by previous scholarship.[42] Furthermore, she spells out the danger posed by the "bad women" of Proverbs and even notes the correspondence between Prov 31 and Ruth, but chooses the extrabiblical frame of Persian era urban middle class women instead of the context she has elucidated from the canon to establish the source category for *Lady Wisdom*.[43]

While her speculative provenance in the era of Ezra-Nehemiah and her association of *Strange Woman* with sexual dissolution and loss seems apt for Proverbs, the reasoning is circular and does not take into account the breadth of possible meanings for "foreigner/ outside woman" (נכריה). Furthermore, losing track of the proximate canonical context and of positive

---

40. Shupak's insight on this point is brilliant and will be considered more below. Feminine imagery functions as a *double entendre*, it operates both on the "figurative" and "non-figurative" plane. Therefore, the *Strange Woman* references a *real* stereotypical danger, but also represents *infidelity to YHWH* through prophetic language and metaphor. Likewise, Wisdom represents the mental state and quality and fidelity to YHWH, but is also directly linked to the *wife* of the young man through concatenation of key terms and images. See Shupak, *Where can Wisdom be found?*, 323.

41. Yoder, *Wisdom as a Woman*, 71.

42. Yoder, *Wisdom as a Woman*, 76–78.

43. Yoder, *Wisdom as a Woman*, 102–5.

characterization of the male/female relationship makes her conclusion incomplete.[44] In the end she states: "The juxtaposition of Woman Wisdom and the Woman of Folly perpetuates the stereotyped polarization of women as 'madonnas' or 'whores.'" Second she says the PRICE metaphor, which she borrows largely from Persian documents, objectifies woman and wisdom. Third, she says that, "What women can do for men defines what is positive and desirable about them." Finally, since the women are types and composites that are unspecific they are "not unlike some contemporary portraits of women in photo and film."[45] While Yoder avoids the pitfalls of reading Wisdom as a deity, anchoring the feminine trope in social phenomena of the Persian Empire shifts the context and criteria for meaning. Her reading of the documents and realia becomes the norm governing the metaphor which thereby both accepts and perpetuates ancient and modern misreading of feminine metaphor and the gendered relationship presented in Proverbs.

While Shupak retains the canonical integrity of the book of Proverbs and uses Egyptian documents mostly as a foil, both she and Yoder color the presentation of *Lady Wisdom* via a palette not provided by the text itself. For Shupak, the personification of *Lady Wisdom* still retains the cast of foreign deity. For Yoder, the personification is bound up in the experience of Persian Jewry.

Canonical Treatments that Maintain WOMAN as the Metaphorical Source for Wisdom

Carol Fontaine's book, *Traditional Sayings in the Old Testament*, endeavors to use insights from the young discipline of orality to study the performance aspects of wisdom as they are preserved in the pages of scripture. While the work provides a number of interesting possibilities, speculative oral provenance is difficult to substantiate.[46] Claudia Camp builds on the work of Fontaine by proposing that Prov 1–9 and 31 constitute a "frame" whereby

---

44. Without the positive element of gendered relations in Proverbs and the broader canon Yoder is led to the conclusion that sexually attractive women constitute only danger to the young man, and that the primary purpose of wisdom was to attain riches and material security. Yoder goes so far as to say, "Money thereby becomes an objective means to evaluate human worth. Economic success is the mark of superior moral character whereas poverty signifies moral deficiency" (Yoder, *Wisdom as a Woman*, 102–4). To say that such an idea could have existed in Ancient Israel is very different from saying that this is the theological message intended by the literary and canonical presentation of Proverbs.

45. Yoder, *Wisdom as a Woman*, 108–9.

46. Fontaine, *Traditional Sayings in the Old Testament*.

the original oral materials of chapters 10–30 are transformed into a literary work. Her primary concern, however, is to "understand the function of a highly exalted female figure in a canon that is patriarchal in source and monotheistic in perspective."[47] Camp argues that since women are portrayed as mothers, wives, lovers, harlots or wise women in the broader text of scripture, these motifs may be assumed to have informed the imagery of Proverbs. She asserts that biblical narrative points to women in positions of authority, or wielding power through indirection as numerous women are noted for "subverting the male hierarchy for God."[48] "Dangerous women" are such because they utilize indirection to disrupt the covenant between Israel and God.[49]

Camp argues that *Lady Wisdom* should be understood not only as a conceptual metaphor of ancient Israel but that she existed as a religious symbol emerging from the exilic period when women obtained more egalitarian positions in society. Finally, she asserts that this reconstruction of religious symbolism should be understood as providing helpful and normative theological insight. Since the personification of wisdom as woman combined both divine and human aspects of wisdom, the personified figure takes on the nature of a mediatrix between God and mankind.[50]

Camp's second volume, *Wise, Strange and Holy: The Strange Woman and the Bible*, extends the notion of personified wisdom as a religious

47. Camp, *Wisdom and the Feminine*, 14.

48. Camp, *Wisdom and the Feminine*, 124–25.

49. While it may seem to North American scholarship that Lady Wisdom is a foundational element in the feminist corpus, this has not long or globally been the case. Siliva Schroer writes, "Since its beginnings feminist theology has been interested in the figure of the goddess in Israel and in the few images of YHWH as mother in the Bible. However, it has concerned itself only recently (and then peripherally) with what is certainly the most developed female image of God in the biblical writings, namely personified ḥokmā. In 1986 an initial monograph appeared in North America with the title Sophia: The future of Feminist Spirituality. Otherwise Sophia ekes out a bare existence, appearing mainly under inappropriate chapter titles like 'God, our Mother,' or 'The appropriation of the Goddess in Jewish and Christian Monotheism.' . . . It is noteworthy that up to the present time there have been very few European feminist exegetical contributions on the subject of personified Wisdom that investigate this figure in the context of the individual writings—that is, using the methods of historical-critical analysis. North American publications reveal a different profile; their scholarly quality is attested, for example in the field of Second Testament studies, by the presence of authors such as Elisabeth Schüssler Fiorenza, while for research into ḥokmā in the First Testament literature I want to give special mention to Claudia V. Camp, whose 1985 book *Wisdom and the Feminine in the Book of Proverbs* served as a trailblazing contribution to critical feminist study of personified Ḥokmā" (Schroer, *Wisdom Has Built Her House*, 15).

50. Camp, *Wisdom and Feminine Imagery*, 253–55

symbol but now expanded through the addition of imagery associated with the *Strange Woman*. Camp believes that: (1) the metaphor of *Strange Woman* is situated in the tensions and upheavals of postexilic Israel and (2) by using the *Strange Woman* as a hermeneutical guide other texts may be "de-constructed" and the situation of the post-exilic period may be understood.[51] She argues against the traditional understanding that *Lady Wisdom* and *Lady Folly* are binary oppositions for a number of very sound reasons. First, the lexical opposite of "strange" is not "wise" but "holy." Second, the opposition is not male and female but female and female.[52] Third, Biblical narrative does not disambiguate wise and strange (i.e., those women who act cleverly through indirection might as well be deemed "strange.")

Stuart Weeks's exceptional book, *Instruction and Imagery in Proverbs 1–9*, dwells precisely upon the rhetorical function of metaphor within the book Proverbs.[53] Weeks shows how *ROAD* metaphor is not so much a "predetermined route" but a caution to "travel straight."[54] Furthermore, in conjunction with the *ROAD* metaphor he is able to show how different characters interact with this metaphor in different ways. First, while the Father and *Lady Wisdom* both refer to *ROAD* metaphor in their speeches, none of the negative characters make any such reference. In contrast the main function for the "bad guys and girls" of Proverbs is to cause the youth to "turn aside" from the path of wisdom. "In short, all the settings involve interest in the figurative use of ways and roads, it seems unlikely to be a coincidence that the speeches of significant characters are associated with them in this way."[55] On the other hand the ambiguity that remains in the depiction of the women (i.e., using the same terminology for embrace, using similar settings and invitations) is also purposeful. "The point of the contrast between Wisdom and the woman is not merely to demonstrate the superiority over the foreign woman. The individual—assumed to be male and thus vulnerable to the attractions of both—cannot easily tell them apart . . . It is the instructed who can recognize true and perverted speech, and the contrast is thus associated with the strong emphasis on instruction elsewhere in Prov 1–9."[56] In summary, the *ROAD* metaphor is the central trunk of the instruction, the negative types exist as practical exercises along that path that demonstrate the need to maintain the *ROAD* and illustrate

---

51. Camp, *Wise, Strange, and Holy*, 38.
52. Camp, *Wise, Strange, and Holy*, 17.
53. Weeks, *Instruction and Imagery*, 66.
54. Weeks, *Instruction and Imagery*, 77.
55. Weeks, *Instruction and Imagery*, 79.
56. Weeks, *Instruction and Imagery*, 85.

the dangers of turning aside. The women of Proverbs are central to showing the need for wisdom to discern right action. By virtue of this discernment they then function by training the desire for wisdom by virtue of the male/female relationship and its associated desires and impulses.

For both Camp and Weeks, *Lady Wisdom* is informed by the broader corpus of scripture and conscious of the role of metaphor. For both scholars the presentation of the Wise versus the Strange/Foreign is an ambiguity that must be accounted for. While Weeks argues that the ambiguous presentation of the women is part of the educative function of the book, Camp seems to argue that the distinction is a frequently dubious one. In Camp's canonical method there is no clear internal or poetic criteria for determining which canonical exemplars are included and which are omitted. She draws from the canon in a less-controlled manner than demonstrated by some pre-critical allegorists. Week's poetic treatment is laudable, with the exception that he limits his consideration to Prov 1–9 and includes no treatment of Prov 31 or intervening sentence literature. Second, while both Camp and Weeks are concerned with the role of metaphor, neither one succeeds in providing a consistent and non-reductive treatment of metaphor. Camp claims to employ Cognitive Metaphor Theory (CMT) as outlined by Lackoff and Turner but in practice uses it only as a means of justifying her canonical construction of *WOMAN* as a source metaphor which allegedly constituted a conceptual symbol in the post-exilic period. Weeks is much more successful in explaining the metaphorical force of different source categories (particularly *ROAD* and *WOMAN*) but he struggles because he is still bound by the rhetorical/ornamental constraints of traditional rhetoric.

Research Project

First, I intend to provide a stable basis for considering the underlying metaphor of *Lady Wisdom* (i.e., WISDOM IS A WOMAN), by improving terms and methodologies that impede the understanding of the metaphor and likewise isolating cultural assumptions that may hinder an approach to wisdom as the goal of that metaphor. Second, based upon these reformed definitions, methods, and assumptions I pursue a close exegesis of selected texts in Prov 1–9 with special attention to *source* categories that are associated with *womanhood* and how these are mapped onto the target concept of *wisdom*. This analysis will illuminate numerous parallel metaphors that participate in the larger *conceptual* blend of wisdom, but specifically with regard to woman as a source category the use of feminine metaphor is to highlight *relational and covenantal fidelity* as the central components for discerning, obtaining and maintaining wisdom from YHWH. Throughout the exegesis, the *form* provided by the MT will be understood and normed in light of the identity of the Trinity expressed in the life, death, and resurrection of Jesus.

Summary

As noted above, this work is divided into two parts. The first half seeks to discern and then resolve those issues which have frustrated previous efforts to engage womanhood as a metaphorical source category for understanding and obtaining wisdom. The second half seeks to employ more adequate assumptions, definitions, and methods to specific texts in Prov 1–9.

Chapter 2 considers the difficulty presented by poor definitions, reductive methodology, and an ill-suited cultural disposition toward wisdom. The failure of the traditional linguistic definition of metaphor and the dismissal of poetic truth are illustrated by and likely rooted in Aristotle and are treated first. Second, the ascendancy of left-hemispheric modes of thought are introduced via an engagement with Ian McGilchrist.

Chapter 3 proposes two answers to these difficulties. First, new findings in Cognitive Metaphor Theory (CMT) are shown to provide more accurate and adequate tools and terminology for the discussion of metaphor in an inspired text. Second, the theological aesthetics of Balthasar is shown, not only to combat the reductive forces of our present cultural disposition but also shows itself to be singularly well-suited for the interplay of theology and feminine imagery in Proverbs.

The second half of the work endeavors to apply these new concepts and terms to the study of feminine imagery in Proverbs. If there were no constraint on page limit, each paragraph of the MT of Prov 1–9 that contains feminine imagery would be listed in full, since the aesthetic perception of the text is key to the proposed methodology of this work. However, since we are subject to limits, texts are selected that are evocative of the larger movements and developments in Prov 1–9.

Chapter 4 focuses upon the presentation and then dissolution of personified Wisdom in Prov 1–4, as illustrated in Prov 1:20–33; 2:1–11. The first component of the conceptual blend is that of the corporate and covenantal. The metaphor WISDOM IS A WOMAN is supplemented by prophetic and divine imagery that makes it clear that wisdom as an abstract concept is first and foremost about YHWH's historic relationship with his people and simultaneously about the youth learning what makes this people wise (Deut 4:5–6). Then, in Prov 2 the poet overturns the unified presentation of divine and prophetic *Lady Wisdom* in favor of reshaping wisdom in light of a diversity of metaphors that center upon the personal, individual and *human* elements of wisdom. In these, parental instruction is blended with the covenantal obligations of Torah, while the *WOMAN* metaphor takes on new elements of gendered attachment and personal protection.[57] Wisdom is about conforming the desire of the youth as an individual to that of YHWH's covenant community.

The fifth chapter of the work focuses particularly upon the consideration of "real women" in Prov 5 and 6 wherein we are introduced directly to elements of feminine characterization that are meant to inform the source category of *WOMAN*. The prophetic coloring, context and metaphor of the "strange/foreign woman" (Prov 6:20–35) juxtaposed with the "wife of your youth" (Prov 5:15–23) shows that *marital fidelity* is central to understanding the depiction of women in Proverbs. The issue of *marital fidelity* is figured as *covenant fidelity* according to the prophetic metaphor of *COVENANT IS MARRIAGE* or *IDOLATRY IS ADULTERY*. Delight, blessing, security and wisdom are attributes and byproducts of this marital and covenantal faithfulness. As such, a man's *wife* is given typological and ontic correspondence with wisdom while simultaneously modelling the correct disposition toward YHWH.

The sixth chapter of the work, uses the progressive development of the *Strange/Wise* dichotomy to show that the difference between destructive *cleverness* and genuine *Wisdom* lies precisely in the domain of faithfulness to YHWH. Prov 7 (in concert with Prov 9:13) fuses unfaithfulness and *stupidity*. The *Strange Woman* is provided with a canonical framework that depicts her as *divine judgment* upon the covenant violator. Where *Lady Wisdom* continues to expand outward into universal domains of speech, rule, creation, order and delight, the *Strange Woman* collapses even human goods into their corruption and reversal. Each of these female figures are considered in light of their invitation, and their house as destination.

In each of these chapters, we will consider what elements of the source category of *WOMAN* are being mapped onto the target category of *WISDOM*. Then, we will consider the influence of associated canonical imagery

---

57. While space does not allow for the treatment of Prov 3–4, these chapters continue the development and fusion of individual and relational commitment to the corporate and covenantal Wisdom. Prov 3 adds the maintenance of right ethical behavior in the road of life by "acknowledging the LORD" (3:6) while deepening the relationship between wisdom, woman, treasure, and life (3:13–19) as well as adding aspects of creation that will be revisited in Prov 8. Prov 4 intensifies the personal and romantic attachment to wisdom as a woman (Prov 4:6–8) while adding dimensions of honor and ethical safety.

on the larger conceptual blend. As noted above, each different role casts different light upon *WISDOM* and also may alter our understanding of the source category of *WOMAN*. The overall personification of *Lady Wisdom* is in turn altered by these developments which shapes our attitudes toward wisdom as an abstract entity.

Exegesis is organized in tiers that correspond to Balthasar's two stages of aesthetic vision. The first portion of the exegesis is dedicated to *perceiving the form* as it is communicated in the selected Hebrew texts of Proverbs. After a close consideration of Hebrew text in translation, elements of the text lead to a discussion of the metaphors and canonical entailments that enable us to "see" how *Lady Wisdom* develops through these chapters. The second stage of vision is the movement and transport of the whole person toward God. In deference to Balthasar, this portion of the theological aesthetic will be attempted by demonstrating parity between elements of Proverbs and the New Testament wherein wisdom forms obtain their splendor in Jesus. The unity of diversity of these images in turn provide substance for a balanced engagement with the beauty of the person of our Triune God. In short, stage one perception helps us to apprehend the beauty of the text. Stage two guides us to apprehend the beauty of God and accords with ultimate expression in Jesus (Heb 1:1–2).

Projected Significance

This work should contribute to the following: (1) in the field of theological interpretation of scripture it should constitute clarification of the conceptual and neurological basis for theological enquiry; (2) in the field of metaphor study it should represent a novel avenue for the discussion of metaphor and conceptual blending as these function within Hebrew Wisdom Literature; (3) in the field of Proverbs research, this study should provide a clearer, textually, canonically and metaphorically based engagement of *Lady Wisdom*; and (4) the aptness of the approach should contribute to similar work in the Megilloth.

Conclusion

The first three chapters of the work aim at providing a conceptually consistent and methodologically feasible understanding of metaphor which will enable us to more reasonably grapple with the personification of wisdom in Proverbs 1–9. First, with regard to the source category of *woman*, we will be able to discern not only the entailments, but also associated imagery that is *blended* with this metaphor and how these affect the overall personification. Second, with regard to the target of the metaphor, WISDOM, a consideration of our cultural blinders will clear the path so that the metaphor may function as it ought; as a *vehicle* for understanding and attaining wisdom. All the same, both components of the problem are complicated by the *manner* by which we study and perceive. In this Balthasar's theological aesthetics provides not only a full framework for hemispheric balance but also Christocentric, Trinitarian and canonical reflection. As such the "double gaze" of aesthetics leads us inexorably to the beauty of Christ. Exegesis in chapters 4–6 of this work aim to accent the formal beauty of the Masoretic Text, while seeing through to the captivating reality of Trinitarian love.

In Proverbs the poet's decision to employ WOMAN as a controlling metaphor for WISDOM centers upon fidelity to divine covenant and human relationships as the central components for discerning and obtaining wisdom, yet even this wisdom is transcended by the depth of beauty witnessed in the reality of divine love expressed in the sacrificial death of Jesus.

Now we proceed to clarifying the problems inherent in traditional models and definitions of metaphor, as well as the left-hemisphere captivity of the western mind.

2

Methodological Challenges

Inconsistency in the Definition of Metaphor and the Implications of Hemispheric Imbalance

Introduction

THERE are two kinds of impediments to present considerations of the metaphor of *Lady Wisdom*. The first are bound up in traditional western linguistic and philosophical approaches to metaphor. Since Aristotle's *Rhetoric* and *Poetics* underwrite not only modern western terms and assumptions, but also much of our hierarchy of philosophical values, his work is used as a dialogue partner. As will be shown below, Aristotle's definition of the terms "metaphor" and "analogy" are not only arbitrary but self-contradictory. Second, Aristotle's categorization of metaphor as an element of rhetoric forces the concept of "metaphor" into an insoluble division between "pragmatics" and "semantics." Furthermore, the subordination of poetry to rhetoric diminished the entire genre to the status of "mere ornament" in order to negate the practice of reading poetry as a means of obtaining truth.

The second class of impediment deals with underlying philosophical defect and cultural assumptions. Through a careful survey of philosophy in conjunction with recent neurological research, Ian McGilchrist argues that Western culture is predicated upon the ascendancy of left hemispheric thinking at the expense of the right. In short, his work suggests that both modern critical and post-modern approaches to theology simply cannot approach Wisdom at all.

Chapter 3 will be dedicated to remedying these hindrances. First, more adequate definitions and methods will be drawn from Conceptual Metaphor Theory. Second, the theological aesthetics of Hans Urs von Balthasar will be employed to compensate for the present ascendancy of left-hemisphere assumptions in theological interpretation. In turn, these assumptions, definitions, and methods will inform the practice of exegesis in chapters 4–6.

Aristotelian Definitions of Metaphor and Analogy

Introduction: The Problem with Definitions

> What is important is that we insist upon an understanding that the overall notion of metaphor is no more a pre-given datum than are metaphors themselves, but is responsive to historical and linguistic development; we construct metaphors for our times, but we also construct a concept of the metaphorical for our times.[1]

The principle difficulty in producing a clear and singular definition of metaphor is quite similar to the difficulty in producing a clear and singular definition of "wisdom." First, the term and definition of "metaphor" is a mental model, which is cognitively, linguistically, socially structured, and diverges widely through time and therefore can have no absolute and objective meaning.[2] Second, in the words of John Middleton Murray, "metaphor is as ultimate as speech itself, speech as ultimate as thought. If we try to penetrate them beyond a certain point we find ourselves questioning the very faculty and instrument with which we are trying to penetrate." The process of clarifying the definition of metaphor pulls at the rug on which we are standing. Third, there has been a surpassing and nearly exponential growth in metaphor research, without consistency in definition or theoretical framework. Van Noppen's bibliography of metaphor for example, covers the years 1970–1985 and has no fewer than 4,000 entries yet contains nothing of the explosion in research in the last thirty years.[3] Given this

---

1. Punter, *Metaphor*, 138.

2. As to the multiplication of applications for the word "metaphor," W. Stanford laments, "If the term metaphor be let apply to every trope of language to every result of association of ideas and analogical reasoning, to architecture, music, painting, religion, and to all the synthetic process of art, science, and philosophy, then indeed metaphor will be warred against metaphor . . . and how then can its meaning stand?" (Stanford quoted in Turbayne, *Myth of Metaphor*, 13).

3. It is not to say that the work in metaphor research has been all bad, but rather proceeding from a multitude of vantage points. As Guttenplan rightly assesses, "What

surfeit, what follows can in no wise be considered a summary of present philosophical or linguistic approaches to metaphor. Rather what follows is a targeted consideration of the root of many if not most later "traditional" definitions and assumptions. While Cognitive Metaphor Theory (CMT) and Conceptual Blending sidestep the difficulties summarized below and provide an elegance and utility that will be employed for the study of Proverbs, this selection should not be deemed a dismissal of the many excellent works in this area of research.[4]

Aristotle on Metaphor

Until the last fifty years or so, the typical definition of metaphor treated it as a *rhetorical* trope and as an *ornamental* function of *words*. Most standard definitions of metaphor as a rhetorical trope are rooted in Aristotle: Metaphor is "the application of an alien name by transference either from genus to species, or from species to genus, or from species to species, or by analogy, that is proportion."[5] This points to an immediate difficulty that will be treated in greater length below. In modern parlance, the word "analogy" has largely been considered a synonym for the word "metaphor." However, it was originally intended as a mode of *ontological* comparison *contrary* to metaphor as a linguistic ornament or trope.

For Aristotle language which was fit for usage in dialectic had a singular and literal meaning. Any use of language that provided for polyvalence of meaning or ambiguity was to be strictly avoided in dialectic. "We must add that dialectical disputation must not employ metaphors, clearly metaphors and metaphorical expressions are precluded in definition: otherwise dialectic would involve metaphors."[6]

---

justifiably brings one low in confronting [metaphor research] is neither its quality nor its scale, but rather the sense that, even though so many sensible things have been said about metaphor, it seems impossible to see how they might form any sort of single, coherent picture. It is as if a lot of very clever people, confronted with a huge jigsaw puzzle, all set to work in different places. Pieces, often many, are fitted together, and if you watch them being assembled, it is easy enough to share the satisfaction that comes from each additional piece snapping into place. But if you stand back to try to get some sense of the whole, what you see are only small sections, jagged in outline, which do not suggest that they themselves fit together" (Guttenplan, *Objects of Metaphor*, 1).

4. See, e.g., Black, *Models and Metaphors*; Guttenplan, *Objects of Metaphor*; Soskice, *Metaphor and Religious Language*, and others too numerous to mention.

5. Aristotle, *Poetics* 1457b4 [74].

6. Aristotle, *Posterior Analytics* 97b37 [241].

The justification for Aristotle's condemnation of metaphor lies precisely in the fact that metaphor endangers stable definitions of things. However, simply because metaphor was inappropriate for dialectical pursuits did not therefore render it verbal detritus.[7] If not used properly, however, metaphor could become a kind of unregulated equivocation, in which words and images may take on a variety of seemingly arbitrary meanings.[8] Therefore, Aristotle gave complete and careful delimitation of criteria to define and regulate metaphor as a *rhetorical* trope beginning in 1457b of *Poetics*. A word may be employed in eight different ways: common, proper, strange, metaphorical, ornamental, newly-coined, extended, contracted or altered. Again, Aristotle's definition of metaphor, "is the application of an alien name by transference either from genus to species, or from species to genus, or from species to species, or by analogy, that is proportion."[9]

Aristotle on Analogy

Aristotle did not assume that all comparative statements were ornamental, quite the contrary, he recognized that the process of recognizing similarities was critical to logical argumentation and experimental verification. However, beyond being the ontological cousin of metaphor, the definition of analogy is no singular entity, even in Aristotle himself. "What philosophers have come to treat under the aegis of 'analogy' has no single stable meaning. Although an identifiable, coherent stream of philosophizing eventually emerges, it begins, historically and conceptually, from two distinct and quite separate tributaries."[10] Unfortunately, these "two distinct tributaries" are nowhere stated explicitly in Aristotle, but may be deduced from particular usages in his writings. It is important to note, however, that the term *analogia*

---

7. After all, Aristotle famously remarked that "it is a great matter to observe propriety in these several modes of expression—compound words, rare or strange words, and so forth. But the greatest thing by far is to have a genius for metaphor. This alone cannot be had from another; it is the mark of a gifted nature—for to make good metaphors implies an eye for resemblances" (Aristotle, *Poetics* 1459a9 [81]).

8. In *De Sophisticis Elenchis*, Aristotle discusses a number of "sophistical tricks" that may be used to gain the upper hand in argumentation. Beginning around 175a32 he explains how equivocation and universal definition may be used to steer the argument without altering the premises, by virtue of using multiple sense a single word or phrase. This form of equivocation, in some sense is very similar to the notion of *pros hen* equivocation.

9. Aristotle, *Poetics* 1457b4, [74]. For a list of Aristotle's delineation of metaphor please see Appendix A.

10. Hochschild, *Semantics of Analogy*, 1.

and discussions of likeness and sameness are entirely positive in their usage and similarly confined to the genres that are governed by dialectic.

The first dialectical usage of analogy is foundational to Aristotle's philosophical and scientific endeavor and may be referred to as his *metaphysical use of analogy*.[11] Aristotle, contra Plato, desired to argue not for the primacy of nebulous forms but of clearly defined substances. His study of "being as being" therefore set out to formulate stable and linear definitions. Unfortunately, therein lay the first problem. The word "being" has no singular stable meaning, but rather can be used in a number of different contexts with vastly differing senses. If Aristotle merely took these as polysemic usages, his first philosophy would be undermined by equivocation.[12] Therefore, in place of polysemy, Aristotle asserted a different kind of equivocation, wherein the thing itself constitutes the core and root definition and the vast array of linguistic usage only points "toward the one" (πρὸς ἕν). This *pros hen* equivocation, or "focal meaning" in recent parlance, constitutes the first and most basic dialectical use of analogy by Aristotle. He illustrates this form of equivocation with regard to health:

> Everything which is healthy is related to health, one thing in the sense that it preserves health, another in the sense that it produces it, another in the sense that it is a symptom of health, another because it is capable of it. And that which is medical is relative to the medical art, one thing in the sense that it possess it, another in the sense that it is naturally adapted to it, another in the sense that it is a function of the medical art. And we shall find other words used similarly to these. So, too, there are many senses in which a thing is said to be, but all refer to one starting-point; some things are said to be because they are substances, others because they are affections of substance.[13]

---

11. Lloyd, *Aristotelian Explorations*, 13, 139.

12. "There is a science which investigates being as being and the attributes which belong to this in virtue of its own nature. Now this is not the same as any of the so-called special sciences; for none of these others deals generally with being as being. They cut off a part of being and investigate the attributes of this part—this is what the mathematical sciences do. Now since we are seeking the first principles and the highest causes, clearly there must be something to which these belong in virtue of its own nature. . . . Therefore it is of being as being that we also must grasp the first causes. There are many senses in which a thing may be said to 'be,' but they are related to one central point, one definite kind of thing, and are not homonymous" Aristotle, *Metaphysics* 1003a22 [1584].

13. Aristotle, *Metaphysics* 1003a22 [1584]

Pros hen equivocation, therefore, makes the substantial referent of a word itself the core definition in which word uses participate in different manners. Therefore, words come to mean by analogy with the substance to which they are associated. These lexical entities then become the stable foundation upon which demonstrations and syllogisms are constructed.[14]

The second tributary of analogy is that which is expressed in the word itself. The Greek word *analogia* derives from the geometric concept of *ratio* which is extended by Aristotle as a depiction of *nongeneric likeness*. In the same way that the ratio 6:3::2:1 communicates that 6 is to 3 as 2 is to 1, *analogia* attempts a similar strategy for discovering a common denominator in relation to non-mathematical entities.[15] In his discussion of matter, Aristotle is able to categorize different things *analogically* into three or possibly four elements: form, privation, and matter, with the fourth possible element being a moving cause.[16] His first example of "health" includes: health (as form), sickness (as privation of form), and matter (the body) with the moving cause being the discipline of medicine. This is related then *by analogy* to building (form), disorder of materials (privation), and bricks (matter) with the moving cause being the work of construction.[17]

This "zoological" function of analogy as described by G. Lloyd is one of the main scientific methodologies that Aristotle employs in the discussion and categorization of plants and animals throughout the *Physics,* but is not given a precise definition in either *Prior* or *Posterior Analytics*.[18] Analogy is

---

14. Lloyd, *Aristotelian Explorations*, 139–40.

15. "The Greek word analogia was reserved, for Aristotle as well as other Greek thinkers, for the phenomenon of nongeneric likeness. (This is NOT a logical device but a proportion of the things themselves). Analogia was originally a mathematical term for the comparison of ratios. It is captured in the familiar schema A:B::C:D (A is to B as C is to D). While originally describing quantitative comparisons, the notion of analogia and its four-term schema was easily extended to areas of reflection that are not strictly mathematical. Aristotle himself describes this schema in nonmathematical contexts (e.g., at *Topics* 108a)" (Hochschild, *Semantics of Analogy*, 5).

16. "The causes and the principles of different things are in a sense different, but in a sense, if one speaks universally and analogically, they are the same for all. For we might raise the question whether the principles and elements are different or the same for substances and for relatives, and similarly in the case of the categories. But it is paradoxical that they should be the same for all. . . Since not only elements present in a thing are causes, but also something external, i.e., the moving cause, clearly while principle and element are different both are causes, and principle is divided into these two kinds; and that which moves a thing or makes it rest is a principle and a substance. Therefore analogically there are three elements and four causes and principles" (Aristotle, *Metaphysics* 1070a31–35, 1070b22–26 [1691]). See also Lloyd, *Aristotelian Explorations*, 139–45.

17. Aristotle, *Metaphysics* 1070b22–35 [1691].

18. Contra analogy, Aristotle provides a very rigorous set of criteria for the

defined in passing (as mentioned above) by reference to the geometric notion of a ratio, but is more so defined by Aristotle's usage. For example, bone and fish spine, nail and hoof, hand and claw, and feathers and scales are held to be *in proportion* to one another by analogy:

> Once again, we may have to do with animals whose parts are neither identical in form nor yet identical save for differences in the way of excess or defect: but they are the same only in the way of analogy, as, for instance, bone is only analogous to fishbone, nail to hoof, hand to claw, and scale to feather; for what the feather is in a bird, the scale is in a fish.[19]

Therefore in summary, analogical function in Aristotle plays a pivotal role in providing definitional stability for demonstration and syllogism (via *pros hen* equivocation) and the core scientific methodology for determining and differentiating species (via proportional analogy).[20]

The Inconsistency and Collapse of Aristotelian Categories and Definitions

First, it should be noted that in the quotations provided at the beginning of this section, Aristotle soundly rejected the possibility of metaphors being used in dialectical genres, but especially in definition. Stability of meaning was the absolute pre-requisite for all further philosophical pursuits. Second, the definition of "metaphor" provided by Aristotle reads "the *application of an alien name by transference either from genus to species*, or *from species to genus*, or *from species to species*, or *by analogy, that is proportion.*"[21] On close reading, the words "alien" and "transfer" are both metaphorical. "Alien" comes from the semantic domain of domestic society and "transfer" is always used of the transport of physical objects. "The basic vocabulary for describing *metaphora* is thus full not just of what *we* might term the

---

definition and usage of "demonstration." A demonstration must be "true, primary, immediate, better known than, prior to, and causative of the conclusion" (Aristotle, *Posterior Analytics* 71b20 [31]). See also Lloyd, *Aristotelian Explorations*, 12.

19. Aristotle, *History of Animals* 486b19–21 [3].

20. Hochschild, *Semantics of Analogy*, 5. As will be seen below, Aristotle's conception of *analogia* is remarkably similar to some of the recent developments in cognitive linguistics. Hochschild writes, "A recent suggestion of the ubiquity of metaphor in everyday discourse is George Lakoff and Mark Johnson, *Metaphors We Live By*. The authors apparently don't realize that their thesis is not new, and could be attributed to Aristotle." See Hesse, "Aristotle's Logic of Analogy," 328–40.

21. Aristotle, *Poetics* 1457b4 [74].

'metaphorical' but of what Aristotle himself treats as *metaphora*."[22] In summary, therefore, Aristotle is inconsistent in his own assessment and definition of metaphor to the degree that his dialectical explanation employs the very phenomena which he denies dialectical usage.

To further complicate the possibility of stable definition consider Aristotle's allegedly dialectical use of analogy in *De Generatione Animalium*. In this passage Aristotle attempts a scientific explanation for gray hair by comparing it with a non-generic parallel.

> But the greyness of hair which is due to age results from weakness and deficiency of heat. For as the body declines in vigour we tend to cold at every time of life, and especially in old age, this age being cold and dry. . . . It is white because mould also, practically alone among the decayed things is white. The reason of this is that it has much air in it, all earthly vapour being equivalent to thick air. For mould is, as it were, the antithesis of hoar-frost; if the ascending vapour be frozen it becomes hoarfrost, if it be decayed, mould. Hence both are on the surface of things, for vapour is superficial. And so the comic poets make a good metaphor in jest when they call grey hairs "mould of old age" and "hoar-frost."[23]

In this example Aristotle is using *analogia* to establish a non-generic likeness between hoar frost and grey hair. In this example, the proportion, predicated as it is on form, deprivation, and matter, is a dialectical analogy belonging to the genre of scientific and philosophic inquiry. Ironically, he commends comic poets for their lowly "metaphor" that uses the same likeness to beget a word picture.[24] Aside from the fact that the graying of the hair is a loss of coloration in the shaft caused by age and not by temperature, it becomes apparent that the distinction between analogy and metaphor is one that arises from Aristotle's definitions and not from the things themselves.

Even though, noticed or unnoticed, metaphors appear with great frequency, in all of his writings (including his metaphysics and his natural science) his official view is that they are contrary to proper argumentation. Just as we found that the analogical use of terms seemed to have, in the

---

22. Lloyd, *Aristotelian Explorations*, 211–12.

23. Aristotle, *Generation of Animals* 784a31–34 [124].

24. "Aristotle is as keen as any ancient Greek writer to contrast the high style of his philosophizing that he advocates with the inferior would-be 'wisdoms' he associates with the poets and the rhetoricians, let alone with the 'sophists'" (Lloyd, *Aristotelian Explorations*, 210).

final analysis, insufficient theoretical basis in Aristotle's explicit discussion of that question, so too the same may be said with regard to his theory and practice of *metaphora*.[25] In short, Aristotle's distinction between ontological analogy and "mere" metaphor are products of faulty definition and circular argumentation.

The Bulk of Modern Traditional Approaches Are Rooted in Aristotelian Paradigms

The history of metaphor from the Renaissance until the dawn of post-modernity can be summarized as the eventual triumph of Aristotle. Despite the fact that the humanism that underwrote the Reformation did so partially in antagonism toward the Aristotelian and Scholastic captivity of the church, Aristotelian definitions and methods provided the foundation for the fledgling modern approach to the New Testament.[26] Aristotle's definition of metaphor as a rhetorical trope was accepted as part of the literary package which promised stable conclusions via objective scientific language. Through time this became entrenched as the "traditional theory."[27] Insofar as metaphor has been considered a *linguistic* (therefore either semantic or pragmatic) problem for a number of centuries, philosophers of language have endeavored at great length to discern, *how* metaphor means with little reflection upon the fact that it might not really be a matter of language.

Apart from the difficulties of circular definition, a linguistic approach also frames the problem of metaphor study in a manner that makes it nearly insoluble. By traditional divisions, accounting for metaphor according to its actual occurrence is precluded by definition.

---

25. Lloyd, *Aristotelian Explorations*, 219.

26. "Breaking with the medieval tradition, failing to anticipate the Reformation style, the humanists exhibited continuity instead with the modern world with respect to New Testament scholarship. Humanist philology came to dominate New Testament study and created a brand of scholarship that has worked a profound influence on modern culture. Humanist philology not only made possible a more accurate understanding of the New Testament, but also led to a new vision of Christian antiquity itself. With the humanists' works, the New Testament world began to retreat into history, and the Christian scriptures would figure in later centuries less as the arbiter of doctrine, more as the object of professional philological and historical analysis" (Bentley, *Humanists and Holy Writ*, 218).

27. For example, Lakoff writes elsewhere, "The classical theory was taken so much for granted over the centuries that many people didn't realize that it was just a theory. The theory was not merely taken to be true, but came to be taken as definitional" (Lakoff, "Contemporary Metaphor Theory," 202).

The central mistake is in the characterization of "semantics" in terms of the Literal Meaning Theory, and the use of the Literal Meaning Theory in drawing the traditional semantics-pragmatics distinction. Once that distinction is drawn, metaphor must be a matter of pragmatics, that is, purely a matter of language use rather than conceptual structure.[28]

Since the bulk of modern treatments of metaphor are situated in the pragmatic/semantic dichotomy and function according to the assumptions of Literal Meaning Theory they generally fail to provide a balanced assessment for a working definition and theoretical frame.[29]

Conclusion

In conclusion, the legacy of Aristotelian methods and definitions proves an essential difficulty to many traditional approaches to metaphor. Tracing these difficulties into present research is beyond our limits, but a few general notes commend a side-stepping of linguistic and philosophical models. First, the unreflective use of linguistic and rhetorical models rooted in Aristotle are predicated in contradictory and circular definition. Moreover, the supposed bifurcation between analogy (ontological, dialectic and scientific) and metaphor (semantic, ornamental, and poetic) proves to be a false one predicated in Aristotelian genres and definitions. Proverbs scholarship, assuming Aristotelian definitions and categories, in some cases dismissed or diminished metaphor as mere verbal ornament. Second, forcing "metaphor" into a linguistic stance that is insoluble through conventional linguistic paradigms (i.e., semantics or pragmatics) is methodologically self-defeating. For example, certain comparative approaches endeavored to search for *meaning under* or *behind* the metaphor in some combination of "objective" entities rather than finding meaning in the metaphor as a conceptual entity. Our definitions and model for metaphor must be of a different kind.

Before continuing to the next section, it is important to note that Aristotle's *Poetics* should be seen not as an articulation of interpretive practice

---

28. Lakoff and Turner, *More Than Cool Reason*, 126.

29. While Lakoff and Turner do provide a relatively detailed critique of current approaches to metaphor, their division provides seven categories that are perhaps less balanced and complete. Shibbles' masterful survey is well-respected and referenced in the field. Nonetheless, however modern theories are grouped, all but the most recent share in the assumptions of Literal Meaning Theory and Objectivism that force the study of metaphor into an insoluble dichotomy as well as the methodological oversights that will be mentioned below. To consider Lakoff and Turner's review, see Lakoff and Turner, *More Than Cool Reason*, 120–27, 217–18.

up until that point, but rather a polemic against well-accepted traditional mores of poetic interpretation.[30] Before Aristotle poetry was deemed to provide the reader with ultimate and ontological truth via the interpretive practice of allegoresis.[31] Philosophy needed language to provide stable and unambiguous meanings for stable and clear categories for scientific inquiry. Aristotle understood poetry and all poetic modes as dialectically opposed to this aim.[32] Therefore in his *Poetics*, Aristotle shuffles poetry into a subcategory of rhetoric and the goal of poetry is utterly changed. "The ascendancy of a rationalized view of poetic language [i.e., in Aristotle's transfer theory, subgroups, and definitions] is meant, quite literally, to demystify it. These different visions of what counts as poetic underpins profound differences in the questions readers see fit to ask a given poetic text."[33]

Aristotle argued that truth should not be sought in poetry. Thereby poetry became an empty and ornamental genre. This marks the last shift in the Aristotelian appraisal of poetry: the movement from appraisal of poetic meaning to poetic method. The epistemological status of poetry was simultaneously demoted from "vehicle of divine truth" to "manipulation of others through language." In Struck's words, "this gives Aristotle the fulcrum to shift the field away from the question of interpretation—*what* the poem means—and toward analysis—*how* the poem produces meaning."[34]

---

30. "Diverse witnesses point to a commonsense view in the archaic and classical periods, well before the time Aristotle is writing, that great poetry is by definition unclear, or more precisely, that it is made up of *ainigmata*, riddles hinting at some hidden truth. Such a predisposition, which sees poetry as enigmatic and defines the reader chiefly as a decipherer, is part and parcel of allegorical reading" (Struck, *Birth of the Symbol*, 24).

31. Up until relatively recently allegorists and ancient reading practices were "exempted" from the history of literary criticism, despite ample extant material that proves that allegorical interpretation was the major mode of criticism in antiquity. As recently as 1986 allegory was not deemed a mode of criticism in its own right, but merely a tool of religious and philosophical "use" of poetry. See Struck, *Birth of the Symbol*, 7. While the argument about who may or may not be considered a "κριτικὸι" falls somewhat outside the pale of our discussion, it is pertinent to note that most scholars in the modern age have chosen to mirror Aristotle's contempt for allegorical interpretation and therefore unconsciously opted for etic approaches to arcane literature. See Struck, *Birth of the Symbol*, 9.

32. "And as the poets, although their utterances were devoid of sense, appeared to have gained their reputation through their style, it was a poetical style (of oratory) that came into being first, that of Gorgias" (Aristotle quoted in Struck, *Birth of the Symbol*, 64).

33. Struck, *Birth of the Symbol*, 65–67.

34. Struck, *Birth of the Symbol*, 66.

Aristotle provides the impetus and apparatus for the devaluation of poetic understanding which arises in McGilchrist's assessment of the impoverished modern western mind.

> Only a man harrowing clods
> In a slow silent walk
> With an old horse that stumbles and
> Nods
> Half asleep as they stalk
>
> A poem of Hardy, which, if it had not existed could never have been imagined and which cannot be substituted by anything else in the universe, is reduced to a heap of general sentiments I could have found anywhere else a hundred times over, apparently clothed in language that is clunky, quirky and far from properly polished. And yet when understood and experienced implicitly, his poetry inescapably alters your life.[35]

It is in the experience of beauty that we obtain empathy predicated in imagination and metaphor. If we reduce the poem rhetorically to a "how of words," then we have not only defeated the purpose of poetry, but as will be seen in greater detail below, we have cut ourselves off from the experience of meaning. This assumption is one that underwrites many of the approaches surveyed in the literature review. Benjamin Jowett's dictum that "scripture be read as any other book," is merely a re-assertion of Aristotle. While communicated via language, scripture, tradition, and reason all attest to deeper ontological moorings. In another way rhetorical methods *close* us to the experience of God in scripture, as we dwell upon the "how of words" we not only frequently overlook the "what" but also fail to address the "whom." Now we turn to the final difficulty: the inherent imbalance and reductionism of scientific culture.

Left-Hemisphere Approaches to Knowledge at the Expense of Meaning: A Précis of Ian McGilchrist's *The Master and His Emissary*

> Our problem is not that we have failed to find an answer to the question of the meaning of life that would satisfy the left hemisphere—in the nature of things, no such answer could exist. Our problem is that we have allowed ourselves to respond to this

---

35. McGilchrist, *Divided Brain*, loc 189.

> failure by deriding the question as meaningless. We shouldn't be trying to find a glib, explicit answer to it, since any such answer would be bound to be wrong. Meaning emerges from engagement with the world, not from abstract contemplation of it. . . . It comes from the world as process, not from the world as thing, and relies on patient and consistent attention to whatever might remind us of what meaning might be like.[36]

The ultimate problem in approaching wisdom does not depend upon shortcomings in terminology or methodology or even in the Aristotelian subordination of poetry to rhetoric. These are but symptoms of a deeper difficulty. Due to a cultural ascendance of left-hemisphere modes and methods of thought, we, as a society, no longer think in ways that *allow* an approach to Wisdom. Rather than discovering the dynamic, ambiguous and relational being expressed by *Lady Wisdom*, we prefer left hemisphere values of static, clear and "objective" propositions that logically inhibit, if not utterly preclude the possibility of finding meaning. McGilchrist's assertions require both justification and clarification, however.

In his book, *Master and His Emissary*, Ian McGilchrist begins from a metaphor originally proposed by Nietzsche about a benevolent master who is overthrown by his trusted emissary. McGilchrist argues that this metaphor is an apt depiction of the relationship between the left and right hemispheres of the brain.[37] Surveying a vast compass of neurological studies McGilchrist explores brain function specifically with the aim of demonstrating that the dominance of the left hemisphere has yielded western cultural ascendancy.[38] However, this ascendancy has not been without cost since the true master of cognition and human activity (i.e., the right hemisphere) has been betrayed.

Using research provided from split brain patients, scholars have been able to determine that the simple dichotomies provided by earlier research (e.g., "the left hemisphere is logical/verbal and the right is relational/visual") are partially true, but mostly false.[39] In actual fact, *most* activities require a

---

36. McGilchrist, *Divided Brain*, loc 412.

37. McGilchrist, *Master and his Emissary*, 14.

38. "My thesis is that for us as human beings there are two fundamentally opposed realities, two different modes of experience; that each is of ultimate importance in bringing about the recognizably human world; and that their difference is rooted in the bi-hemispheric structure of the brain. It follows that the hemispheres need to cooperate, but I believe they are in fact involved in a sort of power struggle, and that this explains many aspects of contemporary Western culture" (McGilchrist, *Master and His Emissary*, 3).

39. McGilchrist notes studies that both hemispheres participate in reason and creativity. See McGilchrist, *Master and His Emissary*, 2.

sort of *independent cooperation* between the hemispheres provided for by the coordinated function of different parts of each hemisphere.[40] The left or right brain dominance in regard to a particular activity is governed by a sort of "winner-take all" operation in which one hemisphere asserts dominance.[41] This is important, because it allows for the phenomenon of *conflict* between the hemispheres, as has been shown repeatedly in split-brain patients.[42] Moreover, this allows for one hemisphere to dominate in activities that really may be more effectively handled by the other hemisphere.

Despite the continuous cooperation between the hemispheres, McGilchrist is able to summarize findings of present research that demonstrate the general *character* and *functional disposition* of the left hemisphere vs. the right.

The Left Hemisphere—The Emissary

In the realm of perception, the left hemisphere is primarily concerned with focal attention of particulars with undue attention to the right visual field.[43] This seems to be because the left hemisphere is concerned with the acquisition of food and avoidance of threat.[44] As such the key values for left hemispheric thinking are *utility* or *profit*.[45] All the same, the left hemisphere

---

40. The *corpus callossum* is given an extended explanation by McGilchrist. This connective tissue allows for limited communication between the hemispheres while allowing each to remain somewhat ignorant of the function of the other. See McGilchrist, *Master and His Emissary*, 34–40.

41. McGilchrist, *Master and His Emissary*, 10–11.

42. "On several occasions while driving, the left hand reached up and grabbed the steering wheel from the right hand. The problem was persistent and severe enough that she had to give up driving. She reported instances in which the left hand closed doors the right hand had opened, unfolded sheets the right hand folded, snatched money the right hand had offered to a store cashier, and disrupted her reading by turning pages and closing books" (Baynes et al. cited in McGilchrist, *Master and His Emissary*, 211).

43. McGilchrist, *Master and His Emissary*, 37–40, 43–46. In particular, McGilchrist notes that in patients with right brain deficits, drawings: (1) are not predicated upon visual experience of the thing but are reduced to a sort of symbolic representation, frequently with the parts dis-integrated from one another and (2) frequently completely omit the left hand side of the subject to be represented. The left hemisphere is unable to integrate the visual field contributed by the right. The result is a drawing of *half* a clock, *half* a cat, etc. In short, the right hemisphere *perceives* the whole. The left hemisphere *grasps* only part. See McGilchrist, *Master and His Emissary*, 45–46.

44. McGilchrist, *Master and His Emissary*, 25–27, 209–11.

45. "Not only does the right hemisphere have an affinity with whatever is living, but the left hemisphere has an equal affinity for what is mechanical. The left hemisphere's principal concern is utility. It is interested in what is has made, and in the world as a

does not process primary sense data, which is borrowed from the right hemisphere. The left hemisphere filters perceptions and grasps only those objects that accord with its primary directives (i.e., utility, profit, right visual field). As a result, the left hemisphere is both literally and figuratively unable to perceive depth. It typically ignores broader context and form in the realm of visual but also verbal and cognitive material.[46] Moreover, since the left hemisphere is ill equipped for processing sense data, the left hemisphere is singularly ungifted with *new experience*. It prefers the *familiar* and is quick to place new experience in known and familiar categories.

This reflex has ramifications on the character of left hemisphere cognition. It prefers to deal only with "known" data. All cognition is "re-cognition."[47] Because of this preference for familiars which are then cataloged as "facts," left brain epistemology constitutes a closed, theoretical idea of the world built upon "knowns."[48] Therefore it tends to be abstract and decontextualized.[49] Since the left hemisphere prefers abstractions and cataloged ideas to direct perception, it typically understands general categories rather than unique individuals. Also, the left-hemisphere is impersonal and shows preference for mechanical and non-living objects.[50] Relationships with the world, her creatures, and other people are typically viewed according to profit and utility and are understood according to inanimate and mechanical conceptions (i.e., the human body is understood as a number

---

resource to be used. It is therefore natural that it has a particular affinity for words and concepts for tools, man-made things, mechanisms and whatever is not alive. The left hemisphere codes for tools and machines" (McGilchrist, *Master and His Emissary*, 55). "Where the left hemisphere sees an agglomerate of parts: there is an intuitive relationship between cutting things up and depriving them of life. It is the left hemisphere alone that codes for non-living things" (McGilchrist, *Master and His Emissary*, 55).

46. McGilchrist, *Master and His Emissary*, 77–79

47. McGilchrist, *Master and His Emissary*, 92–93.

48. "In general the left hemisphere is more closely interconnected with itself, and with regions of itself than the right hemisphere. This is all part of the close focus style, but it is also a reflection at the neural level of the essentially *self-referring* nature of the world of the left hemisphere: it deals with what it already knows, the world it has made for itself" (McGilchrist, *Master and His Emissary*, 42).

49. "The left hemisphere, because its thinking is decontextualized, tends toward a slavish following of the internal logic of the situation, even if this is in contravention of everything experience tells us. This can be a strength, for example in philosophy, when it gets us beyond intuition, although it could also be seen as the disease for which philosophy itself must be the cure; but it is a weakness when it permits too ready a capitulation to theory. The left hemisphere is the hemisphere of abstraction" (McGilchrist, *Master and His Emissary*, 50).

50. McGilchrist, *Master and His Emissary*, 54–56.

of discrete "systems" governed by "processes," nature in all her manifold wonder is equal to "natural resources").

While it is broadly assumed that the left hemisphere is the master of speech, the reality is much more complicated and requires a great deal of hemispheric cooperation. The selection of lexical focus in particular is a left hemisphere domain, as well as the ability to focus metacognitively upon the words themselves.[51] However, despite the giftedness with specific lexical data, the left hemisphere has utterly no capacity for understanding metaphor, humor, sarcasm, and most non-verbal or implied communication. In short, all other *context driven* word uses are handicapped due to the left hemisphere penchant for abstraction and decontextualization.

Finally, the left hemisphere is able to maintain a degree of *emotional neutrality* and distance in comparison with the right hemisphere.[52] In actual fact, however the left hemisphere is optimistic in bent to the point that it is more accurate to describe its disposition as one of *hubris*.[53] This arrogance of left hemisphere modality is worsened on two points. First, because the left typically decides from a world of abstractions and *not* from the world of perceptions it cannot tolerate ambiguity or uncertainty of any kind.[54] Therefore, the left hemisphere rationalizes to remove *aporia* from its abstract

---

51. "The left hemisphere is attached to language *per se*: language where it is at home. It seems to be ... actually less concerned about meaning than the right hemisphere, as long as it has control of the form and the system. In conditions of right hemisphere damage, where the left hemisphere is no longer under constraint from the right, a meaningless hypertrophy of language may result" (McGilchrist, *Master and His Emissary*, 70).

52. "It has to be said that, though it is involved with emotion, the left hemisphere remains, by comparison with right, emotionally relatively neutral, something which is evidenced by its affinity for 'non-emotional' abstract paintings. Emotional stimuli are not incorporated into mood—not adopted personally—when offered to the left hemisphere rather than the right. The whole business seems more conscious, more willed, more deliberate, and that is keeping with the left hemisphere's need to influence and manipulate, as well as its role in reflecting experience" (McGilchrist, *Master and His Emissary*, 62).

53. "The left hemisphere is ever optimistic, but unrealistic about its short-comings. When patients who have had a right-hemisphere stroke are offered constructive guidance about their performance it makes little impact. In the words of one researcher into head injury, 'children with right-brain deficit disorder ignore task obstacles, accept impossible challenges, make grossly inadequate efforts, and are stunned by the poor outcomes. These children act fearless [sic] because they overlook the dangers inherent in the situation'" (McGilchrist, *Master and His Emissary*, 84).

54. "More explicit reasoning is underwritten by the left hemisphere, less explicit reasoning (such as is involved in problem solving, including scientific and mathematical problem solving) by the right hemisphere" (McGilchrist, *Master and His Emissary*, 65).

"objective" construction of the world without recourse to sense data.[55] Second, the right hemisphere is in charge of sense perception which includes bodily awareness. The left hemisphere is distant from the physical body and is over-confident in its own abilities and unaware of its limitations.[56]

Finally, and devastatingly, the left hemisphere is incapable of empathy which is required for nearly all moral, ethical, religious, and aesthetic pursuits.[57]

The Right Hemisphere—The Master

The right hemisphere is characterized by global attention and the maintenance of context.[58] As noted above the right hemisphere is privileged with access to sensory data. This is perhaps clearest in regard to perception and reproduction of what is seen. The right hemisphere perceives the whole, is better able to judge distance and relationships and is able to perceive depth.[59] Where the left hemisphere processes the world as a closed system of knowns, the right hemisphere is specially equipped for the perception of *new* experience.[60] Since the right hemisphere is tuned to sensory perception

---

55. McGilchrist cites a number of experiments wherein the left hemisphere develops a rule of prediction that is quite simply *wrong*. The right hemisphere deficit patients "went on to describe fanciful and elaborate systems that 'explained' why they were always right. So the left hemisphere needs certainty and needs to be right" (McGilchrist, *Master and His Emissary*, 82).

56. "For the left hemisphere . . . the body is something from which we are relatively detached, a thing in the world, like other things . . . devitalized, a 'corpse'" (McGilchrist, *Master and His Emissary*, 67). McGilchrist cites a number of fascinating studies in right hemisphere deficient patients who no longer recognize ownership of their limbs after a stroke. See McGilchrist, *Master and His Emissary*, 67–69. Moreover, as in the case of a right-hemisphere stroke, "when the right hemisphere is no longer available to bring the left side of the body into being, the left hemisphere may substitute only a mechanical structure of inanimate parts down that side" (McGilchrist, *Master and His Emissary*, 55).

57. "Patients with right frontal deficits, but not left frontal deficits, suffer a change of personality whereby they become incapable of empathy" (McGilchrist, *Master and His Emissary*, 58).

58. "To sum up, the right hemisphere is responsible for every type of attention except focused attention. Even where there is divided attention, and both hemispheres appear to be involved, it seems probable that the right hemisphere plays the primary role" (McGilchrist, *Master and His Emissary*, 39).

59. McGilchrist, *Master and His Emissary*, 77–79.

60. "Novel experience induces changes in the right hippocampus, but not the left. So it is no surprise that phenomenologically it is the right hemisphere that is attuned to the apprehension of anything new" (McGilchrist, *Master and His Emissary*, 40).

it avoids abstraction but focuses rather upon the particular characteristics of unique individuals.[61] Therefore where the left prefers stable, objectified, and *non-living* subjects driven by abstract propositions, the right hemisphere prospers with regard to *living* and *dynamic* subjects.[62] Rather than an abstract "system" the right chooses epistemology that is predicated upon *relationship* rather than *use* or *profit*.[63]

While the left hemisphere does have a structural priority in language and consciousness, the right hemisphere is key to the use of language. The right processes context. First, the right hemisphere provides the broader lexical context needed in considering word usage.[64] Second, the right hemisphere provides the pragmatic context for particular speech acts. Without right hemisphere processing the agent is unable to discern implied or non-explicit elements of verbal communication.[65] In particular metaphor, sarcasm, and jokes become impossible, because the right hemisphere provides

---

61. McGilchrist, *Master and His Emissary*, 51–52.

62. "The right temporal region appears to have areas not only specific for living things, but additionally for all that is specifically human. . . . The right hemisphere prioritises whatever actually *is*, and what concerns us. It prefers existing things, real scenes and stimuli that can be made sense of in terms of the lived world" (McGilchrist, *Master and His Emissary*, 56).

63. "The right hemisphere's view of the world in general is construed according to what is of concern to it, not according to objective impersonal categories, and therefore has a personal quality. This is both its strength and its weakness in relation to the left hemisphere. It deals preferentially with whatever is approaching it, drawing near, into relationship with it. The right temporal lobe deals preferentially with memory of personal or emotionally charged nature, what is called episodic memory, where the left temporal lobe is more concerned with memory for facts that are 'in the public domain'" (McGilchrist, *Master and His Emissary*, 54).

64. "The left hemisphere operates focally, suppressing meanings that are not currently relevant. By contrast, the right hemisphere processes information in a non-focal manner with widespread activation of related meanings. Whereas close lexical semantic relationships rely on the left hemisphere, loose semantic associations rely on the right" (McGilchrist, *Master and His Emissary*, 41).

65. "The right hemisphere sees things as a whole, before they have been digested into parts, it also sees each thing in its context, as standing in a qualifying relationship with all that surrounds it, rather than taking it as a single isolated entity. Its awareness of the world is anything but abstract" (McGilchrist, *Master and His Emissary*, 47). Also, it is "particularly important wherever non-literal meaning and particularly where irony, humor, indirection or sarcasm are involved. Patients with right-hemisphere damage have difficulty understanding non-literal meaning. They have difficulty with indirect meaning, such as is implied by metaphor and humor. In fact, those with right-hemisphere damage cannot make inferences, an absolutely vital part of understanding the world: they do not understand implicit meanings whatever their kind, but detect explicit meanings only" (McGilchrist, *Master and His Emissary*, 71).

the bridge between the world of language and the world of perception.[66] Therefore, the right hemisphere is in a privileged place to provide for the consideration of *meaning*.[67]

Finally, since the right hemisphere proceeds from sensory data the nature of its processing is perhaps best described as deductive reasoning. It moves from particular knowns or particular problems to particular solutions.[68] Due to this particularity the disposition of the right hemisphere toward propositions and conclusions is tentative and ambivalent. This is in part because the right hemisphere has much deeper and innate experiential memory through space and time.[69] Moreover, since the right hemisphere is so closely allied with sensory perception it is also much more *embodied* and therefore aware of physical and mental limitations.[70] Finally, the right hemisphere is primarily associated with emotions and affections. Where the left understands the emotions as a *secondary hindrance* to thinking, it has been

---

66. "Only the right hemisphere has the capacity to understand metaphor. That might not sound too important—like it could be a nice thing if one were going to do a bit of lit crit. But that is just a sign of the degree to which our world of discourse is dominated by the left-hemisphere habits of mind. Metaphoric thinking is fundamental to our understanding of the world, because it is the *only* way in which understanding can reach outside the system of signs to life itself. It is what links language to life" (McGilchrist, *Master and His Emissary*, 115).

67. McGilchrist, *Master and His Emissary*, 133–34.

68. "The right hemisphere appears to be crucially involved in the process of deductive reasoning, a process which is independent not only of left-hemisphere language areas, but also of right-hemisphere visuo-saptial areas" (McGilchrist, *Master and His Emissary*, 65). Although McGilchrist describes this process as deductive it is probably more correct to describe the process with Pierce and McGrath as an *abductive process*. Abduction is a dynamic and iterative process in which a "surprising fact" (i.e., a new perception) interrupts and reframes existing knowledge. The new perception generates a new logical inference which in turn provides a better "empirical fit." See McGrath, *Fine-Tuned Universe*.

69. McGilchrist notes how the right hemisphere allows for more durable attention and long term memory. "This broader field of attention, open to whatever may be, and coupled with greater integration over time and space, is what makes possible the recognition of broad or complex patterns, the perception of the 'thing as a whole,' seeing the wood for the trees. In short, the left hemisphere takes a local short-term view, whereas the right hemisphere see the bigger picture" (McGilchrist, *Master and His Emissary*, 43).

70. "In keeping with its capacity for emotion, and its predisposition to understand mental experience within the context of the body, rather than abstracting it, the right hemisphere is deeply connected to the self *as embodied*. Although each side of the brain has both motor and sensory connections with the opposite side of the body, we know that the left hemisphere carries an image only of the contralateral (right) side of the body—when the right hemisphere is incapacitated, the left part of the individual's body virtually ceases to exist for that person" (McGilchrist, *Master and His Emissary*, 66).

shown that emotional disposition actually *precedes* and *guides* later reasoning or rationalization.[71] Since the right hemisphere is the seat of emotions it is also *essentially empathetic*[72] and allows humans to imagine the thoughts and feelings of others, and is therefore foundationally *moral* in its bent.[73]

Finally, though the left brain is more broadly associated with the judgments of conscious thought, it is the *right* hemisphere that is constitutive of the sense-of-self due to its signal role in affections and the preservation of personal episodic memory through time.[74] Though right hemisphere dominance is frequently associated with depression, it provides a more accurate appraisal of self and environs. In place of *hubris*, right hemisphere dominance tends toward despair.[75]

McGilchrist's characterizations provide a functional paradigm which is amply supported by experimental data, much better nuanced than this oversimplified précis. The right hemisphere is clearly better suited to theological interpretation of Scripture and particularly to the consideration of the metaphor of *Lady Wisdom*. Sadly, McGilchrist makes another argument that while the right hemisphere may be better suited for *many* things, our Western Society has fallen into a sort of Babylonian captivity of the right hemisphere.

---

71. "The right hemisphere has by far the preponderance of emotional understanding. It is the mediator of social behavior" (McGilchrist, *Master and His Emissary*, 58). "The right hemisphere is in general more intimately connected with the limbic system, an ancient subcortical system that is involved in the experience of emotions of all kinds, and with other subcortical structures, than is the left hemisphere" (McGilchrist, *Master and His Emissary*, 66).

72. "Because of the right hemisphere's openness to the interconnectedness of things, it is interested in others as individuals, and in how we relate to them. It is the mediator of empathetic identification. If I imagine myself in pain I use both hemispheres, but your pain is in my right hemisphere" (McGilchrist, *Master and His Emissary*, 57).

73. Morality is connected intrinsically to empathy. See McGilchrist, *Master and His Emissary*, 84.

74. McGilchrist, *Master and His Emissary*, 88–90.

75. "The right hemisphere is also more realistic about how it stands in relation to the world at large, less grandiose and more self-aware, than the left hemisphere. . . . Although relatively speaking the right hemisphere takes a more pessimistic view of the self, it is also more realistic about it. There is evidence that (a) those who are somewhat depressed are more realistic, including in self-evaluation and . . . that (b) depression is (often) a condition of relative hemisphere asymmetry, favoring the right hemisphere" (McGilchrist, *Master and His Emissary*, 84).

The Growth of Left-Hemispheric Values in Western Culture

In his effort to demonstrate the cultural ascendancy of left-brain dominance, McGilchrist first argues that the control gained by the left-hemisphere is partially genetic, insofar as it is predicated upon the human ability to *imitate*. It is this process which allows for epigenetic development (not macro evolution) by which individuals within a culture are also affected by the culture at large. By this process each succeeding generation builds upon not only the genetic, but cultural traits that have allowed for greater success in survival. Since the left hemisphere is the one dedicated to control over the environment, it is only reasonable to assume these traits were valued by individuals within the culture. In practice, however, the genetic and cultural processes which might allow for the ascendance of one hemisphere take a back seat to the *characterization* of the hemispheres as set forth in his previous research. Certain eras and movements in the west *do* seem to demonstrate not only a closer affiliation with left hemisphere values, but also betray a growth and fortification of the same.

McGilchrist charts the initial development of right/left hemisphere imbalance to ancient Greece where he believes that the "necessary distance" of hemispheres allowed for the flowering of balance in art, literature and culture. However, soon afterward a number of social and technological advancements led to left hemisphere imbalance. Among these he notes how phonological language and the development of written vowels reduced the import of context. The use of money and competitive economic system favored left hemisphere modes of perception and cognition. More importantly, the hemispheric balance visible in philosophers like Heraclitus was decimated by the ascendance of Platonic philosophy that not only despised right brain modes like poetry and art, but also dismissed perceptions of the physical world as meaningless and illusory. Moreover, while the early Roman Empire evinced some truly great literature that demonstrated hemispheric balance (i.e., Ovid, Virgil, etc.), the empire's value of stasis and utility eventually led to calcification that not only led to Rome's demise but demonstrated the triumph of left hemispheric dominance.[76] Art became flattened

---

76. Even though Roman civilization as a whole is marked by the ascendancy of left-hemisphere modes, at the same time there was remarkable generativity found in the theology of Augustine of Hippo. In his *City of God*, he employs the image schema of CITY to exemplify the antagonism between the real world embodiments of the figurative CITY OF MAN versus the divinely intended reality exemplified in references to the CITY OF GOD. Augustine sets in motion a movement that connects metaphor to the real world which will continue through the Reformation. Augustine's creative balance of perception and abstraction is perhaps best exemplified in McGrath's illustration of Augustine's discussion of creation. See McGrath, *Fine-Tuned Universe*, 97–108.

and abstract. Perception was replaced by dogma. This state of affairs was culturally dominant until the Renaissance/Reformation. McGilchrist does not reduce the Renaissance to the causal outcome of the rediscovery of Greek art and literature in the west, but more the sense of beauty and awe generated by the contact which then re-ignited right hemispheric realization of the world at large. The turn toward the right hemisphere is evident not only in the art of the period, but in the decay of closed and static conceptions of the world and a renewed feeling of *longing*. With regard to his understanding of the Reformation, the picture is less optimistic. While the impetus for Reformation originated in a return to authenticity, experience, balance and life, it was quickly reversed in favor of left hemisphere values.[77] Emergent Protestantism had little patience for art or the metaphorical but sought "unambiguous" doctrinal certainty and a distrust not only of art and the imagination, but of sacred places. In particular, McGilchrist argues that the removal of sacred places buttressed the power of the state.[78]

> Protestantism being a manifestation of left-hemisphere cognition is—even though its conscious self-descriptions would deny this—itself inevitably linked to the will to power, since that is the agenda of the left-hemisphere. Bureaucratisation and capitalism, though not necessarily themselves the best of bedfellows, and at times perhaps in conflict are each manifestations of the will to power, and each is linked to Protestantism. . . . Removing the places of holiness, and effectively dispensing with the dimension of the sacred, eroded the power of the princes of the Church, but it helped to buttress the power of the sacred state. The capacity for religion to crystalize the structures of power and obedience was soon allied under the Reformers to the power of the state.[79]

Therefore, according to McGilchrist, early Protestantism, despite intentions to the contrary, slipped into left-hemispheric imbalance, and thereby, "the cardinal tenet of Christianity: The Word is made Flesh—becomes reversed, and the Flesh is made Word." In balance then:

---

77. McGilchrist, *Master and His Emissary*, 314–15. "What I wish to emphasize is the transition, within the Reformation, from what are initially the concerns of the right hemisphere to those of the left hemisphere: how a call for authenticity, and a reaction against the undoubtedly empty and corrupt nature of some practices of the medieval Roman Catholic Church, an attempt therefore to return from a form of re-presentation to the true presence of religious feeling, turned rapidly into a further entrenchment of inauthenticity" (McGilchrist, *Master and His Emissary*, 323).

78. McGilchrist, *Master and His Emissary*, 321.

79. McGilchrist, *Master and His Emissary*, 321.

As the renaissance progresses, there becomes evident, however, a gradual shift of emphasis from the right hemisphere way of being towards the vision of the left hemisphere, in which a more atomistic individuality characterized by ambition and competition becomes more salient; and originality comes to mean not creative possibility but the right to "free thinking," the way to throw off the shackles of the past and its traditions, which are no longer seen as an inexhaustible source of wisdom, but as tyrannical, superstitious and *irrational*—and therefore wrong. This becomes the basis of the hubristic movement which came to be known as the Enlightenment.[80]

In the Enlightenment, it is not difficult to see left hemisphere values at work, not only in a debasement and distaste for art and poetry, but more importantly in a preference for closed, disconnected, and totalitarian theoretical systems.[81] Moreover, there is not only a demand for "systemic facts" but also an impatience for those elements which resist systemization.[82] In the worst case scenario, the desire for abstract ideals and the innate inability to attain them may lead to violence, barbarity, and revolution.[83]

---

80. McGilchrist, *Master and His Emissary*, 329.

81. A case in point of this abstraction from the body and physical world is Rene Descartes, which bears particular similarity to right hemisphere dysfunction (i.e., schizophrenia). "I would argue that in all its major predilections—divorce from a body, detachment from human feeling, the separation of thought from action in the world, concern with clarity and fixity, the triumph of representation over what is present to sensory experience, in its reduction of time to a succession of atomistic moments, and in its tendency to reduce the living to the devitalised and mechanical—the philosophy of Descartes belongs to the world as construed by the left hemisphere" (McGilchrist, *Master and His Emissary*, 335).

82. As Isaiah Berlin notes three lingering propositions of the Enlightenment are: "That all genuine questions can be answered, that if a question cannot be answered it is not a question; that all these answers are knowable, that they can be discovered by means which can be learnt and taught to other persons; and that all the answers must be compatible with one another" (Berlin quoted in McGilchrist, *Master and His Emissary*, 336).

83. McGilchrist, *Master and His Emissary*, 347–49. McGilchrist notes that the American Revolution did not see the degree or nature of barbarism of the French, in part because of the mediation of right hemispheric values. All the same, he cites de Tocqueville's disturbing prophecy about the roots of American culture in which: "It will be a society which tries to keeps its citizens in 'perpetual childhood'; it will seek to preserve their happiness, but it chooses to be the sole agent and only arbiter of that happiness." This in turn will develop a servitude which, "covers the surface of society with a network of small complicated rules, through which the most original minds and the most energetic characters cannot penetrate . . . it does not tyranise but it compresses, enervates, extinguishes and stupefies a people, till each nation is reduced to be nothing better than a flock of timid and industrious animals, of which government is

The Enlightenment leads to and engages the era of Romanticism, however in unexpected ways. Certain elements are contiguous (i.e., idealism) however, others are reversed (i.e., relation to human embodiment, nature, and the sublime).[84] Causally, McGilchrist sees the Romantic Movement as being the unintended consequence of the study of classical authors and a rediscovery of Shakespeare which brought about a return to the recognition of beauty, longing, and depth. Thinkers began to concentrate upon the unperturbed relationship of object and subject.[85] In the Enlightenment and Romanticism, we witness the swing of the pendulum from left to right, in a way similar to the aftermath of the Reformation.

McGilchrist sees the next swing of the pendulum in the birth of logical positivism and the dawn of the industrial revolution. Where the right had come into flower in Heidegger, Herder, Wordsworth, and Blake, it now swung the other way in Feuerbach and company in a revolutionary fashion.

> The young Hegelians wished to rescue the realm of sensory experience, what can be seen and touched, from what they saw as a subjection to the realm of concepts and ideas, and more generally experience from a representation of experience, and religion from mere theology. Experience was not the same as ideas about experience, true enough. But as with the ideologues of the Reformation, they ended by destroying the bridge between the two realms, and reducing the complexity of existence to something simple and clear. Whereas at the Reformation it had been the Word, in this case it was Matter.[86]

In short, logical positivism provided for the smooth transition from the worship of God to the worship of science.[87] McGilchrist notes that the enthronement of science was enabled by a set of assumptions. First, it was

---

the shepherd" (De Tocqueville quoted in McGilchrist, *Master and His Emissary*, 346).

84. McGilchrist, *Master and His Emissary*, 353.

85. "The romantic acceptance that there is no simple 'fact of the matter'—a reality that exists independent of ourselves and our attitude towards it—brought to the fore the absolutely crucial question of one's disposition towards it, the relationship in which one stands to it'" (McGilchrist, *Master and His Emissary*, 359).

86. McGilchrist, *Master and His Emissary*, 383.

87. "Science preached that it was exempt from the historicisation or contextualization that was being used to undermine Christianity in the nineteenth century, a way of enabling science to criticize all other accounts of the world and of human experience while rendering itself immune to criticism. This doctrine of the infallibility of science is also a result of the Enlightenment failure to understand the conceptual nature of all thought, what Dewey called 'the dogma of immaculate conception of philosophical systems'" (McGilchrist, *Master and His Emissary*, 385).

assumed that there was only one logical path to knowledge. Second, the scientific method was the only sure way on that path. Third, science is above morality and should be conceived of as the "brave hero" standing against forces of religious dogma, usually figured as the church.[88]

With these unquestioned and unquestionable assumptions in place, technology provided for the industrial revolution, which McGilchrist describes as "obviously, colossally, man's most brazen bid for power over the natural world, the grasping left hemisphere's long-term agenda. It was also the creating of a world in the left hemisphere's own likeness."[89]

The Modern and Post-Modern eras therefore, are not marked by a radical bifurcation as some might argue but rather a contiguous line that demonstrates continued left hemisphere gains that only exacerbate those elements introduced by the Enlightenment and Industrial revolution.[90] As mobility reduced the individual's sense of social and physical belonging, urbanization removed them both from nature and relationship, diminishing right hemisphere correction and solidifying left hemisphere gains. McGilchrist's chief evidence in this argument, is first of all human experience of the "look around" variety, but supplemented by a host of studies wherein he shows that disorders of right hemisphere deficit are prevalent mainly in the West and are consistently on the increase.[91] Moreover, in a powerful argument from exemplars he shows that art in the modern and post-modern eras has not only been reduced to left hemisphere values of commodity and utility, but that the subject and form of the art corresponds to the values and modes of the left hemisphere. Rather than finding originality by standing in meaningful relationship to tradition, modern art must *shock* the left

---

88. McGilchrist, *Master and His Emissary*, 385.

89. McGilchrist, *Master and His Emissary*, 386. Almost audaciously, McGilchrist argues, "Is it over-stated to say that this would lead to a position where the pre-reflectively experienced world, the world that the right hemisphere was to deliver, became simply 'the world as processed by the left hemisphere'? I do not think so. I would contend that a combination of urban environments which are increasingly rectilinear grids of machine-made surfaces and shapes, in which little speaks of the natural world; a worldwide increase in the proportion of the population who live in such environments, and live in them in greater degrees of isolation and an unprecedented assault on the natural world, not just through exploitation, despoliation and pollution, but also more subtly, through excessive 'management' of one kind or another, coupled with an increase in the virtuality of life, both in the nature of work undertaken, and in the omnipresence in leisure time of television and internet, which between them created a largely insubstantial replica of 'life' as processed by the left hemisphere—all these have to a remarkable extent realized this aim, if I am right that it is an aim, in an almost unbelievably short period of time" (McGilchrist, *Master and His Emissary*, 387).

90. McGilchrist, *Master and His Emissary*, 390.

91. McGilchrist, *Master and His Emissary*, 393–408.

hemisphere with the juxtaposition of familiar images in bizarre or grotesque context.[92] Rather than art being *bound up in the concrete world of experience* and *translucent* of that experience; modern art is reduced either to material or abstract ideal with no possibility of "in-betweeness." Tragic exemplars of the modern-utilitarian contempt for art are found in Nazi and Leninist "uses" of art.[93]

However, where some have argued for the post-modern "turn to imagination" McGilchrist sees, correctly I believe, nothing of the sort. Rather, the *boredom*, which first appeared in the Modern era during the Enlightenment continues unabated.[94] "Life is a game, which lacks both meaning and joy." The possibility of meaning is undermined by materialist reductionism.[95] McGilchrist, summarizes the matter concisely.

> The post-modern revolt against the silent, static, contrived, lifeless world displayed in the fresco on the wall is not because of its artificiality—the fact that it is untrue to the living world outside—but because of its "pretence" that there exists something outside to be true to. The contrast is not between the fixity of the artificial and the fluidity of the real, but between the fixity and the chaos of two kinds of artificiality.
>
> Post-modern indeterminacy affirms not that there is a reality, towards which we must carefully, tentatively, patiently struggle; it does not posit a truth which is nonetheless real because it defies the determinacy imposed on it by the self-conscious left-hemisphere interpreter (and the only structures available to it). On the contrary, it affirms that there *is* no reality, no truth to interpret or determine. The contrast here is like the difference between the "unknowing" of a believer and the "unknowing" of an atheist. Both believer and atheist may quite coherently hold the position that any assertion about God will be untrue; but their reasons are diametrically opposed. The difference is not in what is said, but in the disposition each holds toward the world. The right hemisphere's disposition is tentative, always reaching

---

92. McGilchrist, *Master and His Emissary*, 408–9, 413.

93. McGilchrist provides a quote from Lenin, "I'm no good at art, art for me is something like an intellectual appendix. And when its use as propaganda, which we need at the moment, is over, we shall cut it out, as useless—snip, snip" (McGilcrhist, *Master and His Emissary*, 412).

94. Patricia Spacks asserts that *boredom* is the offspring of the Enlightenment. See Spacks, *Boredom*. McGilchrist argues that boredom is due to a left-hemisphere experience of time. Rather than "a lived narrative . . . it is static, eternal, unchanging" (McGilchrist, *Master and His Emissary*, 336).

95. McGilchrist, *Master and His Emissary*, 424.

painfully (with "care") towards something which it knows is beyond itself. It tries to open itself (not to say "no") to something that language can only by subterfuge, to something that reason can reach only in transcending itself; not, be it noted, by the abandonment of language or reason, but rather through and beyond them. This is why the left hemisphere is not its enemy, but its valued emissary. Once, however, the left hemisphere is convinced of its own importance, it no longer "cares." Instead it revels in its own freedom from constraint, in what might be called, in a phrase of Robert Graves's, the "ecstasy of chaos." One says "I do not know," the other "I know—that there is nothing to know." One believes that one cannot know: the other "knows" that one cannot believe.[96]

McGilchrist's arguments are important because they suggest that the current preference for methods and models is predicated on more than mere academic fashion. Rather, through the passage of time and event our culture has become less receptive to meaning itself. The present "turn to imagination" is not a reversal of values but rather the appearance of change without the underlying substance.

What Is the Import for Our Study?

First, theology is implicated in hemispheric imbalance. Even if one refuses the severity of McGilchrist's characterization of the Post-Reformation, the reality of objective scientific approaches to theological interpretation of scripture is difficult to avoid. In the previous review of literature, nearly all of those of the modern era mark an affinity for scientific methodologies and materialist assumptions. However, if more evidence is needed Ignacio Carbajosa conducted a diachronic survey of OT historical-critical scholarship in the modern era in response to the Pope's call for a consideration of the increasing gap between "scientific" exegesis and theology. Carbajosa concludes: "In the area of the teaching of Scripture, this radical division contributes to sustaining and strengthening the reason-faith dualism with which students of theology, influenced by the cultural context, frequently begin their course of study. Exegesis in the scenario described is presented as a 'scientific,' 'objective' discipline that operates on a literary work with a method appropriate to it: the historical-critical method."[97] In this model, theological interpretation becomes a *diminution* of the message of scripture.

---

96. McGilchrist, *Master and His Emissary*, 426–27.
97. Carbajosa, *Faith, the Fount of Exegesis*, 243.

More pressingly however, "Theological discourse, which is based on faith, would eventually be pushed aside (in the context of the radical division described) into the realm of 'believing' (linked to feeling), far from that other territory where the truths of man and history are at stake, which is 'knowing.'"[98] Carbajosa's terminology and metaphor independently mirror the language of McGilchrist.

In short, to call something, "theological" is to make it *immaterial* which in our era is synonymous with being *inconsequential*. This does not mean that theological reflection needs to avoid material consideration, nor descend into the realm of "pre-critical" allegoresis. It merely requires a degree of circumspection about the nature of our theological endeavor and the assumptions, terms, and methods we employ. These will be discussed in the next chapter.

Second, to the degree we disbar right hemisphere modes and values; to that same degree our pursuit of wisdom is *precluded* both by definition and intent. If we grant that present theological scholarship is dominated by left hemisphere assumptions, definitions, and methods, the likelihood of approximating *anything like* an approach to wisdom is hobbled.[99] First of all, the left hemisphere has little facility with metaphor, art, beauty or desire beyond utility or profit. Second, by ignoring the dynamic, organic, and relational *essence* of the book of Proverbs, left hemisphere rationalization will be utterly unable to *perceive* the message as it is in fact *delivered* by the book of Proverbs. Finally, wisdom is not the sort of value that can be arrived at by the explicit, self-interested, and hubristic left-hemisphere. Like humility, awe, or even *happiness*, wisdom cannot be obtained via a direct and explicit route.[100]

As noted above, the sort of attention we pay determines the sort of observations and experiences we make about the world. Where the left hemisphere endeavors to determine "how" meaning comes to be (as in Aristotle's

---

98. McGilchrist, *Master and His Emissary*, 244.

99. McGilchrist offers a description of what would happen if left hemisphere modes were applied to wisdom. It is a startling parallel to what has happened in the study of Lady Wisdom in Proverbs. "Ever more narrowly focused attention would lead to an increasing specialization of knowledge. This in turn would promote the substitution of information gathering, for knowledge, which comes through experience. Knowledge, in its turn, would seem more 'real' than what one might call wisdom, which would seem too nebulous, something never to be grasped. One would expect the left hemisphere to keep doing refining experiments on detail, at which it is exceedingly proficient, but to be correspondingly blind to what is not clear or certain, or cannot be brought into focus right in the middle of the visual field" (McGilchrist, *Master and His Emissary*, 429).

100. McGilchrist, *Master and His Emissary*, 436.

rhetorical approach to poetry) the right hemisphere considers *the whole context* and the web of relationships within that context.[101]

> The right hemisphere, the one that believes, but does not know, has to depend on the other, the left hemisphere, that knows but doesn't believe. It is as though a power that has an infinite, and therefore intrinsically uncertain, potential Being needs nonetheless to be delimited—needs stasis, certainty, fixity—in order to Be.[102]

This is the way of wisdom.

Conclusion

In conclusion, the culturally prevalent definitions, methods, and assumptions present in traditional metaphorical models are insufficient for treatment of poetic metaphor in Proverbs. The reduction of poetry to a rhetorical and ornamental use of language to persuade is neither necessary nor appropriate to the study of inspired scripture. The unalloyed preference for left hemisphere approaches to study is not only inappropriate, but destructive to our ends.

In the next chapter we will endeavor to explore more adequate assumptions, definitions, and methods. First, the work of Hans Urs von Balthasar provides for hemispheric balance and allows for engagement of the metaphor of *Lady Wisdom* in light of the target category of *Wisdom* by providing an *aesthetic* model of perception centered in Jesus Christ. Second, definitions, and models of metaphor drawn from Cognitive Metaphor Theory and Conceptual Blending will be shown to be adequate replacements for traditional definitions, models, and methods of metaphor.

---

101. McGilchrist, *Master and His Emissary*, 5.
102. McGilchrist, *Master and His Emissary*, 428.

3

Hemispheric Balance and Methodological Stability

Theological Aesthetics and Conceptual Metaphor Theory

IN this chapter the first aim is to provide for right hemispheric engagement in theology and exegesis through a survey of Balthasar's theological aesthetics. Theological Aesthetics rebalances many of McGilchrist and Carbajosa's criticisms and is well-suited to the consideration of feminine metaphor in Proverbs. It provides for the reintegration of perception and faith, and the relational disposition required for Wisdom. Finally, by anchoring true beauty in the triune revelation of Christ it provides a canonical anchor for engagement with *Lady Wisdom*.

After a summary consideration of theological aesthetics, we will note how recent work in cognitive metaphor theory (CMT) and conceptual blending provide a philosophically and cognitively accurate model for the function of metaphor which in turn provides an excellent apparatus for considering not only *how* metaphor works in poetry, but *why*. The second part of the chapter introduces the conceptual framework and terms adequate necessary to begin exegesis in chapter four.

Theological Aesthetics Provides Balance in Perception and Cognition Rooted in the Reality of Jesus Christ

Introduction: Protestant Resistance to Beauty in Theology

In considering the metaphor of *Lady Wisdom* and her antithesis, the *Strange/Foreign Woman*, gendered desire and feminine beauty play a significant role (Prov 2:16; 4:5–6; 5:15–20; 6:24–35; 7). Furthermore, the *education* of desire functions as a central purpose in the book. However, the notions of "beauty" and "desire" have not traditionally been deemed theologically useful concepts by Protestants:

> The idea of the beautiful is of no significance in forming the life of Christian faith, which sees in the beautiful the temptation of a false transfiguration of the world which distracts the gaze from "beyond." . . . If the beautiful is an image in which, in a certain sense, the puzzling, confused motion of life is brought to a halt and is made surveyable for the eye set at a distance from it, thus disclosing its deeper meaning for him (i.e., for man), then it is true for the Christian faith that it is not art that discloses the depths of reality, and that this is not grasped in a distanced act of seeing, but rather this is grasped in *suffering*. The reply to the question posed in the human lot can never be objectified in a work of art but is always to be found in the enduring of suffering itself. The beautiful . . . is therefore, as far as the Christian faith is concerned, always something that lies beyond this life.[1]

Bultmann's criticism may be overstated, but beauty is not a category that has traditionally been associated with Protestant theology.[2] While Bultmann's sentiment bears witness to the truth of suffering in the life and growth of the Christian both individually and corporately, it does not do justice to the reality of the joy of the Christian life. As Barth suggests:

> That which attracts us to joy in Him, and our consequent attraction is the inalienable form of His glory and the indispensable form of the knowledge of His glory. But this being the case, how

---

1. Bultmann cited in Balthasar, *Seeing the Form*, 27n11.

2. Stephen Garrett provides a concise treatment of modern European aesthetics, which essentially provides the categories and definitions for theology from Baumgartner to Derrida. See Garrett, *God's Beauty-In-Act*, 17–36. In summary, he writes, "Tracing beauty's history from the Enlightenment to the contemporary situation reveals beauty's slow dismissal from the real and later to its demise. . . . At worst, beauty has been treated as a meretricious Hellenistic import, who will distract and indeed corrupt good Christians" (Garrett, *God's Beauty-In-Act*, 36–37).

can we dispense with the idea of the beautiful, and therefore with the statement that God is also beautiful? It is again to be noted that we use the cautious expression that God is "also" beautiful, beautiful in His love and freedom, beautiful in His essence as God and in all His works, beautiful, that is, in the form in which He is all this. We shall not presume to try to interpret God's glory from the point of view of His beauty, as if it were the essence of His glory. But we cannot overlook the fact that God is glorious in such a way that He radiates joy, so that He is all He is with and not without beauty. Otherwise His glory might well be joyless.³

While Barth does associate beauty with the being of God, he *does not* allow that beauty is attributed to God's *essence*, therefore "also" beauty. This is, first of all, because *beauty* is not significantly associated with the LORD in scripture.⁴ Second, and perhaps more importantly, Barth avoids beauty because he deems it an act of "philosophical willfulness."⁵ "The Bible neither requires nor permits us, because God is beautiful to expound the beauty of God as the ultimate cause producing and moving all things, in the way which we can and must do this in regard to God's grace or holiness or eternity, or His omnipotent knowledge and will."⁶ In short, Barth understands the use of beauty as the third transcendental in scholastic theology and wishes to avoid the constraining influence of Thomistic philosophy. However, while beauty may not be listed among other scriptural qualities and attributes of the LORD it is philologically associated with the *Glory* of the Lord. Glory, then, is the means for the consideration of the beauty of God.⁷ Moreover, despite the danger that aesthetics occasions, if beauty is omitted

---

3. Barth, *CD* 2/1:655.

4. "Attention should also be given to the fact that we cannot include the concept of beauty with the main concepts of the doctrine of God, with the divine perfections which are the divine essence itself. In view of what biblical testimony says about God it would be an unjustified risk to try to bring the knowledge of God under the denominator of the idea of the beautiful even in the same way as we have done in our consideration of these leading concepts. It is not a leading concept. Not even in passing can we make it a primary motif in our understanding of the whole being of God as we necessarily did in the case of these other concepts" (Barth, *CD* 2/1:652).

5. Barth, *CD* 2/1:652.

6. Barth, *CD* 2/1:652.

7. "We must now point to the purely philological fact that the significance of the word 'glory' and its Hebrew, Greek, Latin and even German equivalents, at least includes and expresses what we call beauty" (Barth, *CD* 2/1:653). Also, as a sort of caveat, Barth cites Augustine with approval (Barth, *CD* 2/1:656).

from theology then joy, humor, desire, and interest go along with it.[8] Perhaps most importantly, however, Barth figures the beauty of the LORD most explicitly with the expression of the Trinity in the reality of Jesus. As Garrett writes:

> Barth's decision to incorporate the rhetoric of beauty into the doctrine of God through the person and work of Christ acknowledges and accounts for the aforementioned concerns and fears. Yet, if the concept of beauty is to be serviceable, he insists that "we speak of God's beauty only in explanation of His glory," where divine glory, Barth surmises, is "the sum of the divine perfections and ... the divine self-sufficiency ... which overflows and declares itself." It is this over flow for which Barth desires to account, not as some ethereal, abstract divine force but as the persuasive and convincing part of God's glorious self-revelation, "giving pleasure, awakening desire, and creating enjoyment" in his creatures. Hence, beauty plays an essential, yet subservient role to explicating God's glory.[9]

The divergent views of Bultmann and Barth introduce a key problem in the initial consideration of theological aesthetic: accommodating beauty in the context of Protestant theology is a tenuous endeavor. Balthasar's theological aesthetics seems to be at odds with central Protestant assumptions and confessions. For example, for Balthasar classical philosophy is accorded a kind of authority beneath but alongside scripture.[10] Beauty is key because it is one of the three transcendentals of scholastic theology of being and is therefore both primary and central.[11] Moreover, underlying and surrounding the entire work *some* notion of Platonic form is held at least tentatively

---

8. "The theologian who has no joy in his work is not a theologian at all. Sulky faces, morose thoughts and boring ways of speaking are intolerable in this science. May God deliver us from what the Catholic Church reckons one of the seven sins of the monk—*taedium*—in respect of the great spiritual truths which theology has to do. But we must know, of course, that it is only God who can keep us from it" (Barth, CD 2/1:656).

9. Garrett, "God's Beauty-in-Act," 461.

10. See Balthasar, *Seeing the Form*, 154–60. Also, all of Balthasar, *Realm of Metaphysics*, is dedicated to classical metaphysics.

11. "In a world that no longer has enough confidence in itself to affirm the beautiful, the proofs of truth have lost their cogency. In other words, syllogisms may still dutifully clatter away like rotary presses or computers which infallibly spew out an exact number of answer by the minute. But the logic of these answers is itself a mechanism which no longer captivates anyone. The very conclusions are no longer conclusive. And if this is how the transcendentals fare because one of them has been banished, what will happen with Being itself? Thomas described being (*das Sein*) as a 'sure light' for that which exists (das Seiende)?" (Balthasar, *Seeing the Form*, 19).

in mind.¹² Finally, the entire endeavor is *heavily* philosophic and takes very seriously the role of perception and "natural theology."¹³ Doesn't all of this negate the possibility of thorough-going Protestant acceptance of Balthasar's work?

First, bearing in mind the criticisms of McGilchrist, the criteria for considering the beauty, desire, or glory of the LORD should not be judged upon the left hemisphere criteria of utility or profit but rather on the basis of the more appropriate categories of *relationship* and experience. So while it is true that Catholics have the benefit of a legacy that embraces the beauty of God, Protestant interpretation is not thereby bound to accept beauty as an *essential transcendental* of God's character in absence of scriptural reference. However, if the perception of beauty and therefore "longing" are not qualities of *relationship* with God, then we are in open contradiction not only of scripture but of good sense.¹⁴ Therefore, a consideration of what is beautiful and desirable about God should be no offense to Protestant sensibilities.¹⁵ Second, theological aesthetics breaks out of the self-referential,

---

12. While an allegation of Platonic influence cannot be ruled out, Garrett points out that there are significant differences between Balthasar's aesthetics and those offered by Platonism. "Balthasar's notion of *Gestalt* differs from Plato's theory of forms (*eidos*) because Plato jettisons particularity in order to ascend to some ethereal ideal. He differs from Aristotle's notion of form (*morphe*) in that form is not the pinnacle of being but rather revelatory of it. If theological discourse is to do justice to God's self-revelation and thus speak truly of God, it must attend to the particularity of his self-revelation while also accounting for his universality and singularity" (Garrett, *God's Beauty-In-Act*, 40).

13. For example, Garrett writes: "By rooting human ontology first in the created order, Balthasar appears to posit a continuous, unbroken relationship between God and humanity, for even 'a negative relationship to the God of grace is still a relationship, even a very real relationship, to him!' But, such a claim seems to minimize the depth, depravation, and destructive character of the human condition, of human sin" (Garrett, *God's Beauty-In-Act*, 85).

14. Garrett writes: "To exclude God's beauty from our understanding of that encounter makes his truth and goodness unattractive, lifeless, boring, and cold. In fact, by ignoring or sneering at God's beauty, we actually delimit our understanding, closing off the possibility of experiencing the triune God himself. If, however, his beauty attracts, persuades, and draws us out of ourselves and into something greater—participation in his divine life—then his beauty shapes and forms our imaginations such that we can envision how to perform our part in his drama of redemption, all by the power of the Holy Spirit (John 6:65)" (Garrett, *God's Beauty-In-Act*, 44).

15. While as a whole Protestantism may be guilty of neglecting the consideration of the beauty of God, there are many exceptions to the rule. For example, beauty is a controlling element of the theology of Jonathan Edwards who relates it especially to God's glory much like Balthasar. "For it appears that all that is ever spoken of in the Scripture as an ultimate end of God's works is included in that one phrase, 'the glory of God'; which is the name by which the last end of God's works is most commonly called

abstract, and propositional theological box in part through reference to classical philosophy and partially through recourse to human perception of creation. While doubts about the distorting role of Platonic or Aristotelian philosophy are perfectly reasonable, there is a scientific plank in the eye of Protestant theological scholarship. While perhaps avoiding Platonism we have plunged headlong into vacuous scientific empiricism. If we believe scripture then there is something above, beyond and behind creation (e.g., Eph 6:12; Rom 8:20–23, 38). Moreover, at some level we are given to understand these supra-natural things (e.g., 1 Cor 6:1–3; 13:11–12). Whether we speak of these things as "forms, types, archetypes" or some other set of terms, we may agree about our purpose. We intend to discuss ontology. Empty materialism is an option that is denied us by scripture.

So rather than a grudging allowance of beauty as a sort of necessary evil, I hope we may proceed with an openness to a different kind of thinking than has been typical of modern or post-modern theology. It is not therefore less scriptural, rigorous, true, or serious. It is merely a different way of paying theological attention. However, before arriving at McGilchrist's goal of a "unified hemispheric approach,"[16] there are a number of pre-requisite components that *provide* for such: (1) appropriate disposition of the subject, (2) the cooperation of faith and reason, and (3) the life, death, and resurrection of Jesus as the ultimate expression and norm for beauty.

Perception: The Appropriate Disposition of the Subject

> Objectivity [which] *requires* interpretation of what one finds, depends on imagination for its achievement. Detachment has a deeply ambiguous nature. The cool, detached stance of the scientific or bureaucratic mind ultimately lead where we do not wish to follow. And the relationship implied by the left-hemisphere attention brought to bear through the scientific method, with its implied materialism, is not *no* relationship—merely a disengaged relationship, implying incorrectly, that the observer does not have an impact on the observed (and is not altered by what he or she observes). The betweeness is not absent, just denied, and therefore of a particular—particularly "cold"—kind. . . . The

---

in Scripture: and seems to be the name which most aptly signifies the thing" (Edwards, *Ethical Writings*, 526).

16. "Ultimately, we need to unite the ways of seeing yielded by both hemispheres. Above all the attention of the left hemisphere needs to be reintegrated with that of the right hemisphere if it is not to prove damaging" (McGilchrist, *Master and His Emissary*, 174).

right hemisphere's gaze is intrinsically empathetic, by contrast and acknowledges the *inevitability* of "betweeness."[17]

Relationship through the Self-disclosing Spirit

One of the most important contributions of Balthasar's theological aesthetics is the accent placed upon relational modes of knowledge. Instead of an "objective observer" the theologian is deeply engaged as a subject with God as a subject. Balthasar, like the church fathers, requires the essential unity of spirituality and theology. "Objectivity" unbalanced by the subjectivity required by the totalizing love relationship between God and human beings is inappropriate to the whole nature of the endeavor. Even more, however, Balthasar does not only commend a relational subjectivity, he commends the *correct disposition* of subject to subject.[18]

Left-hemisphere approaches to knowledge that pretend an objective "God's-eye" view also tend toward a disposition of *hubris*, a disposition repeatedly and soundly reproved in Proverbs. Balthasar argues that *all* theology must proceed not from the light of reason, but from the light of faith. By an "obedient surrender to the radiant light in which alone by faith and not by vision he partakes in the wisdom of the self-revealing God," the theologian is able to think and therefore *see* obediently.[19] Obedience and deep yielded-ness to God in turn allows for the fusion of *gnosis* and *pistis* that characterizes the relationship that becomes the norm of the Christian's entire existence.

> Only when by "will" and "affect" we understand the engagement of the person in all his depth—only then does intellectual faith become a genuine answer to God's disclosure of his depth as person; for God too does not primarily communicate "truths" about himself, but rather bestows *himself* as absolute truth and love. This is why the deepening and revitalization of the person

---

17. McGilchrist, *Master and His Emissary*, 166.

18. The problem is not with objectivity per se, but by the imbalance of objective and subjective approaches. "It is not permissible simply to exclude this objective structure of faith, which for every Christian belongs to the very content of faith, from the analysis of faith's conscious aspect, in order then to describe this aspect as a purely psychological process. . . . The light of being envelops both subject and object, and, in the act of cognition, it becomes the overarching identity between the two. The light of faith stems from the object which, revealing itself to the subject, draws it out beyond itself (otherwise it would not be faith) into the sphere of the object" (Balthasar, *Seeing the Form*, 175).

19. Balthasar, *Seeing the Form*, 160.

which occurs within the act of faith (as a living act which includes love and hope) has been described by Thomas, along with the whole tradition, as the unfolding of the living Spirit of God in the spirit of man.[20]

The concentration on God's identity as *subject* within the relational paradigm for epistemology also shifts the work of knowing away from active efforts driven by left-hemisphere methodology and into more passive models that are predicated not on reason, but on attentiveness to this essentially imbalanced relationship.[21] For example Balthasar argues: "We must, rather, never lose from sight the permanent one-sidedness, fundamental to the process of Christian revelation, of God's act whereby he grants us participation in his being, which is his act in Jesus Christ, who can be approached only with personal categories."[22]

Theological epistemology has therefore been reframed from primarily *abstract-propositional* (left hemisphere) to primarily *contextual-relational* (right hemisphere). As such, Balthasar provides yet another service to theology by dissolving the partition between the scholar and saint.[23] Theology, then, must proceed more along the lines not of emotional detachment to an object, but intimately motivated admiration of the ultimate subject.

The ramifications for an approach to *Lady Wisdom* are not subtle. As scholars and students we must take our place not only *in conversation* with the God of the text but we must likewise maintain the correct inward disposition. There is no safe place from which we can talk *about* scripture

---

20. Balthasar, *Seeing the Form*, 161.

21. "Christian faith, being God's witness in us, can be understood only as the answer to this interior and intimate self-witnessing of the God who opens up the secrets of his Heart as he gives himself to humanity. . . . Faith is participation in the free self-disclosure of God's interior life and light, just as the spiritual nature of the creature means participation in the unveiled-ness of all reality. The created spirit does not 'deduce' this reality (in which God is included in whatever way) from indication and logical premises; as spirit, it is from the very start already set in the light of this reality, at the same time thinking from within it and directing its thought toward it" (Balthasar, *Seeing the Form*, 152).

22. Balthasar goes on to write, "This should not be interpreted in the extreme extrinsicist Protestant sense, as if faith and the justification proper to it remain 'external' to man and can be 'imputed' to him only juridically. The participation bestowed by God, rather, is highly efficacious; God achieves what he will, just as he achieved it in the miracles of the Gospel: the blind really see, the deaf really hear, the dead really rise and live. But he who is spiritually dead rises to life of God in him. 'In him' here means that he lives, but only by virtue of the fact that God lives in him. He lives subjectively because the objective God, who he is not, lives in him" (Balthasar, *Seeing the Form*, 175–76).

23. Garrett, *God's Beauty-In-Act*, 79.

without being addressed *by God*. There is no point of remove at which we are not addressed. Our study makes us not masters of material but youths vulnerable to the content of the conversation.

Cognition: The Cooperation of Faith and Reason in Theological Aesthetics

"As things become dulled and inauthentic they become conceptualized [left hemisphere] rather than experienced [right hemisphere]; they are taken out of their living context, a bit like ripping the heart out of a living body."[24] McGilchrist warns that the abstraction from *lived* reality and perception is the hallmark of left hemisphere approaches to perception. Balthasar requires that subjective and objective experience must be unified. For Balthasar beauty is not primarily a subjective phenomenon, but rather a subjective response to the reality of objective beauty. "[The] absolute determination (and, hence, also concordance effected by the object of faith) is an essential component of the aesthetics of revelation. In this we can see both an opposition to an inner-worldly aesthetics and a surpassing of it which perfects it, since the truly beautiful is not magically 'conjured up' from man's emotive states, but, rather, surrenders itself on its own initiative with a graciousness that man cannot grasp."[25]

In this Balthasar provides for the unity of philosophy and theology in the physical, existential, and divine person of Jesus. Perception and reason cooperate with that which is known by grace through faith, because in Jesus objective and subjective are joined.

Furthermore, Balthasar critiques the notion that "faith" is a mere "acceptance of truth" and thereby a *decision* predicated upon certain "preliminary knowledge."[26] This is not the model presented by scripture. Rather, Balthasar asserts that faith should be understood as a "kind of knowledge" that functions differently from, "human intellectual modes."[27] It is not for "spiritual knowledge" to destroy the "natural" (as Kierkegaard or Hegel), nor is it for "natural" knowledge to reduce faith "into a "scientifically comprehensible structure."[28] "Man's ultimate attitude in response to God's self-revelation can stand only in the most intimate connection with that other

---

24. McGilchrist, *Master and His Emissary*, 154.
25. Balthasar, *Seeing the Form*, 305.
26. Balthasar, *Seeing the Form*, 305.
27. This sort of knowing is reflected in St. Anselm's prayer of knowing found in chapter 1 of his *Proslogion*. See Anselm, *Prayers and Meditations*, 239–40.
28. Balthasar, *Seeing the Form*, 138.

ultimate attitude of man which is the philosophic."[29] Therefore, faith is not antithetical to reason but both productive and constituent to it.[30]

Likewise, Balthasar corrects the reductive notion of reason as "an innate, self-contained, and *entirely* empirical cognitive process." Rather, reason functions, and is *intended* to function, at a *more than natural or empirical* level. The human spirit works *with* the mind to grant understanding. "If the [human] spirit is to see and understand the facts as indicators of revelation, then it must receive as well the faculty to see what the signs are intended to express: it must include in anticipatory fashion that point of convergence which makes the signs comprehensible." More importantly, however, without the agency of the Holy Spirit, full reason is hobbled.

> Just as in the inductive process the universal law is suddenly seen in a particular case or in a group of cases, so too do the signs of revelation crystallize about a centre which becomes visible in the light of faith. The act of faith is, thus rational precisely at the moment that it is made truly as an act of *faith*. The extent to which an individual believer can justify his vision rationally and reflectively is secondary. The act of faith does not derive its central rationality from a previous exercise of naked reason: this could not be the case, since its rationality really emerges only in the act of faith itself.[31]

By providing for a more balanced and holistic definition of both faith and reason Balthasar not only provides for a more *correct* and *soluble* framing of the problem, he also echoes the criticisms of Left-hemisphere rationality.[32] It is not that faith and reason are adversarial and competitive, but

---

29. Balthasar, *Seeing the Form*, 138.

30. "The act of faith, in its very roots, is both 'supernatural' (because sustained by the light of grace) and 'natural' (as the perfect fulfillment of all spiritual aspirations); both founded objectively upon God's revelatory act and established subjectively and existentially, since everything now is construed in terms of the spirit's dynamic orientation to its formal object" (Balthasar, *Seeing the Form*, 145).

31. Balthasar, *Seeing the Form*, 170.

32. For example McGilchrist notes the critical role that the right hemisphere plays in maintaining a connection with reality and dismissing false premises. Patients who suffered right hemisphere deficiencies generally accepted the truth of syllogisms *despite ridiculous premises* because the premises were internally consistent (i.e., [1] all monkeys climb trees; [2] the porcupine is a monkey; [3] the porcupine climbs trees). McGilchrist explains, "In the left-hemisphere situation, it prioritizes the system, regardless of experience: it stays within the system of signs. Truth, for it, is coherence, because for it there is no world beyond, no Other, nothing outside the mind, to correspond with. . . . The right hemisphere prioritizes what it learns from experience: the real state of existing things 'out there.' For the right hemisphere, truth is not mere coherence, but

rather they are mutually and necessarily interdependent. For example, anyone who asks, "What basis acceptable to reason can we give to his [Jesus'] authoritative claims?" has become "enmeshed in an insoluble dilemma" because if someone believes on the basis of reason "then his is not believing on the basis of divine authority, and his faith is not Christian faith." Likewise, the subject may dismiss all reason and probability, "but then his faith is not really rational."[33] "Such a danger, it is true, is never far off when the existential dimension is played off against the 'historical-critical' dimension (which occurs when the modern scientific concept of truth is accepted for theology) and the result is a 'Christ of faith' versus an 'historical Jesus.'"[34]

In theological aesthetics, Jesus is key in the balance of faith and reason. He is distinct from any other object or subject in creation. Jesus finds man externally and objectively in history. "The believer cannot dissolve this objective form by assimilating it into himself in an interior existential sense, nor can he ever succeed in rarefying the Jesus of history into a mere Christ of faith."[35] The reality of the incarnation is not to be deemed one event among many in the history of creation. It is the in-breaking of super-reality and the fusion of the absolute with the natural. Therefore, it is not merely that the incarnation reframes philosophy, but rather Jesus provides its true end. Natural reason can only find its fulfillment in relation to the objective form of Jesus.[36]

---

correspondence with something other than itself. Truth, for it, is understood in the sense of being 'true' to something, faithfulness to whatever it is that exists apart from ourselves" (McGilchrist, *Master and His Emissary*, 193).

33. Balthasar, *Seeing the Form*, 168.

34. Balthasar goes on to write, "This tragic dialectic, into which Protestant theology has largely fallen, lacks exactly the same thing as the rationalistic school of Catholic apologetics: Namely, the dimension of aesthetic contemplation. The figure which confronts us in Holy Scripture is more and more dissected in 'historical-critical' fashion until all that is left of what was once a living organism is a dead heap of flesh, blood and bones. In the field of theology this means at every step the same inability to perceive form which a mechanistic biology and psychology reveal with regard to the unitive phenomenon of a living being. Nothing expresses more unequivocally the profound failure of these theologies than their deeply anguished, joyless, and cheerless tone: torn between knowing and believing, they are no longer able to *see* anything, nor can they, therefore, be convincing in any visible way" (Balthasar, *Seeing the Form*, 169).

35. Balthasar, *Seeing the Form*, 176.

36. Balthasar writes: "Because of that final securing of reality which the believer who encounters God in Christ experiences, the theological vision makes it possible for the first time for the philosophical act of encounter with Being to occur in all its depth. It is only the man who has encountered the living God in the particular form of revelation chosen by him who can really find God in all things and, thus, who can truly and constantly philosophise. And, because it is the declaration of eternal life for the world, this form of revelation gains universal significance and determines all aspects of the

The immediate significance of these points in light of the approach to *Lady Wisdom* in Proverbs cannot be overdrawn. Trinitarian and Christological approaches to Wisdom are not to be merely cataloged as later theological allegories imposed on a text. Rather, what Proverbs strives to attain at its place in history is the reality of a Trinitarian God expressing himself to his chosen people. It would be strange, indeed, if a scriptural work failed to express the ontological reality of this Creator, since it is not the text, but all reality which leans toward the incarnation. We should expect, therefore, that elements of each of the divine persons will be present in one way or another. If the substance of Wisdom is the diverse description of God's search for humanity and humanity's search for God it is only reasonable that personified Wisdom will have a great deal in common with the experienced and historical reality of the Son.

Basis: The Life, Death and Resurrection of Jesus as the Ultimate Expression and Norm for Beauty

Introduction: True Beauty vs. "This-Worldly" Beauty

Beauty as an absolute quality may seem to be "self-defining" but this is not entirely so. First of all, Balthasar recognizes that there is a significant difference between beauty as a divine absolute and cultural ideals of beauty. Culturally beauty may be reduced to utility, physical form, or many of a diverse set of attributes. All of these amount to what Balthasar calls a "this-worldly form" of beauty.[37] Regardless of how self-evident our cultural ideals about beauty may *seem* they fall short of the biblical and theological ideal provided in Christ. Balthasar writes: "A theology that makes use of such concepts [i.e., "this-worldly" beauty] will sooner or later cease to be a 'theological aesthetics'—that is, the attempt to do aesthetics at the level and with the methods of theology—and deteriorate into an 'aesthetic theology' by betraying and selling out theological substance to the current viewpoints of an inner-worldly theory of beauty."[38]

As such Balthasar exhorts that we must, "forbid ourselves every kind of falsifying or minimizing application of aesthetic categories out of reverence for God's Word, for its awesomeness and its, literal, in-comparable pre-eminence."[39] What is at issue for Balthasar is the *substance* of beauty

---

formal object of philosophy" (Balthasar, *Seeing the Form*, 142).

37. Balthasar, *Seeing the Form*, 37.
38. Balthasar, *Seeing the Form*, 37.
39. Balthasar, *Seeing the Form*, 37.

over against human appraisal of it. Since beauty is an absolute quality of the LORD expressed in his being, then that beauty is substantially and *objectively* expressed in particular *physical* form. The very being as well as the particular physical form of Jesus and the history surrounding his appearance then become the normative expression of the absolute beauty of God, by which all other things may then be measured.[40]

The Beauty of Christ as Being

As noted above, rather than maintaining the modern dichotomy between the "Christ of Faith" and the "Historical Jesus" Balthasar argues that Jesus is more than "mere sign" and even more than "mere form." Rather Jesus is "distinguished from all other worldly forms and aesthetic images by the fact that Jesus's form is the Primal Image—the Archetype itself—that 'has life in itself' (John 5:26)."[41] Jesus as God is the "superform" that not only *has* form but is able to communicate being through himself because he *is* being itself. In Christ, we have the divine-human form, ontological centre, and mytho-ethical archetype.

Jesus, as the God-man is able to speak from God and *as* God in the "I-Form." This makes his witness and testimony objectively different than any other human being. His form is therefore *clearly distinguishable from every human teacher*.[42] In him divine absolutes are displayed in all their glory and demand subjective response.[43] However, beyond his testimony is his very

---

40. The physical reality of the incarnation is a key element of Balthasar's theological aesthetics: "The tendency today is towards the destruction of form: whether it is the Bultmannians, anthropocentric transcendentalists, philosophical functionalists, those who emphasize rhythm alone (E. Przywara) or Teilhardian evolutionists, they are all following the trend to the formless, though they could never be reconciled with each other. Against this strange univocity of the moderns, the character of *form* of the revelation must be maintained—in an unmodern manner—for only when we accept the unique incarnation of the Logos can the infinite dimensions of the Pneuma be understood as his glorification (John 16:14) and not as his dissolution" (Balthasar, *Realm of Metaphysics*, 37).

41. Balthasar, *Seeing the Form*, 176.

42. "The man who is placed before the phenomenon of Christ sees both things at the same time—the proximity and the distance. These belong to the contour of this figure, and they are utterly visible to the unprejudiced glance. If a person lacks such a vision, then some other person who does see can demonstrate exactly where it is that the person in questions has failed to see the object" (Balthasar, *Seeing the Form*, 180).

43. So Garrett, "these transcendentals are interconnected and interpenetrating triad that should not be compartmentalized. To separate beauty, truth, and goodness results in distortion not only of the triad but also of Christ himself. Thus, to see the act of Christ on the cross as merely beautiful is to turn towards sentimentality. To see

being which orients all creation toward himself. It is not so much that his person cannot exist without context, but rather context *exists* because of his person. Balthasar writes:

> A statue can be placed anywhere; a symphony can be performed in any concert-hall; a poem of Goethe's can be understood and enjoyed without any knowledge of its biographical context. The form of Jesus, however, cannot be detached from the place in space and time in which it stands. He s what He Is only by fulfilling, on the one hand, all the promises that point to him, and, on the other, by himself making promises which he will at some time fulfill. To the horizontal power with which he encompasses all time and rules all space "even to the ends of the earth," centering world history on himself, there corresponds the vertical power with which he makes the Father visible and with which he makes present, in his witness concerning the Father, the Father's witness to him. The double, cross-like pattern, in which his form reaches beyond itself and which is precisely what makes him to be what he is, demands that a person who sees him come to understand him within this spiritual space which he has encompassed.[44]

All things stand in essential relation to Jesus as God. As the ontological center, Jesus orients the universe *epistemologically* and provides the very means by which God can be known.[45] At the same time, Jesus as man becomes the ultimate archetype who fulfills the hopes and requirements of humankind as well as providing both demonstration of the character of God and example for the substance of human living.[46]

---

the act of Christ on the cross as merely good is to understand Christ as a good moral example incapable of transforming humanity" (Garrett, *God's Beauty-In-Act*, 150).

44. Balthasar, *Seeing the Form*, 192–93.

45. "The synthetic power of the active 'faculty' of believing (*as habitus and virtus fidei*) does not reside primarily in the believer himself, but in God, who indwells him even as he reveals himself and in whose light and act the believer participates.... It is not that Christ simply facilitates the *initium fidei* by his prompting; rather he bestows faith on the believer in such a way that the centre permanently remains in Christ—and not only the centre of the object, without which the act could not come to be, but also the centre of the act, without which the object could never be attained. God can be known only by God" (Balthasar, *Seeing the Form*, 174).

46. "Christ, the full and perfect man, has in his own totality the experience of what God is. He is, with body and soul, the embodiment of this experience. And, as God-become-man who reveals God to man, Christ, even as God, has the experience of what man is.... This archetype is both things at once: the inimitable and what must be imitated. It determines both itself and what is alien to itself, without both things being able to come under the common head" (Balthasar, *Seeing the Form*, 296).

The Beauty of the Cross of Christ

However, while absolute beauty encompasses much of what can be recognized and embraced from a "this-worldly" aesthetic vantage point, it is the reality of the crucifixion of God that troubles and transforms theological aesthetics. Beauty must not only *include* the Cross, but be *normed* by it. Balthasar writes:

> [Theological aesthetics] embraces the most abysmal ugliness of sin and hell by virtue of the condescension of divine love, which has brought even sin and hell into that divine art for which there is no human analogue. The conclusion to be drawn from all this is that, just as we can never attain to the living God in any way except through his Son become man, but in this Son we can really attain to God in himself, so, too, we ought never to speak of God's beauty without reference to the form and manner of appearing which he exhibits in salvation-history. The beauty and glory which are proper to God may be inferred and "read" off from God's epiphany and its incomprehensible glory which is worthy of God himself.[47]

The crucifixion likewise constitutes an ultimate aesthetic form because it encapsulates the *death* of absolute beauty because of the depth and means of divine love.

> All other conditions—the incarnation of the Word, his death and Resurrection, the Church, its structures, the Christian life—are but means that make possible the Trinitarian depth and breadth of faith. All other conditions are contained within the movement and the event of the Lord's death and resurrection; the Trinitarian aspect alone encompasses every event of salvation-history as its essential ground and goal. To use an aesthetic analogy: every beautiful form is perceived as the expression, frangible within space and time, of more than temporal beauty, and this supratemporal beauty is able both to contain and to vindicate the death of the beautiful, because death, too, belongs to the form in which immortal beauty becomes manifest, and it is dying which in the end truly impresses immortal beauty upon the spirit that contemplates it.[48]

The cross beckons us to the love of the Trinitarian life, or as Garrett summarizes the movement: "God's beauty is real and not to be relegated

---

47. Balthasar, *Seeing the Form*, 121.
48. Balthasar, *Seeing the Form*, 192.

to the realm of the ornamental and innocuous pleasant whereby humanity seeks such beauty in order to escape from its painful existence. On the contrary, God's beauty becomes *deformius* on the cross in order to bring about *transforatio* in the resurrection."[49]

Ultimately then, the apex of beauty is perfectly figured in and fills the cross of Christ. It is the perfect, harmonious, loving association of the Trinity, objectively and subjectively tuned to capture and enrapture fallen humanity. Beauty is the substance and character of the God who went to such lengths. The *only* appropriate human response to the beauty of our Trinitarian God is *desire*. In the words of Saint Thomas:

> [God is] vehement in his manifold and beneficent Eros toward all beings, and he spurs them on to search for him zealously with a yearning *eros*, thus showing himself zealous for love inasmuch as the things that are desired are considered worthy of zeal and inasmuch as he allows himself to be affected by the zeal of all beings for which he cares. In short, both to possess *eros* and to love erotically belong to everything Good and Beautiful, and *eros* has its primal roots in the Beautiful and the Good: *eros* exists and comes into being only through the Beautiful and the Good.[50]

The reality of Christ's ministry and death must engage with wisdom, both as a personification and as an expression of human experience of creation. If Wisdom would be truly beautiful and desirable, it must reckon with the cross.

Conclusion

Finally, turning to aesthetics itself, Balthasar understands the discipline with Thomas Aquinas under the terms *species* ("form" or *Gestalt*) and *lumen* ("splendor" or *Glanz*). The "form" is that external, physical, and therefore "objective" element of the Gospel:

> As form, the beautiful can be materially grasped and even subjected to numerical calculation as a relationship of numbers, harmony and the laws of Being. . . . God manifests himself in his creation and in the order of salvation.[51]

---

49. Garrett, *God's Beauty-In-Act*, 144.

50. Aquinas quoted in Balthasar, *Seeing the Form*, 119. Here, the translation is altered.

51. Balthasar, *Seeing the Form*, 115.

The "effect of the form" is however, not a function of the psychology of the subject, but rather is a manifestation of *being* which is best understood as the "splendor" of the thing itself.

> Psychologically, the effect of beautiful forms on the soul may be described in a great variety of ways. But a true grasp of this effect will not be attained unless one brings to bear logical and ethical concepts, concepts of truth and value: in a word, concepts drawn from a comprehensive doctrine of Being. The form as it appears to us is beautiful only because the delight that it arouses in us is founded upon the fact that, in it, the truth and goodness of the depths of reality itself are manifested and bestowed, and this manifestation and bestowal reveal themselves to us as being something infinitely and inexhaustibly valuable and fascinating. The appearance of the form, as revelation of the depths, is an indissoluble union of two things. It is the real presence of the depths, so the whole of reality, *and* it is a real pointing beyond itself to these depths.[52]

This then, is where Balthasar's perception engages McGilchrist's call for a unified vision. For Balthasar, there are two different and necessary stages in which we "see." The first stage deals with the apprehension of God's self-revelation in scripture and creation, and is therefore addressed to perceiving that form.[53] In this aesthetic theory of vision "the facts of revelation are perceived initially in the light of grace, and faith grows in such a way that it allows the self-evidence of these facts."[54] The second stage, however, deals not with *mere perception* but with the *transport* that is characteristic of engagement with true beauty. This stage is most adequately summed up in Paul's theological aesthetics wherein vision and *rapture* are understood as a single process.[55]

> This is a movement of the entire person, leading away from himself through the vision towards the invisible God, a movement, furthermore, which the word "faith" describes only imperfectly, although it is in this movement that faith has its proper "setting

---

52. In the same passage Balthasar surveys Protestant aesthetics: "Protestant aesthetics has wholly misunderstood this dimension and even denounced it as heretical, locating the total essence of beauty in the event in which the light irrupts. Admittedly, form would not be beautiful unless it were fundamentally a sign and appearing of depth and a fullness that, in themselves and in an abstract sense, remain beyond both our reach and our vision" (Balthasar, *Seeing the Form*, 115–16).

53. Balthasar, *Seeing the Form*, 115–16.

54. Balthasar, *Seeing the Form*, 123.

55. Balthasar, *Seeing the Form*, 122.

in life" (*Sitz im Leben*). The transport of the soul, however, must here again be understood in a strictly theological way. In other words, it must be understood not as a merely psychological response to something beautiful in a worldly sense which has been encountered through vision, but as the movement of man's whole being away from himself towards God through Christ, a movement founded on the divine light of grace in the mystery of Christ.[56]

Theological aesthetics is grounded in unified perception and the meaningful correlation of faith and reason. It commends the sort of subjectivity and personal disposition prescribed by Proverbs. Finally, it provides criteria for distinguishing "this-worldy" beauty from the ultimate beauty of Trinitarian harmony expressed by the historical person of Jesus in his crucifixion.

The use of feminine figures and imagery in Proverbs will illustrate a number of different elements of theological aesthetics. First, the role of the female in relation to the implied male audience shows that one of the primary goals of this imagery is to *educate* desire, specifically with respect to relational fidelity and *being* as opposed to *superficial attraction*. The role of the "strange/foreign" woman vs. positive personifications and characters will demonstrate the hope of "absolute beauty" against the lure of "this-worldly" aesthetics. Finally, the combination of *eros* and relational metaphor in conjunction with the canonical frame highlights the totalizing disposition of love and desire toward YHWH. Ultimately, theological aesthetics places Christ as the ultimate form toward which all scripture and all history lean. Therefore, *Lady Wisdom* anticipates and "leans toward" Christ.

With the reintegration of left and right hemispheric modes provided for we may now turn our attention to the more mundane concerns of the tools and terms adequate to the explication of poetic metaphor in Proverbs. For this we turn toward the constellation of approaches that may be broadly termed Cognitive Metaphor Theory (CMT). In what follows we will briefly introduce defining features and terms central to our study of Proverbs.

Cognitive Metaphor and Blending Theory Contribute to a More Balanced Definition and Methodology of Metaphor

> The Cognitive Theory of Metaphor is important for investigations into the phenomenon of figurativeness because it provides

---

56. Balthasar, *Seeing the Form*, 113.

the researcher with a well-developed metalinguistic apparatus, including heuristically significant concepts such as source domain, target domain, metaphoric model, conceptual mapping, conceptual correspondences, metaphoric entailment, etc. In many cases, applying this apparatus allows us to explain many real properties of figurative units which could not be captured in the framework of any traditional approach. The explanatory power of CTM is especially high in cases where an explanation is needed as to how a particular novel metaphor works. Speakers creating a new metaphor in order to be able to talk about a difficult, barely structured situation, propose, by using such a metaphor, a way of structuring the given situation, i.e., an original view on it. The metaphor is therefore not just a means of naming, but an instrument of conceptualizing the world. [CMT] is the only theory which points to this fact and comes with appropriate tools of analysis.[57]

Lakoff and Turner define metaphor as "conceptual mappings because they are what is responsible for the phenomenon traditionally called metaphor. It is the conceptual work that lies behind the language that makes metaphor what it is. Metaphorical language is not something special. It is the language that conventionally expresses the source—domain concept of conceptual metaphor."[58] For example, considering a metaphor like, "the foundation of the argument," the source domain for the metaphor comes from the concept of a building. In the same way that a building must stand upon a stable basis so must a logical argument.

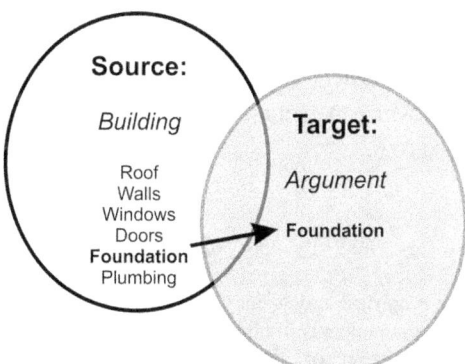

Figure 2. Source—Target Mapping

57. Dobrovol'skij and Piirainen, *Figurative Language*, 142.
58. Lakoff and Johnson, *More Than Cool Reason*, 137.

Certain elements of this metaphorical construction are accepted and "mapped" onto the target category (i.e., "argument"). In turn, certain entailments of a metaphorical construction may be broadly accepted and conventionalized (i.e., an argument has a foundation), while others may not (i.e., an argument has windows) (cf. fig. 2). In the book of Proverbs the metaphor LIFE IS A ROAD is a basic metaphor in which the elements of "choice," "manner of movement," "obstacles," and "destinations" are mapped from the source category of ROAD onto the target category of LIFE. One of the key concerns of this work will be to consider which elements of the source domain WOMAN are mapped onto the target category of WISDOM and why.

In the following section key methodological and terminological refinements will be surveyed. First, key terms basic to CMT and blending provide for greater clarity and function. Second, the hierarchy of metaphor described by CMT explains how poetic metaphors are frequently unified because they are founded in a more basic underlying metaphor. Third, the basic apparatus of conceptual blending not only clarifies the epistemological basis for metaphor but also explains how multiple and mixed metaphors can work together in a single conceptual blend.

Terminological Clarification Provided by CMT

Metaphor

There are a number of terminological distinctions provided by Turner, Johnson, and Lakoff that are helpful. First, the authors maintain but redefine the word "metaphor." Rather than a function of *words*, metaphor is the cross-mapping of concepts according to a controlling image. Maintenance of the term "metaphor" is helpful for the sake of convention, but requires an understanding that while metaphors are frequently expressed in language they are not limited to it.[59]

---

59. In relation to empirical and scientific approaches to metaphor as a cognitive phenomenon, the most complete and stable treatment is by Dobrovol'skij and Piirainen. They avoid the term "metaphor" altogether and prefer to speak instead of "figurative language" or more specifically "Conventional Figurative Units" that are defined by (1) image content and (2) additional meaning. Their concern is primarily linguistic and weighted toward clarifying the conceptual role of figurative language within and between cultures. While their work is laudable, their methodological apparatus and metaphorical framework are inapt for poetic analysis. See Dobrovol'skij and Piirainen, *Figurative Language*, 14–29.

Metonymy

Metonymy is traditionally understood as an "other naming," as in cases when the "White House" is substituted in a sentence describing a statement from the executive branch. Lackoff and Turner point out that metonymy, like metaphor is: conceptual, constituted by a mapping, extends linguistic resources, and can become conventionalized. The primary distinction between conceptual metaphor and metonymy is that in conceptual metaphor a source is being mapped onto a target. In metonymy, there is only one domain. One element from the source/target is being used to represent a constellation of ideas from the same domain.

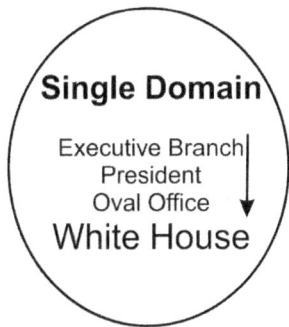

Figure 3. Metonymy

Therefore, while metaphor seeks to elucidate the target space in light of the image or logic of the source, metonymy is used mainly as a referential entity to highlight or expand certain components within the same source domain as in fig. 3.[60] The terminological boon to this insight cannot be overstated. First, it maintains and clarifies the force of conventional language. Second, in a single stroke it both accommodates and obviates a number of terms that have lost reasonable definitions, most particularly, *symbol* and *icon*.[61]

---

60. Lakoff and Turner, *More Than Cool Reason*, 101–3.

61. Despite the fact that these two terms carry two millennia worth of divergent meanings Dmitri Dobrovol'skij and Elisabeth Piirainen, still maintain their use as a central component in their analysis of figurative language in culture. See Dobrovol'skij and Piirainen, *Figurative Language*, 243–351. I would argue that the distinction between "symbol" and "icon" is perhaps definitional rather than conceptual. Conversely, as stated by Lakoff and Turner, *metonymy* does exactly what it says it does and though it is expanded to include other occurrences of "source to source" or "target to target" mappings, it is terminologically stable.

Image Schema

An *image schema* is the imaginary figure which structures basic and conventional metaphors. So the image schema for the metaphor LIFE IS A ROAD is a road. However, the image schema may have very little *image* content. For example in the metaphor TIME IS MOVEMENT wherein we conceive of things "ahead of us in time" as "ahead of us" positionally, there is no concrete entity. In these cases the metaphor may be deemed more accurately a *conceptual schema*.[62]

Basic Metaphor

Lakoff and Turner recognize a class of conceptual mappings that are "basic" to a culture, because without the conceptual structuring provided by the source category, certain abstract concepts would be difficult to discuss.[63]

> Basic conceptual metaphors are part of the common conceptual apparatus shared by members of a culture. They are systematic in that there is a fixed correspondence between the structure of the domain to be understood (e.g., death) and the structure of the domain in terms of which we are understanding it (e.g., departure). We usually understand them in terms of common experiences. They are largely unconscious, though attention may be drawn to them. Their operation in cognition is mostly automatic. And they are widely conventionalized in language, that is, there are a great number of words and idiomatic expression in our language whose interpretations depend upon those conceptual metaphors.[64]

---

62. There are exceptions to the "image requirement" for metaphor. For example, consider the metaphorical comment, "time is running out on us," in regard to a love relationship. There is no explicit figure that is provided by "time is running out." Lakoff and Turner provide *conceptual schemas* for cases when the image component of a conceptual metaphor seems to be absent. "Conceptual schemas organize our knowledge. They constitute cognitive models of some aspect of the world, models that we use in comprehending our experience and in reasoning about it. Cognitive models are not conscious they are unconscious and used automatically and effortlessly. We cannot observe them directly, they are inferred from their effects. Of course, we can consciously consider and try to get at what our unconscious models might be, as we have done throughout this book in the case of metaphorical mappings" (Lakoff and Johnson, *More Than Cool Reason*, 66).

63. Lakoff and Johnson figure the "basicness" of a conceptual mapping based on "its conceptual indispensability" for structuring communication (Lakoff and Johnson, *More Than Cool Reason*, 56).

64. Lakoff and Johnson, *More Than Cool Reason*, 51.

While the cognitive placement and role of "basic" metaphors are contested, the proof of concept can be established merely by attempting to speak or even conceive of "time" without reference to linear space (i.e., yesterday is behind/ tomorrow is ahead) or motion (tomorrow is coming, yesterday is falling behind).[65] While it is a problematic concept, it does appear to be true that in cases basic conceptual metaphors are extended or altered in ways which form new conventional conceptual metaphors, in so far as they are expressed through "a range of everyday linguistic expressions."[66] In *Tanakh*, and also in the book of Proverbs, LIFE IS A ROAD is a basic metaphor, as are depictions that modify the road like GOOD IS LIGHT or MORALLY UPRIGHT IS STRAIGHT and their antitheses EVIL IS DARK and MORALLY BAD IS CROOKED.

Stereotype

Typified entities function as metonymy. They are used to represent a member of one class of persons by reference to a group in which membership is predicated not upon identity but upon the possession or absence of generic qualities typical to that set. In Proverbs types are used to provide a schema for condemnation or approbation. McGarty et al., explain that stereotypes (1) aid in explanation, (2) simplify cognition and perception, (3) are part of a group's shared beliefs. Therefore, a stereotype first exists to help the subject "make sense of a situation," while both streamlining their thought process and enabling them to act in accordance with the mores of their society.[67] The purpose of this process is not for direct reference or precise catalog, but to provide a conceptual grouping which is then used as a rubric for personal reflection and the evaluation of behavior within a community. It is not, of itself, a negative mental process, but rather *the* basic process wherein one

---

65. See Lakoff and Johnson, *Metaphors We Live By*, 34–49.

66. The "hierarchy of conceptual metaphor" is shown to be an incredibly helpful correlate in poetic analysis, but is also *inherently subjective* and nearly impossible to falsify. While Lakoff and Johnson argue for a "few *basic* conceptual metaphors" they consider there to be a near infinite possibility for conventional metaphors. "The reason why there are so many conventional metaphors for life, death, and time is that these are very rich concepts for us. When we try to conceptualize the wealth of our experiences of these domains, no single, consistent structure of that experience is possible; instead we need to import structure from a wide variety of source domains if we are to characterize anything approaching the full richness of the target domains" (Lakoff and Johnson, *More Than Cool Reason*, 52–53).

67. McGarty et al., *Stereotypes as Explanations*, 2.

group of people structures perceptions—rightly or wrongly—about other groups.[68]

The stereotype that will preoccupy much of the discussion below is that of the "foreign/strange" woman. In line with the research of McGarty, the function of this abstraction is primarily to explain social placement with relationship to the *familial* and *relational* mores of the young man. It is an educational structure.[69] As Weeks has pointed out the purpose of the stereotype is to diffuse the specific and "[exemplify] a potential temptation that the son may face at some point, and this is illustrative or figurative, rather in the way that a parable is."[70] In metaphorical terms, a stereotype supplies an image schema which in turn becomes the "source" category for people in the real world, which are then placed as "targets" against that conception.

Personification

In Proverbs personification is mainly with regard to Wisdom.[71] The purpose is a conceptual one. Some element of the world is reconceived in light of personal agency. Lackoff and Turner argue first of all, that personification functions according to the basic conceptual metaphor EVENTS ARE ACTIONS and thus may be given causality attributed to an agent.

---

68. The idea that "stereotype" is strictly negative is a problem with recent research. "Individual people have limited capacities to perform cognitive tasks such as processing information. Nevertheless they exist in a complex, multifaceted world that places enormous demands on that limited capacity. This complexity is certainly true of the social environment, and the resulting overload of human information processing capacity leads people to take shortcuts and to adopt biased and erroneous perceptions of the world. Stereotypes are simply one example of the biases that can develop. Over time this negative view of stereotypes has become the perceived wisdom. Stereotypes are not so much aids to understanding but aids to misunderstanding. Stereotypes have received such a bad press in social psychology for a very long time. As Asch (1952) noted, 'The term stereotype has come to symbolize nearly all that is deficient in popular thinking.' ... In particular, stereotypes have often been seen as rigid distorted mental structures that lead people to make serious errors. The negative view has been rekindled in the last thirty years by the rise of social cognition in social psychology" (McGarty et al., *Stereotypes as Explanations*, 5).

69. Weeks discusses stereotypes under the broader rubric of "characters" but likewise asserts that they exist to make the experience of the life as path seem less "random," and thereby provide structure. See Weeks, *Instruction and Imagery*, 83.

70. Weeks, *Instruction and Imagery*, 70.

71. There are a few cases in which other non-human subjects are personified: However, in most of these cases a concrete object receives human characteristics (e.g., the ant [6:6]; the daughters of the leech [30:15]; the earth [30:16]; etc.).

> The power of poetic composition to create complex new ideas from simpler conventional ideas reveals itself in especially clear form in personification—metaphors through which we understand other things as people. As human beings, we can best understand other things in our own terms. Personification permits us to use our knowledge about ourselves to maximal effect, to use insights about ourselves to help us comprehend such things as forces of nature, common events, abstract concepts, and inanimate objects.[72]

As stereotypes constitute a mental schema that structures our perceptions, expectations and associations with *people* in the realm of the "real world," personification endeavors to reframe our feelings and perceptions of a concept. Lackoff and Turner explain that personification is restricted by our conception of events which in turn determines our choice of metaphor.[73]

> The way we feel about the appearance and character of the personification must correspond to the way we feel about the event. For example, if we feel that the event of healing is benign and comforting, then Time the healer cannot appear terrifying and malicious to us. Time the devourer may be portrayed as a monster, but time the healer had better not be.... There is also a common tendency for people to project their feelings about events onto the actors who cause them. If we get angry at the breaking of a window, we typically get angry at the person who broke it. Correspondingly, since healing is benign, in "Time is healer" we see the agent of healing, time, as benign. Thus, constraints on the appearance and character of a personified agent follow from the nature of the personification process.[74]

In the presentation of personified wisdom in chapters 1–9 of Proverbs very different feelings are invoked. In Prov 1 she is a numinous divine agent. In Prov 2–6, she and her compatriots are familiar and attainable agents saddled with the responsibility of guiding and protecting the youth as an individual.[75] In short, the feminine personification of wisdom is neither unitary nor monolithic. Discovering how and why the personification of

---

72. Lackoff and Turner, *More Than Cool Reason*, 72.
73. Lackoff and Turner, *More Than Cool Reason*, 77.
74. Lackoff and Turner, *More Than Cool Reason*, 79.
75. Weeks notes that Wisdom should *not* be classed with the stereotypes (Weeks, *Instruction and Imagery*, 70), and also notes explicit links between YHWH, parental instruction and wisdom personified (101), and the differences in the characterization of personified wisdom in chapters 2–6 (108), but does not provide a discussion of each appearance to consider growth through the book.

wisdom is characterized so differently will be key to developing a clear and balanced concept of wisdom as a target category.[76]

Hierarchy of Metaphor: Extension and Transformation

While it remains a debated element of CMT, the assumption of skeletally abstract autonomous semantic concepts is important to the function of the model and is a key component in structuring and naming conceptual metaphors.[77] "Each specific—level schema has such generic—level structure, as well as structure at the lower, specific level. Specific level detail is, therefore, of two types: first, there is the detail that comes from specifying the generic—level parameters; second, there is lower—level detail."[78]

Consider, for example, the conceptual metaphor of LOVE IS A JOURNEY.[79] Each of the entailments of this "lower level" metaphor can exist and be stated as metaphorical titles. Therefore, LOVERS are TRAVELERS. Their RELATIONSHIP is a VEHICLE. COMMON GOALS become COMMON DESTINATIONS. Finally, DIFFICULTIES in their relationship are figured as IMPEDIMENTS TO TRAVEL (i.e., we could speak of a relationship "hitting

---

76. Loader's note here is exemplary: "The central question as to the style of the poem is the use of the חכמות—figure as a trope. Her name means 'wisdom' and she is presented as a female person who acts independently. She goes about town, calls out and addresses the public. So, the concept of wisdom is personified in such a way that her authority is manifested in her conduct and words. That does not mean that she is to be seen as a goddess or godlike or as having originally been a goddess as scholars have been suggesting for decades. As a trope she can combine the features of a lover (4:6, 8; 7:4; 8:17) with those of a mother (8:32), even a primordial divine being (8:22–31) and a prophetess (1:20–33) without having to be identified with any one of them" (Loader, *Proverbs 1–9*, 89–90). The difficulty in his approach is that rather than being founded in *metaphor as concept* which can allow for the *blending* of these diverse metaphors, he is forced to rely on the rhetorical term *trope* which forces these images into *ornaments* that must be "either/or" elements.

77. For a brief survey of the history and previous models employed in CMT please see Appendix B.

78. Lakoff and Turner, *More Than Cool Reason*, 82.

79. "It is important to note that the name for a mapping is not to be understood as a propositional substitution for the substance of the metaphor but rather a statement of perceived ontological correspondence between two domains. Names of mappings commonly have a propositional form, for example, LOVE IS A JOURNEY. But the mappings themselves are not propositions. If mappings are confused with names for mappings, one might mistakenly think that, in this theory, metaphors are propositional. They are anything but that: metaphors are mappings, that is, sets of conceptual correspondences" (Lakoff, "Contemporary Theory of Metaphor," 207).

a road block," or "going nowhere," or trying to "fix the relationship").[80] All of these apparently different metaphors are all dependent upon the "lower level" metaphor of LOVE IS A JOURNEY (see fig. 4).

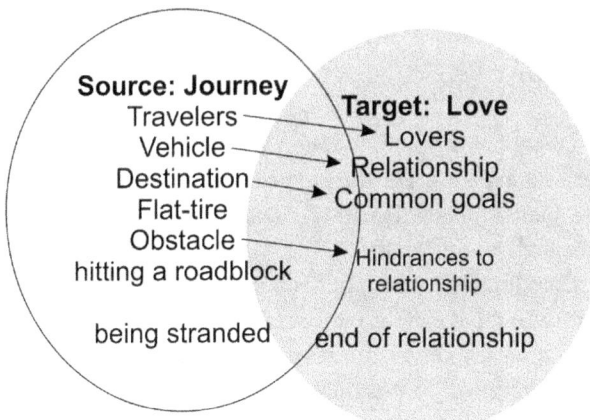

Figure 4. Hierarchy of Metaphor

Recognizing the hierarchy allows us to discern how metaphoric elements are extended or transformed in the course of a poetic work.[81]

In Proverbs the basic metaphor LIFE IS A ROAD, is extended into a number of additional but related metaphors. For example, MANNER OF WALKING IS MANNER OF LIVING is attested in numerous verses (Prov 1:15; 2:7, 13, 20; 4:14; 8:20; 9:6). In a similar way, hazards and pitfalls are recognized as OBSTACLES TO LIFE ARE OBSTACLES TO MOVEMENT (Prov 3:23; 4:12; 6:22; 7:23; 18:7; 20:25; 21:6; 22:25; 29:25). Finally, if LIFE IS A ROAD then DEATH IS A DESTINATION (Prov 2:18; 5:5; 7:27; 12:28;

80. Lakoff, "Contemporary Theory of Metaphor," 207–8.

81. Lakoff and Turner, *More Than Cool Reason*, 67–72. This does not suggest that the analysis of poetry is an easy task, however. "If we often have the same conceptual metaphors in ordinary language as in poetry, why is it that the poetry should seem so much harder? There are a number of reasons. First, poetic uses are often conscious extensions of the ordinary conventionalized metaphors. . . . Because they are conscious, they can draw upon different cognitive resources than the automatic and effortless use of fully conventionalized modes of metaphorical expression. Second, authors may call upon our knowledge of basic conceptual metaphors in order to manipulate them in unusual ways. The unusual use of a normally automatic and unconscious metaphor takes effort. . . . Third, in everyday language, it is unusual to find two or more basic metaphors for the target domain in a single clause, although one may find them in adjacent clauses. . . . Fourth, poetry may be complex for reasons independent of the use of metaphors. It may be phonologically or syntactically or otherwise complex or unusual" (Lakoff and Turner, *More Than Cool Reason*, 53–55).

13:14; 14:12, 27; 16:25; 24:11). All of these conceptual metaphors are rooted in the same source and image schema. The notion of the hierarchy of semantic concepts allows us to recognize the growth of poetic metaphor into new but related domains.

Conceptual Blending

One of the greatest contributions of conceptual blending as a theory is that it simplifies as it explains. For the pioneers of CMT, metaphor was understood as *the* foundational element of cognition, this confusion of roles resulted in justified opposition to CMT as a theory of cognition.[82] For Lackoff and Faucconier, linguistic metaphor is part of a more basic human predisposition to understand new experiences in terms of previous experience in attempt to *achieve human scale*. Conceptual blending is the imaginative process whereby human beings metaphorically inform perception in order to comprehend.[83] In summary, things too large to be comprehended (i.e., the solar system) are reduced. Things too small to be understood (i.e., an atom) are enlarged. Abstract things are made concrete or personal. What is more, these metaphorical models then in turn *structure* our perception.

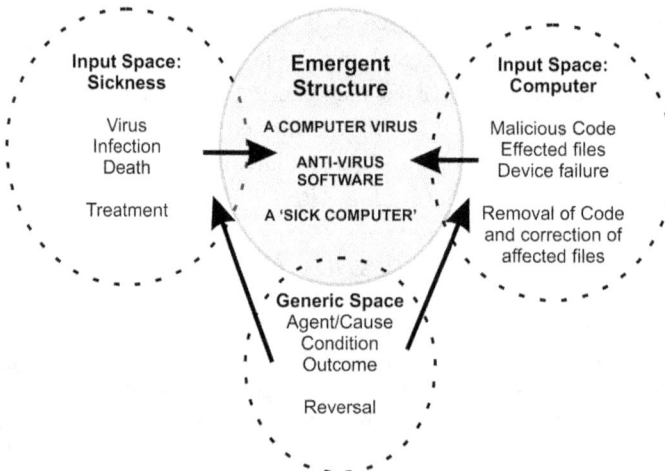

Figure 5. Virus Integration Network

---

82. For greater engagement with shortcomings and criticisms of early attempts in CMT please see Appendix C.

83. Fauconnier and Turner, *Way We Think*, 322–27. It should be noted that treatment of subgoals, *vital relations*, and assumed mental operations obtaining between mental spaces is here omitted. Most of the proposed conceptual machinery is related to the "how" of meaning instead of the "what."

So for example, if a bit malicious code was encrypted in an incoming electronic correspondence and in turn replicated itself within the active processes of a computer, the diagram of the conceptual blend might be as represented in fig. 5 above.

The domain of "sickness" is held in parallel with the action and domain of computer function. The generic space holds the items which needs to be borrowed from one input to the other and in this way an entirely new conceptual integration network is formed, along with entirely new terminology to *achieve human scale* by finding likenesses within dissimilar entities. Electronic correspondence is simplified to "email." The malicious code is figured with relation to a similar entity in human health. What results is a new entity that arises from the juxtaposition of generic categories. So what began as an esoteric and specialized mechanical problem (i.e., self—replicating malicious code) is brought into human scale by reference to the biological domain of "viral infection." This metaphor now not only *describes* but also *defines* further perception.

The main methodological refinement of conceptual blending relates to the model used to represent concepts. Conceptual Blending Theory does not dwell upon source or target domains as fixed semantically autonomous concepts. Rather, it is organized in relation to "mental spaces," which are spontaneous and temporary fields established by perception.[84] Different from CMT, Blending Theory has no limit to the number of input spaces involved in a blend, which is more reflective of the natural environment of spoken or written metaphor. These input spaces are structured according to a common conceptual frame in which elements from the input spaces are related by *cross space mapping* as in CMT. Distinct from CMT, however, is that blending theory provides two additional "mental spaces." The "generic space" is a process/space which determines what elements of the input spaces are activated. The "emergent structure" is not a space in itself but rather is yielded through the perception of the blended space. The elements from the input structure generate a new framing of both elements that are entailed but not determined by the inputs, thereby yielding new meaning. The new meaning is then completed by the blend and may be further elaborated by drawing additional elements from the inputs.[85] This arrangement of inputs, generic space, and emergent structure (sometimes called the blend) constitutes what Fauconnier and Turner call a *conceptual integration network*.

---

84. "Source" and "domain" may be considered to be latent, long-term archives which supply the more ad hoc "mental spaces" with content. See Grady et al., "Blending and Metaphor," 102.

85. Fauconnier and Turner, *Way We Think*, 44–45.

As mentioned above, there is no limit to the number of input spaces, nor is there any limit to what an input space may contain. Anything that can be conceived can be reconceived in light of something else, which can in turn reframe the original, or something altogether different. While their heuristic cannot be validated by any empirical means Faucconier and Turner provide a good model that explains how metaphor and other figurative language is consistent with human thought and experience. Different elements of our cognition and experience can be imaginatively reappropriated in a number of different ways to allow us to understand and express our place in the world. They propose four basic ways in which we as humans combine "input spaces" to understand or create understanding: simplex, mirror, single scope, and double scope, mirror, and simplex networks use a single frame to organize all of the inputs. Single and double scope use multiple frames (i.e., image schemas) to obtain human scale.[86]

Conceptual blending is necessary for a consideration of *Lady Wisdom*, because she exists as and in the context of competing and sometimes contradictory metaphors. As will be seen in greater depth below, *Lady Wisdom* is first presented as a woman, and therefore has certain elements of this source category (Prov 1). However, she is simultaneously presented in language and metaphor typically reserved for YHWH. At the same time she mirrors prophetic language and metaphor. Each of the input spaces provide certain elements of the blend which in turn affects how each of the source categories are understood in light of the whole.

Conclusion

Theological aesthetics will provide a theological framework for the balance of left and right hemisphere function, while urging greater engagement between *Lady Wisdom* and the absolute beauty of the Trinity. Cognitive Metaphor Theory will provide an acceptable terminology and methodological framework for appraising the content, function and interrelation of metaphors that make up *Lady Wisdom*. We now turn to the work and joy of exegesis.

---

86. For a discussion of Simplex, Mirror, Single Scope, and Double Scope Networks, see Appendix D.

4

The Diversity and Paradox of Lady Wisdom in Proverbs 1–2 and the Diversity and Paradox of the Triune God

Introduction

The way the poet presents *Lady Wisdom* colors how we feel about not only the character, but about the entity she represents.[1] As noted by Lakoff and Turner, personification is meant to shape our attitudes toward the abstraction. *DEATH AS GRIM REAPER* induces fear and dread, while *DEATH AS FRIEND* directs us toward affection. The difficulty in the initial chapters of Proverbs is not only in the interweaving of diverse metaphors, but the fact that personification of Wisdom moves in two very different directions.

In Prov 1:20–33, *Wisdom* is presented not only as a woman but as a prophetic ambassador and as an extension of the person of YHWH. The overall conceptual blend shows Wisdom as personal and relational but not in the human domain. Rather, she is bound to the person of YHWH and speaks with the voice of the prophet. She is not desirable as a lover, mother, friend or protector; but rather seems to speak under divine unction. As a poetic personification, the YHWH portion of the conceptual blend does not depict her as a hypostasis or consort to YHWH, but rather to front the importance of the ongoing and prophetic conversation between YHWH and the םכ (you, masculine plural) of Israel. Wisdom in the abstract then, is attentiveness to the corporate and relational covenant of YHWH. The youth is being told, in so many words, "your relationship with Wisdom is seen

---

1. Lakoff and Turner, *More Than Cool Reason*, 72–80.

in maintaining *our* relationship to the covenant of YHWH." The readers' apparent relationship to the personification is one of distance and awe, passivity, and attendance to the divine covenant.

In the second stage of development (Prov 2:1–11), wisdom and related lexemes retain personal agency and therefore feminine personification. However, the vaunted and marginal mediatory presence of *Lady Wisdom* disappears. In place of the quasi—divine and prophetic voice of the Lady, wisdom personified (חכמה) is fragmented into a string of homonymic lexemes. Where the personification of wisdom in Prov 1 was a numinous divine agent, here she is a familiar protector and a possible object not only for the son's affections, but also an end that could be gained. As new metaphors for wisdom (i.e., WORD, SHIELD, TREASURE, etc.) are piled on the existing base of WISDOM IS A WOMAN, she is figured as a protection and guide against stereotypical threats in the life of the young man. Familiar wisdom takes on elements of characterization that evoke those of a wife. This woman will protect the young man from the danger posed by the "strange/foreign woman." The readers' apparent relationship to *this* personification is one of intimacy, desire, and active pursuit.

The dichotomous presentations of personified wisdom highlights the divine and human, passive and active components of wisdom, which accent both obedience to and desire for wisdom which is rooted in covenantal relationship with YHWH.

The first element of this chapter is a close annotated translation of the MT of Prov 1:20–33 and Prov 2:1–11. Much like a work of art, this is the center of our perception as well as the vehicle for transport. With these texts in mind we then proceed to the first stage of aesthetic perception of each paragraph separately. In Prov 1:20–33, we see that WOMAN contributes only the categories of personhood and relational appeal to the personification of WISDOM. The more significant contributions come from the conceptual domains of PROPHET and YHWH. Wisdom is an active and transcendent divine agent and near embodiment of covenant fidelity. In Prov 2:1–11, personified wisdom is diversified into a string of related metaphors that will receive greater extension in the remainder of the book. Simultaneously, she is depicted in familiar categories more alike to those of mother and wife. Rather than overhearing an appeal to Wisdom as covenant obedience, the father exhorts the youth to *desire* for that which is beneficial, desirable, and familiar. These two different presentations of wisdom present us not with contradiction but with the necessary tension required for *paradox*. In the final section of chapter 4, we consider the second stage of aesthetic beauty, that in which the chosen texts transport us toward the person of YHWH as revealed in the person and cross of Jesus. So we are brought to the appeal, rejection, prophetic person, promise of providence, and protection in the ultimate paradox of the life-giving death of Jesus.

Proverbs 1:20–33

> 20 חָכְמוֹת בַּחוּץ תָּרֹנָּה בָּרְחֹבוֹת תִּתֵּן קוֹלָהּ
>
> *Wisdom* in the street[2] will call shrilly.[3] In the public squares she will give her voice
>
> 21 בְּרֹאשׁ הֹמִיּוֹת תִּקְרָא בְּפִתְחֵי שְׁעָרִים בָּעִיר אֲמָרֶיהָ תֹאמֵר׃
>
> At the head of the noise[4] she will call out. In the opening of the gates into the city her words she will say.
>
> 22 עַד־מָתַי ׀ פְּתָיִם תְּאֵהֲבוּ פֶתִי וְלֵצִים לָצוֹן חָמְדוּ לָהֶם וּכְסִילִים יִשְׂנְאוּ־דָעַת׃
>
> "How long, will naive ones love naivety and scoffers desire scorn for themselves and stupid ones hate knowledge?

---

2. Most translations prefer to translate "Wisdom cries aloud in the streets" (cf. Murphy, *Proverbs*, 8; Fox, *Proverbs 1–9*, 96; Waltke, *Proverbs: 1–15*, 201). Given the placement of the word in the context of "squares" and public places this is assuredly the best translation. All the same, however, it is important to note that the idea of "outdoors" or "outside" is still assumed within the translation.

3. This lexeme appears to possess a "pseudo-cohortative" (not plural) form. Grimm endeavors to explain the complexity of form by recourse to comparative grammar, suggesting that the lexical form here is not רנן but רנה on analogy with the formation of כלל and כלה. See Grimm, "Form tārŏnna," 192–96. While possible, such a conjecture is far from certain. Regardless, the parallel verb נתן is singular as is the pronominal suffix associated.

4. The choice has been made to retain the difficulty of the reading in English. Most scholars translate this phrase with regard to a busy intersection. Murphy translates, "a corner of bustling streets," (Murphy, *Proverbs*, 7), but provides the back translation, "at the head of noisy (places)" (Murphy, *Proverbs*, 8). Waltke emends הֹמִיּוֹת to הֹמוֹת following the LXX to provide a better parallel with the heights mentioned in Prov 8:2 (Waltke, *Proverbs: 1–15*, 197). Fox agrees with Waltke, but provides "at the bustling crossroads" in translation (Fox, *Proverbs 1–9*, 7). The original genitival reading of הֹמִיּוֹת also accords with the designed ambiguity between *Lady Wisdom* and the *Strange Woman*. The singular form (הֹמִיָּה) is found in association with the *Strange Woman* in Prov 7:11; 9:13. For this reason the attested reading is maintained.

23 תָּשׁוּבוּ לְתוֹכַחְתִּי הִנֵּה אַבִּיעָה לָכֶם רוּחִי אוֹדִיעָה דְבָרַי אֶתְכֶם׃

You (mp) should return[5] to my rebuke! Look, I would pour out to you my spirit.[6] I would cause you to know my word.

24 יַעַן קָרָאתִי וַתְּמָאֵנוּ נָטִיתִי יָדִי וְאֵין מַקְשִׁיב׃

Because I have called[7] and you (mp) have refused. I have stretched out my hand[8] and none consider.

25 וַתִּפְרְעוּ כָל־עֲצָתִי וְתוֹכַחְתִּי לֹא אֲבִיתֶם׃

And[9] you (mp) have ignored all my counsel and my rebuke you (mp) did not desire.

5. Murphy argues that v. 23 is still governed by the "how long" (עַד־מָתַי) of v. 22a. He therefore, translates this initial imperfect as a participial modifier of the former verse which then reframes the rest of v. 23 into a statement of consequences: "Turning away at my reproof? Now I will pour out my spirit to you; I will make known my words to you" (Murphy, *Proverbs*, 23). However, this reading (1) gives no weight to the *soph pasuch*, (2) removes the impression of promise that seems explicit in the context, and (3) does not accord with the "pouring out my Spirit" metaphor (discussed below). I have translated the verse in agreement with Waltke, Fox and Loader as a string of subjunctives expressing the possibility of discourse with Wisdom that is spurned by the naïve audience. Whether or not the subjunctive form may be deemed a "call to repentance" or not, it is difficult to avoid the assertion that whether here or at some earlier point the naïve had the option of choosing wisdom. Longman notes that Wisdom's offer is substantially in agreement with those gifts poured out to Bezalel in building the tabernacle (Exod 31:3) and also the depiction of Messiah (Isa 11:23).

6. Waltke following Emerton argues against McKane that "pour out my spirit" is a metonymy for speech. Murphy, Fox, and Loader argue that "spirit" is a metonymy for "temper" (cf. Murphy, *Proverbs*, 10; Fox, *Proverbs 1–9*, 100; Loader, *Proverbs 1–9*, 95). Both of these options will be discussed at greater length below.

7. While it is possible to translate קָרָאתִי as a gnomic perfect (Waltke, *Proverbs 1–15*, 199) it is not necessary especially in light of the preterite forms that follow (Loader, *Proverbs 1–9*, 86). Moreover, the syntax also clarifies the relation to the subjunctive imperfects in the previous line. Wisdom called and the audience refused.

8. Fox argues that "stretched forth my hand" should be viewed not as entreaty, but as an idiom of impending judgment (Fox, *Proverbs 1–9*, 100). This reading will be considered more below.

9. The appearance of the preterite puts this line in relation to the former. The LXX translates ἀλλὰ possibly due to a perceived emphasis or extension of the verbal ideas (i.e., that פרע and אהב are more active disavowals than מאן). If this were the poet's intention it is likely that גם or כי עם would have been chosen to express the adversative idea (as in v. 26). I think it best to read v. 25a either with a conjunction or with a comma (Waltke, *Proverbs 1–15*, 199; Loader, *Proverbs 1–9*, 86; Fox, *Proverbs 1–9*, 95) to note that it is a continuation of the previous list of offenses.

THE DIVERSITY AND PARADOX OF LADY WISDOM AND OF GOD

26 גַּם־אֲנִי בְּאֵידְכֶם אֶשְׂחָק אֶלְעַג בְּבֹא פַחְדְּכֶם׃

Also I, in[10] your (mp) disaster I will laugh. I will mock in the coming of your (mp) dread.

27 בְּבֹא כְשַׁאֲוָה פַּחְדְּכֶם וְאֵידְכֶם כְּסוּפָה יֶאֱתֶה בְּבֹא עֲלֵיכֶם צָרָה וְצוּקָה׃

In the coming of your terror like a storm[11] and your disaster will come as a gale. In the coming upon you of adversity and distress.

28 אָז יִקְרָאֻנְנִי וְלֹא אֶעֱנֶה יְשַׁחֲרֻנְנִי וְלֹא יִמְצָאֻנְנִי׃

Then they will call upon me and I will not answer. They will seek me but they will not find me.

---

10. As Waltke notes, this should not be translated with the English idiom "laugh at" since a similar idiom exists in Hebrew using the preposition ל. In this case, the idiom is avoided by the use of the ב preposition (Waltke, *Proverbs 1–15*, 199). "Wisdom does not laugh at disaster, but at the triumph of what is right over what is wrong when your disaster happens" (Waltke, *Proverbs 1–15*, 207).

11. Fox provides a concise depiction of the chiastic form of the text, but does not consider larger lexical and metaphorical correspondences (Fox, *Proverbs 1–9*, 101). Waltke notes the correspondence of judgment with offense and even notes the presence of the lexemes in Deuteronomy, but he classes the storm metaphor as mere simile (Waltke, *Proverbs 1–15*, 207). Limiting the metaphor to a function of words hobbles the larger canonical linkages. The combination of terror (פחד) and STORM metaphor is present not only here, but also again in Prov 3:24–25. In Prov 3 the image schema of travel is shifted toward repose in v. 24, with an accent upon sleep, but also the terrors of 1:25–27 are resurrected along with STORM metaphor in the shared lexeme for "ruin" (שׁאוה). In walking the young man will not strike his foot. In lying down, the young man's sleep will not be troubled by "sudden terror." While this terror (פחד) may be of a general kind (cf. Job 3:25), the word is most widely employed with regard to either divine presence or divine judgment, sometimes coming in the form of calamity. More particularly, dread is to be visited upon those who violate the covenant in Deut 28:65–67. In each of these contexts terror (פחד) is purchased through disobedience. The basic metaphor, STORM IS JUDGMENT therefore is deemed as "coming" to the wicked and therefore unavoidable. The STORM IS JUDGMENT metaphor, ultimately provides another hitching point of covenant faithfulness as expressed in the Prophets and unifies the personified treatment of Wisdom in Prov 1, with the more abstract configuration in Prov 3.

> 29 תַּחַת כִּי־שָׂנְאוּ דָעַת וְיִרְאַת יְהוָה לֹא בָחָרוּ:
>
> Because[12] they have hated knowledge[13] and the fear of YHWH they have not chosen.
>
> 30 לֹא־אָבוּ לַעֲצָתִי נָאֲצוּ כָּל־תּוֹכַחְתִּי:
>
> They did not want my counsel. They spurned all of my rebuke.
>
> 31 וְיֹאכְלוּ מִפְּרִי דַרְכָּם וּמִמֹּעֲצֹתֵיהֶם יִשְׂבָּעוּ:
>
> And they will eat from the fruit of their road[14] and from their plans they will be satisfied.

12. The construction תַּחַת כִּי appears in this form in only one other context in Tanakh (Deut 4:37). All other contexts where these words appear together תַּחַת functions as a previous prepositional phrase (1 Kgs 1:30; 1 Chr 4:41; 2 Chr 22:1; Isa 51:6). Since Deut 4:37 also contains the root בחר it is possible that this is a purposeful activation of the image scheme of God's Choice of Israel as an antithesis to the naïve person's rejection of God. וְתַחַת כִּי אָהַב אֶת־אֲבֹתֶיךָ וַיִּבְחַר בְּזַרְעוֹ אַחֲרָיו וַיּוֹצִאֲךָ בְּפָנָיו בְּכֹחוֹ הַגָּדֹל מִמִּצְרָיִם: (Deut 4:37). Most commentators note that disposition toward God is herein synonymous with the appeal of Wisdom although they differ as to how directly this condemnation should be related to relationship with YHWH. Waltke is most explicit in connecting the Fear of YHWH with the person of YHWH expressed in Torah and bound by the covenant. "Their willful indifference and hostility are against Israel's God, not against an impersonal order or even a hypostatized human wisdom. Submission to Wisdom is equated with submission to God" (Waltke, *Proverbs 1–15*, 210).

13. Longman notes that "knowledge" and the "Fear of YHWH" is paralleled in Isaiah 11:2–3a as a depiction of Messiah (Longman, *Proverbs*, 112). Following the Masora, this is the only other precise occurrence of וְיִרְאַת יְהוָה in Tanakh. More broadly, the relationship between "knowledge" (דעת) and the "fear of God" (ירעת יהיה) is most pronounced in the book of Hosea, although the parallel there is typically with the "knowledge of God" (דעת אלהים). However, the connection between the "knowledge of God" and "knowledge" seems to be fluid. For example in Hosea 4, the first appearance is "knowledge of God" alongside אמת and חסד. In v. 6, the reference is simply "knowledge." נִדְמוּ עַמִּי מִבְּלִי הַדָּעַת כִּי־אַתָּה הַדַּעַת מָאַסְתָּ וְאֶמְאָסְךָ: "My people are destroyed for lack of knowledge because you (ms) that knowledge have rejected, I will reject you." In a similar manner, the "knowledge" lexeme turns up again in Hos 6:4–6. מָה אֶעֱשֶׂה־לְּךָ אֶפְרַיִם מָה אֶעֱשֶׂה־לְּךָ יְהוּדָה וְחַסְדְּכֶם כַּעֲנַן־בֹּקֶר וְכַטַּל מַשְׁכִּים הֹלֵךְ: What shall I do with you, Ephraim? (What) shall I do with you Judah? Your covenant love is like the clouds of morning and like dew passing away early in the morning."כִּי חֶסֶד חָפַצְתִּי וְלֹא־זָבַח וְדַעַת אֱלֹהִים מֵעֹלוֹת: "For I desire covenant love and not sacrifice [and] the knowledge of God more than burnt offering." The LORD's complaint through Hosea rings not only of typical sapiential concerns, but also of the failure of relationship. The overall prophetic metaphor provides a constellation of (1) the lack of knowledge, (2) the rejection of YHWH by the people, and (3) a concern for relationship over against cultic observance. Again, each of these are consonant with the prophetic and covenantal coloring of Wisdom below.

14. Murphy notes that the metaphor of EATING IS CONSEQUENCE appears fairly frequently in the latter half of Proverbs (cf. 12:10; 13:2; 18:20–21). He points

> 32 כִּי מְשׁוּבַת פְּתָיִם תַּהַרְגֵם וְשַׁלְוַת כְּסִילִים תְּאַבְּדֵם:
>
> For the falling away of the simple will kill them and the ease of the stupid ones will destroy them[15]
>
> 33 וְשֹׁמֵעַ לִי יִשְׁכָּן־בֶּטַח וְשַׁאֲנַן מִפַּחַד רָעָה: פ
>
> But one listening to me will dwell securely and will be without anxiety from dread of evil."[16]

Proverbs 2:1–11

> 1 בְּנִי אִם־תִּקַּח אֲמָרָי וּמִצְוֹתַי תִּצְפֹּן אִתָּךְ:
>
> My son, if you will[17] take my words[18] and my commandments[19] you will treasure with you.

---

out "the fruit will correspond to the conduct" (Murphy, *Proverbs*, 11). Loader furthers Murphy's argument that this metaphor is also found frequently in the Prophets (Isa 3:10; Jer 17:10; 21:14; Mic 7:13) (Loader, *Proverbs 19*, 99). However, it is important to note that in the second half of the verse EATING metaphor is fused with ROAD metaphor in an absolutely novel way. For a fuller treatment, see Appendix E.

15. The terms מְשׁוּבַת and וְשַׁלְוַת will be treated under the consideration of Prophetic vocabulary below.

16. Toy argues that the final verses do not describe internal peace and security, but rather are a restatement of the deed-consequence nexus (Toy, *Book of Proverbs*, 39). Fox's retort is worthwhile: "When Toy asserts that security from fear of harm here means merely freedom from outward misfortune . . . he has neatly stated the opposite of the truth. Proverbs is directly and deeply concerned with shaping attitudes, beliefs, and feeling for the sake of both internal and external well-being. . . . Wisdom's speeches, which give the essence of her demands, describe attitudes: on the one hand, stubborn, smug disregard; on the other, love and desire for Wisdom" (Fox, *Proverbs 1–9*, 103).

17. I preserve the imperfect tense in agreement with the subjunctive particle and the overall structure of the passage. Waltke, Murphy and Fox drop "will" as it is not strictly necessary in English

18. As in other passages, references to the father's words and commandments are not limited to the immediate context, but rather, "Verse 2 refers to the father's words and precepts taught elsewhere in the lectures of Part I, while "wisdom" (v. 2) embraces all wise teaching" (Fox, *Proverbs 1–9*, 107).

19. While Murphy argues that "commandments" (מִצְוֹתַי) is not to be understood in light of Deuteronomic usage, but rather limited only to the instructions of the Father, the close association between the father and Wisdom, especially within a canonical context, complicates such a reading. As mentioned in greater depth below, the parallel of "words" with "commandments" (מצות) are both framed with reference to the commandments of YHWH. "Instead of the prophetic 'Thus saith the LORD,' the father speaks authoritatively of *my words* . . . which he equates with wisdom (2:2) proceeding from God himself (v. 6). The father bases his authority not on his patriarchal position

2 לְהַקְשִׁיב לַחָכְמָה אָזְנֶךָ תַּטֶּה לִבְּךָ לַתְּבוּנָה׃

By making your ear attentive[20] to wisdom[21] you will incline[22] your heart to understanding.

3 כִּי אִם לַבִּינָה תִקְרָא לַתְּבוּנָה תִּתֵּן קוֹלֶךָ׃

Moreover,[23] to discernment you should call. To understanding you should give your voice.[24]

---

or on tradition, but on the LORD himself'" (Waltke, *Proverbs 1-15*, 220). See also Fox, *Proverbs 1-9*, 108. The metaphor WISDOM AS WORD will be treated in greater depth below.

20. Translated as a gerund identifying the manner of the preceding action. "The infinitive with ל is very often used after a verb to express an action which gives more details about or explains the preceding action ... [as in English] *by doing* ... (This process is very frequent in rhetorical phraseology, especially Deuteronomistic)" (Joüon and Muraoka, *Grammar of Biblical Hebrew* §1240). See Gen 18:19; Exod 31:16; Deut 13:19; 15:5; 28:13, 15; 30:10; 1 Sam 12:17; 14:33; 19:5; 1 Kgs 14:8; Jer 44:3.

21. The means of attaining wisdom is predicated upon taking and treasuring the words of the father. Therefore: "The father's words are not only the way to wisdom, but wisdom itself" (Fox, *Proverbs 1-9*, 108).

22. נטה is primarily concerned with desire and disposition toward the object (cf. Judg 9:3; 1 Kgs 1:3; Ps 119:36). It "is not an appeal for attention only; it is a demand for a certain attitude; an eager receptivity toward the teachings" (Fox, *Proverbs 1-9*, 109) Waltke suggests a few possible metaphorical image schemas that provide the ground for meaning (e.g., Num 21:15; Gen 24:14; 49:15) (Waltke, *Proverbs 1-15*, 221).

23. Fox and Murphy both leave כִּי untranslated but as an asservative (GKC §159ee). Waltke translates כִּי in order to provide greater emphasis (Waltke, *Proverbs 1-15*, 213). In similar appearances in Proverbs (cf. Prov 18:2; 19:19; 23:17-18), the phrase seems to suggest a translation of "but rather," or perhaps "surely." Likewise in this case, in the first line the father has instructed the youth to be attentive, here he radicalizes that command. Not only should he be attentive, which suggests a passive engagement, but *moreover* he should himself *call out* to Wisdom. He should take an *active* and not passive approach to obtaining Wisdom. Plöger describes this in terms of logical/rhetorical escalation, however, it is more neatly explained with regard to metaphor. See Plöger, *Sprüche*, 25. Making femininity passive and masculinity aggressive is not a necessary component of the interpretation. Waltke notes that the repetition of "understanding" (תְּבוּנָה) unifies these initial verses, even as the shift in metaphor from "listening" to "calling" recommends a more aggressive approach to Wisdom (Waltke, *Proverbs 1-15*, 221). Fox also notes the incremental increase in requirement: from attentiveness to desire and then from desire to desperate search in v. 4. See Fox, *Proverbs 1-9*, 110.

24. Murphy translates the b colon as "and summon understanding." While this strengthens feminine personification it is not an apt translation of the idiom "give voice" (תִּתֵּן קוֹלֶךָ). See Murphy, *Proverbs*, 13. The further development of the metaphor WISDOM IS A WOMAN will be treated below.

THE DIVERSITY AND PARADOX OF LADY WISDOM AND OF GOD 91

4 אִם־תְּבַקְשֶׁנָּה כַכָּסֶף וְכַמַּטְמוֹנִים תַּחְפְּשֶׂנָּה׃

If you will seek her[25] as (the) silver and as (hidden?) treasure[26] you will search for her.

5 אָז תָּבִין יִרְאַת יְהוָה וְדַעַת אֱלֹהִים תִּמְצָא׃

Then you will discern (the) fear of YHWH and knowledge of God[27] you will find.

6 כִּי־יְהוָה יִתֵּן חָכְמָה מִפִּיו דַּעַת וּתְבוּנָה׃

For YHWH will give wisdom, from His mouth[28] knowledge and understanding

7 (וְצָפַן) [יִצְפֹּן] לַיְשָׁרִים תּוּשִׁיָּה מָגֵן לְהֹלְכֵי תֹם׃

And he will treasure up[29] for the upright well-being[30] a shield to the walkers of integrity.

25. I have translated the 3fs pronominal suffix as "her" to preserve the continuity and ambiguity of the text (following Murphy). Given the parallels of WOMAN and TREASURE in the rest of the book I think it best to preserve the linkage. Waltke notes correctly that this pronoun makes the three different feminine nouns (i.e., "wisdom," "understanding," "discernment") co-referential. See Waltke, *Proverbs 1–15*, 214.

26. Though the root מטמון appears first in Gen 43:23 with regard simply to "treasure." The word more frequently refers to hidden treasure (cf. Job 3:21; Isa 45:3; Jer 41:8). See Hamilton, "מטמון," 927. Moreover, in context it makes more sense as the subject of "search" (בקש).

27. The curious construction, "knowledge of God" (דַּעַת אֱלֹהִים), "refers, at least in part, to entering into a personal relationship with the Creator (cf. 1:2; Hos 4:1; 6:6). . . . 'Knowledge of God' refers to personal intimacy with him through obedience to his word (cf. 1 Sam 3:7); the notion of cognitive response to his revelation and existential intimacy and obedience are inseparable" (Waltke, *Proverbs 1–15*, 223). Likewise, Fox writes: "Knowledge of God (or knowledge of Yahweh, as well as verbal constructions) is a concept of great importance throughout the Bible, especially in prophecy. Its incorporation in Wisdom literature and its identification with wisdom are among the earmarks, and probably the innovations of Proverbs 1–9" (Fox, *Proverbs 1–9*, 112).

28. Fox and Waltke provide the English idiom "come" (i.e., "From his mouth comes knowledge and understanding"). See Waltke, *Proverbs 1–15*, 224. There is no necessity for providing an additional verb. The syntax can easily be read as a string of direct objects (i.e., YHWH will give wisdom, knowledge and understanding). The prepositional phrase functions as an appositional phrase defining the source of the gift.

29. I have translated "treasure up" largely in accordance with the prevalence of TREASURE lexemes in the passage and in consonance with Fox's comment: "[It] implies setting something aside for a favored person . . . who alone can benefit from it" (Fox, *Proverbs 1–9*, 114). The metaphor WISDOM IS TREASURE will be treated below.

30. Fox argues that "[תּוּשִׁיָּה] is an inner power that can help one escape a fix. It is not an inherently intellectual faculty, nor is it a moral virtue; in fact, many honest

> 8 לִנְצֹר אָרְחוֹת מִשְׁפָּט וְדֶרֶךְ (חֲסִידוֹ) [חֲסִידָיו] יִשְׁמֹר׃
>
> To protect[31] ways of justice[32] and (the) road of his faithful he will guard.[33]
>
> 9 אָז תָּבִין צֶדֶק וּמִשְׁפָּט וּמֵישָׁרִים כָּל־מַעְגַּל־טוֹב׃
>
> Then you will discern righteousness, justice, and rectitude, all good paths.[34]

people lack the gift.... But the sage insists that God himself imbues the upright with the useful endowment of mental dexterity" (Fox, *Proverbs 1–9*, 114). However, given the fuller constellation of terms there are many that appear to have a positive connotation in context (cf. with reference to Job [Job 6:13; 26:3]; God [Job 11:6; 12:16; Isa 28:29]. Moreover, the quality is promised on the basis of *integrity*, which would imply "dissimulation will be given to the upright." Especially in light of the LXX translation (σωτηρίαν), I think it is better to translate in accordance with HALOT, "like hk'r'b. indicates the productive skill in an action, as well as at the same time the action itself" (*HALOT* s.v. "תּוּשִׁיָּה")

31. Fox places direct agency for "protection" and "keeping" with YHWH. Waltke's reading is more nuanced and apt: "With objects in the semantic domain of concrete persons or things (e.g., a vineyard [Isa 27:3]; a fig tree [Prov 27:18]; paths [2:8]; or son [2:11]) nṣr and šmr signify 'to keep' from danger so as to preserve (cf. Isa 27:3; Prov 2:8, 1; 4:13; 5:2; 13:6; 20:28; 22:12; 23:26; 24:12; 27:28; 28:7), but with the object in the semantic domain of wisdom and commands it signifies to preserve them carefully by faithful obedience and compliance (see 3:1, 21; 4:6, 13; 6:20; 16:17), 'to protect' them from being damaged. The double meanings allow a pun on both senses that encapsulate the book's teaching: keep the commands, and they/the LORD will keep you (e.g., 3:21, 26). Here it explains the purpose of the shield, which is the LORD himself" (Waltke, *Proverbs 1–15*, 225).

32. Fox notes that the object of protection is not the righteous themselves, but upon the path which they maintain. "The verse thus teaches that people are not left to their own resources when they strive to be upright. Once they step onto the right path, God helps them remain on it. He protects them by guarding their behavior" (Fox, *Proverbs 1–9*, 115).

33. As in 2:11 the pun on different senses of שמר is in play. "As they protect/guard the sage's words, the teachings guard/protect them" (Waltke, *Proverbs 1–15*, 226).

34. Fox maintains that the minor nature of the word "course" (מַעְגַּל) plus the explicit mention of their plurality indicates, "that there are numerous worthy tracks of behavior" (Fox, *Proverbs 1–9*, 115). In a similar but related manner Weeks argues that the overall purpose of the *ROAD* metaphor does not have to do with a simple dichotomy between "good and bad" ways but rather the emphasis is upon "walking straight" (Weeks, *Instruction and Imagery*, 75). In this context such assertions are entirely appropriate. However, there is nothing to prevent the poet from employing the metaphor as a dichotomy in some contexts and as a diversity in others. For example, Waltke notes that in the road metaphor it is typical that the "good road" is singular contra the plurality of "bad roads" (e.g., Prov 7:27; 14:12) (Waltke, *Proverbs 1–15*, 226). There is no necessity of maintaining unmixed metaphor throughout.

THE DIVERSITY AND PARADOX OF LADY WISDOM AND OF GOD 93

> 10 כִּי־תָבוֹא חָכְמָה[35] בְלִבֶּךָ וְדַעַת לְנַפְשְׁךָ יִנְעָם׃
>
> For[36] Wisdom will come in your (ms) heart[37] and knowledge to your soul will be pleasant.

11 מְזִמָּה תִּשְׁמֹר עָלֶיךָ תְּבוּנָה תִנְצְרֶכָּה׃

Prudence will watch[38] over you. Understanding will protect you.

---

35. Note that the gifts of YHHW (v. 6): wisdom (חכמה), knowledge (דעת) and understanding (תבונה) reappear in the same order (vv. 10–11) only with the addition of מזמה. The passive gifts are refigured as active and likely personified protections to the young man.

36. Syntactically, Waltke proposes that this כי "explicitly validates and explains the promised ethical discernment (v. 9) is due to a regenerate heart. The parallelism between vv. 6 and 10 shows that the *wisdom* . . . from the LORD's mouth through the father's words (2:6) will now *enter* . . . your heart. The relationship between the LORD and the son could not be closer" (Waltke, *Proverbs 1–15*, 227).

37. Waltke parallels the coming of Wisdom into the heart with the transformation of the heart in the prophets via the metaphor of the "new heart" (cf. Jer 24:7; 31:31–34; 32:37–41; Ezek 36:27) (Waltke, *Proverbs 1–15*, 227). However, the NEW HEART metaphor is altogether different. In most of the prophetic passages, the heart is not viewed as a container or domicile which something enters. Rather the heart is a metonymy for the seat of emotions and will. The heart is not entered—it is removed and replaced. Moreover, the metaphor includes a significant blend of *GIFT* or *BLESSING* source categories. It is a gift of YHWH that is listed with a series of other blessings (Jer 24:7). It is *not* obtained through instruction or even covenant obedience. It is established by the divine will alone (Jer 31:31–34). It is understood in a collective sense with all of the people of YHWH, again by his unilateral action as a gift (Jer 32:37–41). Only the Ezekiel passage includes both *GIFT* and *REPLACEMENT* components (36:26) in conjunction with the entry of the Spirit of YHWH (36:27) even while continuing to list these in the context of covenant blessings (36:28). Wisdom is not presented as a unilateral blessing, and it is contingent upon the subject in a way that the "new heart" is not. Both however, are connected to the transformation of appetites, desires and especially in the case of the NEW HEART, the will. Where Wisdom approaches through obedience and instruction that is then graced with divine beneficence, the NEW HEART of prophecy is a miraculous action of God establishing a sweeping ontological spiritual change. Wisdom changes the desire through obedient knowledge. The NEW HEART changes knowledge through obedient desire. Fox notes the function of the metaphor in context admirably: "There is a causal relationship between wisdom entering ones heart (v. 10) and the ability to perceive what is right (v. 9). Absorbing wisdom—not just memorizing it but learning to love it—allows one to recognize 'every good course.' Like the fear of God, the understanding of justice is a stage of development beyond the simple doing of good" (Fox, *Proverbs 1–9*, 116).

38. As in 2:8, "The pun on *šmr* and *nṣr* is structured chiastically . . . to bring closure to the first half of the lecture on the development of the godly character that defends the disciple against the wiles and tactics of the apostate man and woman (vv. 12–19). There is no tension between the Lord protecting saints . . . and the saints' character guarding

Stage 1 Perception: Part I: The Personification of Wisdom in Proverbs 1 as a Conceptual Blend of WOMAN, PROPHET, and YHWH

Introduction

In Prov 1 *Lady Wisdom* (חָכְמוֹת) is presented speaking with a prophetic voice and acting in ways typically reserved for YHWH. The poet blends metaphor and imagery to show that the roots of wisdom are found in the past and ongoing covenant between YHWH and his people. As such, these lexical and metaphorical elements dominate the personification of *Lady Wisdom*. In fact, the elements of the source category of *WOMAN* are shallow and oblique by comparison with the robust imagery of YHWH and the prophets. Elements of her femininity that might evoke gendered desire do not appear. The only elements of *WOMAN* that are mapped onto *WISDOM* relate simply to (1) being a person and (2) making a relational appeal.

First, with regard to her person, there might be some expectation that wisdom should be personified as a person of some dignity, power, and majesty. Loader, for example, argues that *Lady Wisdom* is presented as an authoritative figure due to her placement and speech.[39] There are a number of complications with such an assertion. First, her placement is shared not with kings and nobles, but rather is the shared domain of the *Strange Woman* and her emissaries.[40] Moreover, while the "city gate" by itself may stand as a metonymy for elders or leadership, the broader context indicates that this is not the intent here. It is more likely that her placement does not signal magisterial import but rather public activity. She is outside (חוּץ), in the markets (רְחֹבוֹת), and in the bustle (הֹמִיּוֹת). Her person and her message

---

them against evil. As the wisdom of God became incarnate in the teacher's words, so God's protection becomes effective through the son's formed character" (Waltke, *Proverbs 1–15*, 228).

39. Alfred Loader writes, "She is a woman of stature. Both her name and the places she goes indicate her eminence (which will stand her in good stead, given the contents of her speech that can only be delivered by a person with authority" (Loader, *Proverbs 1–9*, 91).

40. "On the other hand it may also seem very dangerous for a woman to do this kind of thing, which might be construed as searching for sexual partners (cf. 7:12). These are indeed the places where prostitutes (Gen 38:14; Ezek 16:25) and Madame Folly (Prov 9:14) are also to be found. Even though it may be daring for a dignified lady to go out in public and call to men, the danger is offset by the fact that she does it publicly and of course also by the contents of her calls. Addressing all the men of the city, or all who are present in the public venues, on their failure to listen to wisdom and rejection of the Fear of Yahweh, is rather unlikely to be construed as soliciting" (Loader, *Proverbs 1–9*, 92–93).

are neither private nor privileged.⁴¹ Despite the poet's unlimited potential for creative expression, he decided to make Wisdom a woman and moreover, he decided to maintain the substance of divine message and character within a jarring condescension of imagery.⁴² Even beyond the question of the social status of women in the ANE, is the simple question of *any* single human person standing and making vaunted declarations in a public place.

This condescension in imagery then is the substance of the second difficulty. While *Lady Wisdom*'s entreaty squarely accords with prophetic parallels, the innate authority of her relational appeal and person is not recognized by her audience who are quite happy to ignore both.⁴³

> Her communication does not only take place on the level of a concept or a set of truths or a strategy, but on that of a person. Therefore it acquires a personal dimension. This has a profound effect on the power of the poem in that the urgency of the message and the impossibility of escaping the consequences of ignoring Wisdom are heightened. This, in turn, makes room for an emotional aspect. Calling out like Jeremiah, making a scene in public, angrily telling people of the wish to give them a piece of one's mind, exclaiming, "how long is this still going to go on?" and threatening like a prophet of doom is anything but a matter of cool, rational and reflectively thought through sapientialising.⁴⁴

Despite her status, despite her true and authoritative message, she is found in the muddle of human society and communication. First, therefore, Wisdom is not an angel or goddess. Wisdom is neither a prince nor priest. Despite Wisdom's vaunted claims she is first presented as a woman in a particular and public space.

Second, with regard to her "relational appeal" this is not expressed in domains typical of gendered relationships. She speaks to men in plural, publicly. As will be seen in greater detail below, there is overlap between the call for relational attentiveness and the prophetic call to covenant fidelity. The

---

41. See Fox, *Proverbs 1–9*, 97.

42. While BH has a decided tendency toward conceiving of abstract entities as females (Fox, *Proverbs 1–9*, 110) it would be difficult to argue that this coerced the poet into employing female imagery for personification. The element could have been avoided altogether.

43. Many commentators make distinctions between the negative lexemes for simple (פתי), fool (נבל), and scoffer (לץ) and that these are presented in increasing severity from the merely naïve to the hardened rebel (i.e., Fox, *Proverbs 1–9*, 98; Loader, *Proverbs 1–9*, 94).

44. Loader, *Proverbs 1–9*, 91.

parity between these two will provide for the fusion of *covenant* appeal with *relational* appeal which provide the avenue for love and desire to inform the development of wisdom.[45] While the metaphorical source WOMAN provides very few mapped elements to the personification in Proverbs 1:20-33, the poet includes chooses images and metaphors that add both PROPHET and YHWH as elements of the overall personification of Wisdom. Thus, WISDOM AS PROPHET and WISDOM AS YHWH become a part of the blend. Each of these will be considered in turn below.

Wisdom as a Prophet

Within the context of Prov 1, a number of scholars suggest that there is some sort of a recontextualization of the prophets at work, but especially with reference to Jeremiah.[46] First of all, her initial declamation, "How Long!" is typically a divine reproach found in Jer 4:14; 21; 31:22; Hos 8:5.[47] Second, the metaphorical image schema of a "call without an answer" is a common feature in a number of prophetic books (Hos 5:6; Isa: 1:15; Jer 11:11, 14; Ezek 8:18).[48] Third, like the prophets, there is no great expectation that the human audience of her divine message will heed (Isa 6:9; Jer 1:19; Ezek 3:7).[49] Fourth, even the shape of the protasis—apodosis syntactic structure is similar to that found in the prophets (Jer 7:13; Hos 8:1; Amos 5:11).[50] Fifth, the construct form "apostasy of" (מְשׁוּבַת) (v. 32) is a marker

---

45. Van Leeuwen, "Book of Proverbs," 40.

46. "Several modern scholars, including Robert (1934, 172-81), Gemser (1963, 23), Kayatz (1966, 122-29) and, most carefully, Harris (1994, 87-109), have traced correspondence with prophetic speech, particularly Jeremiah's (chapters 7 and 20) and Zechariah's (chapter 7). There are numerous similarities in diction and phrasing (listed in Harris 1995, 93-95). For example, Jeremiah complains that everyone 'laughs' (śḥq) and 'mocks' (לעג) him (Jer 20:7) ... the most important parallel is thematic, in God's recurrent complaint that he spoke but they did not listen; that he called but they did not answer" (Fox, *Proverbs 1–9*, 105). See also Loader, *Proverbs 1–9*, 90.

47. Loader, *Proverbs 1–9*, 93. See also Prov 6:9; Num 14:17; 1 Sam 1:14; 1 Kgs 18:21. The phrase is also found in the mouth of God in Ps 6:4; 74:10; 80:5; 90:13.

48. Loader, *Proverbs 1–9*, 98.

49. Loader, *Proverbs 1–9*, 98.

50. Loader, *Proverbs 1–9*, 95-96. Waltke notes each of the above, but also includes formal grammatical similarities with the Prophets: "Examples of this phenomenon includes, first, the accusatory question 'how long' (v. 22). It is unknown in other sapiential literature but is at home in prophetic preaching (cf. Jer 4:14; 31:22; Hos 8:5). Second, the call for repentance (v. 23) and the use of *šub* with this meaning (113 times), is found exclusively among the prophets (cf. Jer 15:19; 18:11; 25:5). Third, the scolding accusation of not listening, formally introduced with *ya'an* (vv. 24-25) is prophetic (cf.

for significant lexical association with the prophets. While this is the only case where this word appears as a feminine construct without pronominal suffixes, there are nine uses of this root in Jeremiah and two in Hosea.[51] In every case it regards the apostasy of the children of Israel. There is no secular or sapiential meaning that can be applied.[52] Likewise the word glossed "being at ease" (שַׁלְוַת) also suggests association with the punishment of the exile. In each case it evokes the consequences of covenant infidelity. While textual dependence may be possible, the more demonstrable case is that the presence of such a number of lexical associations serve to frame the sapiential content not as correct action or propositional knowledge but in the reality of both expressed in terms of faithfulness to YHWH.[53]

Both contrary and consonant with the Prophets, *Lady Wisdom* "deals with people's attitudes rather than deeds.... In all of her speeches, rather than explaining what deeds are good or bad, Wisdom demands a basic stance toward wisdom itself: a loving openness to wisdom's message, whether this is sweet or harsh, alongside a dread of the consequences of rejecting."[54] The notion of relationship evoked by feminine imagery reverberates in that relational space which is rightfully called *covenant*.

In this is found a sort of functional equivalent between Wisdom and the human prophets. She is portrayed in the midst of daily human activity, but simultaneously set apart from it by her message and person. While

---

Isa 65:12; 66:4; Jer 7:13; 11:8; 17:23; 25:7; 32:33; 34:17; 35:14, 17). Fourth, the rigidly coined sequence of a substantiating accusation with either *ya'an* 'since/because' (vv. 24–25; cf. Isa 8:3; 30:12) or *tahat ki* (vv. 29–30; cf. Judg 2:3) or *waw* (cf. Isa 37:29), followed by the judicial sentence 'so . . . then,' is not encountered in the sapiential Gattung but is met with in prophetic threats. Fifth, the motif of a judicial sentence to destruction introduced by 'I' (v. 26) is also prophetic (cf. Jer 4:18; 21:14; 35:17; 48:16; 49:8). Sixth, the motif of calling in vain at the time of judgment (v. 28), though not found elsewhere in sapiential literature, is met with in the prophets (Mic 3:4; Isa 1:15; Jer 11:11, 14; Hos 5:6; Ezek 8:18; Zech 7:13). And seventh, the condemnation of faithlessness (v. 32) occurs also in the prophets (Jer 2:19; 3:6; 8:12; 14:7; Hos 11:7; 14:5)" (Waltke, "Lady Wisdom as a Mediatrix," 13).

51. Jer 2:19; 3:6, 8, 11–12, 22; 5:6; 8:5; 14:7; Hos 11:7; 14:5. Fox argues that מְשׁוּבַת should be understood as a "psychological disposition" or "disorder" "more than to a sinful deed" (Fox, *Proverbs 1–9*, 103). While it is assured that the issue is more than *deed*, understanding it as a component of the *human psyche* will reduce wisdom to a mental-social deficiency in human agents without respect or concern for their relation to the LORD.

52. See Job 3:18; Jer 48:11 (without *waw*); Jer 30:10; 46:27 (with *waw* and nearly identical).

53. Moreover, Lady Wisdom's metaphor "they will eat of the fruit of their roads" is a novel extension of Deuteronomic and prophetic retribution metaphors. For a larger consideration of this peculiar metaphor, see Appendix E.

54. Fox, *Proverbs 1–9*, 105.

Wisdom warns of impending judgment, this comes not as a threat which she will execute, but more like the warning of the prophets.[55] As such then, Wisdom takes on the color not of deity, but of intermediary.

Wisdom as YHWH

Lady Wisdom (חכמת) speaks and acts in ways that are typically reserved for YHWH in the Tanakh. First, the image of "pouring spirit" is consonant with imagery of YHWH in the prophets. Second, she is depicted with a similar *Schadenfreude* at the poetic justice that visits her rebellious audience. Finally, in a similar manner to YHWH, *Lady Wisdom* offers humans life and is rejected.[56]

Wisdom "Pours Out Her Spirit"

While both Loader and Fox argue that "pour forth my spirit" has to do with a display of temper, context and innerbiblical exegesis impedes such a reading.[57] First, the immediate parallel with "pouring forth spirit" is with speech.

55. Fox, *Proverbs 1–9*, 105.

56. Again, Waltke provides a neat summary of the novelty of the portrayal of *Lady Wisdom*: "The motifs of calling and not hearing and of seeking and not being found (v. 28), which are found in prophetic literature, in fact refer in those texts to Yahweh as an expression of His reaction to punish mankind's disobedience and self-will (cf. Mic 3:4; Isa 1:15; Jer 11:11; Hos 5:6). Both Yahweh and Lady Wisdom withdraw themselves from sinners in the time of judgment. These motifs, which consciously express the speaker's awesome authority, move Lady Wisdom into the closest association with Yahweh. As Yahweh's word demands obedience and as disobedience to Him provokes His judgment, the same is correspondingly valid for Lady Wisdom. Her withdrawal as a savior in the time of judgment has decisive weight. Her refusal to respond signifies judgment in the same way as Yahweh's withdrawal. When she laughs, mocks, and no longer listens, the person is helplessly given over to his self-afflicted, hopeless situation. Fourth, her statement, 'I will cause my spirit to bubble over to you,' resembles the relationship of Yahweh to His Messiah through the Spirit. No vizier and no prophet ever spoke like that. Finally, both promise security to those that obey them. In sum, Lady Wisdom's speech contains forms and motifs that did not originally belong together. She brings together into a new speech form elements that were originally diverse and thus creates a form that expresses divine revelation with the highest authority" (Waltke, "Lady Wisdom as a Mediatrix," 14).

57. Loader argues that "it can also mean spiritual capacity as an aspect of the Hebrew view of mind. Therefore she quite literally wishes to give the crowd 'a piece of her mind,' which includes anger and irritation. This is clear both from the semantics of רוּחַ and from the emotional level of the poem" (Loader, *Proverbs 1–9*, 95–96). This is likely through reference to Fox, "As a constituent of mind, *ruaḥ* (when it refers to a component of mind) is usually associated with emotion and matters of the 'spirit,'

As the verb is generally associated with "pouring out speech," it could be that רוחי is meant to be somehow metonymic to אמריה.⁵⁸ However, the word is never utilized in this way.⁵⁹ Instead, I think that the poet has mixed metaphors. The Lady does not move from "words" to "spirit" but exactly the reverse. Her spirit is poured forth *first*. If this were meant to be a metonymic understanding of "speech" then it stands to reason that *speech* should have been introduced as the lead referent to provide context. Instead, the poet present the image scheme: SPIRIT IS LIQUID. This imagery is consonant with that witnessed in the prophets.⁶⁰

> כִּי אֶצָּק־מַ֙יִם֙ עַל־צָמֵ֔א וְנֹזְלִ֖ים עַל־יַבָּשָׁ֑ה אֶצֹּ֤ק רוּחִי֙ עַל־זַרְעֶ֔ךָ וּבִרְכָתִ֖י עַל־צֶאֱצָאֶֽיךָ׃
>
> For I will pour water upon (the) thirsty and flows upon the dry land. I will pour my spirit upon your seed and my blessing upon your offspring. (Isa 44:3)
>
> וְלֹא־אַסְתִּ֥יר ע֛וֹד פָּנַ֖י מֵהֶ֑ם אֲשֶׁ֨ר שָׁפַ֤כְתִּי אֶת־רוּחִי֙ עַל־בֵּ֣ית יִשְׂרָאֵ֔ל נְאֻ֖ם אֲדֹנָ֥י יְהוִֽה׃ פ
>
> And I will no longer hide my face from them [that] I have poured my Spirit upon the house of Israel, says the LORD YHWH. (Ezek 39:29)
>
> וְהָיָ֣ה אַֽחֲרֵי־כֵ֗ן אֶשְׁפּ֤וֹךְ אֶת־רוּחִי֙ עַל־כָּל־בָּשָׂ֔ר
>
> And it will come to pass after thus, I will pour my Spirit upon all flesh
>
> וְנִבְּא֖וּ בְּנֵיכֶ֣ם וּבְנֽוֹתֵיכֶ֑ם זִקְנֵיכֶם֙ חֲלֹמ֣וֹת יַחֲלֹמ֔וּן בַּח֣וּרֵיכֶ֔ם חֶזְיֹנ֖וֹת יִרְאֽוּ׃
>
> And your sons and your daughters will prophesy and your old men will dream dreams and your young men will see visions.

---

while *leb* 'heart' is the organ of faculties and thoughts we identify with cognition" (Fox, *Proverbs 1–9*, 100).

58. See Ps 19:3: י֤וֹם לְי֨וֹם׀ יַבִּ֣יעַֽ אֹ֑מֶר וְלַ֥יְלָה לְּ֝לַ֗יְלָה יְחַוֶּה־דָּֽעַת

59. In Isa 59:21 YHWH "gives" his Spirit and it results in speech, but this is more similar to the giving of the Spirit in Ezek 36:27; 37:13.

60. While each of these phrases do not share in the verbal root of Prov 1:23 (נבע) they do all participate in the image schema of Spirit as a sort of fluid which can be "poured out."

> וְגַם עַל־הָעֲבָדִים וְעַל־הַשְּׁפָחוֹת בַּיָּמִים הָהֵמָּה אֶשְׁפּוֹךְ אֶת־רוּחִי:
>
> And also upon slaves and maidservants in those days I will pour out my Spirit. (Joel 3:1–2)

The precise nature of the "outpouring of spirit" in each of these contexts is beyond our present purposes. At the very minimum, however, the image schema of "pouring spirit" contains a communicative component that alters the understanding of humanity. More importantly the only subject who performs this "outpouring" is YHWH. Again, Lady Wisdom is being attributed with actions that are reserved for YHWH in the broader Tanakh.

Wisdom Mocks

The representation of *Lady Wisdom* "mocking" at those who scorn her counsel is reminiscent of the depiction of YHWH in Psalms. Her response is entirely commensurate and possibly even lexically dependent upon similar depictions of YHWH in the Psalms.

> יוֹשֵׁב בַּשָּׁמַיִם יִשְׂחָק אֲדֹנָי יִלְעַג־לָמוֹ:
>
> The one sitting in the heavens will laugh. My Lord will mock at them. (Ps 2:4)
>
> וְאַתָּה יְהוָה תִּשְׂחַק־לָמוֹ תִּלְעַג לְכָל־גּוֹיִם:
>
> But you YHWH will laugh at them. You will mock at all the nations. (Ps 59:9)

Therefore, even while there seems to be distinction from YHWH imaged by the lack of personal responsibility for judgment, Wisdom is still directly associated with YHWH in person and agency, specifically in that her dignity or value appear to be rooted in him.[61]

---

61. Van Leeuwen provides a helpful characterization of *Lady Wisdom's* "mocking": "The laughter of Wisdom is shocking. It is perhaps to be understood as a response to the absurdity of those who flaunt reality, who 'spit into the wind' and are puzzled when they get wet. It is also, perhaps, a fierce joy that the goodness of the world order and justice have been vindicated when the wicked reap what they have sown" (Van Leeuwen, "Book of Proverbs," 41).

Wisdom Offers Life and Is Rejected

The use of the "call and answer" image schema by *Lady Wisdom* in Prov 1 is lexically and metaphorically similar to a number of reported speeches and portrayals of YHWH in the prophets.[62] The phrase (גַם־אֲנִי) (cf. 1:26), "also, I" which appears six times in Tanakh in the initial position provides a clear parallel in Isa 66:4.[63] After a string of comparisons in which typical cultic activities are figured in terms of murder and idolatry, in verse four, YHWH condemns empty religious observances and states:

> גַּם־אֲנִ֞י אֶבְחַ֣ר בְּתַעֲלֻלֵיהֶ֗ם וּמְגֽוּרֹתָם֙ אָבִ֣יא לָהֶ֔ם
>
> Therefore, I, I will choose their ill-treatment and their terrors I will bring to them.
>
> יַ֤עַן קָרָ֙אתִי֙ וְאֵ֣ין עוֹנֶ֔ה דִּבַּ֖רְתִּי וְלֹ֥א שָׁמֵ֑עוּ
>
> Because I called and there was no one answering. I spoke and they did not listen.
>
> וַיַּעֲשׂ֤וּ הָרַע֙ בְּעֵינַ֔י וּבַאֲשֶׁ֥ר לֹֽא־חָפַ֖צְתִּי בָּחָֽרוּ׃
>
> And they have done the evil in my eyes and in that which I do not delight they have chosen. Isa 66:4

Likewise, the complaint of "no one listening" is found in the reported speech of YHWH in Ps 81:12–14.[64]

> 12 וְלֹא־שָׁמַ֣ע עַמִּ֣י לְקוֹלִ֑י וְ֝יִשְׂרָאֵ֗ל לֹא־אָ֥בָה לִֽי׃
>
> My people did not listen to my voice. Israel was not willing.

---

62. The Masoretes note that "they will call me" appears nowhere else in Tanakh with the present morphology, but also as noted the lexeme has frequent occurrences in similar contexts in the prophets. Likewise, "they will seek me" (יְשַׁחֲרֻֽנְנִי) is noted to have only one other like appearance in Tanakh in Hosea. Despite the fact that the "seeking without finding" image is found in a number of prophetic contexts (Isa 1:15; Jer 11:11, 14; Ezek 8:18). See Loader, *Proverbs 1–9*, 98. There are only two cases that match this particular string of words: The first is in Hos 6:1 אֵלֵ֤ךְ אָשׁ֙וּבָה֙ אֶל־מְקוֹמִ֔י עַ֥ד אֲשֶֽׁר־יֶאְשְׁמ֖וּ וּבִקְשׁ֣וּ פָנָ֑י בַּצַּ֥ר לָהֶ֖ם יְשַׁחֲרֻֽנְנִי. Likewise, the word glossed, "they will find me" also occurs in only one other context, this time in the longer wisdom speech in 8:17. However, and perhaps more tellingly, the words for "seeking" and "finding" also appear in the speech of the *Strange Woman* (Prov 7:15).

63. Cf. Judg 2:21; Job 7:11; Ps 71:22; Prov 1:26; Isa 66:4; Ezek 20:23

64. Without the conjunction the phrase appears again in Proverbs 8:34 providing continuity between this speech and the conclusion. See also the speech of Job (Job 31:35) and the speech of Elihu in (Job 34:34).

> 13 וָאֲשַׁלְּחֵהוּ בִּשְׁרִירוּת לִבָּם יֵלְכוּ בְּמוֹעֲצוֹתֵיהֶם׃
>
> And I sent him away in the stubbornness of their heart. They went in their counsels.
>
> 14 לוּ עַמִּי שֹׁמֵעַ לִי יִשְׂרָאֵל בִּדְרָכַי יְהַלֵּכוּ׃
>
> If only my people were listening to me. (If only) Israel would walk in my path. (Psa 81: 12–14)

Based upon the shared vocabulary of "willing" (אבה), and "plan" (עֵצָה) there may be basis to suggest a purposeful literary allusion at work. However, the more basic question regards the metaphorical function in this and the related passages. This passage does not constitute a prophetic judgment, but rational, though emotionally charged, argumentation. Wisdom, as YHWH in Ps 81:14, is featured as the frustrated patron of a disobedient subordinate.

Conclusion

Given the strength of these innerbiblical allusions and metaphors it is not difficult to see that the conceptual blend of *Lady Wisdom* is largely composed of elements common to the canonical characterization of the PROPHET and YHWH, but also maintains the strand of personal relationship provided by WOMAN as a conceptual input. The personification of WISDOM contains the vaunted qualities of YHWH himself and prophetic mediation of the covenant in the condescension and vulnerability of a human woman.

Stage 1 Perception: Part II: The Personification of Wisdom in Prov 2 as a Woman and a Shield

Introduction

Over against the strong, unified, prophetic, and divine personification of wisdom in Prov 1:20–33 the second stage of development (Prov 2:1–11) diversifies and fragments the personification not only to introduce metaphors that will be basic to the rest of the book, but also to highlight WOMAN metaphor and her role as a familiar and desirable protector to the youth. The more familiar presentation of personified wisdom begins accruing qualities that will be associated with the wife of the young man. Thereby, personified wisdom begins to be blended with the good woman who will serve to guard the young man's desire from the wiles of the "strange/foreign woman." This personification draws wisdom into a nearer orbit of intimacy, desire, and active pursuit, rather than the passive and numinous disposition set forth in Prov 1.

The Syntax of Prov 2 Contributes to the Development and Diversification of Metaphor

While earlier scholarship generally understood Prov 2 as a syntactic and redactional hodgepodge (i.e., Toy, Whybray, Michel) current interpretation largely follows Meinhold in understanding the chapter as a single and well-designed sentence.[65] After careful grammatical and rhetorical analysis Loader's conclusion is apt, "So on neither the logical nor the grammatical or the stylistic level or their integration can we speak of a muddled text."[66] Rather it is quite the reverse, "On the linguistic level, the syntactic structure is not as complicated as is often claimed. It may be extended and involve many more clauses than usual in Hebrew poetry, but these are all clearly identifiable and describable."[67]

---

65. Whybray, for example, undertakes significant redactional criticism in order to uncover what he deems to be the original discourse (Whybray, *Composition of the Book of Proverbs*, 38–40). See also Meinhold, *Die Sprüche*, 1:43–47.

66. Loader, *Proverbs 1–9*, 110. While the grammatical, syntactic and rhetorical scheme of the poem are remarkable, scholarly assertions that Prov 2 is a non-alphabetic acrostic (i.e., Van Leeuwen, Clifford, and Murphy) is difficult to substantiate. The "key letters," א and ל, do open the first and last three strophes, but are also found in other opening lines.

67. Loader, *Proverbs 1–9*, 106.

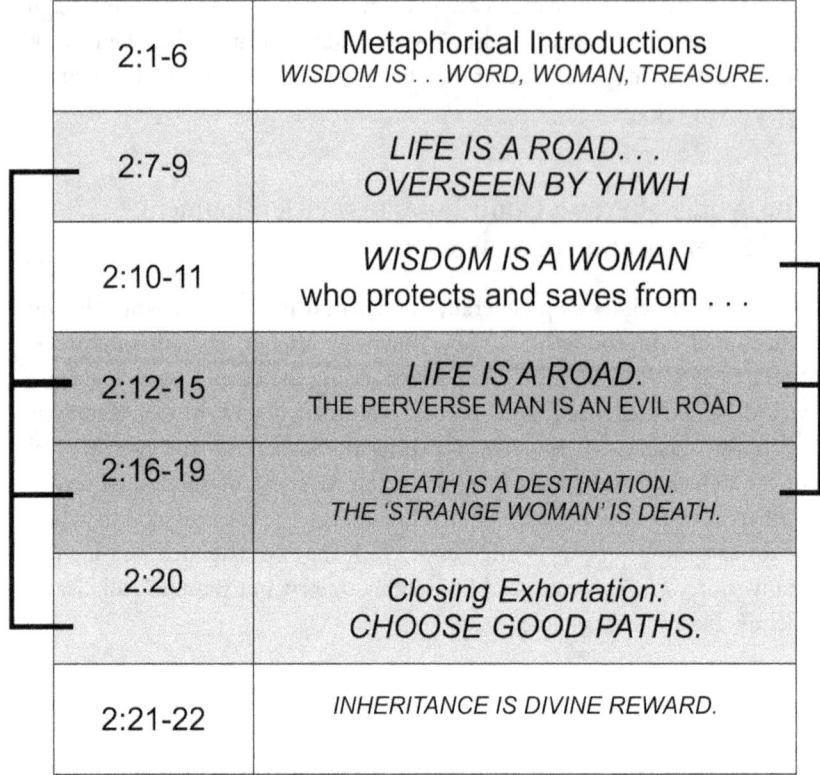

Figure 6. Metaphor and Structure in Proverbs 2

In addition to the sophisticated syntactic structure, the metaphors appearing in Proverbs 2:1-22 are interwoven within the syntactic chain around reference to "fear of YHWH."[68] Where Proverbs 1:20-33 was a strong, unified personification of Wisdom as a woman, Proverbs two splits wisdom into three basic metaphors.[69] The protases in 2:1, 3, and 4 introduce each

---

68. "The whole chapter can be read as one long conditional sentence with a whole series of clauses and sub-clauses" (Loader, *Proverbs 1–9*, 108).

69. The assertion of "basic metaphor" is perhaps an oversimplification. These metaphors are the most explicitly stated and lexically anchored. However, it could also be argued that each of these is balanced by a passive counterpart (i.e., TREASURE-GIFT, WORD-DEED, WOMAN-ROAD). Van Leeuwen actually notes each of these metaphors in his commentary, but does not mark the correlation. In regard to WOMAN metaphor, "Wisdom's call to humans is echoed by the call of humans for Wisdom" (Van Leeuwen, *Proverbs*, 43). In regard to TREASURE metaphor, "The opening verses also play upon the search for treasure. The son is to 'treasure up' the words of the father (2:1 a; cf. 1:11, 19; 2:7 Hebrew), and to 'seek' and 'search' for wisdom 'like silver' and 'hidden treasures' (v. 4), which the Lord 'stores up for the good' (v. 7)" (Van Leeuwen, "Book of

metaphor in turn. In the first protasis, "if you will take my word and treasure my command," the basic metaphor is *WISDOM IS WORD* which will be perhaps the most frequent metaphor for Wisdom in the book. Thus, "the first condition for the acquisition of wisdom is the acceptance of authoritative utterances made by the teacher."[70] This initial clause is then further qualified by the condition of conforming the *will* to understanding by being *attentive* to the father's word in 2:2.[71] In the second protasis (2:3a), "if you will call to insight," the basic metaphor is *WISDOM IS A WOMAN*, which had been introduced in the previous section.[72] In the third protasis (2:4a), "if you will seek (her/it) like silver," the added metaphor is WISDOM IS TREASURE, which will appear throughout the book in combination with other metaphors.[73] The apodosis and epexegetic clause in 4:5-6, provides

---

Proverbs," 43). Finally, in regard to *WISDOM AS WORD*, "The search for wisdom begins with master of parental 'words' and 'commandments' (v. 1)" (Van Leeuwen, "Book of Proverbs," 43).

70. Loader, *Proverbs 1-9*, 110. Loader also makes an important contribution to the understanding of "sapiential authority." It is *not* so much that parental instruction must be deemed in precisely the same manner as Torah. "Authority is not at all just a matter of using the command mode, but presupposes the categorical validity of a statement being made. The concept of authority (not the *term*) occurs in the expressions אמרי תכח and מצותי used in the respective hemistichs of v. 1. The speaker makes no claim to speak on behalf of God. Whereas the prophets speak in the name of Yahweh ... and bring his word ... the wisdom teacher offers his own words. He has received no revelation and expects to be taken seriously in his own right" (Loader, *Proverbs 1-9*, 111). See also Longman, *Proverbs*, 120-21, 126.

71. Loader, *Proverbs 1-9*, 112. "Striving for understanding implies not (yet) having it. Neither aspect of understanding is *required* of the pupil, which stands to reason, for understanding is the *result* of the enterprise, not its condition (cf. the apodosis, vv. 5, 6 and 9, 11 where the root occurs four times). All of this suggests that the condition for the acquisition includes the acceptance of the authoritative utterances of the teacher (v. 1) as a matter of attentiveness of the will (v. 2). Even if education in Israel was a matter of discipline, it could not achieve its purpose if the pupils themselves were unwilling" (Loader, *Proverbs 1-9*, 113).

72. Loader argues that the verbs in this protasis (i.e., "call" and "give voice") indicate that attaining wisdom is an active pursuit. He argues that this verse is dialectically opposed to the absolute divine dependence of Ps 127:2. "Prov 2 emphasizes the necessity of human effort as a condition for the divine gift of wisdom (cf. v. 5).... The youth here is required to look for wisdom/insight in the same way used by Wisdom to reach to him" (Loader, *Proverbs 1-9*, 114). While Loader is correct in pointing to v. 6 as highlighting YHWH's role as the *giver* of Wisdom, I am not sure that he is correct in seeing the relational model as highlighting *human* initiative. As he, himself, has pointed out our action is only *re*-action.

73. As noted above Loader misplaces human agency, therefore, he sees v. 4 as a statement of *valuation* more than of effort. Since the metaphor is placed alongside verbs for *diligent search* (i.e., בקש and חפש) it is clear that while value *motivates* the metaphor, the accent is upon human agency (cf. Loader, *Proverbs 1-9*, 114). In later paragraphs,

the central idea that unifies these metaphors and then inverts the order in reply to each protasis: "THEN you will understand the fear of YHWH (unparalleled) and the knowledge of God you will FIND (*TREASURE*) and YHWH will give WISDOM (*WOMAN?*), from HIS MOUTH (*WORD*) knowledge and understanding."[74] Perhaps the item of key significance is the lack of parallel in "the fear of YHWH" (2:5).[75] As the first element after the apodosis and the only member of the apodosis not linked lexically to *any* of the metaphorical models, it would appear that it is the basis each.[76] Therefore, the WORD of parental instruction and Torah is paired with WOMAN and TREASURE as desirable ends. Second, each of these more active components of attaining and desiring wisdom are still rooted in the fear of YHWH. Third, each of these metaphors will become associated with the conceptual blend of wisdom personified and will in turn be more deeply entwined and integrated throughout the book.[77]

The Role of Conflicting Personifications of Wisdom in Prov 1 and 2

This second appearance of the metaphor WISDOM AS A WOMAN is first of all contiguous with the personification of wisdom in Prov 1. The word "wisdom" (חָכְמָה) with continuing personification retains the influence of feminine metaphor from chapter 1.[78] Also, the language and metaphor of

---

the metaphor of TREASURE will shift from an accent on "effort of obtaining" to "essential value and profit." Therefore the metaphor WISDOM IS TREASURE will be treated in greater detail below.

74. Verse 5 "reminds us that wisdom and relationship with Yahweh are integrally entwined" (Longman, *Proverbs*, 120).

75. "Understanding the Fear of Yahweh *follows* the search for wisdom. This does not contradict the famous claim in 1:7 that the Fear of Yahweh is the *beginning* of knowledge. In the context of chapter 1 acceptance of the authority of human teachers would be unthinkable if its foundation were not the acceptance of the source of all authority, which is of course God as the ultimate authority" (Loader, *Proverbs 1–9*, 116).

76. Loader notes that this "strophe of the poem coincides with the first part of the composite result clause" (Loader, *Proverbs 1–9*, 116). He does carefully note how the syntax relates in a chiastic parallel and the special placement of the fear of YHWH, but does not mark the correspondence of metaphorical models. Cf. Loader, *Proverbs 1–9*, 121.

77. The sundering of the strong and unified personification of wisdom into these metaphors is different from Meinhold's argument that this chapter is used as an "introduction" to the rest of Prov 1–9. Here the correspondences are neither topical nor systemic. Rather, these are the basic image schemes that are used as a conceptual mold for wisdom. See Loader, *Proverbs 1–9*, 107–12 for a nice treatment in the weaknesses in Meinhold's argument.

78. Lexically the connection between this paragraph and other contexts can be

"calling out" (קרא) and "giving voice" (תִּתֵּן קוֹלֶךָ) is not at all arbitrary, but evokes the immediately preceding context of chapter 1, wherein wisdom has "raised her voice" (תִּתֵּן קוֹלָהּ). Also when her audience attempts to "call upon [her]" (יִקְרָאֻנְנִי) (1:28) they will not "find" (מצא) her (1:28). All of these terms are chosen to solidify the relationship to that passage. The parents are exhorting their child, not to initiate a conversation with wisdom, but to respond to the conversation already begun. As such the personal and response-able person of Wisdom is retained, as is the close association with YHWH and by extension his covenant. The movement is from corporate exhortation to the formation of a singular desire.

There are a number of ways the metaphor of *WISDOM IS A WOMAN* is either transformed or overturned in Prov 2: (1) by disjunction in formal presentation (2) disjunction in presentation as singular or plural (3) the absence of juridical and prophetic metaphor and vocabulary (4) difference in function.

First, the piling of feminine nouns (2:2–3) generates ambiguity as to the identity of the feminine subject. The simple syntax points toward a singular feminine subject while her "personal" nature is scattered by refusing to maintain חכמת or even חכמה as a singular referent.[79] In addition to scattering reference to her as a single person, wisdom lexemes are linked to justice, righteousness, and equity which appear to be parallel means to parallel ends.

---

demonstrated by unusual lexical forms. The Masoretes note a number of peculiar forms which demonstrate connections between feminine figurations in the first nine chapters. First, the note in 2a, indicates the construction לְחָכְמָה ("to wisdom") appears only in one other context in the book at 7:4. Likewise in 2:3a לַבִּינָה ("to discernment") is limited to the same context, with regard to personified wisdom as a foil for the *Strange Woman* of chapter 7.

79. After the כי, the first clause is the entirely conventional order of verb, subject, and a prepositional phrase functioning as a locative. "Wisdom will come in your heart." The next colon is syndetically related to the first, and renames "Wisdom" as "knowledge" (דעת) via the same switching of diction already witnessed in 2:2–3. The order of syntax fronts "knowledge" as the direct object and follows with a prepositional phrase that includes both the subject and reflexive verb "to your soul will be pleasant." It is interesting to note that the movement metaphor is maintained in the a colon, and abstracted into stasis in the b colon through the choice of verbs. Verse 11 contains no explicit syntactic marker to show that it is in series with 10, however, the presence of the wisdom lexemes in both a and b cola cause the reader to group the lines together. The syntax across the final line is subject fronted and followed by an imperfect verb, to be read as future/subjunctive. In the a colon the direct object is provided by the על preposition, where in the b colon the direct object is provided by the pronominal suffix. The relationship across the lines therefore is extension from 10a to 10b, where the welcomed Wisdom becomes sweet. This "discernment" then remains and guards in line 11a and is restated essentially synonymously as "understanding" in the b colon.

Second, the poet's peculiar word choices and metaphors that highlighted a connection with the prophets noted above do not reappear in Prov 2. Rather, in their place we find language that is more typical of Torah (specifically association of שמר and מצות) blended with the profusion of sapiential terms.

Third, *Lady Wisdom* shifts from the role of prophet and divine mediator in Prov 1 to the role of a guard and protector in Prov 2.

The Metaphor *YHWH IS A SHIELD* Is Added to the Conceptual Blend of Personified Wisdom

Lady Wisdom is repeatedly associated with protection in this paragraph. But she is not the protector of the crowd of the simple as in Prov 1. Rather wisdom is said to protect and guard the youth as an individual (Prov 2:11). Moreover, by virtue of the larger argument she acts as a guide to the youth as he endeavors to maintain straight paths in life and most particularly to *deliver* the youth (נציל) from stereotypical dangers on that path (2:12, 16).[80] Finally, by the repetition of the verbs נצר and שמר in Prov 2:8 and Prov 2:11 personified wisdom is drawn into association with the metaphor *YHWH IS A SHIELD* (2:6–9).

Outside of the poetic/sapiential books reference to the "shield" (מגן) is not used in metaphor directly, but frequently may be used in concert with other weaponry as a metonymy for "warfare."[81] Within the poetic and sapiential corpus, the metaphor of *[x] IS A SHIELD* is common enough perhaps to be considered a basic metaphor in the Tanakh. In nearly all of these contexts it is YHWH who is identified with the shield, as a physical protection to the speaker or entity. As such the protection of YHWH is imaged as a divine, personal, and frequently *physical* protection established by

---

80. The metaphor LIFE IS A ROAD is the basic structure that underlies not only all of the different qualifications of life (i.e., crooked, smooth, dark, bright, etc.) but also underlies other expressions like MANNER OF LIVING IS MANNER OF WALKING and CHOICES ARE PATHS. Road and movement are the prevalent image schema for this paragraph and are variously transformed to account for the threat of emulation found in the "perverse man" and the threat of relationship and association found in the *Strange Woman*.

81. See Judg 5:8; 2 Sam 1:21; 1 Kgs 10:17; 14:26–27; 2 Kgs 19:32; 1 Chr 5:18; 2 Chr 9:16; 12:9–10; 14:7; 17:17; 23:9; 26:14; 32:5, 27; Neh 4:10; Job 15:26; 41:7; Song 4:4; Isa 21:5; 22:6; 37:33; Jer 46:3, 9; Ezek 23:24; 27:10; 38:4–5; 39:9; Nah 2:4. Of these uses SHIELD is used as the source category for metaphor in only a few cases (e.g., Job 41:7; Song 4:4).

God's personal agency.[82] In this case, YHWH's protection is modulated first by the metaphor of LIFE IS A ROAD but also with the regard to the role of personified wisdom as a guide and protection from dangers that inhabit that road.[83]

By this blend of lexical and metaphorical associations not only does PROTECTION become part of the conceptual blend for personified wisdom, but also influences the presentation of the input category of WOMAN.

Conclusion

In Prov 2, Wisdom is not the projection of a human quality, nor is she a transcendent external divine property. She enters the heart of the youth and blends the preservation inherent in obedience to parental instruction with the might of divine protection. The experience of the youth is one of delight in the depth of his person.[84] YHWH shields the youth by shielding his path. The youth maintains that path through the transformation of his desires through being captivated by *Lady Wisdom*.

Conclusion: The Diverse and Dichotomous Personifications of Wisdom Lead to Paradox

The diversification and blending of familiar and divine metaphors associated with familiar and desirable *Lady Wisdom* does not cease in Prov 2. In Prov 3 the personification develops associations with WISDOM IS TREASURE (3:10–16) but is balanced with divine mediatorial components of the metaphor WISDOM IS LIFE (3:8, 16, 18). As in this paragraph, the pursuit of wisdom balances relational and objective components but also is heavily

---

82. See Gen 14:20; 15:1; Deut 33:29; 2 Sam 22:3, 31, 36; Ps 3:4; 7:11; 18:3, 31, 36; 28:7; 33:20; 35:2; 47:10; 59:12; 76:4; 84:10, 12; 89:19; 115:9–11; 119:114; 144:2; Prov 2:7; 6:11; 24:34; 30:5.

83. "What God guards, is the way of justice as practiced by the faithful, not their welfare. In terms of the nexus of deed and consequence, however, this must also indirectly benefit their day-to-day interests, because if God keeps them on the path of justice, it must eventually result in the reward of success. But that is not the focus of the verse [2:8]" (Loader, *Proverbs 1–9*, 120).

84. "When wisdom enters the heart, it enters the central organ of the human mind. ... Not a mere dexterity, but the deep wisdom of judgment between right and wrong, an insight with ethical implications. [Prov 10:2b] bears this out, since this knowledge is said to be pleasing to the human soul. This is an aesthetic judgment and means that the sage conceives of wisdom with its religious ramifications as a deep-seated aesthetic experience" (Loader, *Proverbs 1–9*, 121).

self-interested. This time not for protection from negative stereotypes, but of the maintenance of the road of blessing. At the same time, covenantal associations of Torah and parental instruction are drawn into closer association (3:1–5, 11–13). This profusion and fusion of metaphors will continue to grow and blend until we find the beautiful statement of romantic attachment for the human, divine, prophetic, faithful, cognitive, and feminine personification of wisdom in Proverbs 4:5–9.

> 5 קְנֵה חָכְמָה קְנֵה בִינָה אַל־תִּשְׁכַּח וְאַל־תֵּט מֵאִמְרֵי־פִי:
>
> Get Wisdom. Get insight. Do not forget and do not turn aside from the words of my mouth
>
> 6 אַל־תַּעַזְבֶהָ וְתִשְׁמְרֶךָּ אֱהָבֶהָ וְתִצְּרֶךָּ:
>
> Do not abandon her and she will keep you. Love her and she will protect you.
>
> 7 רֵאשִׁית חָכְמָה קְנֵה חָכְמָה וּבְכָל־קִנְיָנְךָ קְנֵה בִינָה:
>
> The beginning of wisdom [is] get wisdom, and in all that you obtain, get insight.
>
> 8 סַלְסְלֶהָ וּתְרוֹמְמֶךָּ תְּכַבֵּדְךָ כִּי תְחַבְּקֶנָּה:
>
> Prize her and she will exalt you. She will honor you because you embrace her.
>
> 9 תִּתֵּן לְרֹאשְׁךָ לִוְיַת־חֵן עֲטֶרֶת תִּפְאֶרֶת תְּמַגְּנֶךָּ:
>
> She will give to your head a wreath of grace. A crown of beauty she will bestow on you. (Prov 4:5–9)

The parallel of the human and sapiential dimension is neatly stated by Raymond Van Leeuwen:

> Human wisdom is fostered by pointing to Wisdom as something "out there" to be gotten hold of, to be loved, embraced, and prized (vv. 6, 8), like the wife in 5:15–20. Human wisdom is love of realty, of the world, and of its excellent "norms." And those who embrace Wisdom are in turn kept, guarded, and honored by her reality (vv. 6, 8; for the imagery of v. 9, cf. 1:9). The love affair of humans and Wisdom is reciprocal and mutual.[85]

---

85. Van Leeuwen, "Book of Proverbs," 59.

This blending of human and divine metaphors produce a balance of passive and active image schema that yields *paradox,* which is one of the hallmarks of right-hemisphere thinking.[86] Left-hemisphere thinking sees in these two personifications a contradiction which is to be understood as basic error; things must be one thing or another. There can be no polyvalence of truth.[87] Rather than seeing the world in terms of singular and propositional "right answers," it is rather that we are called to understand the world as Heraclitus's bow. "The taut string, its two ends pulling apart under opposing forces, that for bow or lyre is what gives its vital strength or virtue, is the perfect expression of a dynamic, rather than static equilibrium."[88]

So in Prov 1 and 2 wisdom is presented as paradox. Wisdom is a divine gift calling out in consonance with the covenant. Wisdom is a desperate human search for the highest human good. The "taut string" is the truth of the paradox.

> Wisdom as such, then, is a human undertaking, but has its ultimate source in God.... The ambivalence of wisdom as the result of both human industry *and* divine generosity (Murphy) is well established in Hebrew narratives. In the Book of Esther, success is achieved by human planning, but the series of unbelievable coincidences at precisely the right junctures makes it clear that a divine power is at work behind the scenes. The Book of Ruth exemplifies the same, though with explicit reference to God. In the Joseph story (Gen 37–50) Joseph saves Egypt by his own wisdom, yet ascribes it to God's plan with him (cf. Gen 50:20).

---

86. For example, McGilchrist argues that Heraclitus seems "to have grasped the essence of the balance between the hemispheres, while remaining aware of the primacy of the right hemisphere's world" precisely because Heraclitus understood the world primarily by an inward consideration of paradox. Heraclitus balanced the hemispheres in "his insistence on the importance of perception, despite the difficulties of truly understanding what it is that we perceive; in his prioritizing of experience over our theories about experience; in his insistence that opposites need to be held together, rather than inevitably cancelling one another out; in his sense that all is in the process of change and eternal flux, rather than stasis or completion; and in his sense that all things contain an energy or life. In addition he sees the *logos* as something 'shared,' reciprocal perhaps even reciprocally coming into being, rather than, as he says we tend to see it, something achieved through 'private,' isolated thought processes" (McGilchrist, *Master and His Emissary,* 270–71).

87. McGilchrist, *Master and His Emissary,* 271. In Zeno, for example, movement is impossible because if things could move, "they would move into the void" (McGilchrist, *Master and His Emissary,* 271). For post-modern linguists, since words apparently change meaning based on context and audience, they therefore can have no meaning at all. Both are examples of left-hemisphere theories ruling right hemisphere perception.

88. McGilchrist, *Master and His Emissary,* 270.

The Succession Narrative (2 Sam 9–1 Kgs 2) develops according to a chain of human causality, but at specific junctures refers to God's decisive providence (e.g., 2 Sam 17:14). Humans and God are fully "responsible" for what transpires in life.[89]

In a similar fashion, the diversification of metaphor also generates a sort of cyclical reasoning. Longman notes, "Wisdom leads to the fear of Yahweh/knowledge of God, but then surprisingly, this knowledge of God leads to wisdom (v. 6). This is the circular paradox: Seek wisdom and find God. Seek God and find wisdom. And once one does find wisdom, one is to thank God for it."[90] The seemingly irreconcilable personifications of wisdom, then point us to a truth too big for us. These dichotomous presentations of personified wisdom present a balanced but paradoxical wisdom: divine and human, passive and active, distant and desirable. Ultimately, however, both personifications reflect different aspects of the covenantal relationship with YHWH.

Stage 2: Jesus Is the Substance Echoed by Lady Wisdom

The recognition of the complex blend of canonical images and allusions in the personification of *Lady Wisdom* is formally beautiful in itself. The beauty of the characterization only deepens when we discover how she reflects the reality and process of discerning and obtaining WISDOM as an abstract target category: the dance of human and divine; the blend of law and prophets; the individual and communal. However, Balthasar's theological aesthetics beckons us further and higher, to recognize that all earthly beauty is partial and transitory and ends with the pangs of *Sehnsucht*. In the person of Jesus we find the substance which wisdom personified mirrors and the true sound

---

89. Loader, *Proverbs 1–9*, 116.

90. I appreciate how Longman connects this realization with the spiritual life of everyman: "On a practical level, what does this mean for someone who wants to heed the admonition of the father and become wise? Work hard at it. Study the book of Proverbs and the rest of the Bible. However, the acknowledgment that whatever wisdom we have comes ultimately from God chastens our pride and leads to humility. It does not allow the pursuit of proverbial wisdom to lead to the pride that separates us from God. It also reminds those who are wise to be thankful for whatever wisdom they have" (Longman, *Proverbs*, 127). Moreover, Longman also connects the "circular paradox" with the metaphor YHWH IS A WARRIOR, wherein the LORD commands the Israelites to fight, but requires their praise for victory. Human agency works in concert with divine grace (Longman, *Proverbs*, 127). Van Leeuwen also notes this circularity, but points out that it is a circle that *begins* with YHWH, then continues through human agency and interaction (i.e., Exod 20:1–7; Matt 6:8–10; 11–13; Hos 4:1–2). See Van Leeuwen, "Book of Proverbs," 45–46.

of which she is only an echo. The prophetic and mediatorial strands of *Lady Wisdom* are substantiated in the life, ministry, death, and resurrection of Christ. The divine components of *Lady Wisdom* are grounded in the reality Jesus as YHWH. The intimacy of the *Lady Wisdom* is only a foreshadowing of the promise fulfilled in Jesus. Wisdom, as the personification of the rightly understood created order, is diverse and paradoxical as she stretches toward the numinous and personal reality of our triune God. It is not that Jesus looks like *Lady Wisdom*. It is that *Lady Wisdom* along with the created order she personifies, reflects the substance of the triune God demonstrated in Jesus: in his role as prophetic mediator, his divine person, his role as personal protector and his paradoxical identity as God made man.

Prophetic Wisdom Echoes Rejected Jesus

> God's entrance is signaled by the beginning of Christ's public activity, with the double *exousia* it exhibits: the prophetic "power of the word" and the "power of miracles" (Luke 24:19). God himself resounds and acts through the prophetic task of this man. . . . Through Christ's prophetic word and miracles, God wishes now no longer to reveal the judging God but rather wishes to descend into the judged human flesh whose suffering and death is everything but make-believe. *This* is what the Incarnation is, no longer now as a state but as an event, or, if you wish, as the dynamic and eventful measuring of one's own static reality.[91]

Christ's ministry is steeped in Prophecy objectively with regard to his birth and ministry (cf. Matt 1:23; Luke 1:67–79; 3:4) but also with regard to his message and demeanor. Moreover, Jesus frames his entire ministry as a continuation of the prophetic message: "Well did Isaiah prophesy of you hypocrites, as it is written, 'This people honors me with their lips, but their heart is far from me; in vain do they worship me, teaching as doctrines the commandments of men'" (Mark 7:6–7; Isa 29:13; cf. Ezek 33:31). But more than a prophetic messenger he declares that he is a prophetic fulfillment. In Nazareth, he begins his public ministry by reference to Isa 61:1, and declares "these words have been fulfilled in your hearing." More particularly, the prophetic metaphors employed by *Lady Wisdom* are also employed by Christ. He appeals to humanity. He promises that the one who asks will receive and the one who seeks will find. (Matt 7:7; Luke 11:9–10) Moreover, much of Jesus' early and primary address is prophetically aimed at those who would not hear. They are the לצים and the כסילים who have not been seduced by

---

91. Balthasar, *Seeing the Form,* 461–62.

pleasure to a shortcut but by pride into self-righteousness (Matt 23). The opposition to Wisdom is consonant with the reception of Jesus. The message is identical to the messenger and their claims transcend earthly categories (John 5:43–47).

He met the simple with a message much the same as *Lady Wisdom*. He came, reiterating the long cry, and extending once again in entreaty the warning of the upraised arm of YHWH.

> 43 I have come in my Father's name, and you do not receive me. If another comes in his own name, you will receive him. 44 How can you believe, when you receive glory from one another and do not seek the glory that comes from the only God? 45 Do not think that I will accuse you to the Father. There is one who accuses you: Moses, on whom you have set your hope. 46 For if you believed Moses, you would believe me; for he wrote of me. 47 But if you do not believe his writings, how will you believe my words?" (John 5:43–47, ESV)

Even so, as he reached out again in love and warning to the scattered flocks of Israel, he brought the ringing warning of the coming wrath of God to those who chose to reject the offer of the knowledge and *fear* of YHWH.

However, we must be clear about the *reason* for this parity. The claims and depiction of *Lady Wisdom* are precisely the claims and depiction of YHWH set forth in covenant with his people. Therefore, since her metaphorical depiction is *reflective* of YHWH it is only reasonable that she is therefore reflective of the person of the Son. Those who argue for a Wisdom Christology, who find an echo of *Lady Wisdom* in Christ, have reversed the relationship.

Divine Wisdom Echoes YHWH's appeal in Christ

"The unity which Christ himself represents is the opposite of a synthesis of what men imagine to be the best of man and God . . . a unity of the most unpretentious humanity with the one and only divine Sonship."[92] YHWH, in the person of his Son, visited his covenant people who did not receive him (John 1:10–11). He spoke openly in public at the sea (Mark 3:7), in their hills (Matt 5:1), in streets (Matt 20:29; 27:32; Luke 10:38) and synagogues (Matt 4:23; 9:35; Mark 1:39, Luke 4:15, 44; John 18:20).

Even as *Lady Wisdom* speaks with the message of YHWH with the authority of YHWH, and acts in ways reserved for YHWH, so also does

---

92. Balthasar, *Seeing the Form*, 476.

Christ ... because he IS YHWH (John 8:58). He not only claims unity with the Father, but does miraculous works in accordance with the will of His Father (John 10:37). He is given authority not just to heal and raise from the dead, as other prophetic messengers, but he has the divine authority to forgive sin (Matt 9:6; Mark 2:10; Luke 5:24). In all and through all, as the perfect human archetype, he also displays the unity of the Trinity expressed in obedience.

> The "image" of God that Christ concretises for us has its own dynamism which means that here we have someone who can speak and act with divine power and also suffer and die with human impotence. This does not make it into an image of fragmentation but of unification, because the one speaking with God's power and suffering with man's impotence does both things in accordance with an identical disposition: he does both things out of obedience.[93]

While Christ does not threaten mockery of the foolish, he does in reality become the vehicle for pouring forth of the Spirit (John 15:26) and ultimately the providence for a real and abiding life through his sacrificial death (John 3:14–16).

Familiar Wisdom Echoes Christ's Promise of Providence and Protection

In Prov 2, the curious pun on שמר and נצר shows that keeping and protecting WISDOM AS WORD is equivalent to being kept and protected by wisdom. However, the manner of this protection is not one that denies suffering or adversity but merely assures one's place upon those paths overseen by YHWH. In a similar manner, Jesus promises that those who hear and believe his word will be given eternal life and pass from death to life (John 5:24). Likewise, the one abiding in the word of Christ will have Christ abide in him assuring him of fruitfulness and life, even as the branch remains in the vine (John 15). The one who hears and obeys the words of Christ is like a wise person building a house upon the rock, while the fool ignores the word of Christ and suffers disaster (Matt 7:24–29). Attending to the word of Christ, even as one attends to the word of Wisdom is supplied with that measure of protection and blessing that does not do away with the rain, but insures that the hardships of life will not result in ultimate ruin. Even more, Jesus assures us of the beneficent disposition of God. We should not be

---

93. Balthasar, *Seeing the Form*, 466.

anxious for the needs of this world. The LORD provides for creatures who ply no trade for their providence, how much more so for his children (Matt 6:25–34). Finally, we can have no greater certainty of the love and good will of our triune God than the death and resurrection of Jesus.

> 32 He who did not spare his own Son but gave him up for us all, how will he not also with him graciously give us all things? 33 Who shall bring any charge against God's elect? It is God who justifies. 34 Who is to condemn? Christ Jesus is the one who died—more than that, who was raised—who is at the right hand of God, who indeed is interceding for us. (Rom 8:32–34, ESV).

In transcendent Wisdom as in Christ, we see the diversity, paradox, and circularity that are the ground of the human experience of God within the covenant community. The divine is always leaning towards us, beckoning us, but requiring of us not merely ethical action but relational passion. So also, the divine commitment to our good does not preclude hardship but guarantees those hardships will find us well on the road to our ultimate good. Where Wisdom can only offer long life and material blessing, the Son forges a way through sin and death to Life itself.

Wisdom Echoes the Diversity and Paradox of Christ

The characterization of Wisdom personified in Prov 2 is framed as a diversity and paradox. Wisdom is not merely a woman calling. Wisdom is a woman sought. Wisdom is a Word taught by YHWH through parents. Wisdom is hidden treasure.

In like manner, Jesus multiplied metaphors for himself (i.e., bread of heaven, good shepherd, door, vine) and for the kingdom of heaven (mustard seed, treasure in the field, pearl of great price, dishonest manager). He disallows a static and singular perception of the truth. Moreover, paradox is basic to his communicative agenda: Freedom is Slavery (Matt 20:27; Mark 10:44). Love is Hatred (Luke 14:26). First is Last (Matt 19:30; 20:16). Work is Rest (Matt 11:28). In Jesus, the whole traditional framework of divine blessing contingent on human conduct is reversed (Matt 5). Finally, the circular paradox *is* the Christian life. We are "saved by grace and not by works that any should boast" (Eph 2:8) and yet "faith without works is dead" (Jas 2:17). As Christians we are predestined not only for heaven but for good works before the foundation of the world (Acts 4:28; Rom 8:29–30; Eph 1:5, 11), yet we must *believe* as function of will and desire (John 1:12–13; 3:16; 6:29, etc.). Ultimately, even Wisdom and Folly change places, such that foolishness of God is better than the Wisdom of man (1 Cor 1:18–21). In all and through all the dynamic and paradoxical power of Jesus is active. However, and most importantly in the paradoxical nature of Wisdom the death of Jesus forms a keystone. In the death of Christ is life, and hope and the prospect of eternal joy (cf. John 3:16; 8:42; 13:1; 17:23). Likewise, life and death change places for the believer as we follow Christ (Matt 16:25; Mark 8:35; Luke 9:24). The aesthetic of wisdom provides for the paradoxical beauty of the Cross.

Conclusion

The diverse and divergent personifications of wisdom create disequilibrium and paradox in our understanding of wisdom. Wisdom is prophetic, divine, and dependent upon covenant obedience. The dichotomous presentations of personified wisdom highlight the divine and human, passive and active components of wisdom. They accent both obedience to and desire for wisdom which is rooted in covenantal relationship with YHWH and reflected from the reality of Jesus.

However in all of these discussions, the role of the metaphor *WISDOM IS A WOMAN* has been one metaphor among many with the entailments from the source domain of *WOMAN* related mainly to person and appeal. In Prov 5–6 the poet provides us with an interesting turn. Where in the opening chapters *WOMAN* has been a source category for *WISDOM*, in chapters 5 and 6 women become the target category for other metaphors. In short, the poet gives us a hint to those elements of feminine metaphor that are important: desire, delight, and fidelity. It is to this love affair as an image schema to which we turn next in the characterization of the "real women" of Prov 5 and 6.

5

Women and the Divine

The Blending of Canonical Metaphors around the Axes of Desire, Fidelity and Covenant

Introduction

IN paragraphs 11 and 16–17 (Prov 5:15–20; 6:20–35) there is a dramatic shift in the way *WOMAN* metaphor has been employed. In these chapters it is not *WISDOM* that is the target category, but rather *WOMAN*. In this way, the poet provides a window into discovering the purpose for the deployment of feminine metaphor for the book as a whole. The treatment of the "wife of your youth" and "the wife of your neighbor" are purposefully paired around dichotomous image schema (i.e., water and fire) and serve to highlight the place of relational fidelity, not only with regard to gendered relationship, but also to wisdom. The marital dimension of *WOMAN* as a target category will only grow through the course of the book through numerous lexical linkages which refer to both to *finding* wisdom and *finding* a wife (Prov 18:22; 8:35; 3:15; 31:10) as well as the value, protection, and blessing that are related with a good marriage (Prov 19:14; 4:5–10).

After the presentation of the texts, the first part of the chapter of the chapter is dedicated to clarifying the related terms "wife of one's youth" and the "strange/foreign woman." It will be shown that this set of terms is most at home within the prophetic metaphor *COVENANT IS MARRIAGE/ IDOLATRY IS ADULTERY*. In this way, the human dimension of the marital bond is figured as the substance of fidelity to YHWH. These values then become part of the consideration of the conceptual blend of both WISDOM and WOMAN.

The second part of the chapter explores the *WATER* metaphor that is associated with the "wife of your youth" in Prov 5:15–23. In this conceptual blend the poet blends the romantic metaphor *LOVE IS THIRST* as in Song of Songs with the prophetic metaphor *WATER IS LIFE* wherein it is YHWH who is figured as water. In this section we briefly survey the interpretive difficulties that arise by failing to recognize the underlying basic metaphor and then demonstrate the metaphorical and lexical associations whereby the "wife of one's youth" is pictured in relation the LORD. Relational fidelity, filled with desire, delight and blessing is understood as like unto covenant fidelity to the LORD.

In third part of the chapter we consider Prov 6:20–35 wherein the previously ambiguous delineation of the זרה or נכריה is made explicit as the wife of another man (Prov 6:24, 29). As the wife of one's youth is equated with water and blessing in Prov 5, the adulteress (זרה or נכריה) is figured as *FIRE* and *THEFT* in Prov 6.[1] These metaphors are colored not only by reference to the prophets, but also through the blending of materials from the Decalogue and the Song of Songs. Ultimately, the poet intends to identify fidelity to one's wife as fidelity to YHWH and infidelity as the breach of divine covenant. Moreover, this entire treatment blends allusion to Torah with those of Song of Songs and points toward gendered desire not only as a danger to the youth, but also describes the jealousy of the husband as parallel to divine wrath.

Gendered desire is then figured as either the vehicle to the harmonious blending of divine pleasure and human delight, fulfillment and blessing or as the slippery slope that will lead to dissipation and death. The young man's relationship to women acts as a concrete expression of his fidelity to YHWH. Fidelity to the wife of one's youth is consonant with fidelity to YHWH. Infidelity with the wife of another betrays both covenant and wisdom.

Finally, the second stage of perception again beckons us to turn toward Jesus. The New Testament in consonance with Proverbs maintains that fidelity to the LORD is fidelity in human marital relationship (Eph 5), but simultaneously Jesus himself extends and overturns the WATER metaphors of Prov 5 to demonstrate that he, as YHWH, is the source of life and all human longing. The chapter closes with the consideration of Jesus challenging

---

1. *ADULTERY AS THEFT* is a dubious title for the metaphor. However, theft as prohibited in the Decalogue and as punished in Torah does provide the image schema for guiding the analogous consideration. Moreover, the mention of divine blessing in Prov 5:23 provides balance for theft as the human antithesis.

our notions of what it means to be wise and what it means to be "strange," which will be the substance of chapter 6.

Proverbs 5:15-23

> 15 שְׁתֵה־מַיִם מִבּוֹרֶךָ וְנֹזְלִים מִתּוֹךְ בְּאֵרֶךָ׃
>
> Drink water from your cistern and trickling water[2] from the midst of your well.[3]
>
> 16 יָפוּצוּ מַעְיְנֹתֶיךָ חוּצָה בָּרְחֹבוֹת פַּלְגֵי־מָיִם׃
>
> Your springs could[4] flow outside,[5] In the squares streams of water.

---

2. "Formally, there is as distinction between a *bor* ('cistern') which is a reservoir or container, and a *bᵉ'er* ('well'), which is a source of water continually replenished by underground springs, *nozᵉlin* (see, e.g., Hame' iri). This distinction does not, however, seem to be active in the present sense, which uses different synonyms as the metaphoric vehicle" (Fox, *Proverbs 1-9*, 199). I depart from Fox as explained below because there is a growth of metaphoric imagery from cistern, to well, to spring. Each water source has greater volume, which explains the capacitive use of the imperfect verb in 5:16.

3. Murphy asserts that this section is comprised of "advice to the married" but is not delivered with any particular individual in view, and therefore should be heeded by the audience regardless of their status (Murphy, *Proverbs*, 32). Without delving too deeply into the issues of hermeneutics and inspiration, a particular audience would not therefore abrogate wider circulation and meaning (i.e., the Pastoral Epistles). The transgenerational nature of parental instruction has maintained *both* the particularity of the parent-child relationship, *and* universal applicability (via teaching to the grandsons).

4. A number of interpreters and translations read the imperfect of פוץ ("disperse") as an unmarked hypothetical question, "Should your springs overflow?" The implied answer is negative (REB; NIV; ESV; NRS; Waltke, *Proverbs 1-15*, 318). However, there is no formal or contextual marker for the question. Here I translate as a capacitive subjunctive. This will be discussed at greater length below.

5. The mention of "outside" (חוּץ) and "squares" (רחבות) hearkens both back to *Lady Wisdom* (1:20) but also *ahead* to the *Strange Woman* (Prov 7:12). See Fox, *Proverbs 1-9*, 201; Waltke, *Proverbs 1-15*, 319.

> 17: יִהְיוּ־לְךָ לְבַדֶּךָ וְאֵין לְזָרִים אִתָּךְ
>
> Let them be[6] for you, you alone[7] and for no strangers (mp)[8] with you.
>
> 18 יְהִי־מְקוֹרְךָ בָרוּךְ וּשְׂמַח מֵאֵשֶׁת נְעוּרֶךָ:
>
> Let your fountain be blessed[9] and rejoice in[10] the wife of your youth.[11]

---

6. יְהִי may be translated as either jussive (i.e., "Let them be") or in any one of the imperfect tenses (i.e., could, should, will, etc.) since the plural has no formal jussive. Most translations and interpreters choose the jussive in agreement with v. 18.

7. "The privacy of conjugal love is underscored by *for yourself alone* *lᵉkā*, lit. 'for yourself in radical isolation from others'" (Waltke, *Proverbs 1–15*, 319). The duplicated 2ms pronoun, in conjunction with יחד leaves no doubt that this is not a public affair.

8. "The reproductive sources of an adulterer's wife will . . . ultimately be shared by another man—a *zar*, as in v. 10" (Fox, *Proverbs 1–9*, 201). As noted the noun here is masculine plural, so the metaphorical association with WATER is the woman. All the same it is more than "reproductive sources" that are in view here, as will be discussed in greater detail below.

9. Waltke argues that while in other places blessing is related to fertility (cf. Deut 28:4; Ps 128:3–4) in this case the blessing is with regard to sexual gratification (Waltke, *Proverbs 1–15*, 320). Below, I argue that while sexuality is certainly in view the broader issue is not the water source, but the basic metaphor of LOVE IS THIRST. ברך is treated in greater detail below.

10. Fox notes that the use of the preposition מ is unusual with regard to the object of שמח, which is always used in association with ב. Waltke argues that "from is chosen instead of prosaic 'in' (cf. Judg 9:19) to evoke the figure of drawing water from a well. The parallelism with one of the water sources in the series of them provides the key to the allegory's interpretation" (Waltke, *Proverbs 1–15*, 320). While "metaphor" should be substituted for "allegory" the choice of prepositions in view of the image schema is a reasonable assertion.

11. The "wife of your youth" is a purposeful reflection of Mal 2:15 and will be discussed in greater depth below.

19 אַיֶּלֶת אֲהָבִים וְיַעֲלַת־חֵן דַּדֶּיהָ יְרַוֻּךָ בְכָל־עֵת בְּאַהֲבָתָהּ תִּשְׁגֶּה תָמִיד:

[12]A doe[13] of love[14] and a graceful mountain goat[15]—Her breasts[16] should slake your thirst[17] at all times. You should stagger with her love continually.

12. Waltke elides v. 19a into the jussive יהי of v. 18, and therefore reads "May she be a lovemaking doe" (Waltke, *Proverbs 1–15*, 304, 320). While there is no textual evidence to support such an expansion, some sort of copulative verb is implied in the poetic line and the jussive would accord with the preceding.

13. "Gazelles and does connote grace, tenderness, and affection in the Song of Songs, where the girl speaks of her lover running like a gazelle (4:5). The phrase 'ayyelet 'ăhabim a 'loving doe' (lit. 'a doe of lovemaking' or 'love-doe') has strong sexual connotations" (Fox, *Proverbs 1–9*, 202). While these animals are noted for their fleetness and grace in Song of Songs, there is no particular reason that these qualities should be evoked in the middle of an image metaphor dedicated to the image schema of water sources. A better option is provided in those cases where the deer is noted with reference to thirst. Consider Ps 42:2: כְּאַיָּל תַּעֲרֹג עַל־אֲפִיקֵי־מָיִם כֵּן נַפְשִׁי תַעֲרֹג אֵלֶיךָ אֱלֹהִים—"As the deer craves streams of water, so my soul craves you, O God." Likewise in Job 39:1, the only other parallel of יעל and אילת, the context is that of the "dry wild" and YHWH's provision for these creatures. Robert Chisolm's assertion that the young male is being equated with the virile buck who finds his counterpart in his spouse would nicely compliment this imagery, however, such metaphorical usage is not attested in Tanakh. See Chisolm, "'Drink Water,'" 405.

14. Fox argues that 'ăhabim in the present context is limited to the physical dimension of sex because of the parallels in Hos 8:9 and Prov 7:18 which "[signify] loveless sex" (Fox, *Proverbs 1–9*, 202). HALOT argues for the definition of "charm" because of the parallel with חֵן in 19b, which is not associated with sexual intercourse (*HALOT* s.v. "אהב").

15. The word יַעֲלָה is a *hapex legomena* and appears only here in *Tanakh*. Meinhold identifies the creature with the ibex (Meinhold, *Die Sprüche*, 1:105) but any secure referent is difficult to establish.

16. Fox emends "breasts" (דַּדֶּיהָ) to "lovemaking" (*dōddeyhā*) on the presumption that this is the construct formation of דדי that is attested in Prov 7:18; Ezek 16:8; 23:17. "The word *dd* occurs as a Semiticism in Egyptian, where it is written with the phallus sign as the determinative and usually alludes to sexual intercourse. Given these connotations, the advice in Prov 5:19 is quite explicit" (Fox, *Proverbs 1–9*, 202). There is not necessarily any reason to expect such an emendation (Murphy, *Proverbs*, 32) and reading "breasts" will be shown more likely in light of the image metaphor for the chapter below.

17. Here we see the basic metaphor of LOVE IS THIRST in explicit form. The piel form יְרַוֻּךָ has no special jussive form and surpasses mere satisfaction or refreshment and tends toward surfeit (Isa 16:9; Ps 65:11; Sir 39:22; Jer 31:14) (*HALOT* s.v. "רוה"). The form may be an implied imperative (i.e., "drink your fill") (Murphy, *Proverbs*, 32) or jussive (Waltke, *Proverbs 1–15*, 321; Fox, *Proverbs 1–9*, 203). I have translated the imperfect as "should" in light of the phrasing of the question in v. 20 "Why should you be inebriated . . . ?" Also, in an interesting turn, the same verbal form appears in the qal form in Prov 7:18, only in that case it issues from the mouth of the *Strange Woman*.

> 20 וְלָמָּה תִשְׁגֶּה בְנִי בְזָרָה וּתְחַבֵּק חֵק נָכְרִיָּה׃
>
> But[18] why should you stagger,[19] my son with a *Strange Woman*[20] and embrace[21] the bosom[22] of a foreign woman?

18. Waltke translates the initial וְ as "now" (Waltke, *Proverbs 1–15*, 322). Most versions and interpreters choose to leave the וְ untranslated (ESV, NRSV, NIV, Fox, Murphy), however, the disjunction is important to the flow of the argument. "In view of the better way of conjugal bliss with the blessed wife, involvement with the unchaste wife is absurd" (Waltke, *Proverbs 1–15*, 322).

19. The previous verb "stagger" (שׁגה) is repeated here and as noted above, is paired with the "bosom" of the *Strange Woman*. While the THIRST image schema is still in view, the fact that the verb belongs to the image scheme of MOVEMENT will be significant since it provides the transition to the ROAD metaphor in v. 21. The primary nuance of "inebriation" will give way to the new extensions until the verb repeated in v. 23 will be soundly situated in the ROAD metaphor with the primary meaning of "wander" or "be misled." As such שׁגה functions as a "pivot word." See Fox, *Proverbs 1–9*, 204.

20. The pairing of "strange" and "alien" mirrors usage in the prophets with regard to the controlling metaphor *IDOLATRY IS ADULTERY*. The issue is not ethnic or even familial strangeness, as much as the fact that the feminine figure represents marital infidelity as a model of covenant infidelity.

21. "Embrace" (חבק) has strong erotic connotations (Song 2:6; 8:3) and is first used in reference to *Lady Wisdom* in Prov 4:8. The appearance of the word here draws the female images into parity. The "erotic passion" for wisdom is here being overturned and misdirected. "Fascination with the 'stranger' destroys a double love: the love for one's wife, and also for Wisdom" (Murphy, *Proverbs*, 33). I would argue that given the identification of marital fidelity with covenant fidelity, that the betrayal is *triple* insofar as it betrays the covenant and therefore YHWH himself.

22. חוק is provided as the counterpart to the דדים of v. 19. Technically it "designates that outer and somewhat lower part of the body below the breasts where beloved ones, including a son (1 Kgs 17:19), a wife (2 Sam 12:8), or infants (Ruth 4:16) and animals (2 Sam 12:13), are pressed closely. Giving into the bosom is a euphemism for sexual relations (Gen 16:5; Prov 18:22)" (Waltke, *Proverbs 1–15*, 323). The bodily pairing helps to accent the obvious choice between these two women. "Why go astray with another man's wife, when you have your own woman to 'stray' with?" (Fox, *Proverbs 1–9*, 204).

21 כִּ֤י ׀ נֹ֬כַח ׀ עֵינֵ֣י יְ֭הוָה דַּרְכֵי־אִ֑ישׁ וְֽכָל־מַעְגְּלֹתָ֥יו מְפַלֵּֽס׃

For,[23] in front[24] of the eyes of YHWH are the paths of a man and all his tracks he weighs.[25]

22 עֲ֭וֺנוֹתָיו יִלְכְּדֻנ֣וֹ אֶת־הָרָשָׁ֑ע וּבְחַבְלֵ֥י חַ֝טָּאת֗וֹ יִתָּמֵֽךְ׃

His iniquities will catch him[26] the wicked man[27] and with cords of his sin he will be seized.[28]

23. The epexegetic כי introduces the final verses of Prov 5 which provides an inclusio with the ROAD metaphor that closed Prov 4 and continues into the beginning of Prov 5. See Waltke, *Proverbs 1–15*, 323. It appears that 5:21 is essentially a discrete proverbial unit in so far as it appears again in Prov 15:3 (Murphy, *Proverbs*, 33). The image scheme of YHWH overseeing and judging all paths is then expanded in v. 22–23 explicitly with regard to the movement and capture of the one who has rejected wisdom and embraced the *Strange Woman* via infidelity. His lack of discipline is figured as folly (v. 23) but he himself is labeled as *wicked* (v. 22). See Waltke, *Provbers 1–15*, 323.

24. The poet has chosen *not* to employ the more common idiom "before" (לנפי), but rather has chosen the word נכח that more frequently means "opposite" in a locative sense (e.g., Exod 26:25) or may be used with reference to something "directly ahead of" (Prov 4:25). In this case, the term functions as a preposition that implies direct presence and oversight (cf. Judg 18:6; Jer 17:16) but also seems to be used with reference to purposed action (Lam 2:19; Ezek 14:3–4, 7). See Waltke, *Proverbs 1–15*, 323.

25. מְפַלֵּס recalls v. 6 where the *Strange Woman* "refused to go" in the paths of life (Fox, *Proverbs 1–9*, 204). The parallel is likely purposeful, even as the meaning of שגה is shifted from v. 20 to v. 23.

26. Here the ROAD metaphor is combined with imagery of animal trapping that will be developed more in Prov 6:24–26; 7:22–23. In these passages the *Strange Woman* is figured as the HUNTER. Here however, the culprit is not the woman, but rather the sin of the young man. "As elsewhere in Proverbs, no distinction is made, nor is any tension felt by the sage, between the LORD who upholds the moral order and the moral order of act-consequence itself. . . . No thunderbolt from heaven strikes him down. Rather, sin will *catch him* (*yilkedunô*; see 3:26) like a hunter's trap." Waltke argues that the young man's sin is personified "possessing the cords that capture the victim" (Waltke, *Proverbs 1–15*, 324). While personification is possible, there is no evidence either preceding or following, nor is there any clear reason for the poet to employ personification with regard to iniquity.

27. Fox views אֶת־הָרָשָׁע as a secondary gloss added by a later hand and "unnecessary since anyone's iniquities trap him." The assertion is not unreasonable since there is no parallel in the LXX or *Peshitta*. See Fox, *Proverbs 1–9*, 205. However, the choice of רשע as a gloss does add emphasis to the poetic line. Where v. 23 concentrates upon the "folly" (אִוַּלְתּוֹ) of the man's action, in this case the accent is upon his *sin* and *wickedness* which are ethical/covenantal terms. Where "folly" would normally be the antithesis of "wisdom," "wicked" is the opposite of "righteous," thereby folly and wickedness are presented as synonymous parallels.

28. This usage of the verb תמך is the capstone of the three previous uses in Prov 4 and 5. First, in Prov 4:4, the young man who "holds fast" (תמך) to the words of parental instruction should obtain wisdom, embrace her and cling to her. If he should be lax,

> 23 הוּא יָמוּת בְּאֵין מוּסָר וּבְרֹב אִוַּלְתּוֹ יִשְׁגֶּה׃
>
> He, he will die[29] without discipline[30] and in the abundance of his folly[31] he will be staggered[32]

Proverbs 6:20-35

> אִמֶּךָ׃ תּוֹרַת וְאַל־תִּטֹּשׁ אָבִיךָ מִצְוַת בְּנִי נְצֹר 20
>
> Protect,[33] my son, the commandment of your father and do not leave unheeded[34] the torah[35] of your mother[36]

---

he may fall victim to the wiles of the *Strange Woman* whose foot "holds fast" (תמך) to the paths of Sheol (Prov 5:5). In the third case, it is not with regard to the antithesis of *wisdom* that the youth acts, but the antithesis of righteousness. His sin and wickedness will "hold him fast" (תמך). Thereby wisdom and righteous, folly and wickedness are joined. See Waltke, *Proverbs 1–15,* 324.

29. Waltke notes that "death" provides the fusion point for religious and sapiential language. "Death is frequently the outcome and destination for those who refuse instruction (cf. 10:21; 15:10; 19:16; 23:13). Likewise, the immoral are robbed of life which is rooted in the true love and loyalty found in God and his people both now and forevermore" (Waltke, *Proverbs 1–15,* 324).

30. "While this verse is in harmony with the generalization in v 22, it can also reflect back on the hopeless remorse of the guilty young man in vv 11–14. Where there is no מוסר ('discipline'), there is death" (Murphy, *Proverbs,* 33).

31. The seduction of the youth marks a transition from פתי to לץ. He has moved from naivety and lack of experience to moral perversity. "He does not lack the intellectual capacity to attain discipline, he lacks the moral capacity to want it" (Fox, *Proverbs 1–9,* 205).

32. The final occurrence of שגה ("stagger") may still retain some sense of "inebriation" from the previous occurrences (Murphy, *Proverbs,* 33), but it seems more likely that the image schema of ROAD now dominates usage and seems to lean more toward the abstracted meaning of being "misled" or "lost" in the road overseen by YHWH. See Fox, *Proverbs 1–9,* 205.

33. The notion of "protecting" (נצר) or "keeping watch" (שמר) connects this chapter with the fusion of Torah, personified Wisdom and parental instruction in Prov 3; 4; 5.

34. This notion of "spurning" (נטש) appears first in Prov 1:8, parallel usage in the Torah is found in Deut 32:15.

35. Although most interpreters choose to translate תורת as "instruction" in this case, the reference to "binding" (v. 21), followed by reference to "walking," "lying down" and "talking" are a fairly clear allusion to the *Shema* in Deut 6 (Murphy, *Proverbs,* 39). For this reason "Torah" is left untranslated.

36. It is important to note that *both* mother and father are involved in teaching the son (cf. Prov 1:8) though it is likely that their "command" and "law" are not differentiated. See Fox, *Proverbs 1–9,* 228.

21 קָשְׁרֵם עַל־לִבְּךָ תָמִיד עָנְדֵם עַל־גַּרְגְּרֹתֶךָ׃

Bind[37] them upon your heart continually.[38] Tie[39] them upon your neck.

22 בְּהִתְהַלֶּכְךָ ׀ תַּנְחֶה אֹתָךְ בְּשָׁכְבְּךָ תִּשְׁמֹר עָלֶיךָ וַהֲקִיצוֹתָ הִיא תְשִׂיחֶךָ׃

In your walking she will lead you. In your lying down she will guard you. In your waking she, she will converse[40] with you.

23 כִּי נֵר מִצְוָה וְתוֹרָה אוֹר וְדֶרֶךְ חַיִּים תּוֹכְחוֹת מוּסָר׃

For the commandment is a lamp[41] and law is light. The rebuke of discipline[42] is the road of life.[43]

---

37. Waltke argues that the metaphor of "fixing" the commandments is by "memorizing them in such a way that they are permanently impressed on his essential mental and spiritual being that prompts his every action" (Waltke, *Proverbs 1–15*, 351). The parallel appearance of the image schema in Deut 6:4–7 seems to indicate just such an idea.

38. Cf. Prov 5:19; Isa 57:13; Jer 52:3; Ps 16:8. See also Waltke, *Proverbs 1–15*, 351.

39. ענד ("fasten" or "bind") appears only here and in Job 31:36 where it refers to affixing a "crown" (עטרה). Waltke asserts that the image here therefore may relate to exaltation as well as protection as in Prov 4:9. See Waltke, *Proverbs 1–15*, 351.

40. The verb שיח "fluctuat[es] between the act of speaking and thinking" as governed by context. See Diamond, "שיח" (NIDOTTE 4:1234). In some settings it takes a general meaning of "talking" (e.g., Judg 5:10) but quite frequently it is associated with *complaint* (e.g., 1 Sam 1:16; 1 Kgs 18:27; Job 7:11, 13; 9:27; 10:1). This particular context bears more in common with the meditation and recitation of YHWH's mighty deeds in Psalms (e.g., Ps 77:4, 7, 13; 104:34). Fox cites a parallel metaphor in *b. Soṭa 21a* where it is not parental instruction, or wisdom, but rather *Torah* that will continually watch and protect, "'And when you wake up, it will converse with you'—in the world to come" (Fox, *Proverbs 1–9*, 230). It is difficult to determine if connotations of the recitation of YHWH's saving deeds is alluded to in light of the broader context of the poem.

41. Fox asserts that the underlying image metaphor here is that "life as a journey through the dark and pitted landscape" (Fox, *Proverbs 1–9*, 229). The imagery of "lamp" (נר) and "light" (אור) function according the basic metaphor LIGHT IS PERCEPTION or perhaps LIGHT IS KNOWLEDGE and they are used in a similar manner in Prov 20:27 and 21:24, but may also be used following the metaphor LIGHT IS LIFE (Prov 13:9; 20:20; 24:20) or with regard to personal industry (31:18).

42. Fox argues that תוכחות מוסר is a "doubled noun" and he translates as "instruction that reproves" (Fox, *Proverbs 1–9*, 229). Maintaining the construct formation "rebuke of discipline" amounts to the same thing, rebuke which continues and maintains discipline. See Waltke, *Proverbs 1–15*, 352.

43. The nearest parallel to "road of life" (דרך חיים) is found in the "paths of life" of Prov 2:19 and 5:6. "In sum, the parental teaching illuminates the way the LORD watches over, the way of the full and abundant life, and the way on which the son will be protected from hidden pitfalls" (Waltke, *Proverbs 1–15*, 352).

24 לִשְׁמָרְךָ מֵאֵשֶׁת רָע מֵחֶלְקַת לָשׁוֹן נָכְרִיָּה׃

To guard[44] you from the wife of a neighbor[45]—from the smooth[46] tongue[47] of a foreigner.[48]

25 אַל־תַּחְמֹד יָפְיָהּ בִּלְבָבֶךָ וְאַל־תִּקָּחֲךָ בְּעַפְעַפֶּיהָ׃

Do not desire[49] her beauty[50] with your heart and do not be taken[51] with her eyelashes[52]

---

44. Syntactically, v. 24a is parallel to 2:16—infinitive of purpose (protection/delivery) + direct object followed by a mem-preposition indicating the identity of the threat. The subject of that lecture was also parental instruction equated with Torah (2:1-6).

45. The text may be read literally as "woman of evil" (מֵאֵשֶׁת רָע). Either through mis-pointing or through a purposeful paronomasia the "evil woman" is closely allied with the "wife of his/your neighbor" (e.g., Prov 6:29 אֵשֶׁת רֵעֵהוּ). While it departs from convention, the text is here translated in agreement with consonantal text, "wife of *a* neighbor."

46. Though the lexemes are different the substance is the same as Prov 2:17 (מִנָּכְרִיָּה אֲמָרֶיהָ הֶחֱלִיקָה) the particular threat posed by the woman is associated with her smoothness of speech (cf. also 5:3).

47. "Tongue" (לשון) is used as a metonymy for speech in this case. Waltke argues that the usage is the same as in 2:17 and 5:3 (Waltke, *Proverbs 1-15*, 353). However, in chapter 5 in particular the metonymy becomes a conceptual blend of MOUTH FOR SPEECH (5:3) and MOUTH FOR CONSUMPTION (5:9-14). The blend is further complicated by the fact that there is a possibility of sexual innuendo as well.

48. As above, "foreigner" (נכריה) is consistent with prophetic usage and refers to a faithless wife as discussed at length below.

49. The prohibition אַל־תַּחְמֹד appears to have two possible translations: "desire" or "covet." However, due to the force of covenant language and the paucity of usage with the אַל prohibitive, "covet" provides the most likely gloss, as will be discussed in greater detail below.

50. The nominal form יפי ("beauty") "may be used of a tree (Ezek 31:8), a woman (Esth 1; 11; Ps 45:11[12]; Prov 6:25; 31:30; Isa 3:24), the [messianic?] king (Isa 33:17), Jerusalem (Lam 2:15; Ezek; 16:14-15, 25), Zion (Ps 50:2), Tyre (Ezek 27:3-4, 11) and its ruler (Ezek 28:7, 12, 17), or the redeemed remnant (Zech 9:17). In the instances the nom., like the adj., describes the outward appearance. While Scripture speaks of God's 'glory' and Zion's beauty, nowhere does it connect the root *yph* with God." Williams, "יפה" (NIDOTTE 2:495-96). Note particularly that Israel is depicted as a faithless spouse in accordance with the prophetic metaphor IDOLATRY IS ADULTERY (Ezek 16:14-15, 25).

51. Waltke rightly notes that there is an ironic reversal in "coveting" (חמד) and "being taken" (לקח) in which the verb "*changes* the perspective from the man's role in the A verset to the woman's role of getting him into her possession and control" (Waltke, *Proverbs 1-9*, 354). While the young man's covetous desire is for *acquisition*, the beauty of the seductress captures and subdues him.

52. "The traditional rendering of *ap'ap*, which only occurs in the dual construct and sing. Fem. forms, is 'eyelid.' This is probably because it is a derivative of '*wp* I, fly,

> 26 כִּי בְעַד־אִשָּׁה זוֹנָה עַד־כִּכַּר לָחֶם וְאֵשֶׁת אִישׁ נֶפֶשׁ יְקָרָה תָצוּד׃ פ
>
> Because the price[53] of a woman of prostitution[54] is scarcely a loaf of bread but the wife of a man hunts[55] the precious soul.
>
> הֲיַחְתֶּה אִישׁ אֵשׁ בְּחֵיקוֹ וּבְגָדָיו לֹא תִשָּׂרַפְנָה׃
>
> Can a man snatch up[56] fire[57] in his lap[58] and his garments not be burned?

---

flap, but out of 10x in the OT, 5x it is parallel to ʿēnayim (Ps 11:4; 132:4; Prov 4:25; 6:4; Jer 9:18[17]). It may be better to assume it means '(flashing) eyes" (Harman, "עַפְעַפִּים" [NIDOTTE 3:471]). Waltke assumes that the adulteress employs cosmetics to draw attention to her eyes (cf. 2 Kgs 9:30; Jer 4:30; Sir 26:9) and that the eyes play a special role in the process of seduction. See Waltke, Proverbs 1–15, 354.

53. The meaning of עד ... בעד is very difficult and broadly contested. HALOT takes the root to be a hapex legomena meaning "exchange price" through the influence of the LXX and Vulgate (HALOT s.v. "בְּעַד"). Contrarily, Fox argues in favor of reading the string as two prepositions: עד ... בעד with "the literal translation of 6:26a is 'because for [bᵉad] a harlot—up to [ʿad] a loaf of bread.' Though difficult, this makes sense as an ellipsis 'because for a harlot (one pays only) as much as a loaf of bread'" (Fox, Proverbs 1–9, 231). However, the particle בעד only appears in a handful of cases with עד and these bear no meaningful similarities to the present context (cf. Lev 16:17; 1 Chr 15:29; Isa 26:20; 32:14). It is best to read the root as an unattested root associated with price.

54. The key element in the parallel is between the "woman of prostitution" and the "woman (wife) of another man." Where the first requires only nominal payment, the second leads ultimately to ruin and death. The poet, "does not condone prostitution, [but] he does insinuate that it is safer to resort to harlots than to married women" (Waltke, Proverbs 1–15, 231).

55. The basic metaphor WOMAN IS A HUNTER appears here and 7:22–23.

56. "Snatch up" (חתה) has only scant usage in Tanakh (Ps 52:7; Prov 6:27; 25:22; Isa 30:14) and may already have taken up the technical meaning "remove coals from a fire" as in LBH and Aramaic. See Waltke, Proverbs 1–15, 356.

57. The poet seems to be making deliberate play upon "fire" (אש) and "man" (איש) (Waltke, Proverbs 1–15, 356). Moreover, the assonance and alliteration, "are evocative of the hissing and crackling of fire" (Waltke, Proverbs 1–15, 233).

58. "Fire (ʾēš) should be carried in a firepan (Exod 27:3; Lev 10:1) or a clay shard (cf. 25:22; Isa 30:14), not in his bosom" (Waltke, Proverbs 1–15, 356). The "bosom" (here translated "lap") is equated with the Strange Woman in Prov 5:20. The fire snatched "into his lap" (חיקו) can mean "in the folds of his garment" as is the case of receiving a bribe in Prov 17:23; 21:14. However, the word is also used for the embrace of a foreign woman in 5:20 and refers not to the "bosom" but nearer to the "lap." Used in parallel with what is glossed as "garment" (בגד) there is an interesting possibility in the homonym for "faithlessness" or "treachery." This possibility is underlined by the fact that the final verb in the line cannot be used with either of the nouns in this line. תִשָּׂרַפְנָה is a niphal third person feminine plural. חוק is a masculine singular noun. בגד is a masculine plural construct with 3ms suffix. Therefore, the line actually reads (as above) "Can a man snatch fire in his lap (atnaḥ) and in his garments (they) will not be burned. In either case the subject for the verb is problematic. However, the ambiguous word choice

> 28 אִם־יְהַלֵּךְ אִישׁ עַל־הַגֶּחָלִים וְרַגְלָיו לֹא תִכָּוֶינָה׃
>
> Or can a man walk[59] upon the embers and his feet not be scorched?
>
> 29 כֵּן הַבָּא אֶל־אֵשֶׁת רֵעֵהוּ לֹא יִנָּקֶה כָּל־הַנֹּגֵעַ בָּהּ׃
>
> Thus the one coming[60] to the wife of his friend,[61] anyone touching her will not be held innocent.[62]
>
> 30 לֹא־יָבוּזוּ לַגַּנָּב כִּי יִגְנוֹב לְמַלֵּא נַפְשׁוֹ כִּי יִרְעָב׃
>
> They[63] will not despise a thief when he steals to fill his soul[64] because he is starving.

continues into the next line, where the word "feet" occurs, which in this case is a 3fp. It could be that there is insulation that "they will get burned" is a parallel and euphemistic usage of "feet" as is proposed to occur in Exod 4:25; Isa 6:2; 7:20, which are also all dual in morphology with an appended 3ms suffix.

59. Saʿadia believes that there is an escalation from v. 27 to v. 28 that is reflected in v. 29. The man who "snatches up fire" only faces damage to his garments corresponds to the one who "touches" a woman. Conversely the one who walks on coals touches fire directly and therefore is burned, this parallels the one who "comes to" his neighbor's wife. See Fox, *Proverbs 1–9*, 223.

60. The target of the metaphor has been suspended until this point in the poem in a way similar to that in Prov 5:15–23. Here we discover that fire is a married woman. "Coming to" (בָּא אֶל) may be used as a euphemism for sexual intercourse (Waltke, *Proverbs 1–15*, 357). While this is possible, it makes more sense in light of the image schema to view it more generally. As will be noted in greater length below, the WOMAN IS FIRE metaphor suggests that distance and care should be employed with woman in a manner similar to the treatment of fire. Waltke's idea that only *sex* is in view actually weakens the warning expressed in the metaphor.

61. "This phrase makes it clear that the 'strange woman' is strange in the sense of belonging to another man, not in being foreign or socially marginal" (Fox, *Proverbs 1–9*, 234). While Fox is certainly correct in establishing the ontological referent the selection of the terms, נכריה and זרה, are influenced by prophetic usage. This is given fuller treatment below.

62. While related to the Akk. *naqû* ("libation" or "sacrifice"), "the derived juridical meaning, to be acquitted, or to be free from punishment, is exclusive to the OT . . . The root *nqh* conveys the notion of freedom in a forensic sense: on the one hand, the exemption from obligations and duties that have been legally imposed; on the other, the acquittal of guilt incurred and punishment deserved on account of God's forgiveness. By declaring a person *nāqî* he is set free" (Olivier, "נקה" [NIDOTTE 3 152–53]). This word introduces the judicial and cultic portion of the conceptual blend in the following verses.

63. The imperfect verb assumes a general subject (i.e., "people").

64. The phrase "to fill his soul" or to "satisfy his appetite" (לְמַלֵּא נַפְשׁוֹ) appears at first blush to be a comparison of sexual and dietary appetite. However, the closing of the colon—"because he is starving"—points to desperate hunger (cf. Gen 41:55; Isa 8:21;

> 31 וְנִמְצָא יְשַׁלֵּם שִׁבְעָתָיִם אֶת־כָּל־הוֹן בֵּיתוֹ יִתֵּן׃
>
> But when he will be found[65] he will repay seven times. All the substance of his house he will give.
>
> 32 נֹאֵף אִשָּׁה חֲסַר־לֵב מַשְׁחִית נַפְשׁוֹ הוּא יַעֲשֶׂנָּה׃
>
> Committing adultery with a woman[66] is empty-headed.[67] Destroying[68] his soul, he[69] will do this.

9:20) (Waltke, *Proverbs 1–15*, 358).

65. Many English translations (ESV; KJV; NAS; NRS) and most interpreters translate וְנִמְצָא as an implied protasis ("but if he is found"). However, the particle אִם, which would normally introduce the protasis is absent. More importantly, why would the poet wish to insert an element of uncertainty at this point in the argument? Since the form can also be translated as "but he *will* be found."

66. Most English translations and versions (NIV; NEV; NRSV; KJV; etc.) translate נֹאֵף אִשָּׁה as a substantive, "one committing adultery." While there are cases in *Tanakh* that appear to support this usage (cf. Job 24:15; Lev 20:10), the piel participle would be more typical of a substantive (cf. Ps 50:18; Prov 30:20; Isa 57:3; Jer 9:1; 23:10; Ezek 16:32; Hos 3:1; 7:4; Mal 3:5). Fox argues that the addition of the superficial "woman" is added for poetic ballast (Fox, *Proverbs 1–9*, 235). If this were the case, there is even less explanation for why the poet would avoid the piel participle as a substantive. Waltke argues that אשה is added to clarify the nature of the offense (Waltke, *Proverbs 1–15*, 358). However, the nature of this clarification is unclear. Regardless, in either case the substantive is translated as a gerund phrase where אשה functions as the implied object of the participle in a gerund.

67. The phrase חסר־לב means literally, "lacking heart." The basic metaphor for "heart" however does not relate to emotion or courage as in Anglo-American parlance, but rather refers to the heart as the seat of intelligence and volition. Therefore, most English translations read "lacking sense," making heart a metonymy for intelligence (NIV; NRSV; NAB; NEV). This is certainly an acceptable translation. I have chosen the idiomatic translation "empty head" because the חסר־לב functions as a stereotypical pejorative in Proverbs, and especially in Prov 7.

68. The form is morphologically undifferentiated from the masculine singular form (cf. Prov 18:9; 28:24; Isa 54:16; Jer 5:26; 51:1; Ezek 21:36) or the adjective (cf. Jer 2:30) or the hiphil masculine singular participle (cf. Gen 19:4; 1 Chron 21:12). Therefore, this phrase could be translated as either of two forms of the participle ("one destroying his soul" and "destroying his soul") or a genitive construct ("the destruction of his soul"). Especially given the force of the imperfect verb in 32b, the 3fs pronominal suffix is typically translated as a relative pronoun relating to this "destruction."

69. The phrase הוּא יַעֲשֶׂנָּה makes it clear that the culpability for the sin of adultery does not lie with the woman, but rather through the doubling of the pronoun places emphasis upon the young man. HE will accomplish the destruction of his own soul. See Waltke, *Proverbs 1–15*, 359; Fox; *Proverbs 1–9*, 235. However, the poet's choice of both verb and pronominal suffix is much more difficult. These will be treated in greater detail below.

33 נֶגַע־וְקָלוֹן יִמְצָא וְחֶרְפָּתוֹ לֹא תִמָּחֶה׃

A blow and dishonor he will find and his disgrace will not be wiped away.

34 כִּי־קִנְאָה חֲמַת־גָּבֶר וְלֹא־יַחְמוֹל בְּיוֹם נָקָם׃

Because jealousy is the rage[70] of a man[71] and he will not have compassion in the day of vengeance.[72]

35 לֹא־יִשָּׂא פְּנֵי כָל־כֹּפֶר וְלֹא־יֹאבֶה כִּי תַרְבֶּה־שֹׁחַד פ׃

He will not accept[73] any ransom and he will not be appeased that you should multiply the bribe.

Stage One Perception: Part I: The "Wife of Your Youth" and the *Strange Woman* Activate the Prophetic Metaphor of *MARRIAGE IS COVENANT*

In the same way that the poet has presented wisdom personified along two seemingly contradictory axes in Prov 1–4, so also the presentation

---

70. The root for "rage" (חמת) is associated mainly with *heat* and apparently belongs to the basic metaphor *ANGER IS FIRE* or *ANGER IS HOT*. This would well accord with the image schema of "fire" and "coals" in 6:27–28.

71. "The jealous husband is designated *a man . . .* because this word designates the human male in his strength and competency. By nature wrath is cruel and merciless and exceeds all bounds when excited by jealousy (27:4). Song 8:6 compares it with the inexorable hardness of the unyielding and unforgiving grave" (Waltke, *Proverbs 1–15*, 360).

72. The "day of vengeance" (יוֹם נָקָם) appears as a construct phrase in the prophets (Isa 34:8; 61:2; 63:4; Jer 46:10) specifically with reference to the vengeance that YHWH was to visit upon the nations. However, there does not appear to be enough common lexical or metaphorical association to assume that YHWH's "day of vengeance" is echoed in Prov 6:34. Rather, Peels points out that the phrase points to the *legitimate* action of the community acting on behalf of the wronged husband that will bring about the death of the perpetrator (Lev 18:20; 20:10; Deut 12:22; Ezek 16:38; 23:45). "Consequently, the expression byóm näqäm does not imply the idea that on a certain day the revengeful husband will strike a blow, but refers to the day of discovery, condemnation and public punishment of the crime. The 'day of vengeance' is the day on which the husband makes the case public after which the community (accuser included?) is to execute the sentence" (Peels, "Passion or justice?," 272).

73. The phrase יִשָּׂא פְּנֵי appears frequently enough in Tanakh to be deemed a Biblical idiom and is usually associated with "acceptance" or "forgiveness" but also betrays a usage similar to that of "being held guiltless" (נקה) (cf. Gen 19:21; 32:21; Lev 19:15; Deut 10:17; 28:50; 1 Sam 25:35; 2 Sam 2:22; 2 Kgs 5:1; 9:32; Job 11:15; 22:8; 32:21; 34:19; Prov 6:35; 18:5; Mal 1:8). See Waltke, *Proverbs 1–15*, 361.

of women is not singular, but dichotomous and complex. In Prov 5-6 we are introduced to "the wife of your youth," who is paralleled with "the wife of your neighbor" who is revealed as a synonymous representation of the *Strange/foreign Woman* opposed to *Lady Wisdom* in Prov 1-4. What began as a simple comparison of two concrete or stereotypical referents is therefore transposed into the plane of divine Wisdom.

Moreover, the transcendent and covenantal importance of fidelity is further accomplished by the poet's choice of diction. These word choices change the coloring of feminine characterization, but also helps to fix the axis of comparison for *Lady Wisdom*. The stereotype figures not only in opposition to *Lady Wisdom*, but also as an antithesis to the "wife of your youth." Below I argue that the poet chooses the unusual terms "wife of your youth" (5:18), "strange" (זרה) and "foreign" (נכריה) in order to activate the metaphor of *IDOLATRY IS ADULTERY* or *COVENANT IS MARRIAGE* as it is found in the prophets (particularly Jeremiah and Ezekiel, but also Hosea and Malachi).

The "Wife of Your Youth" and the *Strange Woman* Activate the Prophetic Metaphor of *MARRIAGE IS COVENANT* or *ADULTERY IS IDOLATRY*

The "Wife of Your Youth" is consonant with Mal 2:14-15

First, the phrase "wife of your youth" (אֵשֶׁת נְעוּרֶיךָ) appears in only two other contexts in Tanakh.[74] The most pertinent of these is Mal 2:14-15 where fidelity to this wife is featured analogously to YHWH.[75]

> וַאֲמַרְתֶּם עַל־מָה
>
> And you will say, "For what reason?"

---

74. In Isa 54:6 the phrase is again used with relation to YHWH, and again with connotations of covenant fidelity, but in this context the accent is upon the joy of the people being renewed to YHWH's favor.

75. The overall message of the oracle Mal 2 is dedicated to the covenantal ramification of marital infidelity. "The basic message of the oracle is twofold: God detests (religious) intermarriage and divorce (vv. 11, 16). Both are despicable crimes before YHWH, and an affront to the essence of covenant relationship socially and religiously—faithfulness and loyalty. These covenant transgressions have defiled the people of Judah and polluted their worship of God, thereby desecrating his temple (2:11). The emphasis on one in the disputation (vv. 10, 15) indicates that the entire community stood under the prophet's condemnation and the threat of judgment—a threat announced in the fourth disputation" (Hill, *Haggai, Zechariah, Malachi*, loc 5091).

> עַל כִּי־יְהוָה֙ הֵעִ֣יד בֵּינְךָ֗ וּבֵין֙ ׀ אֵ֣שֶׁת נְעוּרֶ֔יךָ
>
> Because YHWH bears witness between you and between the wife of your youth
>
> אֲשֶׁ֥ר אַתָּ֖ה בָּגַ֣דְתָּה בָּ֑הּ וְהִ֛יא חֲבֶרְתְּךָ֥ וְאֵ֖שֶׁת בְּרִיתֶֽךָ׃
>
> That you (ms) you have been faithless with her but she (is) your companion and the wife of your covenant.[76]
>
> וְלֹא־אֶחָ֣ד עָשָׂ֗ה וּשְׁאָ֥ר ר֨וּחַ֙ ל֔וֹ וּמָה֙ הָֽאֶחָ֔ד מְבַקֵּ֖שׁ זֶ֣רַע אֱלֹהִ֑ים
>
> And did he not make one?—and yet he had the residue of the Spirit![77] Why the one?—seeking a godly seed.[78]
>
> וְנִשְׁמַרְתֶּם֙ בְּרֽוּחֲכֶ֔ם וּבְאֵ֥שֶׁת נְעוּרֶ֖יךָ אַל־יִבְגֹּֽד׃
>
> And you (mp) keep watch with your (mp) spirit and with the wife of your youth do not be faithless. (Mal 2:14–15)

76. The phrase "wife of your covenant" is unique to Malachi and is given as a hendiadys to "wife of your youth." Although the precise referent for covenant is debated by commentators the constellation of references to the wife serves to highlight the closeness and sacredness of the marital union. See Hill, *Haggai, Zechariah, Malachi*, loc 5194).

77. The phrase "residue of spirit" is a difficult one but seems to be bound up in the marriage and creation imagery of Gen 2:24. Hill writes: "The word for 'residue' or 'remnant' in the MT (Heb. šĕ'ār) is sometimes emended to šĕ'ēr, flesh or 'body,' making the word pair 'body and spirit' (cf. NAB, 'Did he not make one being, with flesh and spirit'; NIV, In flesh and spirit they are his; NLT, 'In body and spirit you are his'; NRSV, 'Both flesh and spirit are his'). The word spirit (Heb. rûaḥ) in this context refers to the 'life force' or 'life principle' animating all living things (cf. NJPS, 'So that all remaining life breath is his'). The gist of the first portion of verse 15 seems to be that God created man and woman to be one being (assuming the marital relationship of Gen 2:24?), and that all life belongs to God (implying that the union of man and woman is fixed in the creation principle and is not to be violated or severed?)" (Hill, *Haggai, Zechariah, Malachi*, loc 5194).

78. The broader emphasis on the production and preservation of "godly seed" is not limited to the marital union, but extends to the people as a whole. "The core issue is not human procreation or Hebrew ethnic purity, but the religious and social implications that the treachery and betrayal of intermarriage and divorce have for Israel's covenant relationship with YHWH. God is seeking faithful children: that is, descendants of Abraham, Isaac and Jacob who love him, obey him and hold fast to him (Deut 30:19–20), and those who love justice, hate wrongdoing and act faithfully (Isa 61:8–9)" (Hill, *Haggai, Zechariah, Malachi*, loc 5236).

In this case, infidelity to the marital covenant was counted as a breach of relationship with YHWH.[79] From 5:19 on the poet draws the "wife of your youth" into opposition with the wiles and outcomes of the *Strange Woman* via lexical and metaphorical correspondences. The shaping power of this allusion will be strengthened by the poet's choice of the terms זרה and נכריה.

The Use of "Strange" (זרה) and "Foreign" (נכריה) Is Associated with the MARRIAGE IS COVENANT Metaphor in the Prophets

First, it should be noted that references to the *Strange Woman* are contiguous and consistent, and are therefore intended to be read as a singular stereotypical entity. References to the "strange" woman and "foreign" woman are (1) consistently used with reference to "smooth speech," (2) frequently employed with explicitly sexual imagery (e.g., Prov 7; 5), (3) or sexual or relational metaphors, and (4) are linked closely to one another by context, lexeme, and metaphor.

Second, these terms are largely inconsistent with the usage of these roots in the rest of Tanakh and are seldom used in parallel.[80] Moreover, in addition to the infrequency of parallel usage, the feminine forms of the adjectives are even more unusual within Tanakh.[81] Outside of the book of

---

79. Weeks also notes the striking parallel in the passage. He says that language is "strikingly close to Mal 2:14, where God does not accept sacrifices from the priests because he had 'stood witness between you and the wife of your youth, to whom you have acted unfaithfully, although she is your companion and the wife of your covenant'" (Weeks, *Instruction and Imagery*, 86). The notions of covenant parity in Mal 2 are entirely in keeping with that of Proverbs. Andrew Hill describes covenant in Malachi: "The thrust of Malachi's preaching may be placed under the umbrella theme of 'covenant,' specifically the covenant of Jacob (i.e., the patriarchs; cf. Mal 1:2), the covenant of Levi (2:5), the covenant of marriage (2:14) and the covenant of Moses (4:4). The basic idea of a covenant is essentially that of a treaty or pact that establishes a relationship between parties, with attendant obligations and responsibilities. It is not surprising, then, that three of the book's disputations deal with right relationships. We should also take note of the fact that God's messenger works on the premise that proper knowledge of God is essential to maintaining these right relationships (as seen in his first disputation)" (Hill, *Haggai, Zechariah, Malachi*, loc 4523).

80. There are only four cases, all of which employ the roots in masculine form. In Job 19:15, the guests and servants in his house count Job as a "stranger" and a "foreigner," which does not suggest that he has changed ethnicity, but rather is no longer familiar. Similar in force is the usage in Isa 28:21, where the adjectives are used to describe the work of YHWH as "strange" and "alien." However, these contexts are set off by the usage of Lam 5:2 and Obad 1:11, in which "strangers" and "foreigners" plundered and took possession of Zion and Jerusalem. In this case it is certain that ethnic outsiders are in view.

81. More frequently the word זרה appears by itself as a substantive, where it is used

Proverbs נכרי and its related nominal root נכר are almost universally related to referents who are non-Israelite or foreign.[82] Outside of Proverbs the usage for זר is slightly more sophisticated, although as noted previously, these contexts are nearly entirely masculine. The largest semantic domain for זר is associated with non-Israelite ethnicity or foreign-ness generally with a total of 18 occurrences.[83] Of these all are with regard to foreign peoples, or objects or places associated with foreign peoples. The second largest category of usage is a general usage of the word with the meaning "unknown," "other" or "strange." Of these 11 usages, a few seem to play with the notion of "unknown" as "foreign" (e.g., Hos 8:12; Isa 18:21) but each context speaks primarily of the "otherness" without particular markings that bear on ethnicity.[84]

---

four times in the book of Proverbs (Prov 2:16; 5:3, 20; 7:5). In each of these cases with the exception of 5:3, the word occurs in parallel with "foreign woman" (נכריה). Outside of the book of Proverbs the word has no substantive usage, but is used adjectivally to describe unauthorized incense (Exod 30:9), and the "unauthorized fire" offered by at the Nadab and Abihu barbecue (Lev 10:1; Num 3:4; 26:61). It is doubtful, however, that there is any allusion here. Against the ten total occurrences of זר as a feminine adjective, are sixty cases where the word has masculine reference.

82. The following references all are clearly marked with relation to ethnic identity or locale: Exod 2:22; 18:3; 21:8; Deut 14:21; 15:3; 17:5; 23:21; 29:21; Judg 19:12; Ruth 2:10; 2 Sam 15:19; 1 Kgs 8:41, 43; 11:1, 8; 2 Chr 6:32–33; Ezra 10:2, 10–11, 14, 17–18, 44; Neh 13:26, 27; Isa 2:6; Lam 5:2; Obad 1:11; Zeph 1:8. Conversely, general, familial or other uses constitute only a handful of contexts: Gen 31:15; Job 19:15; Ps 69:9; Eccl 6:2; Isa 28:21; Jer 2:21. As for the nominal root, נכר, it is interesting to note that it in all 37 cases it appears as a masculine singular noun in genitive construct, and almost universally as the genitive absolute as בֶּן־נֵכָר. It never occurs in Proverbs. The lead usage in this case is also, "non-Israelite": Exod 12:43; Lev 22:25; 2 Sam 22:45–46; Neh 9:2; 13:30; Ps 18:45–46; 137:4; 144:4, 11; Isa 56:3, 6; 60:10; 61:5; 62:8; Ezek 44:7, 9. Gen 17:12, 27 regard the law of circumcision and while in the narrative Israel was not yet a nation, the word likely means more than "familial outsider." The second, but very similar usage is with regard to "foreign gods" (Gen 35:2, 4; Deut 31:16; 32:12; Josh 24:20, 23; Judg 10:16; 1 Sam 7:3; 2 Chr 14:2; 33:15; Ps 81:10; Jer 5:19; 8:19; Dan 11:39; Mal 2:11; Ezek 44:7, 9). There are two homonymic uses: Obad 1:12; Job 31:3.

83. 2 Kgs 19:24; Ps 54:5; Isa 1:7; 25:2, 5; 29:5; 61:5; Jer 30:8; 51:51; Lam 5:2; Ezek 7:21; 11:9; 28:7, 10; 30:12; 31:12; Hos 8:7; Joel 4:17.

84. See 1 Kgs 3:18; Job 15:19; 19:27; Ps 109:11; Prov 5:17; 6:1; 14:10; 27:2; Isa 28:21; Jer 18:14; Hos 8:12. The semantic domain of cultic out-grouping (i.e., those who should not partake in certain functions or domains) is also around 11 uses, but requires greater discussion. First, there are ten contexts that more or less clearly indicate זר as a sort of technical term frequently used in construct with איש or some other noun to differentiate between priests and laymen (cf. Exod 30:33; Lev 22:12–13; Num 1:51; 3:10, 38; 17:5; 18:4, 7. Also, Lev 22:10 could be grouped with the cultic domain, but also includes references to non-Israelites and thus may also have bearing on ethnicity). These usages are restricted entirely to Torah. It seems most likely that the word is not used metonymically in Proverbs to import cultic associations, but that either ethnicity or some

Why would the poet choose what would amount to a neologism when there are other more conventional phrases that would convey the idea?[85] Especially in light of the word נכריה which appears more than twenty times[86] in *Tanakh* with the consistent meaning of "non-Israelite."[87]

The use and context of "strange" (זרה) and "foreign" (נכריה) in Proverbs are most closely allied with usage in the Prophets that employ marital infidelity to figure unfaithfulness to YHWH. Within the prophets, particularly Jeremiah and Hosea, זר and נכריה are among a special set of lexemes that are particularly associated with the metaphor IDOLATRY IS ADULTERY and thereby take on sexual connotations. In Jer 2:20–26 YHWH conducts an interview with idolatrous Judah who is figured first as a prostitute on every green hill and then as a choice vine who becomes the "disloyal vine of a foreigner" (הַגֶּפֶן נָכְרִיָּה). In the next lines, Judah is reported to say, "Alas, had I not loved strangers (זרים)! But after them I will go" (Jer 2:25). Sexual

---

more general meaning is in view. Camp's choice of the "cultic" domain for the term is not warranted by usage within Tanakh.

85. Historically there has been a considerable disagreement on the *identity* of the Strange Woman. Many of these were touched upon in chapter 1. She has been understood in a number of different ways: (1) She may be a foreign woman then *allegorized* as foreign teaching or heresy (Rabbinic and early Christian interpretation) or as an ethnic outsider (Washington, Plöger). (2) She has been various understood as a representative of a foreign deity (i.e., Clifford, Boström, Perdue) and lately, (3) she has been equated with the "other" or any brand of "social outsider or social deviant" (McKane. Snijders, Blenkinsopp). (4) Only Van der Toorn seems to take the view that she was a home-born prostitute. Fox, Blenkinsopp and Brenner, among others, settle on the notion that the "stranger" is somebody else's wife. Fox notes a few Biblical reference that indicate that such a meaning is permissible (cf. Gen 31:15; Jer 2:21; Eccl 6:2, Prov 5:10; 6:24, 27:13). The only difficulty with Fox's proposal is that *reduces* the complexity of the inner-biblical allusion. Rather than preserving the ambiguity that is inherent in the poem's self-presentation, he chooses the left-hemisphere shortcut to clarity. If clarity were the poet's intention, he would have favored terms for adultery (cf. Prov 6:32 נֹאֵף אִשָּׁה). While feminist scholarship typically is concerned for "the other" (category 3), most scholars fall along other accents. For example, a great number of scholars abstract the Strange Woman into a symbolic and therefore allegorical figure (i.e., Camp, Newsom). Others lean toward the historical-critical referent of the "foreign woman" (i.e., Roy-Yoder, Maier). Finally, with Weeks is a class of "literary" interpretation that allows the referent to remain more nebulous, and understands the Strange Woman as the negative complement to the characterization of wisdom (Habel, Murphy).

86. Gen 31:15; Exod 2:22; 18:3; Ruth 2:10; 1 Kgs 11:1, 8; Ezra 10:2, 10–11, 14, 17–18, 44; Neh 13:26–27; Prov 2:16; 5:20; 6:24; 7:5; 20:16; 23:27; 27:13; Isa 28:21; Jer 2:21.

87. E.g., Prov 2:16; 5:10, 20; 7:5; 20:16; 27:2, 13. Within the book of Proverbs only two additional contexts are different from זר. In the first (Prov 6:24), the word is paralleled not with the Strange Woman (אשה זרה) but with the "evil woman" (אשה רע) with reference to smooth speech and errant sexuality. In the second (Prov 23:27), the parallel is with the prostitute, as will be discussed below.

depravity is the image schema used to describe covenant infidelity. Likewise in Jer 3 Israel and Judah are portrayed as two faithless sisters who "play the whore" with Judah emulating the faithlessness of her sister. Ultimately, Judah is condemned because she has "lavished her 'roads' upon strangers [זרים] beneath every leafy tree" and disobeyed YHWH. Finally, Ezek 16:31 provides the image schema of the harlot compared with the adulterous wife. Judah is portrayed as an adulterous wife who scorns payment and "receives strangers (זרים) instead of her husband" (Ezek 16:32). Judah's shame and punishment is then figured in relation to that set out for adultery in Torah (16:38–63). Again, covenant infidelity is figured as marital infidelity, with the nation playing the part of the bride.

The image schema in all of these contexts depicts the relationship between YHWH and his people as a marital covenant. The cult infidelity of the people is then imaged upon the sexual infidelity of the spouse. These contexts from the Prophets are the only ones that use the words "foreigner" (נכרי) and "stranger" (זר) in sexual contexts and employ similar metaphors in Tanakh.[88] I do not here argue for textual dependence in one direction or another, rather I argue for a shared image metaphor of COVENANT AS MARRIAGE or IDOLATRY IS ADULTERY. This imagery is further borne out by other lexical borrowings in similar contexts.

For example, the word for "close companion" (אלוף) (Prov 2:17) has rare usage in the Tanakh, with most cases being found in Proverbs in agreement with this gloss.[89] However, the only other occurrence of this noun is found in the previously noted context of Jer 3, wherein Israel calls to YHWH as their "father" and "companion of their youth."[90] This leads to the next phrase, "her youth" (נְעוּרֶיהָ), not only does it occur in 3:4 in construct with the rare word אלוף, but it appears twice more in the same chapter (e.g.,

---

88. The contexts that employ נכרי or זר in the context of the IDOLATRY IS ADULTERY metaphor include: Jer 2:21; 3:13; Deut 32:16; Isa 17:10; 43:12; Jer 2:25; Ezek 16:32; Hos 5:7; 7:9. Only Jer 2:21 employs both roots together. The most significant contexts for נכרי as a feminine form include Solomon's love for foreign women (1 Kgs 11:1, 8) and the considerable attention given to "non-Israelite wives" in Ezra and Nehemiah (Ezra 10:2, 10–11, 14, 17–18, 44; Neh 13:26–27).

89. See Prov 16:28; 17:9. All other uses outside of Prov and Jer are for the homonymic root glossed as "tribal chieftain." McKane chooses a reading parallel with this meaning (i.e., "family head") but it is difficult to make sense of it in context. Loader understands the parallel thus, "'the covenant of her God' is a subjective genitive, that is, a covenant imposed on her by her God with respect to her partner, who must then be her husband. This is further supported by the fact that a parallel phrase for אלוף נעוריה is (the wife of your youth) mentioned in 5:18" (Loader, *Proverbs 1–9*, 128). Fox also notes the parallel with Jeremiah 3:4 and the metaphorical context listed above. See Fox, *Proverbs 1–9*, 120.

90. (Jer 3:4) הֲלוֹא מֵעַתָּה (קָרָאתִי) [קָרָאת] לִי אָבִי אַלּוּף נְעֻרַי אָתָּה

3:24–25) and once with reference to Jerusalem as a bride in 2:2. Moreover, in construct with a third person feminine suffix the word appears in two more of the prophetic contexts (Ezek 23:3; Hos 2:17) and one time in association with the cultic usage of זר (Lev 22:3).

In the phrase, "she has forgotten the covenant of her god," (2:17) the covenant in question appears to be related to YHWH, since every usage of ברית אלהיה is in the context of Yahwism.[91] Moreover, the only other occurrence of "she has forgotten me" as a Qal perfect third feminine singular, also occurs within the context of the *IDOLATRY IS ADULTERY* metaphor, this time in Hos 2:15.[92]

Both Weeks and Loader have noted that the identity of the "strange" or "foreign" women is not to be found in a speculative social milieu, but in the poetic associations of the Tanakh.[93] Weeks, for example, points out that the background for the selection and characterization of the type comes from Deut 7:1–5; Exod 34:11–16; Neh 13:25; Judg 2:1–3; 3:6; Ezra 9—wherein foreign wives lead to "whoring after other gods" (Exod 34:11–16). In these passages "Israel had courted divine anger through apostasy."[94]

> According to the predictions of Deuteronomy and Exodus, and also according to certain accounts in Judges and Kings, intermarriage is one way, and perhaps the main way, in which such

---

91. See Exod 34:16; Num 25:2; Ruth 1:15; 1 Kgs 11:8; Isa 21:9; Jer 46:25; Hos 14:1; Zeph 3:2. Fox proposes that the covenant in question is a marriage covenant, which would only solidify ties to prophetic metaphor. Moreover, he insists that there is no evidence that Israel's neighbors made covenants with their gods. See Fox, *Proverbs 1–9*, 120.

92. "The covenant is, then, imposed by Yahweh (or overseen by him, which would amount to basically the same thing). Logically, this could be the Sinai covenant (so Meinhold), but it is unlikely because it would strain the feminine singular suffix if the covenant of Yahweh with the whole people of Israel were meant. Moreover, a reference to the Sinai tradition in Proverbs would, though logically possible, be highly improbable, especially where a less doubtful alternative is available" (Loader, *Proverbs 1–9*, 129). While Loader's interpretation is likely correct, the fact that the *Strange Woman* is so solidly situated in the prophetic metaphor of *IDOLATRY IS ADULTERY* the marriage covenant itself becomes a figure for the larger issue of fidelity to Yahweh.

93. "In a way that other identifications do not, this association supplies a reason for the arch-seductress of Proverbs 1–9 to be called a 'foreign woman,' and for the strong emphasis on her persuasiveness: foreign women, after all, can corrupt and destroy even a Solomon. It would be wrong, however, to start asking whether the woman is supposed to be a lapsed Israelite, a foreign resident, or one of the 'people of the land': there is little in Proverbs 1–9 to suggest that it is simply trying to wade into a debate on intermarriage. Rather it seems likely that the author is using the 'foreignness' of the woman primarily in a poetic way, exploiting the connotations of the term, not setting out an exclusivist agenda" (Weeks, *Instruction and Imagery*, 141).

94. Weeks, *Instruction and Imagery*, 138.

undesirable assimilation to the religious beliefs of these peoples can occur. Whatever the extent of this motif in earlier literature, and whatever the actual socio-political background, the idea of such seduction into apostasy is offered by the principle biblical sources as the key justification for the proposed ban on intermarriage in the community of the return. The term "foreign woman" is not only given prominence in that controversy, therefore, but it is also given very specific associations with the corruption, or seduction of Jewish men into apostasy from YHWH.[95]

The *Strange/Foreign Woman* constitutes a novel extension of the language and metaphors of the prophets.[96] By recognizing that the axis of metaphorical comparison is that of *covenant fidelity* we are granted a new avenue for understanding *Lady Wisdom*.

Marital and Covenant Infidelity Is Associated with the Strange Woman of Malachi 2

The phrase הוּא יַעֲשֶׂנָּה (lit. "he, *he* will do her") in Prov 6:32 also points toward possible prophetic allusion, as well as further reinforcing the *IDOLATRY IS ADULTERY* metaphor. The emphatic repetition of the 3ms pronoun makes it clear that the fault for the consequences of adultery are upon the young man, but otherwise it is syntactically and grammatically awkward. Why use the general verb עשה? Are there not clearer words that relate more closely to the context? Moreover, the pronominal suffix "her" does not have a clear antecedent since the participial forms of both נאף and משית are masculine.[97] Finally, *why* should the poet choose to emphasize the role of the foolish young man? In this case, the reason that the author has employed a strange verb with awkward pronominal suffix is in order to activate another

---

95. Weeks, *Instruction and Imagery*, 140–42.

96. "In the text, this woman's strangeness does not relate to the people of Israel, but to the young man. . . . The smooth words of a female strange from which youths are to be protected can only mean sexually seductive speech (cf. 6:24; 7:5, 21, and especially 5:3 where the imagery of the smoothness of her mouth is not just an obvious reference to her talking, but also carries erotic connotations). So the specific type of woman here intended is not only a woman to whom the young man has no rightful sexual access, but also one who wishes to seduce him into precisely that" (Loader, *Proverbs 1–9*, 127). As noted, if this were the poet's intention, then he has brought along a great deal of unnecessary canonical baggage.

97. Fox, *Proverbs 1–9*, 235.

canonical context. The only other appearance of the morphological form יַעֲשֶׂנָּה is in Mal 2:11–12.

> 11 בָּגְדָה יְהוּדָה וְתוֹעֵבָה נֶעֶשְׂתָה בְיִשְׂרָאֵל וּבִירוּשָׁלָ͏ִם
>
> Judah is faithless and abomination will be committed in Israel and in Jerusalem
>
> כִּי ׀ חִלֵּל יְהוּדָה קֹדֶשׁ יְהוָה אֲשֶׁר אָהֵב וּבָעַל בַּת־אֵל נֵכָר׃
>
> Because Judah has profaned the sanctuary of YHWH whom he loved and married the daughter of a foreign god.
>
> 12 יַכְרֵת יְהוָה לָאִישׁ אֲשֶׁר יַעֲשֶׂנָּה עֵר וְעֹנֶה מֵאָהֳלֵי יַעֲקֹב
>
> YHWH will cut of the man that he, he will do this—waker and one answering[98] from the tents of Jacob
>
> וּמַגִּישׁ מִנְחָה לַיהוָה צְבָאוֹת׃ פ
>
> And one bringing near a gift to YHWH of Hosts. (Mal 2:11–12)

It should be noted that this is the very same context of the "wife of your youth" discussed in Prov 5:18. Moreover it continues and develops the metaphor of IDOLATRY IS ADULTERY. In an interesting twist, the earlier context (Mal 2:10–11) emphasizes that Judah has profaned her covenant by her dealings with one another.

> הֲלוֹא אָב אֶחָד לְכֻלָּנוּ הֲלוֹא אֵל אֶחָד בְּרָאָנוּ
>
> Do we not all have one father? Has not the same one created us?
>
> מַדּוּעַ נִבְגַּד אִישׁ בְּאָחִיו לְחַלֵּל בְּרִית אֲבֹתֵינוּ׃
>
> Why will we act faithlessly each with his brother thereby profaning the covenant of our fathers? (Mal 2:10–11)

---

98. Ross takes the difficult phrase, "waker and one answering" as a merism which relates to "watchmen at either end of the settlement, one calling out and the other answering. In any case, it is a figure to express the totality of the people (a merism), meaning everyone, from one extreme to the other (opposite)" (Ross, *Malachi Then and Now*, loc 2679).

By extension in Prov 6:32, we find the implication that a man will *profane* the covenant of his God by transgressing the covenant with the *wife of his youth*. He, *he* will do this.

Therefore, via the resonance of metaphor and vocabulary with Mal 2, both with regard to "the wife of you youth" and the disastrous outcomes of covenant infidelity, the poet is emphasizing and blending *covenant fidelity* and *marital fidelity*. This coupled with the prophetic usage of the terms "strange" (זרה) and "foreign" (נכריה) makes it is clear that the prophetic metaphor of IDOLATRY IS ADULTERY or COVENANT IS MARRIAGE should be seen as the basic metaphor upon which other blends are joined.

Stage 1 Perception: Part II: The "Wife of Your Youth" Blends the Prophetic Metaphor, *WATER IS LIFE/ YHWH* with the Metaphor *LOVE IS THIRST*

In paragraph 11 (5:7–23) the poet places emphasis on marital and relational fidelity through the juxtaposition of the *Strange Woman* with the "wife of your youth" (אֵשֶׁת נְעוּרֶךָ). First of all, the father debriefs the grandfather's metaphorical teaching with specific warnings about avoiding the *Strange Woman*.[99] From v. 15 the father introduces the speculative referent of the young man's wife as the positive counterpart to the foil provided by the *Strange Woman* in vv. 1–14. She highlights the disparity between the joy and benefits of faithful, covenantal relationship with the loss and harm caused by infidelity. In this section the father adds his own string of metaphorical teachings: WOMAN IS WATER. (DESIRE IS THIRST). WOMAN IS AN ANIMAL (v. 19). WOMAN IS AN INEBRIATE (v. 19). Finally, if the son should fail in his fidelity to his wife, he is pictured as a TRAPPED ANIMAL (vv. 21–23).

In the treatment that follows we will give particular attention to the blending and development of *WATER* and *THIRST* metaphor of Jer 2:13 and the Song of Solomon. In the first part of the section we clarify the source/ target mapping for Prov 5:15–23 with reference to the sources described, argue for a capacitive reading of יפוץ and then survey interpretive difficulties arising from previous mismappings of this metaphor. We then proceed to consider the metaphor *WATER IS LIFE/YHWH* as set forth in Jer 2:13. The

---

99. Not only the return to the plural form "sons" (בנים) (cf. 4:1; 7:24; 8:32) but also the command to "listen to me" (שמע לי) (cf. 7:24; 8:32) fits within the larger framework wherein the audience is figured as a plural. Therefore, the end of paragraph 10 is the end of the grandfatherly quotation, and paragraph 11 begins the father's debrief of that teaching, as the interplay of syntax, lexeme and metaphor make apparent.

image schema which describes the exchange of the "fountain" of YHWH for bad and broken water sources accords with that set forth in the fountain of the "wife of your youth." The erotic thirst for love from Song of Solomon is joined with prophetic associations of *LIFE* with secondary associations of providence and joy. By the blending of these two basic metaphors the wife is depicted as the complete fulfillment the young man's desires and thirst for love in a manner similar to the LORD himself.

Incomplete Mappings for the Metaphor
WOMAN AS A WATER SOURCE

In the opening lines (5:15–17) the metaphorical target is not specified; rather cistern, running waters, well, springs, and streams all contain only a half-meaning. By 5:17, the reader is provided guidance against male strangers and then finally and explicitly "rejoice in the wife of your youth" (5:18). First, it is important to note that the string of referents for *water sources* are not merely a piling up of synonyms.[100] The selection of water sources is purposeful. There are a number of water sources that *are* disincluded, for example all those that refer to rivers or larger sources (נחר,יאר, ים, etc.). The principle of selection has to do with personal ownership. Cisterns, wells, and springs could all be owned by an individual or family, whereas rivers or larger bodies could not.[101] Second, the ordering of the nouns betrays a growth in magnitude and production. The cistern is smaller and only gathers rain water. The "trickling well," "fountain," and "stream" grow in magnitude and production. The parallelism betrays a growth and expansion in quantity and production.[102]

Second, while the verb פוץ in 5:16 has typically been a problem for translators it is also a key to the overall interpretation of the passage. Some traditional rabbinic sources read יָפֻצוּ as a jussive, "let your springs spread abroad." In most cases they deem the metaphorical target to be something other than the woman. Some associate the "springs" with either progeny (Qimḥi, Hame'iri, Radaq) or semen (*Gen. Rab.* §26; cf. Joel 4:18; Isa 48:1; Num 24:7).[103] Another interpretive option incorrectly associates the water sources with some male issue, but provide a negative particle for the verb (as in the LXX) and thereby reverse the force of verb and make the jussive

---

100. E.g., Waltke, *Proverbs 1–15*, 317.
101. Waltke, *Proverbs 1–15*, 317; Fox, *Proverbs 1–9*, 199.
102. Chisholm, "Drink Water," 399–401.
103. Fox, *Proverbs 1–9*, 201.

into a negative admonition. This makes better sense than the former option, especially in light of the content of vv. 16–17.[104] In a similar manner, some interpreters (e.g., Waltke) and most versions (NIV; NRSV; NEV) read the imperfect verb as an implied rhetorical question. In this interpretation the water sources are seen as metaphor for feminine sexuality. However, there is no formal marking to indicate a question. Fox argues that the verse should be read as an unmarked apodosis that serves as a threat of consequence. *If* you "drink from other sources" then "strangers will drink from yours." Therefore, the metaphor pertains to female sexuality. Fox writes, "In both cases [i.e., here and Ahiqar S2 2:6] the idea is an appropriate, tit-for-tat punishment for violating another's wife. The wronged wife's motive, whether it is spite or sexual frustration, is not stated, nor are we told whether she will be acting voluntarily. The only relevant agents are male."[105] However, the proposed subjunctive is difficult to substantiate as also is the motive for omitting any formal marking.

However, all of the problems may be safely circumvented by reading the verb as a capacitive: "they *could* spread out."[106] As the water metaphors move from holding to generating water and grow in volume the image schema of a sources for drinking water requires some sort of consumption or containment. In this way, the wife's motive for faithlessness is less important than her capacity to *fill* all of the son's desires and needs. The emphasis is upon the fact that if the son slakes his thirst elsewhere, the wellspring of his wife is liable to overflow into public places. In this way the culpability is squarely upon the young man and simultaneously highlights the folly of looking outside the marital union for what can be entirely provided within it. So while Fox's assertion, "The only relevant agents are male," should be framed in light of the fact that the father is exhorting the son not to be the *cause* of infidelity by neglecting his wife.[107]

---

104. Fox, *Proverbs 1–9*, 201.

105. Fox, *Proverbs 1–9*, 201.

106. See Gemser, *Spüche Salomos*, 37; Meinhold, *Die Sprüche*, 1:104.

107. The mention of "outside" (חוץ) and "squares" (רחבות) hearkens both *back* to Lady Wisdom (1:20) but also *ahead* to the Strange Woman (Prov 7:12) (cf. Fox, *Proverbs 1–9*, 201; Waltke, *Proverbs 1–15*, 319). Waltke's assertion that the capacitive view of יפוץ "questionably assumes that the virtuous wife will become a harlot if neglected," has merit but is perhaps an oversimplification. The son and his wife mirror one another, as will be seen in greater detail in the sentence literature. The young man's wife has every possibility of demonstrating the qualities of *Lady Wisdom* drawn into association in Prov 1–9 and Prov 31, but it is *unlikely* that she will attain to such heights if *he* is a fool and faithless. In this case, she becomes vulnerable to "strangers." If the youth emulates the way of wicked and duplicitous men, his wife may turn out to be his perfect match. Her fidelity is figured as a mirror of his own.

Interpretive Difficulties Arising from Mis-mapping of Metaphor

As noted above, some interpreters argue that the basic metaphor should be construed as something like CHILDREN ARE WATER. By this basic metaphor then, it is not the woman's sexuality but her reproductive capacity which is the target category of the metaphor. Given the fact that women who are negative stereotypes are figured with reference to "pit" (שחה) and "cistern" (בור) the absence of water would suggest that water was related to the idea of issue (Prov 22:14; 23:27). With this basic metaphor, however, the idea of "rejoicing" (5:18) and the strongly sexual imagery of vv. 18–20 seem disjointed.

Conversely, some interpreters argue that the basic metaphor is something like SEX IS WATER. In this case it is the woman's sexual potential that is made explicit in the target. Such a reading seems to accord with the erotic content of the poem and the further expansion in vv. 19–20 (i.e., the doe and inebriation). However, there seems to be a reductionism in the readings that is unsettling. For example, Fox, citing Lev 20:18 (also 12:7), makes the *FOUNTAIN* a detailed but euphemistic equivalent to the female reproductive system. "Perhaps metaphors have more specific referents, with 'cistern'/'well' being the vagina and the 'fount' or 'source' (*maqor*) being the womb."[108] He cannot be faulted for lack of clarity. While such usage cannot be ruled out as a possibility, reducing the metaphor to the *physical apparatus* of sexuality does not account for all of the elements of the formal presentation.

Ultimately, while sexuality is certainly in view, it is not the *point* of the metaphor. While "drinking" is repeatedly activated in Song of Solomon and Proverbs with reference to sexuality (e.g., Prov 7:18; 9:17; Song 1:2, 4; 4:10; 5:1; 7:2, 9; 8:2) it should not be read as a euphemism and therefore as sort of metonymy. Rather, the metaphor still acts as metaphor and may be combined or blended in any number of different ways. In Prov 5 the basic metaphor appears to be is WATER IS LOVE. This is exactly backwards. Rather, the basic metaphor is that LOVE IS THIRST. At a basic level, the point of all of the listed water sources is that they were for *drinking*.

This is perhaps clearest with reference to the appearance of *FIRE* and *WATER* image schemas in Song 8:6–7, which will be alluded to again in Prov 7:

---

108. Fox, *Proverbs 1–9*, 201.

> שִׂימֵ֨נִי כַֽחוֹתָ֜ם עַל־לִבֶּ֗ךָ כַּֽחוֹתָם֙ עַל־זְרוֹעֶ֔ךָ כִּֽי־עַזָּ֤ה כַמָּ֙וֶת֙ אַהֲבָ֔ה
>
> Place me like a seal upon you're your heart, like a seal upon your arm. For strong as death is love.
>
> קָשָׁ֥ה כִשְׁא֖וֹל קִנְאָ֑ה רְשָׁפֶ֕יהָ רִשְׁפֵּ֕י אֵ֖שׁ שַׁלְהֶבֶתְיָֽה:
>
> Hard as Sheol is jealousy. Her flashes are flashes of fire, a raging flame.
>
> מַ֣יִם רַבִּ֗ים לֹ֤א יֽוּכְלוּ֙ לְכַבּ֣וֹת אֶת־הָֽאַהֲבָ֔ה וּנְהָר֖וֹת לֹ֣א יִשְׁטְפ֑וּהָ
>
> Many waters cannot extinguish love and rivers will not overflow it.
>
> אִם־יִתֵּ֨ן אִ֜ישׁ אֶת־כָּל־ה֤וֹן בֵּיתוֹ֙ בָּאַהֲבָ֔ה בּ֖וֹז יָב֥וּזוּ לֽוֹ: ס
>
> If a man would give all the treasure of his house for love, he would be utterly scorned. (Song 8:6–7)

Here, the metaphorical target of *FIRE* and *FLOOD* may not be reduced to mere sexuality. Moreover while they are tempestuous and seem to signal *LOSS*, *HARM*, and *POWER* the emphasized element is *INSATIETY*. Love is *unrelenting*, *unquenchable* and *inextinguishable*. It lies above and beyond what any person could give in exchange.

With this context activated in Prov 5:18, the parallel usage of water imagery in Jeremiah 2:13 appears in a new light which then makes the best sense of the metaphor as a whole.

Parallels with Jeremiah: WATER IS LIFE and YHWH IS A FOUNTAIN

> כִּֽי־שְׁתַּ֥יִם רָע֖וֹת עָשָׂ֣ה עַמִּ֑י
>
> For two evils my people have done.
>
> אֹתִ֣י עָזְב֗וּ מְק֤וֹר ׀ מַ֣יִם חַיִּ֔ים לַחְצֹ֤ב לָהֶם֙ בֹּאר֔וֹת
>
> Me, they have abandoned, a spring of living water, to hew for themselves cisterns.
>
> בֹּארֹת֙ נִשְׁבָּרִ֔ים אֲשֶׁ֥ר לֹא־יָכִ֖לוּ הַמָּֽיִם:
>
> Broken cisterns that cannot contain water. (Jer 2:13)

The broader context in Jeremiah is that Israel has betrayed YHWH and "exchanged her gods" (v. 11) and "exchanged their glory for that which does not profit" (v. 12).[109] In Prov 5:20, there is a similar exchange of the blessed delight of the "wife of one's youth," for the dissipation and loss found in the *Strange Woman*. Moreover, that exchange is predicated upon misdirected desire. Finally, in both cases, the ultimate source lies in the "fountain" (מקור). While in Jeremiah, YHWH is identified as "a fountain of living water" (מְקוֹר ׀ מַיִם חַיִּים)[110] the parallel in Prov 5 does not accord, but rather is a simple fountain (מקור), that is "blessed."

The Poet Provides Parity between the Depiction of YHWH AS A FOUNTAIN and the WIFE AS A FOUNTAIN

The fountain, which is capable of sating the son's needs and desires is first of all "blessed" (ברך). This term draws the issue of marital fidelity even further into the divine realm. "All usages of *bāruk*, presuppose God as either the ultimate author (of blessing) or receiver (of praise)."[111] As such the present occurrence should be deemed, "a prayer or desire that the individual might

---

109. The image of *JUDAH AS A WOMAN* following the basic metaphor of *IDOLATRY IS ADULTERY* is one of the main themes in Jer 2:1–4:4. As noted by Holladay, "One begins with the assumption that 2:1–4:4 forms a self-contained collection. Though not all of the material deals with the harlotry of the nation, much of it does" (Holladay, *Jeremiah*, 62). Specifically in the beginning of Jer 2, the love and fidelity of the marital relationship is parallel to language and metaphor in Hosea 2. See Holladay, *Jeremiah*, 62.

110. This phrase appears in Proverbs but is associated with the "mouth of the righteous" (Prov 10:11), the "teaching of the wise" (13:14), the fear of YHWH (14:27), good sense (16:22). Outside of Proverbs it usually is identified with YHWH (cf. Ps 36:10; 68:27; Jer 2:13; 17:13). Holladay remarks, "Yahweh is depicted metaphorically as a 'spring of running water' (מְקוֹר ׀ חַיִּים). A מְקוֹר is a natural spring, and מַיִם חַיִּים is normal idiom for running 'running water' (Gen 26:19; Lev 14:5). The adjective חַי does mean 'living,' and Yahweh is the 'living God' (אֱלֹהִים חַיִּים, Deut 5:26), and Jrm plays on the double meaning of חַיִּים here; nevertheless, 'fountain of living water' (RSV and other translations) is misleading, for the contrast between the running water of this spring and the collected water in the reservoirs which must come from some other source even if the reservoirs were tight. Behind Jrm's metaphor could well be Isa 8:6–8: there Israel has refused the waters of Shiloah which supply Jerusalem, so that God must bring over them the waters of the river (the Euphrates).... On the other hand, 'spring/fountain of life' is a standard phrase (Ps 36:10; Prov 10:11; 13:14; 14:27; 16:22) for 'sources of life,' and one wonders whether this is not some otiose phrase with mythological overtones like 'tree of life.' All these intersecting images—running water, soure of life, living God, and a spring as a symbol for Yahweh or his word in Isaiah 8—coalesce in Jrm's phrase, which recurs in the book (17:13)" (Holladay, *Jeremiah*, 92).

111. Brown, "ברך" (NIDOTTE 1:763).

receive special blessing from God in light of their special acts, equivalent to our, 'God bless you!' (cf. 1 Sam 15:13)."[112] However, the specific usage in Proverbs is also enlightening:

> While Prov stresses the causal relationship between right living and a good life, it does so in a God-centered way. Thus, a secure, stable, and satisfied existence is not just the natural result of godly living, it also comes as a direct blessing of God, the tangible consequence of his favor. Blessings crown the righteous (Prov 10:6a; cf. 10:7a), the generous (11:26b; 22:9), and the faithful (28:20a), as opposed to those who "get rich quick" (20:21; cf. 28:20b). Succinctly stated, "The blessing of the LORD brings wealth, and he adds no trouble to it" (10:22). As for Prov 11:11 ("Through the blessing of the upright a city is exalted, but by the mouth of the wicked it is destroyed"), the parallelism seems to indicate that the blessing in v. 11 refers to the blessing that the upright pronounce; as blessed people, they bring blessing to the city.[113]

The *son* is only the indirect beneficiary of the blessing. The blessing is first and foremost upon the water source that is equated with his wife. Second, considering that most interpreters model the jussive of verse 17 directly upon verse 18. In verse 17 the implied syntax is that "in order for the springs to be for you alone . . . you should remain faithful to your wife." Verse 18 seems to reproduce the same argument, "in order for you fountains to be blessed, they should be yours alone . . . you should remain faithful to your wife." In this way, both verses 17 and 18 function as implied apodoses of the former argument. This in turn enlightens *how* and *why* the blessing may function. As noted, since the blessing is typically invoked in light of action or obedience, the son's observation of parental instruction will provide blessing that will yield joy. The breach of such fidelity will break the possibility of blessing and joy.

In Jeremiah, human desire and life is figured not as an outgiving but an intake. Rather than relying on the ever flowing "fountain of living water" of YHWH, the children of Israel made for themselves false sources to slake their human desire.[114] While in Prov 5, woman is not featured as a "fountain of living water" she is featured as being entirely adequate to slake the young man's "thirst for love." While she is not and cannot be YHWH; she is the closest the son will find short of YHWH himself. The "wife of your youth"

---

112. Brown, "ברך" (NIDOTTE 1:764).
113. Brown, "ברך" (NIDOTTE 1:764).
114. Holladay, *Jeremiah*, 93.

is the only licit and beneficial relationship that will provide both satiety and blessing.

Conclusion

The erotic metaphor of LOVE IS THIRST informs the comparison of the "wife of your youth" against the foil of the *Strange Woman* (5:20-23). The "wife of your youth" is described as being completely able to satisfy the young man's thirst for love in all of its entailments where the *Strange Woman* leads only to punishment and death. The possibility of *exchanging* this blessed and licit covenantal association with his wife is like unto the exchange of the "living waters" of YHWH for broken cisterns for in Jer 2. Marital fidelity is the delightful means of maintaining and demonstrating covenant fidelity to YHWH.

Stage One Perception: Part III: The Novel Metaphor *MARRIED WOMAN IS FIRE* and Allusions to Torah and Song of Songs

Introduction

These two paragraphs (6:20-27, 27-35) showcase the poet's talent of blending canonical contexts into the service of extending previously employed metaphors in new directions. First, the romantic metaphor LOVE IS THIRST and the imagery drawn from Song of Songs is contrasted with the image schema of fire with a basic metaphor something like MARRIED WOMAN IS FIRE. The identity of the *Strange Woman* is here anchored in the identity of another man's wife. However, contrary to her villainous appearance in Prov 5, the initial emphasis is upon the young man's failure to maintain proper boundaries.

Second, the poet continues to develop connections with Torah via textual allusion and metaphor. First, from 6:20-22, the author borrows not only words, but also image schemas of ORNAMENT and MOVEMENT that are typical descriptions of the *Shema*. Second, the author alludes to the prohibitions against covetousness, adultery, and theft and then closes the chapter by using the legal framework of judgment as a metaphorical image schema to compare the outcomes of theft and adultery. In all, Proverbs five and six maintain the protective role of wisdom while highlighting the dangers of inappropriate boundaries with married women. The paragraphs conclude by illustrating the severity of breach of covenant by the blend of the Decalogue and the Song of Songs with regard to the rage of the wronged husband.

MARRIED WOMAN AS FIRE—as a Sapiential Frame for Gendered Relationships

In Prov 6:27, the poet provides what may be deemed a textbook model for a proverb. Following the studies of Lakoff and Turner nearly all proverbs can be reduced to a basic metaphor something like *GENERIC IS SPECIFIC*. One element of the image schema provided by the proverb, parable, fable or allegory becomes the map for other *specific* cases.[115] So for example in the English proverb, "That is like the pot calling the kettle black," no lexical element of the metaphor has referential purpose. Rather, the proverb holds up a relationship that is used to frame a particular experience. In the case of the English proverb, it may be employed when one speaker ascribes a particular quality to another that he or she possesses in surfeit. It is used to point out either ironic or hypocritical speech (i.e., a father with poor handwriting lamenting that of his son). The generic structure of the proverb in Prov 6 relates to the treatment of fire. Snatching fire into the lap or garment is not an action that is required by any other activity. It is precisely equivalent to stupidity and self-harm. In the second case, walking upon coals could be deemed an accidental action, however, the choice of the *piel* verb (which otherwise indicates purposeful movement in the figurative domain) makes it clear that stumbling through a cooking fire is not in view. The same generic likeness is maintained. No one decides to make a shortcut through a cooking fire to warm his feet. There is no reasonable cause for such behavior. It is identical with self-harm. The fire is not the culprit. Stupidity is the culprit. Finally, the target input is supplied over the top of the vivid image metaphors. "Coming to the wife of one's friend" is equivalent to the self-harm inflicted by walking on coals.[116] Therefore, the generic structure provided places the young man's experience of married women in the place of sources of fire. In Prov 5:15–23 the young man was exhorted to delight in the wife of his youth, lest he become a victim, not of the *Strange Woman*, but of the LORD's judgment of his sin. Here, the teacher aims at the consequences of the negative behavior itself. If a married woman is fire,

---

115. Lakoff, "Conceptual Metaphor Theory," 235.

116. Also note that "touch" and "movement" are mirrored between the two scenarios. The concern in v. 27 is with a man grasping and therefore touching fire also the last verb in v. 29 reflects "one touching." Likewise, where "walking" is used with reference to the coals, so "the one coming to the wife of his friend."

appropriate boundaries and respect should be maintained. There is no good reason why a man should violate the clear boundaries established by good sense. If he does so the consequences are inherent in the deed itself. The proceeding verses further specify the married woman as a possible adulteress, and anchors defense in the familiar categories of parental instruction and Torah.

The Blend of Torah and Song of Songs and the Desire for Covenant Fidelity

Allusions to Torah

First, it should be noted that the poet maintains and deepens allusion to parental instruction and Torah, by maintaining the circular relationship of "keeping," (שמר) and "protecting" (נצר). In Prov 2:8 it is YHWH who "protects" (נצר) the paths of justice via the wisdom of parental instruction. Discretion will "protect" (נצר) and understanding will "guard" (שמר) the youth (2:11). Then the idea is deepened and extended in Prov 3–4 where there is a double entendre in both "protect" (נצר) and "guard" (שמר). As the son "guards" and "protects" the commands (מצות) of the father (3:1), and thereby "protects" wisdom and discretion (3:21), wisdom will in turn "protect" (נצר) and "guard" (שמר) the young man (4:6). Moreover, "protecting" (נצר) wisdom is equated with defending life itself (4:13, 23). Finally, in Prov 5:2 the son is instructed to "keep discretion" (לִשְׁמֹר מְזִמּוֹת). In each case, the admonition of "keeping" and "protecting" is paired with being granted protection from a threat (e.g., 2:17; 5:3; 6:24). In addition to the maintenance of these terms and metaphor, the author includes a number of textual and metaphorical allusions to the Shema and to the Ten Commandments.

Allusion to the Shema

There are two ways in which the section recalls Deut 6:6–9. First, there is the repeated language of "binding" and "fastening" the teaching (Prov 3:3; 6:21; 7:3) that is very similar to that in Deut 6:8, where the commandments are to be "bound" (קשר) as a sign on the hand. The underlying image schema may be that of an apotropaic amulet or charm that is intended to "ward off harm" (cf. Exod 28:29; Song 8:6).[117] Even by itself the shared metaphor and language are enough to deepen the identification of Torah and Wisdom.[118]

Second, in addition to being "fastened to the neck" the parental Torah is associated with walking (הלך), lying down (שכב), and arising (although the verb is קום) as in Deut 6:7 (cf. Deut 11:18–20).[119] Whether the parallel terms and image schema are the result of allusion or textual dependence, the outcome is the same. It demonstrates the parity between the wisdom of parental instruction and the Torah of Moses.[120]

Finally, the connection between parental instruction and Torah is further emphasized by the inherent ambiguity in the subject of the 3fs verbs in 6:22 (i.e., "she will lead . . . she will guard . . . she will converse"). The fusion of parental instruction, Torah, and wisdom in a female person seems to be precisely the poet's intention. "Wisdom, which here refers to the internalized parental principles, is described in terms suggestive of personification: Wisdom is your friend, protector, and teacher. She will accompany you at all times, protect you from harm, and provide you with worthy and valuable thoughts. Make her—and not the temptress—your companion."[121]

This feminine imagery is then extended by a double entendre with the word "desire/covet" (חמד), the prohibition against adultery, and the comparison with theft as these appear in the Ten Commandments.

Allusions to the Ten Commandments

Three prohibitions in the Ten Commandments are directly or indirectly referenced in these paragraphs. First, the prohibition, "Do not covet" (Exod 20:17; Deut 5:21; Prov 6:25) is cited specifically with reference to one's neighbor's wife who is figured as the *Strange Woman*. Second, the prohibition, "Do not commit adultery" (Exod 20:14; Deut 5:18; Prov 6:26, 29, 32) is activated by the repeated use of the term נאף which is otherwise scant in the book of Proverbs. Finally, the prohibition, "Do not steal" (Exod 20:15;

---

117. Fox, *Proverbs 1–9*, 229. See also Miller, "Apotropaic Imagery," 129–30.

118. For example, Murphy writes, "One may even draw the conclusion that sapiential and 'Yahwistic' teaching do not differ, one from another. The teaching of the parents are on a level with, or better, analogous to the commands of Moses" (Murphy, *Proverbs*, 39).

119. Waltke, *Proverbs 1–15*, 351; Fox, *Proverbs 1–9*, 220.

120. Fox does not assert textual influence in one direction or the other, but asserts rather that, "Prov 6:20–22 formulates a commonplace of education: the teachings must permeate your entire life. If you keep them (Deut 11:22) they will keep you and watch over you (Prov 6:22)" (Fox, *Proverbs 1–9*, 220).

121. Fox, *Proverbs 1–9*, 229. See also Waltke, *Proverbs 1–15*, 351–52.

Do Not Covet

The prohibition אַל־תַּחְמֹד in Prov 6:25 has two possible English glosses. First, it may mean basically "do not desire." Fox takes this reading and supposes that the prohibition sets up the consequence in 25b, "lest you be taken."[122] Conversely, it may mean "do not *covet*" in accordance with usage in the Ten Commandments (cf. Exod 20:17; Deut 5:21). However, in the final assessment the only difference regards the English perception of covenant overtones which are significant in these paragraphs. In either case the issue is of wanting that which rightfully "belongs" to another, and is therefore a breach of covenant. Moreover, since there are only five appearances of חמד with the prohibitive לא (cf. Exod 20:17; 34:24; Deut 5:21; 7:25; Isa 53:2) and two of these appear in the Ten Commandments, it is reasonable to assume that "do not covet" is the appropriate gloss.

Do Not Commit Adultery

The text apparently reads "woman of evil" (מֵאֵשֶׁת רָע). While this reading is not impossible, "this is not the usage with the noun *ra'* elsewhere in Proverbs, and it does not produce a good parallel. The LXX's *gynaikos hypandrou* 'married woman' implicitly vocalizes the phrase as *'ešet rēa'*, lit. 'the wife of a neighbor.' This makes good sense, esp. since v 26 refers to *'ešet 'îš* and v. 29 to *'ešet rē'ēhû*."[123] At the same time, however, Baumgartner has pointed out that this emendation is problematic insofar as it defies typical usage. In every other appearance of the phrase (Prov 6:29; Exod 20:17; Lev 20:10; Deut 5:21; 22:24; Jer 5:8; Ezek 18:6, 11, 15; 22:11; 33:26) the phrase is "wife of *your* neighbor" (אֵשֶׁת רֵעֶךָ).[124] It could be that the poet wrote "bad woman" (מֵאֵשֶׁת רָע) as a deliberate play with אֵשֶׁת רֵעֶךָ and expected the overall context to make this clear. Otherwise, the poet may have written "a neighbor" without the conventional pronominal suffixes (i.e., "his" or "your") which was consequently mispointed. Regardless, the overall argument of the text repeatedly refers to one's neighbor and therefore, it is most likely that it also does so here.

---

122. Fox, *Proverbs 1–9*, 230.
123. Fox, *Proverbs 1–9*, 230.
124. Baumgartner cited in Waltke, *Proverbs 1–15*, 349.

The Blend of the Decalogue and Song of Songs

In verse 30, the poet blends elements of Song of Songs with Torah by comparing theft and adultery to emphasize the severe legal and relational ramifications of marital infidelity. Theft is represented as a legal offense in consonance with the prohibition in the Ten Commandments.[125] Traditional Jewish interpretation struggled with this line, because a thief *was* despised. Both adultery and theft were violations of the Ten Commandments, however, "people's attitudes toward it are mitigated by the circumstances prompting it."[126] As in 6:20 there is likely some hyperbole at work. It is not that a thief was *not* despised. It is more that the adulterer is despised much more.[127] Where the thief may receive pity because he is motivated by hunger, the adulterer has no excuse.[128]

Second, restitution is included in the context of theft. In Exodus, however, the theft of livestock is to be restored five-fold. The "seven-times" reference may be applying hyperbole to present the worst case scenario for one caught stealing.[129] The point of the passage is not to provide sentencing data for theft, but rather to demonstrate the greater gravity of the offense for one who attempts to "steal love."

---

125. While the word גנב is not used primarily in legal contexts in Tanakh, as one of the Ten Commandments it would be difficult to imagine this word without reference to the Law, especially since the concatenation of imperfect verbs denoting consequence gives it the feel of casuistic law. The primary context for "stealing" is in the book of Genesis, with the legal material constituting the second greatest domain. Cf. Exod 20:15; 21:16, 37; 22:1, 6–7, 11; Lev 19:11; Deut 5:19; 24:7.

126. Waltke, *Proverbs 1–15*, 235.

127. Fox, *Proverbs 1–9*, 234.

128. Waltke, *Proverbs 1–15*, 357

129. The "seven fold restitution" departs from that dictated by Torah. "The Covenant Code stipulates reimbursement plus damages of 100 percent for theft or negligence is the animal is recovered (Exod 22:3, 8) or, if the stolen animal is killed fourfold and fivefold compensation (21:37)" (Fox, *Proverbs 1–9*, 234). It seems likely that "seven fold" refers to perfect or complete restitution (cf. Gen 4:15; Lev 26:28). See Waltke, *Proverbs 1–15*, 358. In other contexts, the reference to seven-times seems to be the mark of absolute repayment. "Seven times" (שִׁבְעָתָיִם) appears only six times in Tanakh and none of those cases figure restitution for theft. Rather they figure the punishment to be inflicted upon whoever would kill Cain, the purity of the words of YHWH, and the perfected light of sun and moon in the coming judgment. Cf. Gen 4:15, 24; Ps 12:7; 79:12; Prov 6:31; Isa 30:26.

Finally then, these allusions to Torah are blended with a number of lexical and metaphorical elements that show direct correspondence between Prov 6 and Song of Songs. First, in Prov 6, "despise" (בוז) is a morphological oddity. It has only three occurrences, two of which are found in Song of Songs chapter 8 (8:1, 7). The young woman wishes that her lover was like her brother so she could kiss him and not be despised. Later she says that if one would "give all the property of his house" (יִתֵּן אִישׁ אֶת־כָּל־הוֹן בֵּיתוֹ) for love he would be despised. Since this phrase corresponds closely with that found in the b colon of verse 31 (אֶת־כָּל־הוֹן בֵּיתוֹ יִתֵּן) this appears to be a purposeful inner-biblical allusion. The only other appearance of the phrase, "all the substance of his house he will give" (אֶת־כָּל־הוֹן בֵּיתוֹ יִתֵּן:) is in Song of Solomon 8:7.[130]

Given the fact the overall context is established with relation to the prophetic metaphor MARRIAGE IS COVENANT / IDOLATRY IS ADULTERY the conceptual blend focuses upon the correct disposition of desire. The maintenance of the divine covenant is bound up not only with legal obedience and consequence but in a measured attempt to show that matters of desire and relational fidelity are the substance and basis of that covenant.

Conclusion for Stage 1: Part III

Where Prov 5 holds up the "wife of your youth" as a fountain and water source like unto YHWH, Prov 6 describes the "wife of your neighbor" as a potential *Strange Woman*. The maintenance of words, metaphor, and allusions to the Torah colors the entire treatment of gendered desire. The common sense parable of the fire helps the young man to understand that the maintenance of covenant begins with the wisdom of maintaining appropriate boundaries. Finally, the transport and blending of romantic categories into the domain of the Decalogue shows that desire is not "outside" the demands of Torah, but constituent of it. The foil of fire, theft and punishment provides a neat parallel to the promise of water, satiety and blessing.

---

130. Waltke asserts: "This conventional expression for losing everything (Song 8:7) entails that he loses his fields, his livelihood, and thus his freedom, to become a slave (see Exod 22:3b[2b]; Mic 2:2)" (Waltke, *Proverbs 1–15*, 358). However, the citations he provides do not correspond either lexically or metaphorically.

Conclusion for Stage One Perception: The Women of Proverbs 5 & 6 and Two Types of Gendered Desire

> Let your fountain be blessed, and rejoice in the wife of your youth. (Prov 5:18, ESV)

> Do not desire her beauty in your heart, and do not let her capture you with her eyelashes; (Prov 6:25, ESV)

These two verses illustrate the crux of interpretation for feminine metaphor in these chapters. In the first case, the father exhorts the youth to delight and be captivated by the feminine wiles of his wife and covenant partner. In the second case, the father exhorts his son not to desire the wife of his neighbor lest he be captured and destroyed. While the identity of the women is by no means arbitrary, the underlying exhortation is founded upon obedience and trust and resolves itself around the issue of desire. What the father exhorts is not merely *obedience* but rather *conforming the will* of the son to that which is good. As McGilchrist points out, in this way *will* is very like *belief*. As agents, our values and emotions first shape what we *perceive* as good before we can *pursue* it.[131] However, our perceptions are also altered by the way in which we interact with the world:

> The left-hemisphere disposition towards the world is that of use. Philosophy being a hyperconscious cognitive process, it may be hard to get away from the left hemisphere's perspective that will is about control, and must lie in the conscious left hemisphere. But if our disposition towards the world, our relationship with it, alters, will has a different meaning. The disposition of the right hemisphere, the nature of its attention to the world, is one of care, rather than control. Its will relates to a desire or *longing* towards something, something that lies beyond itself, towards the Other.[132]

---

131. See McGilchrist, *Master and His Emissary,* 171. McGilchrist, citing a study by Damasio points out that what we deem is "our will" is actually only that fraction of our will of which we are conscious. It is not that we are determined because we are unaware of our motives, but rather that our person may be imagined as a tree. The considerable portion that lies below the soil is no less tree than that which is above. In the same way, our *wants* are not informed by reason but rather the other way about. See McGilchrist, *Master and His Emissary,* 170. Therefore, as we consider the instruction of desire in Proverbs, the force of emotive and relational models are particularly well-attuned to engage and instruct the "subterranean" portion of our psyche.

132. McGilchrist, *Master and His Emissary,* 171.

McGilchrist's distinction between "wanting" and "longing" as two facets of desire reflected and informed in the bicameral mind is mirrored not only in the theological aesthetic of Balthasar, but also provides a helpful model for gendered desire in Proverbs. The desire for the *Strange Woman* as with that associated with "unjust gain" are "impelled, as it were 'from behind' toward something which is inert, and from which one is isolated."[133] McGilchrist compares left hemisphere desire to hydraulic force or mechanical pressure. It is a simple, unmixed, and unidirectional force. "One either wants or does not want."[134] In just this way the negative paradigms of Proverbs offer the youth an easy path to obtain pleasure or possession. They guarantee shortcuts for control and use. Longing, however, is an altogether different process. "In longing, one is drawn 'from in front' towards something from which one is already not wholly separate, and which exerts an influence through that 'division with union.'" Rather being a simple "on" or "off," longing is filled with a "between-ness"; a mix of emotions that include satiety, but stretch beyond it.[135]

> Wanting is clear, purposive, urgent, driven by the will, always with its goal clearly in view. Longing, by contrast, is something that "happens" between us and another thing. It is not directed by will, and is not an aim, with the ultimate goal of acquisition; but instead is a desire for union—or rather it is experienced as a desire for *re*-union. . . . Wanting is clear in its target, and in its separation from the thing that is wanted. Longing suggests instead a distance, but a never interrupted connection or union over that distance with whatever it is that is longed for, however remote the object of longing may be.[136]

In short, *wanting* ends either in the frustration of the desire by failing to obtain, or the devastation of desire by shallow fulfillment in the thing itself. The *Strange Woman*/"wife of your neighbor" is equivalent to left-hemisphere wanting with a single purpose which collapses in upon itself. The "wife of your youth" is equivalent to that longing which opens the youth not only to his spouse but also toward YHWH and Wisdom.

Ironically, the "wife of your neighbor" or *Strange Woman*, for all of her seductive wiles does not rise to the level of Balthasar's theological aesthetic

---

133. McGilchrist, *Master and His Emissary*, 367.
134. McGilchrist, *Master and His Emissary*, 367.
135. McGilchrist, *Master and His Emissary*, 367.
136. McGilchrist, *Master and His Emissary*, 308.

at all. However, what McGilchrist terms "longing," possesses most of the qualities that Balthasar describes in the contemplation of "worldly beauty."[137]

Stage 2 Perception: The Beauty of the Triune God Reflected in Christian Marriage and Fulfilled in Jesus

Introduction

The basis for gendered attraction is the "being-together" and "being-for-one-another of man and woman." It is one the beautiful ontic metaphors that the Trinity has provided for humanity to understand our relationship to God.[138] Rightly directed desire becomes a vehicle for understanding the LORD's love for us. "This, in turn, is the mystery that foreshadows the union of Yahweh with Israel, which is so prominently portrayed as a marriage-covenant (and then also as Israel's adultery) and which is finally fulfilled in the relationship between Christ and the Church."[139] Wrongly directed desire, as demonstrated in the *Strange Woman* is the reality and devastating cost of infidelity: dissipation and death apart from YHWH. The poet chooses to figure the youth's faithfulness to YHWH's covenant in his disposition to his wife. In a paraphrase of 1 John 4:20; "for he who does not keep the covenant with his wife that he has seen cannot keep the covenant with God whom he has not seen."[140] The New Testament explicitly maintains the image schema

---

137. For Balthasar, the experience of "worldly beauty" provides a moment of eternity that is filled not only with rapture, but with sadness. "The form, containing eternity, of the beautiful object communicates something of its supratemporality to the condition of the person who experiences it in contemplation. Nevertheless, the 'sorrow of the gods' (Göttertrauer) wafts about the beautiful form, for it must die, and the state of being blissfully enraptured always includes a knowledge of its tragic contradiction: both the act and the object contain within themselves the death that contradicts their very content" (Balthasar, *Seeing the Form*, 231).

138. Cf. Barth, *CD* 3/2:285–319. See also Balthasar, *Seeing the Form*, 374.

139. Balthasar, *Seeing the Form*, 374

140. In particular, Balthasar argues that "our neighbor" is the image of Christ which the LORD has provided for us to perceive. In this context, the "wife of our youth" stands in a similar and profound relation to YHWH. "For in faith I know that I have been redeemed by the blood of Christ, and I know therefore that you equally have been redeemed and that in you faith compels me to see, to respect, and to anticipate in action the supremely real image which the triune God has of you. In our neighbor faith is at each instant tested through the senses, and, if it is authenticated as faith, it immediately receives its sensory corroboration. For, according to John, love that is practiced contains the ability to demonstrate itself as the truth. But such love bears its proof in itself in sensory fashion only in so far as it understands itself to exist in obedience to the God who laid down his life for us. If it is love at all (and not a hidden egotism of whatever

of the marital covenant in Ephesians, even as Jesus deepens and diversifies the metaphors of *LOVE IS THIRST* and *WATER IS LIFE* in John 4.

The Witness of Ephesians 5

First, it must be noted that the parity and unity of covenant fidelity and marital fidelity is maintained in the New Testament, with the clearest example being that set forth in Eph 5:17–33.

> Wives, submit to your own husbands, as to the Lord. 23 For the husband is the head of the wife even as Christ is the head of the church, his body, and is himself its Savior. 24 Now as the church submits to Christ, so also wives should submit in everything to their husbands. 25 Husbands, love your wives, as Christ loved the church and gave himself up for her, 26 that he might sanctify her, having cleansed her by the washing of water with the word, 27 so that he might present the church to himself in splendor, without spot or wrinkle or any such thing, that she might be holy and without blemish. 28 In the same way husbands should love their wives as their own bodies. He who loves his wife loves himself. 29 For no one ever hated his own flesh, but nourishes and cherishes it, just as Christ does the church, 30 because we are members of his body. 31 "Therefore a man shall leave his father and mother and hold fast to his wife, and the two shall become one flesh." 32 This mystery is profound, and I am saying that it refers to Christ and the church. 33 However, let each one of you love his wife as himself, and let the wife see that she respects her husband. (Eph 5:17–33, ESV) .

The actions of husband and wife are not material and situational but are in fact carried up into the same sacramental understanding of covenant

---

form), it bears within itself in sensory fashion the quintessence of dogmatics. In his love for his neighbor, the Christian definitively receives his Christian senses, which, of course are no 'other' than his bodily senses, but these senses in so far as they have been formed according to the form of Christ. Whether or not Christ's historical form thereby becomes explicit to the lover is less important; love itself has this form within itself and communicates it. In a Christian sense, love is not 'act without image'; on the contrary, love is what creates image and bestows shape absolutely. Love is the creative power of God himself which has been infused into man by virtue of God's Incarnation. This is why, in the light of the divine ideas, love can read the world of forms and, in particular, man correctly. Outside of this light, man remains an incomprehensible and contradictory hieroglyph. Cross and Resurrection, understood as the love and the glory of God, bleeding to death and forsaken, render man decipherable" (Balthasar, *Seeing the Form*, 413–14).

fidelity that is witnessed in the prophets and in Proverbs. Our relational fidelity is rooted in the reality of Jesus's sacrificial love that is the foundation of the new covenant.

The Triune God as the Absolute Substance of Our Longing as Demonstrated by Jesus in John 4

Christian theological aesthetics departs and transcends even right hemisphere *longing*. In Jesus, the despair inherent in worldly aesthetic is swallowed up and transformed. "In John there can be no talk of the 'sorrow of the gods,' for the Beloved who dies dies out of love; his death is not a limitation, but the mighty expression of his love (John 10:18). Therefore, the believer does not contain death in himself as 'anguish' (as with worldly beauty) but, rather, if he really believes, he has already left anguish behind (1 John 4:14f)."[141]

This is the sort of desire described by St. Augustine:

> [Whenever man] desires he begins to notice that he is unable to satisfy himself.... But here it becomes evident that genuine and proper desiring can only be desiring God.... In the created world, man with all his neediness is always also the lord and master who knows how to make use of created things. Towards them he is not capable of genuine desiring—or only when he has apprehended that even in his desiring of created things he can first and last desire only their Creator. But in relation to the Created, there is no self-satisfaction ... he can desire and love in general.... In practice, he can and will always desire and love God Himself only in such another, in His witnesses, as the God who is active, visible, audible, and tangible in His works.[142]

Jesus shows this transcendence of longing and also uses the metaphors of *WATER IS LIFE* and *LOVE IS THIRST* in a very similar way in John 4.[143] In this chapter, we find YHWH in the person of Christ, toying with these

---

141. Balthasar, *Seeing the Form*, 231.

142. Augustine quoted in Balthasar, *Seeing the Form*, 412.

143. D. A. Carson suggests that within the book of John, the Samaritan woman exists as a foil against the respectable and learned Nicodemus (John 3). See Carson, *Gospel According to John*, 216. It is interesting to note that wisdom and epistemology play a key role in both narratives and also Jesus' engagement with each. "A religious, male, Jewish aristocrat like Nicodemus, or an untrained, female Samaritan peasant who had made a mess of her life—Jesus converses frankly with both, and happily breaks social and religious taboos to do so" (Carson, *Gospel According to John*, 216).

same metaphors and the boundaries of Wisdom and fidelity provided in Prov 5–9. Jesus, seated by Jacob's well asks a Samaritan woman for a drink, breaching both convention and the accepted mores of propriety (John 4:8–9).[144] In response to the woman's protestation that "he is a Jew," Jesus plunges headlong into the water metaphor of thirst, love, and fidelity, almost as if it is a very old inside joke.

> 11 The woman said to him, "Sir, you have nothing to draw water with, and the well is deep. Where do you get that living water? 12 Are you greater than our father Jacob? He gave us the well and drank from it himself, as did his sons and his livestock." 13 Jesus said to her, "Everyone who drinks of this water will be thirsty again, 14 but whoever drinks of the water that I will give him will never be thirsty again. The water that I will give him will become in him a spring of water welling up to eternal life." 15 The woman said to him, "Sir, give me this water, so that I will not be thirsty or have to come here to draw water." (John 4:11–15, ESV)

Jesus refers to the old metaphors of *LOVE IS THIRST* and *WATER IS LIFE*. He makes the woman aware not of a temporary "want" but of deep seated "longing." The metaphors of Jeremiah's broken cisterns and the waters of YHWH's love are already in full flood, when Jesus turns the question in a completely expected direction: that of marital fidelity.[145]

> 16 Jesus said to her, "Go, call your husband, and come here." 17 The woman answered him, "I have no husband." Jesus said to her, "You are right in saying, 'I have no husband'; 18 for you

---

144. Carson notes Mishnah *Niddah* 4:1 which "reflected [the] longstanding popular sentiment, to the effect that all 'the daughters of the Samaritans are menstruants from their cradle' and therefore perpetually in a state of uncleannees" (Carson, *Gospel According to John*, 217–18). More basically, even conversing with a woman was deemed socially questionable according to *Pirke Aboth* 1:5 and Mishnah *Sotah* 3:4. See Carson, *Gospel According to John*, 227.

145. Carson notes not only the reference to Jer 2:13, but also suggests that the water metaphor here evokes a number of related image schema: "water flowing from Jerusalem" (Zech 14:8; Ezek 47:9) and "water in the desert" (Isa 12:3; 44:3). He also suggests that the metaphor also recalls the related metaphors of *WATER IS SPIRIT* (Isa 1:16; Ezek 36:25–27). Also, following the image schema of "satiety" he suggests, "The language of inner satisfaction and transformation calls to mind a string of prophecies anticipating new hearts, the exchange of failed formalism in religion for a heart that knows and experiences God, and that hungers to do his will (Jer 31:29–34; Ezek 36:25–27; Joel 2:28–32" (Carson, *Gospel According to John*, 219–20). I would argue that while the image schema allows for these associations it is the *THIRST/SATIETY* and *LIFE* metaphors that provide the basic structure for the conceptual blend.

have had five husbands, and the one you now have is not your husband. What you have said is true." (John 4:16–18, ESV)

The question of fidelity to YHWH hinges upon marital fidelity. They are expressions of one another. From this declaration the question turns to that of religious orthodoxy and the place and the manner of worship: Questions which had accepted, orthodox, and scriptural answers, which Jesus articulately ignores.

> 22"You worship what you do not know; we worship what we know, for salvation is from the Jews. 23 But the hour is coming, and is now here, when the true worshipers will worship the Father in spirit and truth, for the Father is seeking such people to worship him. 24 God is spirit, and those who worship him must worship in spirit and truth." 25 The woman said to him, "I know that Messiah is coming (he who is called Christ). When he comes, he will tell us all things." 26 Jesus said to her, "I who speak to you am he." 27 Just then his disciples came back. They marveled that he was talking with a woman, but no one said, "What do you seek?" or, "Why are you talking with her?" (John 4:22–27, ESV)

This parity of metaphor with the *Strange Woman* of Proverbs is only deepened by Jesus reference to his "secret bread" (Prov 9:17; John 4:31–34).[146]

> 31 Meanwhile the disciples were urging him, saying, "Rabbi, eat." 32 But he said to them, "I have food to eat that you do not know about." 33 So the disciples said to one another, "Has anyone brought him something to eat?" 34 Jesus said to them, "My food is to do the will of him who sent me and to accomplish his work" (John 4:31–34, ESV).

Jesus, in obedience to his father, seems to again present his people with the question, "*Who* is strange?" The woman is a despised ethnic outsider, a theological heretic, and apostate even then. She is marginal among the marginal. In a fabulous twist, the Source of all things asks this apparently *Strange Woman* for a drink, and in case we missed the punchline, he makes sure we wouldn't overlook his secret bread. While the disciples respond with quiet shock and dismay, this woman goes with joy and wonder. "Come,

---

146. Carson argues that the reference to bread here is "almost certainly" an allusion to Deut 8:3, in which the LORD provides mana as bread which "you had not known" in order to teach the Israelites not to "live on bread alone buth on every word that comes from the mouth of the LORD" (Carson, *Gospel According to John*, 228). I do not think that allusion to the *Strange Woman* precludes the activation of the allusion to Deuteronomy, especially since both schemas pertain to *learning faithfulness*.

see a man who told me all that I ever did. Can this be the Christ?" (John 4:29, ESV).[147] As if such a thing could have come from anyone else. It is the LORD's prerogative to desire the undesirable, reach to the unreachable and bring beauty from ashes.

Conclusion

In Prov 1–4 the personification of wisdom allowed for a breadth and diversity of different conceptual blends that preserved the numinous, immanent, and paradoxical qualities of Wisdom rooted in the fear of YHWH, while simultaneously providing an avenue for her *desire*. In Prov 5–6, the poet moves away from WISDOM as the target category of the metaphor, and instead places two different kinds of WOMEN in the target space. The goal now is to "obtain human scale" not for wisdom, but for these two different sorts of women. The "wife of your youth" and the *Strange Woman/*"wife of your neighbor" are paired around antithetical image schema (i.e., WATER and FIRE) to highlight the axial role of fidelity. These antithetical images are then supplemented by different inner-canonical allusions.

The WATER image schema in Prov 5 is buttressed by imagery shared with the Prophets, and particularly Mal 2, which imports the metaphor MARRIAGE IS COVENANT and thereby shows that marital fidelity is the substance and demonstration of faithfulness to YHWH. Moreover, this framework is then supplemented with the metaphors LOVE IS THIRST as set out in the Song of Solomon 8 and WATER IS LIFE/YHWH from Jer 2. The coupling of these image schema portray the fulfillment and blessing found in the fountain of the "wife of your youth" as a conceptual parallel to the providence and blessing found in the living waters of YHWH. Marital fidelity is the means of delight, fulfillment and blessing. It is understood as like unto covenant fidelity to the LORD. Anything else is a senseless misdirection of desire.

This point is made even clearer in Prov 6:20–35 wherein the roots of *infidelity* are located in a failure to maintain appropriate boundaries for married women via the proverbial construction A MARRIED WOMAN IS

---

147. Carson notes a final return to the water metaphor that provides for a fitting conclusion in the Samaritan Woman abandoning her water jar: "Whether the woman left her water jar out of nothing more than haste as she hurried back to Sychar, or out of simple courtesy so that at last Jesus might have is drink, is not made clear. Many have suggested that, whatever her reason, John detects a profound symbolism: in her eagerness to enjoy the new and living water, she abandons the old water jar, and thus speaks of renunciation of the old ceremonial forms of religion in favor of worship in spirit and truth" (Carson, *Gospel According to John*, 227–28).

FIRE. This basic image schema is then blended with innercanonical allusions to the Shema, the Decalogue, and finally the Song of Songs. In so doing, the poet provides an undercurrent of passion and desire that fills and motivates the covenant.

Between these two antithetical image schemas gendered desire provides either for a harmonious fusion of divine pleasure and human blessing or a foolish and selfish will to destruction. The young man's relationship to women acts as a concrete expression of his fidelity to YHWH. Desire must be informed by wisdom or it will threaten wisdom. The distinction between shallow "wanting" and transcendent "longing" then becomes a part of our consideration of desire. The longing for the "wife of your youth" finds its ultimate end in the person of YHWH. The misdirected desire for the wife of another, is a shallow wanting that ends only in dissipation and loss.

The New Testament maintains marital fidelity as a vehicle for divine blessing even as the reality of Christ is meant to inform how we relate to our spouses. However, the ultimate substance of our transcendent longing is for Jesus himself, who is that fountain of living water who is capable of quenching our inner longing. In John 4 he employs the same images schemas and metaphor of Prov 5–9, but extends them and overturns them. In particular, by becoming the "living water" to the Samaritan woman Jesus points toward his own ability to bring beauty from utter dissipation, and challenges us to consider what it means to be wise and what it means to be strange. This question will be the substance of chapter 6.

6

Wise or Strange?

The Faithful, Incomparable, and Insufficient Beauty of Lady Wisdom

Introduction

THE presentation for *Lady Wisdom* in Prov 1–4 was aimed at generating an understanding of and desire for parental, covenantal wisdom via paradox. In Prov 5–6 the *Strange Woman* provided a foil for the "wife of your youth" that illustrated disparity of outcomes for the youth based upon a blend of metaphors and vocabulary for *marital* and *covenant* fidelity. This foil is now carried over into the depiction of the *Strange Woman* contra *Lady Wisdom*. Both women activate romantic categories. They employ similar metaphors and ultimately make identical appeals (Prov 9:4, 16). The apparent ambiguity of these similarities is clarified with regard to the axial role of *fidelity* and the outcomes associated.

In the chapter that follows the personification of wisdom in Prov 8 is compared to the parallel presentation of the *Strange Woman* in Prov 7 under three headings: their characterizations, their invitations, and their houses as destinations for the road of life.

The characterization of the *Strange Woman* of Prov 7 is consistent with the rest of the book, however, it is expanded by the witnessed scene between her and the חסר־לב which is structured by the Jael narrative of Judges 5. In this, the youth is portrayed not as her victim but an enemy of YHWH because of his disavowal of the covenant through his choice of infidelity. Conversely, the personification of *Lady Wisdom* continues to deepen and expand. Her personification is extended into realms of leadership and rule even as connections to her role in creation are expanded. The complex interweaving of metaphors for building and construction, childhood and delight, and ultimately *fidelity* are illustrated via a consideration of Prov 8:30.

With regard to the *invitation* of the *Strange Woman* and *Lady Wisdom* we are presented with a comparison of no comparison. The invitation of the *Strange Woman* is first of all one that ensnares with speech and misuses the metaphor and context of the cult. Her invitation is explicitly to adultery with the promise of the avoidance of consequences without the reckoning of the LORD. Conversely, the invitation of *Lady Wisdom* is the same that began in Prov 1, which is finally reissued as the blending of both covenantal and parental categories, "And now sons, listen to me . . ." (Prov 8:32). Her promise is one of lasting blessing and substance.

With regard to houses of the *Strange Woman* and *Lady Wisdom* we are presented with a unique metaphorical difficulty. *Strange Woman*'s house is explicitly associated with *Sheol* and death from Prov 2 onward. She is conceived of as the destination for those who walk in dark and crooked paths. In this way the LIFE IS A ROAD metaphor gives way to the DEATH IS A DESTINATION metaphor. When *Lady Wisdom*'s house is mentioned in the close of Prov 8 and the beginning of Prov 9, it lacks specific points of reference either canonically or with regard to external referent. It is as if the poet refuses to provide a conceptual parallel to the *Strange Woman*'s house of death. This is precisely the case. While Wisdom may allow for the avoidance of premature or unlucky death, her house cannot avoid death altogether. Wisdom's house is unmapped in the metaphor because there is not an antithetical target that can be provided for death. Therefore Wisdom's house is a nebulous something with some elements of the temple, but at the same time defying a direct equation.

Finally, we approach stage two perception by considering the person, invitation, and house of Jesus. Jesus is neither stereotype nor personification, but a divine person. The similarity between the characterization of *Lady Wisdom* and the person of Jesus Christ, is that *Lady Wisdom* is reflecting both the *reality* of YHWH and his covenant (Prov 1) and the cultivation of the best of human aims at keeping this covenant (Prov 2–4). It is not that Jesus looks like Wisdom, it is that Wisdom looks like Jesus. He is one member of the divine person, YHWH. He is the human incarnation of the Triune God. Likewise, the invitation of Wisdom sounds like the invitation of Jesus, because it echoes the invitation of YHWH in the Prophets. Matthew 11:29 provides a clear example of Jesus invitation as a fusion of wisdom, law, and prophets aimed at humanity. Finally, where the house of wisdom is confounded by death, Jesus makes the metaphor LIFE IS A DESTINATION a real counterpart to that offered by the *Strange Woman*. Jesus through the *HOUSE* of his body, founds the *HOUSE* of his church, which will come to his Father's *HOUSE* in Glory.

Imagery shared with the Prophets in tandem with the role of the *Strange Woman* as a foil both for the "wife of your youth" and *Lady Wisdom* demonstrate that the central axis for comparison has to do with covenantal and relational fidelity. Fidelity to divine covenant and human relationship then becomes the criteria for discerning wisdom. The triune person of YHWH then models this fidelity through the ultimate sacrifice in Christ which reconciles divine to human and trumps and transcends all the claims of Wisdom.

Proverbs 7:6–21

6 כִּי בְּחַלּוֹן בֵּיתִי בְּעַד אֶשְׁנַבִּי נִשְׁקָפְתִּי׃

For at the window of my house—behind the window lattice I gazed down.

7 וָאֵרֶא בַפְּתָאיִם אָבִינָה בַבָּנִים נַעַר חֲסַר־לֵב׃

And I looked at the simple ones. I discerned among the sons a young man, an empty head.

8 עֹבֵר בַּשּׁוּק אֵצֶל פִּנָּהּ וְדֶרֶךְ בֵּיתָהּ יִצְעָד׃

Crossing in the street beside her corner and the road to her house he strode.

9 בְּנֶשֶׁף־בְּעֶרֶב יוֹם בְּאִישׁוֹן לַיְלָה וַאֲפֵלָה׃

In twilight, in the evening of the day, at the beginning of night and darkness.

10 וְהִנֵּה אִשָּׁה לִקְרָאתוֹ שִׁית זוֹנָה וּנְצֻרַת לֵב׃

And look! a woman to call him. The garment of a prostitute and watching heart.

11 הֹמִיָּה הִיא וְסֹרָרֶת בְּבֵיתָהּ לֹא־יִשְׁכְּנוּ רַגְלֶיהָ׃

Roaring is she and being stubborn. In her house her feet will not abide.

12 פַּעַם ׀ בַּח֗וּץ פַּ֥עַם בָּרְחֹב֑וֹת וְאֵ֖צֶל כָּל־פִּנָּ֣ה תֶאֱרֹֽב׃

A step in the outdoors, a step in the squares and beside every corner she will lurk.

13 וְהֶחֱזִ֣יקָה בּ֭וֹ וְנָ֣שְׁקָה־לּ֑וֹ הֵעֵ֥זָה פָ֝נֶ֗יהָ וַתֹּ֣אמַר לֽוֹ׃

And she grabbed him and she kissed him and she made a bold face and she said to him,

14 זִבְחֵ֣י שְׁלָמִ֣ים עָלָ֑י הַ֝יּ֗וֹם שִׁלַּ֥מְתִּי נְדָרָֽי׃

Sacrifices of peace (are) upon me. Today I have paid my vow.

15 עַל־כֵּ֭ן יָצָ֣אתִי לִקְרָאתֶ֑ךָ לְשַׁחֵ֥ר פָּ֝נֶ֗יךָ וָאֶמְצָאֶֽךָּ׃

Therefore, I came out to call you, to seek your face. And I have found you.

16 מַ֭רְבַדִּים רָבַ֣דְתִּי עַרְשִׂ֑י חֲ֝טֻב֗וֹת אֵט֥וּן מִצְרָֽיִם׃

Covers I have covered my bed, embroidered yarn of Egypt.

17 נַ֥פְתִּי מִשְׁכָּבִ֑י מֹ֥ר אֲ֝הָלִ֗ים וְקִנָּמֽוֹן׃

I have sprinkled my bed: myrrh, aloe, and cinnamon.

18 לְכָ֤ה נִרְוֶ֣ה דֹ֭דִים עַד־הַבֹּ֑קֶר נִ֝תְעַלְּסָ֗ה בָּאֳהָבִֽים׃

Come and let us drink love until the morning. Let us delight ourselves in the love.

19 כִּ֤י אֵ֣ין הָאִ֣ישׁ בְּבֵית֑וֹ הָ֝לַ֗ךְ בְּדֶ֣רֶךְ מֵרָחֽוֹק׃

Because the man is not in the house. He has gone in a distant road.

20 צְֽרוֹר־הַ֭כֶּסֶף לָקַ֣ח בְּיָד֑וֹ לְי֥וֹם הַ֝כֵּ֗סֶא יָבֹ֥א בֵיתֽוֹ׃

The pouch of silver he took in his hand. On the day of the full moon he will come to his house.

21 הִ֭טַּתּוּ בְּרֹ֣ב לִקְחָ֑הּ בְּחֵ֥לֶק שְׂ֝פָתֶ֗יהָ תַּדִּיחֶֽנּוּ׃

She turns him aside with the abundance of her teaching. In the smoothness of her lips she compels him.

Proverbs 8:1–36

> הֲלֹא־חָכְמָה תִקְרָא וּתְבוּנָה תִּתֵּן קוֹלָהּ׃
>
> Does not Wisdom call out[1]? And Understanding[2] give her voice[3]?

1. Fox translates, "Listen, isn't that Wisdom calling?" because he believes that it is clear that *someone* is calling, but the question is *whom* (Fox, *Proverbs 1–9*, 265). Unfortunately it is difficult to bear out Fox's assertion with reference to canonical context. In 1 Sam 26:14, 26, David does call out to Abner, and is unrecognized. However, in Num 22:37, Balaak inquires of Balaam, "Did I not send . . . Did I not call?" The implication is that he *has* called, and Balaam recognized the call but did not respond. Within the Writings the usage also is not very helpful. In Psalms 14:4; 53:5, the question regards the people's lack of knowledge (i.e., "do you not know?") that causes them not to call out to YHWH. Finally, in Jer 3:4, the vocabulary of *COVENANT IS MARRIAGE* is invoked, but again it is the people who have not called out. Waltke notes that both the LXX and Syriac omit the feminine personification here, however, this does not accord with the 3fs pronoun in the b colon. See Waltke, *Proverbs 1–15*, 386. It is better to translate with Waltke, "Does not Wisdom call out?" "It connotes that Wisdom makes her proclamation heard far and wide and does not wait for an audience to come to her" (Waltke, *Proverbs 1–15*, 394).

2. Due to the 3fs pronoun in 8:2, it appears that personified "Understanding" (תבונה) is co-referential with "Wisdom" (חכמה) as in Prov 2:3. See Waltke, *Proverbs 1–15*, 394; Loader, *Proverbs 1–9*, 325.

3. The phrase "give voice" (נתן קול) seems to be an apparent Hebrew idiom, equivalent to the English "raise one's voice." See Waltke, *Proverbs 1–15*, 394. This is not entirely borne out by usage. There are only a dozen or so occurrences in *Tanakh*. Of these uses, it is associated with the voice of YHWH. Of these cases a number are explicitly associated with thunder (Exod 9:23; 1 Sam 12:17; 2 Sam 22:14; Ps 18:14). Other cases may refer to the actual speech of YHWH (Jer 25:30; Joel 2:11; 4:16; Amos 1:2). In a few contexts it is used to describe the noise of animals: birds (Ps 104:12) and lions (Jer 2:15). The remaining three cases (outside of Proverbs) fall into two contexts. In 2 Chron 24:9, it is used with regard to reporting the content of a command to the community. In Jer 22:20, it is listed as a command in parallel with "cry" (צעק) as a prophetic declamation against Lebanon and Bashan. Likewise in Jer 48:34 (again parallel to צעק) it is used not as an imperative, but rather as a narrative form describing the grief of Moab. Therefore, the two options seem to be of "simple report" or "grief and desperation." While Waltke's assertion that the phrase "escalates fervency" (Waltke, 394) is likely correct, in all other similar contexts that fervency is combined with an element of *grief*. It is, however, important to note that the choice of verbs (נתן קול/קרא) is precisely parallel to the Father's exhortation to the son in Prov 2:3. Wisdom calls to the youth in the same manner that the youth is instructed to call to Wisdom.

> 2 בְּרֹאשׁ־מְרוֹמִ֥ים עֲלֵי־דָ֑רֶךְ בֵּ֖ית נְתִיב֣וֹת נִצָּֽבָה׃
>
> Atop the heights,[4] upon the road[5] between paths[6] she positioned herself.[7]

4. "Some commentators (e.g., Meinhold) identify the $m^e rômîm$ as the city walls; others believe it means thoroughfares (Toy). But $m^e rômîm$ (used literally) denotes only natural high spots—hills or the heavens—not constructed high objects such as highways and city walls. While one can speak of the $mārôm$ ('top') of a man-made structure (see Jer 51:53), only natural objects are themselves called $m^e rômîm$). [sic] The phrase $roš\ m^e rômîm$ is probably to be distinguished from $roš\ derek$, the beginning of a road, which is usually where several roads converge, as in Ezek 21:26" (Fox, *Proverbs 1-9*, 265).

5. In most contexts, "upon the road" (עלי דרך) means either journeying *in* a way or lying beside it (cf. Gen 49:17; Judg 5:10; 1 Sam 6:12; Job 19:12; 22:28; Isa 49:9; Hos 13:7). A few of these appear within the prophetic COVENANT IS MARRIAGE metaphor as well (Jer 3:2; 6:16).

6. Fox correctly indicates that this colon should be seen as an extension and restatement of the a colon and therefore refers to the same place. Ezekiel 16:25 uses the same reference for a prostitute (as does Jer 3:2 for adulterous Israel). See Fox, *Proverbs 1-9*, 266. As in the discussion of Prov 1, the issue at stake is again public exposure.

7. Both Loader and Waltke believe that the verb "positioned herself" (נצב) suggests that Wisdom comes to a place of some prominence to address the public especially since it appears in the perfective form. See Loader, *Proverbs 1-9*, 326; Waltke, *Proverbs 1-15*, 394.

3 לְיַד־שְׁעָרִ֥ים לְפִי־קָ֑רֶת מְב֖וֹא פְתָחִ֣ים תָּרֹֽנָּה׃

To the hand[8] of [the] gates, to the mouth of the city[9] [at] the entrance of the openings[10] she will shout.[11]

4 אֲלֵיכֶ֣ם אִישִׁ֣ים אֶקְרָ֑א וְ֝קוֹלִ֗י אֶל־בְּנֵ֥י אָדָֽם׃

To you[12] [mp] men[13] I will call[14] and my voice to the sons of Adam.

5 הָבִ֣ינוּ פְתָאיִ֣ם עָרְמָ֑ה וּ֝כְסִילִ֗ים הָבִ֥ינוּ לֵֽב׃

Discern, simple ones, subtlety, and stupid ones discern heart.[15]

---

8. There are a few contexts in which "to the hand" (ליד) means "beside" or "with." In a number of cases it refers to being in association or under the supervision of people (cf. 1 Sam 19:3; 1 Chr 18:17; 23:28; Neh 11:24). In only two cases it means "beside": a "track" (Ps 140:6) and "gates" (here).

9. The phrase "mouth of the city" (לְפִי־קָרֶת) finds no parallel occurrence in Tanakh. "Mouth" is used metaphorically for the "entrance" of the city. Due to the proximity of "head" (ראש), "hand" (יד) with "mouth" (פה), Van Leeuwen assumes that the basic metaphor in this case is that CITY IS A WOMAN. See Van Leeuwen, "Book of Proverbs," 89. However, it is unclear what the poet would be intending to accomplish by such a metaphor in this place. It is not the extension of previous metaphor. It does not provide the image schema for any additional metaphor, nor does it activate other scriptural contexts. Likewise, the word "city" (קרת), apparently a loan word from Hittite, has only five occurrences in Tanakh (Job 29:7; Prov 8:3; 9:3, 14; 11:11) and does not provide any metaphorical ground (*HALOT* s.v. "קֶרֶת"). The unique word choice does provide an easy pairing with the women of Prov 9:3 and 14, however.

10. "Lit. the entry of the openings; in other words, not within the gate passageway or chambers, but the outer opening of the gateway, where everyone entering or leaving the city or conducting business in the gate would hear the speaker. Both *lepiy qaret* 'at the city entrance' and *mebo' petahim* 'at the portals' describe the gate from an external perspective. 'Openings' (*petahim*) are the apertures giving access to the gate proper, the *šaar*. This is where Absalom stood when he sought to curry favor with the populace" (Fox, *Proverbs 1–9*, 266).

11. Based on a parallel with 1 Kgs 22:36, Fox believes that the verb for רנן ("cry out" or "shout") indicates that "wisdom is acting the part of a royal herald" (Fox, *Proverbs 1–9*, 266).

12. The audience, "to you (mp)" is fronted for emphasis. See Fox, *Proverbs 1–9*, 267.

13. While it is customary in Phoenician, the peculiar plural of "men" (אִישִׁים) appears only here, Ps 141:4 and Isa 53:3 (Loader, *Proverbs 1–9*, 327). Fox rejects the traditional rabbinic interpretation of איש and בני אדם as a merism for poor and wealthy of mankind. Rather it is to be deemed as a universal call to all mankind. See Fox, *Proverbs 1–9*, 267.

14. The pairing of "calling" (קרא) and "voice" (קול) recall both 8:1 and 1:20.

15. Again, the better English translation would be "discern brain" as the "heart" functions here not as a metonymy for emotion, but of will and intellect.

> 6 שִׁמְעוּ כִּי־נְגִידִים אֲדַבֵּר וּמִפְתַּח שְׂפָתַי מֵישָׁרִים׃
>
> Hear, that direct things[16] I will speak and the opening of my lips is rectitude.
>
> 7 כִּי־אֱמֶת יֶהְגֶּה חִכִּי וְתוֹעֲבַת שְׂפָתַי רֶשַׁע׃
>
> Because[17] truth[18] my palate[19] will mutter and the abomination of my lips[20] is wickedness.

16. The translation of נְגִידִים as "noble" (cf. NRSV; NIV; ESV; KJV) creates difficulty within the parallel line. The underlying metaphor with regard to speech is *TRUE IS STRAIGHT* and it informs not only this line, but also 8:9. See Loader, *Proverbs 1–9*, 328–29.

17. The epexegetic function of the כי signals the justification of the assertion in v. 6, coupled with the fronting of "truth" (אמת) it "emphasizes that the religio-ethical dimension of Wisdom's speech (vv. 6–7) is essential for understanding ultimate truth" (Waltke, *Proverbs 1–15*, 397).

18. "Truth" (אמת) is fronted in order to show emphasis, because "it is axiomatic in Proverbs that genuine intelligence is inherently and inevitably honest" (Fox, *Proverbs 1–9*, 269). M. Gilbert notes that the depiction of Wisdom's speech is lexically and structurally very similar to the portrayal of YHWH's speech in Deut 32:4–5. "Truth" (אמת) is opposed to "wickedness" (רשע) in Prov 8:7 as "trustworthiness" (אמונה) is opposed to "iniquity" (עול) in Deut 32:4. The parallel in Prov 8:8 and Deut 32:5 employs the same roots with "righteousness" (צדק) being opposed to "twisted" (עקש) and "tortuous" (פתל). See Gilbert, "Le Discourse Meneçant de Sagesse," 99–119. "Moreover, the Deuteronomy text uses several similar terms to bolster the argument (תמם [upright], משפט [justice], ישר [right], all of them semantically related to the terminology used in vv. 7–8 and also v. 6" (Loader, *Proverbs 1–9*, 329).

19. The references to the organs of speech: "lips" (שפתים) and "palate" (חק) are metonymies for speech, but also provide an internal allusion to the speech of the *Strange Woman* in Proverbs 5:3. See Van Leeuwen, "Book of Proverbs," 91.

20. The LXX alters the reading to "an abomination before me are untruthful lips" (ἐβδελυγμένα δὲ ἐναντίον ἐμοῦ χείλη ψευδῆ). However, there is no need to alter the text, as the phrase וְתוֹעֲבַת שְׂפָתַי is a genitive construct. See Loader, *Proverbs 1–9*, 330. Moreover, the phrase provides linkages to "abomination to YHWH" which is frequent, especially in the second half of the book (cf. Prov 3:32; 6:16; 8:7; 11:1, 20; 12:22; 13:19; 15:8–9, 26; 16:5, 12; 17:15; 20:10, 23; 21:27; 24:9; 26:25; 28:9; 29:27). See Murphy, *Proverbs*, 50.

> 8 בְּצֶדֶק כָּל־אִמְרֵי־פִי אֵין בָּהֶם נִפְתָּל וְעִקֵּשׁ׃
>
> In righteousness are all[21] the words of my mouth. There is not with among them [one] tortuous[22] and twisting.[23]
>
> 9 כֻּלָּם נְכֹחִים לַמֵּבִין וִישָׁרִים לְמֹצְאֵי דָעַת׃
>
> All of them are straightforward[24] to the discerning[25] and straight to the ones finding knowledge.

21. "All" (כול) appears in parallel with its negative counterpart providing for no loophole provided for dissimulation. Coupled with the repeated "all of them" (כֻּלָּם) in 9a, "underscores that not one of her words is exempted from these six qualifications" (Waltke, *Proverbs 1–15*, 398). Fox argues that the moral component of Wisdom is particular to Proverbs, citing the argument of Eliphaz from the book of Job: "A comparison between Job 5:13 and this verse [v. 8] highlights the distinctiveness of Proverbs' concept of wisdom. Eliphaz says that God 'captures the wise (*ḥăkāmîm*) in their cunning, and the plans of tricky men (*niptālîm*) are dashed.' Eliphaz (whose discourses have many sapiential features) can place *ḥăkāmîm* and *niptālîm* in synonymous parallelism in referring to the same type of people: those whose plans can offend God. (More precisely, *niptālîm* narrows the scope of *ḥăkāmîm*: those wise men who are tricky.) In Prov 8:8, by contrast, Wisdom insists that she speaks only true, straight things; never a contorted word. And as Wisdom speaks, so do the wise, all of them" (Fox, *Proverbs 1–9*, 270). First, there is some question as to whether Eliphaz should be used as the "standard" given his somewhat tenuous role as an authority in the book. Second, the concept of wisdom is not monolithic in definition or metaphor in *Tanakh*. It is better to consider Proverbs not as "deviant" but as *corrective*.

22. "Tortuous" (עקש) and "twisting" (פתל) are frequently listed together or in parallel in Tanakh and may constitute a lexical collocation (cf. Deut 32:5; 2 Sam 22:17; Ps 18:27[28]). Structurally, the binding of the two terms provides for parity with the other verses of 6–9. See Waltke, *Proverbs 1–15*, 398. However, it is important to note that these descriptions are applied metaphorically both to "roads" and "speech."

23. "The physical imagery of ethics throughout Prov 1–9 is consistent: Honesty is bright, straight, directly to the front. Dishonesty is dark, crooked, and off to the side—a departure from the right and bright path" (Fox, *Proverbs 1–9*, 269–70).

24. "The adjective/substantive *nākōaḥ* is almost always used metaphorically in the sense of forthright and honest" (Fox, *Proverbs 1–9*, 270). Cf. Isa 30:10; 59:14.

25. Where v. 8 seems to suggest that wisdom may be learned by all, v. 9 provides an important qualification. "The real issue in this verse is not so much the truth of Wisdom's words (which is declared in vv. 6–8) as how they are to be perceived. Riyqam points out the gist of the verse by stating its obverse: 'But in the eyes of the fool they will seem contrary and contradictory to one another'" (Fox, *Proverbs 1–9*, 270).

10 קְחוּ־מוּסָרִי וְאַל־כָּסֶף וְדַעַת מֵחָרוּץ נִבְחָר׃

Take[26] my discipline[27] and not silver[28] and knowledge before[29] choice gold.[30]

---

26. Waltke translates קְחוּ as "choose" due to its association with שמע ("listen") as a "telic counterpart" (Waltke, *Proverbs 1–15*, 399). However, this English gloss is reserved for בחר and related roots in this translation. It is sufficient to point out that לקח "normally has the educational nuance of accepting what is true (cf. 1:5; 2:1; 24:32) or false (6:25; 7:21; 22:24–25), not of developing an independent critical faculty. Whatever you take takes you" (Waltke, *Proverbs 1–15*, 399).

27. The LXX, Targum, Peshitta, and one Hebrew witness omit the 1cs pronominal suffix. Toy and Fox argue that this omission provides better parallelism with דעת in the second colon. Fox, in particular, argues that the י came about through י for ו dittography (Fox, *Proverbs 1–9*, 270. However, the omission of the pronominal suffix scarcely alters the meaning of the line overall, and is entirely permissible within the conventions of Hebrew poetry. See Loader, *Proverbs 1–9*, 332.

28. Silver (כסף) and gold (זהב) may both be read as metonymic representations of "wealth." There is some question regarding the exact nuance of this line. Does the verse warn against the *love* of money which may usurp the place of wisdom and cast it down? So reads Waltke, "When made the aim of one's life, it corrupts (1 Tim 6:9). Wisdom will brook no rival. If one loves riches—and one loves either wisdom or riches, there is no third way (Matt 6:24)—wisdom will withdraw herself, leaving the person at best a rich fool for a while but headed for eternal death" (Waltke, *Proverbs 1–15*, 399). Fox and Loader both disagree on the grounds that riches are not so figured within the theology of Proverbs. They are a valuable and worthwhile reward, and are merely used to demonstrate the superlative value of Wisdom. In this case, ואל is read not as "instead of" but rather as a comparative like מן in the second colon (see Loader, *Proverbs 1–9*, 331; Fox, *Proverbs 1–9*, 270). Ultimately, the seemingly divergent views are not so divergent. The book of Proverbs states explicitly that the pursuit of riches for their own sake is folly (Prov 23:4). Likewise the NT's cautions regarding riches are aimed at the love of money over the love of God and others. The exhortation is both comparative and cautionary.

29. In order to preserve the comparative element the omparative מ has been translated here with "before" in place of "rather than."

30. Van Leeuwen notes that the direct quotation of 3:15 coupled with that in 8:11 foreshadows the embodiment of Wisdom in the *Woman of Valor* in Prov 31:10, thereby strengthening the connections between WISDOM AS WOMAN and WISDOM AS WIFE (Van Leeuwen, "Book of Proverbs," 91).

> 11 כִּי־טוֹבָה חָכְמָה מִפְּנִינִים וְכָל־חֲפָצִים לֹא יִשְׁווּ־בָהּ׃
>
> Indeed[31] Wisdom is better than pearls and all delights[32] will not compare with her.

---

31. Some scholars believe that v. 11 is a gloss, due largely to the similarity with Prov 3:15 and the fact that the third-person verbs are out of sorts with the larger flow of the first-person argument (Murphy, *Proverbs 1–9*, 50; Waltke, *Proverbs 1–15*, 388; Skehan, "Structures in Poems," 368; Meinhold, *Die Sprüche*, 1:137). However, there are substantial reasons to avoid emending the text. First, the lack of the verse is not attested in Hebrew manuscript. Second, despite the similarities in the generic form (i.e., "better than proverbs") the verses are not identical. Third, the shift from first to third person is by no means unconventional in Hebrew poetry. "The whole poem is a eulogy *on* wisdom *by* Wisdom, the very character of which attenuates the divide between the first-person personified Wisdom and the third person wisdom in its non-personified dimension and makes the use of both forms natural. Precisely for that reason the use of material occurring in another chapter (as, for instance, in 3:3 compared with 6:21 and 7:3) does not have to be a sign of a secondary addition, but can equally well—and here does—testify to sensible intertextuality" (Loader, *Proverbs 1–9*, 333).

32. In Prov 3:15 the word חֲפָצֶיךָ should be translated as "your business" because the broader context and image metaphor dealt with the *profit* of commerce in precious metals and jewels. In this case commerce is not in view, rather the comparative is with regard to the value of the things themselves. It is difficult to determine whether the noun should then be translated as "desires" in parity with "silver" and "gold" or whether it should be translated in analogy with Prov 3:15. Due to the lack of the personal pronoun, and to agree with the parallel it is here translated as "delights."

> 12 אֲנִי־חָכְמָה שָׁכַנְתִּי עָרְמָה וְדַעַת מְזִמּוֹת אֶמְצָא:
>
> I am wisdom.[33] I dwell subtly[34] but[35] knowledge[36] of discernment I find.[37]

33. Fox believes that this self-introduction demonstrates parity with one by Isis in the aretology of Cyme (Fox, *Proverbs 1-9*, 336-40). However, the "self-declaratory" reading of the Egyptian, may be an appositional rather than introductory. Moreover, the following sentences do not strengthen the comparison (Loader, *Proverbs 1-9*, 334). Zaban and Loader both argue that the function of this clause is not so much to introduce Wisdom, but to explain her relationship with the following string of wisdom lexemes (Loader, *Proverbs 1-9*, 334; Zaban, *Pillar Function*, 122).

34. Waltke and Loader both translate שָׁכַנְתִּי as "dwell with" (Loader, *Proverbs 1-9*, 334; Waltke, *Proverbs 1-15*, 400). In this reading, "shrewdness" (עָרְמָה) is read according to the image metaphor of a woman, and "shrewdness" is therefore viewed as a feminine counterpart to Wisdom. Fox translates "shrewdness" not as a feminine personification, but rather as a *locale*. "Wisdom has, as it were, moved into the territory of *'ormah* and made it her own" (Fox, *Proverbs 1-9*, 271). Fox points out that the appearance of the verb + the accusative *without* the preposition in other cases means to "dwell *in* or *at* (e.g., 2:21; 10:30; Isa 33:16; Job 4:19)" (Fox, *Proverbs 1-9*, 271). However, the appearance of the verb "dwell" when referring to location much more frequently appears with a preposition indicating that locale (e.g., Gen 3:24; 9:27; 14:13; 25:18; Exod 29:45). It is more reasonable to assume that the feminine nominal form עָרְמָה is functioning like the ms form בֶּטַח in Prov 1:33 (cf. Deut 33:12; Ps 16:9; Jer 23:6; 33:16). The phrase וְשָׁמַע לִי יִשְׁכָּן־בֶּטַח being glossed as "he will dwell securely" thereby provides an analog in this case, "I will dwell subtly" or "I will dwell cunningly." Not only does this make more sense with the syntax of the line, it also explains the extension in the b colon. Wisdom is subtle and difficult to find, but she *finds* the knowledge of discernment.

35. By reading the first colon as the "subtle dwelling" of Wisdom, the second colon may be read as an antithetical statement introduced by a disjunctive *waw*.

36. Waltke provides a conjunction and thereby separates "knowledge" and "discretion" into compound objects, though he provides no rationale for this emendation. The two terms are listed separately as objects in the prologue (1:4). It is best to take the phrase as a genitive construction, "knowledge of discrete ways to conduct oneself" (Loader, *Proverbs 1-9*, 334). The subtlety of wisdom, coupled with this ability then provides an excellent transition to the next section dealing with leadership.

37. The imperfect form of "find" (מצא) may be translated as a simple future tense, or it may be taken as an iterative, which speaks not of possession, but rather pictures Wisdom "describing herself in terms of wise human behavior" (Fox, *Proverbs 1-9*, 272). However, there is an intensification implied insofar as the qualities promised to be *given* in the Prologue (e.g., 1:4) "are qualities already at the disposal of Wisdom" (Loader, *Proverbs 1-9*, 335).

13 יִרְאַת יְהוָֹה שְֹנֹאת רָע גֵּאָה וְגָאוֹן | וְדֶרֶךְ רָע וּפִי תַהְפֻּכוֹת שָׂנֵאתִי:

The[38] fear of Yahweh[39] [is] to hate evil, arrogance,[40] and pride[41] and the evil road and the mouth of perversity[42] I hate.

---

38. Some scholars view v. 13 as a secondary accretion (as v. 11). Fox, for example, argues that the verse is likely a "pious addition" to offset the possible amoral interpretation of v. 12 (Fox, *Proverbs 1–9*, 272). Like verse 11, the verse bears considerable similarity to parallel statements in Wisdom literature (cf. Job 28:28; Prov 3:17; 16:16) and shifts the voice from first to third-person. However, the reasons for retaining the verse far outnumber those to excise it. First, the context has no need of additional piety. All of the previous verses employ the same metaphorical image schema as employed for parental instruction and Torah. Second, (as in v. 11) the other texts (e.g., Prov 3:17; 16:16) are not identical with this verse, but are adapted. Third, the verse is attested in all ancient versions. See Loader, *Proverbs 1–9*, 336.

39. Camp sees the fs construct "fear of YHWH" (יִרְאַת יְהוָֹה) as a later addition which provides a parallel with Prov 31:30 (Camp, *Feminine*, 95). While this is possible, it is difficult to see how broader textual allusion is at work.

40. "The contrasting association of arrogance (and its mastering) with the Fear of God is so basic that it is incorporated in the trendsetting prologue of 1:1–7. There the Fear of God is not just a pious pendant to go with the opposites of arrogance (cf. 1:2, 3, 7b). Hubris is the basic obstruction to the acquisition of wisdom because it undercuts the acceptance of authority, which ultimately derives from God. Therefore Lady Wisdom's hatred of arrogance harmonises with the motif of the Fear of God" (Loader, *Proverbs 1–9*, 336).

41. This verse is not provided with an *atnaḥ* which complicates the division of the phrase. Since Fox drops the first four words (יִרְאַת יְהוָֹה שְֹנֹאת רָע) he divides after "road" (דרך). Other commentators divide the verse intro tri (Waltke, *Proverbs 1–15*, 263) or tetra colon (Loader, *Proverbs 1–9*, 316) due to the unusual Masoretic accentuation. However, the Masoretes did supply a *Paseq*. By following this accentuation each colon is divided into roughly 11 syllables, with basically two objects on each side, with the "hatred" characteristic of the Fear of YHWH associated on one side and the "hatred" characteristic of wisdom on the other.

42. Reference to both the "evil road" (דֶרֶךְ רָע) and perverse speech (תַהְפֻּכוֹת) activate the previous context of Prov 2:15 (:לְהַצִּילְךָ מִדֶּרֶךְ רָע מֵאִישׁ מְדַבֵּר תַּהְפֻּכוֹת).

WISE OR STRANGE? 177

> 14 לִי־עֵצָה וְתוּשִׁיָּה אֲנִי בִינָה לִי גְבוּרָה:
>
> Mine are counsel[43] and resource. I am discernment.[44] Mine is might.

---

43. The words "counsel" (עצה), "resource" (תושיה) and "might" (גבר) provide the foundation for the discussion of leadership that follows. The plan (עצה) requires "the practical efficiency needed to attain it and גבורה is the power to put it into effect" (Loader, *Proverbs 1–9*, 336). Moreover, vv. 13–14 contain numerous lexical connections to Isa 11:2. While it would be incorrect to suppose that all Israelite kings bore these qualities (Loader, *Proverbs 1–9*, 337; Fox, *Proverbs 1–9*, 273), in Isa 11:2 the coming Davidic King is described in exactly these terms. This parallel becomes important because, "This cluster of attributes brings Wisdom very close to the LORD himself, for according to Job 12:13 he too possess what she claims as her possessions. These heavenly qualities are needed by a ruler (see 8:15). Isaiah attributes the dynamic Spirit of the LORD as their mediator to the messianic King (Isa 11:2), but Wisdom mediates them to those who love her. Jesus Christ alone achieved them perfectly, and he has become 'wisdom' from God for his church" (Waltke, *Proverbs 1–15*, 402). See Van Leeuwen, "Book of Proverbs," 91.

44. Some commentators have endeavored to dissolve this identification and add "understanding" (בינה) to the list of attributes possessed by Wisdom following the LXX. However, בינה is an identification for Lady Wisdom in 2:3; 4:5, 7, where the other nouns are not so identified. See Fox, *Proverbs 1–9*, 273.

> 15 בִּי מְלָכִים יִמְלֹכוּ וְרוֹזְנִים יְחֹקְקוּ צֶדֶק׃
>
> With me[45] kings[46] will king[47] and rulers[48] decree[49] righteousness.
>
> 16 בִּי שָׂרִים יָשֹׂרוּ וּנְדִיבִים כָּל־שֹׁפְטֵי צֶדֶק׃
>
> With me princes prince and nobles[50] are all judges of righteousness.[51]

45. Wisdom asserts in the phrase "with me" (בִּי) that "all royal functions are done in accordance with her authority and gifts" (Van Leeuwen, "Book of Proverbs," 91). Loader argues that the image metaphor employed in this case is that of divine patronage. Referencing a hymn to Marduk and another of Hammurabi he argues, cogently, that the king was responsible to uphold divine justice, and was therefore empowered with divine wisdom and ability. "Similarly, in asserting where Yahweh alone was to be worshiped, Wisdom declares that all kings and rulers on the earth (v. 16b, NIV) carry out their functions 'by/with me'—that is, by using Wisdom's gifts of insight, justice, and state craft according to her cosmic standards, as determined by Yahweh at creation. The cosmic connection with human government is a common presupposition of ancient Near Eastern and biblical thought. In this text it is spelled out by means of a series of wordplays on the thematic Hebrew root חקק ($ḥqq$). Just as the Lord 'marked out' (חקק $ḥāqaq$) the horizon on the face of the dep' and 'gave to the sea its boundary' ($ḥāqaq$), and as God 'marked out' ($ḥāqaq$) 'the foundations of the earth' (vv. 27, 29), so also do human rulers 'decree' ($ḥāqaq$) 'what is just' (v. 15)" (Loader, *Proverbs 1-9*, 338).

46. The poet begins with the most important of the referents to rulers, and then proceeds down this list. A king may rule a city-state, country, territory or tribe (cf. 14:28; 16:10–16; 19:10, 12; 22:29; 24:21; 25:1–7; 29:4, 14; 30:31; 31:4). Waltke, *Proverbs 1-15*, 402–3.

47. Verses 15, 16 both begin with an anaphora followed by a *figura etymologica*, "which suggests and emphasizes the unity of the principle expressed here—not that there are different kinds of rulers, but the principle that their work can only be done justly if it is done in Wisdom" (Loader, *Proverbs 1-9*, 338).

48. The word glossed as "rulers" (רזן) is always found in parallel with "king" (מלך) (with the exception of Isa 40:23) but refers only to foreign officials. See Fox, *Proverbs 1-9*, 273.

49. The word (חקק) may be glossed as "inscribe" or "engrave" (cf. Job 19:23; Isa 10:1; 30:8; Prov 31:5; Isa 10:1; Jer 31:35). See Fox, *Proverbs 1-9*, 274. It is likely that the word is employed to provide a catchword to activate the imagery of YHWH's work in creation (v. 29). See Waltke, *Proverbs 1-15*, 305.

50. This likely refers to officials or members of the royal court (cf. 17:7). See Waltke, *Proverbs 1-15*, 403.

51. Waltke argues that the verb from the a colon "prince" (שר) is gapped into the second colon (Waltke, *Proverbs 1-15*, 403). The *figura etymologica* doesn't work nearly so well in the second colon. Grammatically reading the b colon as a verbless clause with implied copulative provides a much smoother reading and makes better sense with context.

17 אֲנִי (אֹהֲבֶיהָ) [אֹהֲבַי] אֵהָב וּמְשַׁחֲרַי יִמְצָאֻנְנִי׃

I,[52] the ones loving me[53] I will love and the ones seeking me will find me.

18 עֹשֶׁר־וְכָבוֹד אִתִּי הוֹן עָתֵק וּצְדָקָה׃

Wealth and honor[54] are with me[55]—venerable[56] wealth and righteousness.[57]

---

52. The fronted and superfluous pronoun serves to emphasize the speaker and also mark the next movement of the poem. See Waltke, *Proverbs 1–15*, 404.

53. The *qere*, "the ones loving me" (אֹהֲבַי) makes better sense with the fronted pronoun than the *kethib*, "ones loving her" (אֹהֲבֶיהָ). Kayatz argues the third person form preserves an originally Egyptian form, but cites no example. See Kayatz, *Studien Zu Proverbien 1–9*, 102.

54. Fox believes that the stereotypical pair of "wealth" (עשר) and "honor" (כבוד) may here be read as a hendiadys meaning "honorable wealth" citing the fact that the wealth and honor received by Solomon in 1 Kgs 3:13 initially appeared only as "wealth" in 1 Kgs 3:11 (Fox, *Proverbs 1–9*, 277). This would provide for a neat parallel between the first and second colon in which the permanence and substance of wealth is directly linked to the righteous means by which it is attained. See Loader, *Proverbs 1–9*, 341. See also 1 Kgs 3:13; 1 Chr 29:12, 28; 2 Chr 1:11–12; 17:5; 18:1; 32:27; Esth 1:4; 5:11; Ps 49:17; Prov 3:16; 8:18; 11:16; 22:4; Eccl 6:2.

55. In Prov 3:16, the goods of "wealth" and "honor" are catalogued as goods that *belonged* to Wisdom and therefore by implication at her disposal. In this case, the grammar does not clearly express *possession* (i.e., לִי) as it does in 3:16. Rather, Wisdom declares that these goods are "with her." It is possible to read "with me" (אִתִּי) as an implicit declaration of possession (e.g., Judg 17:2; Ps 38:11; 66:20; Prov 8:18) but it is much more common that the declaration is associative (Gen 14:24; 30:29, 33; 33:15; 39:8; 42:33; 43:8, 16; 44:28, 34; Exod 20:23; 33:21; Num 23:13; Josh 8:5; 14:12; Judg 1:3; 7:18; 11:27; 16:15; 1 Sam 16:5; 17:9; 22:23; 24:19; 26:6; 28:1; 29:3, 6; 2 Sam 3:12; 15:33; 19:34, 39; 1 Kgs 12:24; 13:7, 15; 20:36; 22:4, 24; 2 Kgs 3:7; 9:32; 10:16; 18:31; 2 Chr 11:4; 18:23; Job 19:4; Ps 34:4; 109:2, 21; Song 4:8; Isa 36:16; 44:24; 50:8; 51:4; 54:17; 57:8; 63:3; Jer 13:25; 20:11; 40:4; 51:53; Ezek 3:24; Mal 2:6). Therefore, while these are listed as her possessions in 3:16, here, they are attendant values to be found in her company. For a contrary view, see Waltke, *Proverbs 1–15*, 404.

56. HALOT reads as "time-honored" or "venerable" (*HALOT* s.v. "עָתֵק"). "Both *ʿattîq* ʿand *ʿātēq* are adjectival forms from ʿ-t-q, so the equation is reasonable. The ability to endure, demonstrated by something's antiquity, is transposed into the future" (Fox, *Proverbs 1–9*, 277).

57. Although NRSV translates as צדקה "prosperity" based upon a cause-for-effect metonymy, there is no reason to provide any special sense. As noted, the accent in this line is upon material outcomes being predicated by correct moral and ethical means. See Fox, *Proverbs 1–9*, 278.

> 19 טוֹב פִּרְיִי מֵחָרוּץ וּמִפָּז וּתְבוּאָתִי מִכֶּסֶף נִבְחָר׃
>
> Better is my fruit[58] than pure gold and even refined gold. My produce is better than choice silver.[59]
>
> 20 בְּאֹרַח־צְדָקָה אֲהַלֵּךְ בְּתוֹךְ נְתִיבוֹת מִשְׁפָּט׃
>
> In [the] path of righteousness[60] I will walk,[61] in the midst[62] of tracks of judgment.

58. Waltke and Loader refer to the reference of "fruit" (פרי) and "produce" (תבואת) as an "incomplete" or "partial metaphor" (Waltke, *Proverbs 1–15*, 405; Loader, *Proverbs 1–9*, 341). It is easier to see this line as a blend of the "commerce" metaphor of Prov 3:14, which provides for the association of תבואת and the words for precious metals, with the common metaphor FRUIT IS OUTCOME (OF ACTIONS) which is common in Proverbs (cf. Prov 1:31; 8:19; 11:30; 12:14; 13:2; 18:20–21; 27:18; 31:16, 31). Both allegedly "incomplete" metaphors are, therefore, singular. The "fruit" and "produce" (synonyms) are outcomes and values that derive from wisdom. These are to be preferred to treasure. "In the present text, Wisdom takes a precautionary step away from her enthusiastic promise of material blessing to remind us (in an echo of v. 10) that wealth is still inferior to the fruits of wisdom, which are intellectual and ethical, not only material" (Fox, *Proverbs 1–9*, 278).

59. Fox and Waltke both reference "rejected silver" in Jer 6:30 as a parallel to "choice silver" of v. 19 (Fox, *Proverbs 1–9*, 278; Waltke, *Proverbs 1–15*, 405). However, this connection is dubious. In this case, the underlying image of "harvest" is extended with regard to "treasure" specifically with regard to *worth*, though likely preserving the notion of commerce from Prov 3:14. In Jer 6:30, the image schema is not of "gain via harvest" but it is the process of *refinement*. While "value" is indeed a part of the blend, in Jeremiah what is at issue is that of *purity* gained through the process of metallurgy. This in turn becomes a metaphor for filthy Israel.

60. Association with "righteousness" and "justice" are paralleled in Isa 5:16; Jer 9:23–24 (Murphy, *Proverbs*, 51). "The (צדקה) is the principle, the latter (משפט) its practical realization. Syntactically, the verb אהלך does not occupy the first position, thereby giving emphasis to the way of righteousness. The path metaphor again carries the idea of the way of life, conduct (even God himself has his 'ways,' v. 22)" (Loader, *Proverbs 1–9*, 342).

61. Wisdom and not the youth is the walker in the path of righteousness. See Murphy, *Proverbs*, 51. While this is normally prescribed for humans (1:15; 2:13–15, 20; 4:14–15, 26–27), "here Wisdom states that she herself practises what she preaches" (Loader, *Proverbs 1–9*, 343).

62. "In the midst" (בתוך) may indicate that Wisdom is found at the crossroads of just tracks (Waltke, *Proverbs 1–15*, 406) or it may mean that Wisdom is not found "turning to the right or left" in the path, but her tracks are the essential middle of all just ways. See Loader, *Proverbs 1–9*, 342.

> 21 לְהַנְחִיל אֹהֲבַי ׀ יֵשׁ וְאֹצְרֹתֵיהֶם אֲמַלֵּא׃ פ
>
> Bequeathing inheritance[63] to those who love me[64] substance.[65]
> I will fill their store-houses.[66]

63. The infinitive construct provides for syntactic attachment between v. 20 and v. 21. Waltke calls it an "infinitive of purpose" (Waltke, *Proverbs 1–15*, 406), but as Loader points out, "'to give inheritance' is not the sole purpose for Wisdom's 'walking in paths of righteousness.' Rather in parity with Prov 13:22 bestowing inheritance is an attendant consequence of her righteous behavior. The important metaphorical component of vv. 20–21 is that Wisdom is figured as a *parent* to her children. As a good parent, she maintains righteous and just behavior which then benefits her *children*" (Loader, *Proverbs 1–9*, 343). This new extension of wisdom metaphor (i.e., WISDOM AS PARENT) is not a "partial metaphor" (Waltke, *Proverbs 1–15*, 406), but rather is a concept that will gain greater and more explicit articulation in 8:32. The linkage between "love" (אהב) and "find" (מצא) and the romantic metaphor is now seemingly turned in a new direction, away from erotic categories and into familial ones.

64. The substantive participle provides for an inclusio with 8:17 that rounds off this section. "A certain intensification in Wisdom's speech can be detected. From the present, which manifests Wisdom's generosity, she now turns to the past, which will highlight her origins from God before creation" (Murphy, *Proverbs*, 51).

65. The particle of existence יֵשׁ functions as a noun meaning "possessions" or "substance" only here and in Sir 42:3. "The pairing of *yēš* with *nḥlh* in Sir 42:3 suggests that *yēš* is an enduring, stable property, and not just any valuables." In the previous movement, Wisdom was associated with kingship and rule. In this one, she is associated with wealth and power. See Fox, *Proverbs 1–9*, 278.

66. Store houses (אוֹצָר) may refer to rooms for treasure (1 Kgs 14:26; 7:51) or metonymically to the goods which fill these houses (cf. Josh 6:19; Isa 2:7; 39:2; Jer 15:13; 38:11). In this case, it clearly refers to the former. See Waltke, *Proverbs 1–15*, 406. Within the book of Proverbs the word is always used to differentiate between the legitimacy and blessing of righteousness and the fear of YHWH over against the gains of the wicked and foolish (cf. Prov 8:21; 10:2; 15:16; 21:6, 20).

> 22 יְהוָ֗ה קָ֭נָנִי רֵאשִׁ֣ית דַּרְכּ֑וֹ קֶ֖דֶם מִפְעָלָ֣יו מֵאָֽז׃
>
> YHWH[67] obtained me[68] first of his road[69]—oldest of his works at that time.[70]

67. The divine name is fronted for emphasis.

68. First, the basic meaning of קנה in Tanakh means merely "to acquire," frequently through purchase (Fox, *Proverbs 1–9*, 280). Within the book of Proverbs this basic meaning has been employed repeatedly in association with the process of "getting wisdom," with associations of commerce (Prov 1:5; 4:5, 7; 15:32; 16:16; 17:16; 18:15; 19:8; 23:23). Once the word is used only with the association of purchase (Prov 20:14). Outside of Proverbs there are a few other possible meanings. In one context קנה means "beget" (Gen 4:1) (Loader, *Proverbs 1–9*, 346; Fox, *Proverbs 1–9*, 280). In a few contexts, קנה appears to mean "create" (14:19, 22; Ps 139:13). Especially since the b colon places the קנה of Wisdom with other "works" of YHWH, creation could be in view (Loader, *Proverbs 1–9*, 345–48; Fox, *Proverbs 1–9*, 279–80). While this context has a number of references both to the "birth" of Wisdom (vv. 24–25) and to creation generally (vv. 23–29) the verb קנה has not functioned with the meanings of "birth" or "creation" heretofore in Proverbs. The reader's natural association would be to attach it to previous occurrences. It is possible, then, that in the introduction of birth and/or creation imagery the initial reading would be overturned, thereby generating ambiguity about the intended meaning, which would be entirely commensurate with the poet's modus operandi. While any definitive declaration is not possible in context, the general poetic function is straightforward: "The verb *qanah* is chosen to designate divine acquisition of wisdom to show that this is the prototype of human acquisition of wisdom, even though they gain wisdom in quite different ways" (Fox, *Proverbs 1–9*, 280).

69. Because the phrase "first of his road" (רֵאשִׁ֣ית דַּרְכּ֑וֹ) appears without the ב preposition a number of different interpretations are possible. It may be a second accusative "he has created me as the first of his way." It could be an appositive, "he created me, the first of his way." Otherwise, it might be an adverbial qualifier of the verb, "he created me at the beginning of his way." The last option is the most fitting. "The noun ראשית is used as an *accusativus tempori* and therefore functions as an adverbial accusative (cf. GKC 118i). If Wisdom was made at the beginning of God's way, she is chronologically the first. Even so, the suggestion of superiority or excellence is naturally implied, not because the word ראשית provides it, but because the oldest is simultaneously 'number one' (cf. Gen 43:33; 49:3). Since this is the thrust of the whole poem, the temporal interpretation fits nicely into the context" (Loader, *Proverbs 1–9*, 350). For the "road" of God, see Job 40:19.

70. Lit. "from then." Murphy notes that the next few verses are overloaded with the מ preposition, meaning "from" with temporal connotation (22b; 23a; 23b [x2]) and five cases where a particle with the temporal force of "before" is used (באין—8:24a, b; בטרם—8:25a; לפני—8:25b; עד—8:26) (Murphy, *Proverbs*, 52). The poet's concern is with the *antiquity* of Wisdom, even before creation.

> 23 מֵעוֹלָם נִסַּכְתִּי מֵרֹאשׁ מִקַּדְמֵי־אָרֶץ׃
>
> From the most remote time[71] I was woven,[72] from the head, from[73] the primeval time[74] of the earth,

---

71. The noun עוֹלָם "does not mean 'timeless eternity' but the distant past (or the distant future, Ps 90:2)." Especially in context, Lady Wisdom existed *before* the created order (Loader, *Proverbs 1–9*, 351). However, this does not imply that she is declaring co-eternity with YHWH, because she repeatedly speaks of her own "birth" (Waltke, *Proverbs 1–15*, 410).

72. The root of נִסַּכְתִּי is difficult. The first meaning of נסך is "to pour out" and does not fit well with context. However, HALOT provides a secondary/homonymic meaning for the root as a niphal perfect of נסך with an English gloss of "I was woven," however this requires a different vocalization (*nᵉsakkōtî* (HALOT s.v. "נסך"; Fox, *Proverbs 1–9*, 281). Otherwise, the word may derive from the niphal perfect of the root סכך. In Ps 2:6 this word evidently refers to "setting up" or "installing" the king. In Ps 139:13 it refers to "forming" the inward parts (Murphy, *Proverbs*, 48). If the root derived from the latter, there is a possibility of verbal allusion to Psalm 139:13 (cf. Job 10:11).

73. The lack of an *atnaḥ* may assist in the verbal elision of נִסַּכְתִּי to the second colon. See Loader, *Proverbs 1–9*, 351.

74. *HALOT* s.v. "קֶדֶם."

24 בְּאֵין־תְּהֹמוֹת חוֹלָלְתִּי בְּאֵין מַעְיָנוֹת נִכְבַּדֵּי־מָיִם:

When[75] there were no deeps,[76] I was born[77]—when there

75. Here the בְּ preposition is used as a temporal, "when" (*HALOT* s.v. "בְּ").

76. The reference to תהום "deeps" likely engages with the idea of the "primeval deep" which is mentioned in Prov 3:20. While the mention of the "deeps" can sometimes be used as an image metaphor for unsearchable profundity (Job 38:16; Ps 36:7) in context it is clear that "the deeps" are only the beginning of the larger image schema of the "three-tiered universe" as it was conceived by the ancients (Gen 7:11; 8:2). Beneath all lies שאול, the underworld. Next, ארץ, the earth, supported by pillars (Ps 18:8, 16; 75:4; Job 9:6). "Upon these props, the habitable land (*tebel*) lies like a griddle. Around and beneath the *tebel* (and according to Gen 1:7, above the entire earth), there is *t*^{e}*hom* the primeval ocean or abyss, which is sometimes identified with the underworld, Sheol. . . . The sky is a dome or cupola, a two-dimensional 'firmament' resting on the columns of sky' ('*ammudey šamayimi*; Job 22:14). Separating the sky from the flat surface (earth + seas) there is a visible border (namely, the horizon), which is called both 'the circle of the sky' (*ḥug šamayim*; Job 22:14) and the 'circle of the earth' (*ḥug haʾareṣ*; Isa 40:22)" (Fox, *Proverbs 1–9*, 282).

77. The birth of Wisdom at the extremity of time and before creation bears the strong implication that the one giving birth to Wisdom was YHWH (Loader, *Proverbs 1–9*, 352; Fox, *Proverbs 1–9*, 282; Waltke, *Proverbs 1–15*, 412). The metaphorical schema of YHWH as mother is activated by the same root in Ps 90:2 with regard to the earth, and also Deut 32:18 with regard to Israel. As noted by Fox, v. 30 extends the birth schema to include YHWH as a parent. Fox notes that the verb generally refers to "birth labors" and is never used with regard to human males. However, he reserves the possibility of figurative usage, "Since divine productivity is not really sexual, tropes for this activity need not be governed by the constraints of human reproduction" (Fox, *Proverbs 1–9*, 282–83). As previously, there is a confusion of metaphor with ontology. Personified Wisdom had no birth. Birth metaphor is added to the Lady Wisdom metaphor for a poetic purpose. It is likely that as in the Psalms birth imagery is used to show *nearness and maternal affection* between YHWH and his creation (Baumann, "Die 'Männlichkeit JHWH,'" 197–213; Grohman, *Fruchtbarkeit und Geburt*, 113–16). So also here, birth imagery implies the maternity of YHWH, which exists right alongside 3ms verbal and pronominal forms. It is important to note, first, that while there are numerous correspondences between this stanza and ANE cosmogonies, the departures are significant. First there is no pairing of gods with respect to gender that is demonstrated in nearly all other cosmogonies. See Waltke, *Proverbs 1–15*, 412. YHWH is conceived of as a woman, specifically as a mother, in precisely the same manner that he is conceived of as a man, specifically as a father. These are both conceptual structures that allow gendered humanity to "obtain human scale" with different elements of YHWH's person and being.

were no fountains⁷⁸ heavy⁷⁹ with water.

25 בְּטֶרֶם הָרִים הָטְבָּעוּ לִפְנֵי גְבָעוֹת חוֹלָלְתִּי:

Before mountains were sunk,⁸⁰ before hills,⁸¹ I was born.⁸²

78. There is a general consensus that there are similarities between this stanza and the opening lines of *Enuma Elish* (ANET, 60–61) and Egyptian Coffin Texts (Meinhold, *Die Sprüche*, 1:145). See also Waltke, *Proverbs 1–15*, 411; Loader, *Proverbs 1–9*, 352. While there certainly is an element of merism (between depths and heights) the structuring of elements is in some senses similar to Gen 1, which places humanity in the center. "Sea, land, and sky depict the entire universe of the living. Within the unified vv. 24–26 the huge geographical spheres are escalated with reference to human habitation: from the oceans, which is [sic] most remote (v. 24), to mountains, which is [sic] less remote (v. 25), and climactically to land, where human beings dwell (v. 26)" (Waltke, *Proverbs 1–15*, 411).

79. Fox argues that כבד in niphal "never refers to quantity, literally or figuratively, but only to the reception or possession of honor and esteem. Moreover, this chapter shows no interest in the size or majesty of the natural phenomena" (Fox, *Proverbs 1–9*, 283). See Gen 34:19; Exod 14:4, 17–18; Lev 10:3; Num 22:15; Deut 28:58; 1 Sam 9:6; 22:14; 2 Sam 6:20, 22; 23:19, 23; 2 Kgs 14:10; 1 Chr 4:9; 11:21, 25; Ps 87:3; 149:8; Prov 8:24; Isa 3:5; 23:8–9; 26:15; 43:4; 49:5; Ezek 28:22; 39:13; Nah 3:10; Hag 1:8. In place he argues for emendation of *mibbᵉkê* or 'fountains' (Job 28:11; 38:6; 1QHod 3, 15). However, reading the root as another reference to water sources is also problematic. "In the context of the fountains or springs from which the subterranean water saturates the earth, the niphal participle of the root כבד (heavy) is intelligible: the springs are heavily drenched with water from the abyss below, which can be glossed by English 'replete' with its suggestion of a heavy load as well as overflow. A change to נבכי (cf. BHS) would create a tautology (fountains, sources of water), which is not an improvement" (Loader, *Proverbs 1–9*, 353).

80. The hophal perfect הָטְבָּעוּ of the root טבע refers to more than "planting" the mountains, but images them as being "sunk" in sockets as in Job 38:6 (cf. also Job 26:7). This again refers to the image schema of the three-tiered universe. "Bear in mind that poets represent the phenomenal cosmos figuratively. For example, the mountains may be pictured as pillars founded in the ocean to support the earth (cf. Pss 18:7, 16 [8, 17]), but that is no more literal than that they were brought forth in childbirth (Ps 90:2). Job debunks a literal interpretation: 'Upon what are the earth's sockets sunk (*hoṭbā'û*)?'" (Waltke, *Proverbs 1–15*, 413). The issue here is that science represents the cosmos in no less figurative manner. There is *no* conception of ultimate reality apart from mental models. These models then highlight different elements of lived reality. Poet's endeavor to discover metaphors that reflect the experiential reality. Scientists endeavor to generate models that allow for explanation and control of the physical and material elements of creation.

81. "Mountains" (הרים) and "hills" (גבע) are a stock parallel in Hebrew poetry (Waltke, *Proverbs 1–15*, 413). See Deut 12:2; 33:15; Josh 24:33; Judg 19:16; 1 Sam 13:2; Ps 72:3; 114:4, 6; 148:9; Prov 8:25; Song 2:8; 4:6; Isa 2:2, 14; 10:32; 30:17; 31:4; 40:4, 12; 41:15; 42:15; 54:10; 55:12; 65:7; Jer 3:23; 4:24; 16:16; 50:6; Ezek 6:3, 13; 34:6; 35:8; 36:4, 6; Hos 4:13; 10:8; Joel 4:18; Amos 9:13; Mic 4:1; 6:1; Nah 1:5; Hab 3:6).

82. The birth of wisdom is again emphasized by a second repetition of the verb "born" (חיל) in 8:25b which provides for a sort of chiasm with 8:24a. See Waltke,

> 26 עַד־לֹא עָשָׂה אֶרֶץ וְחוּצוֹת וְרֹאשׁ עָפְרוֹת תֵּבֵל׃
>
> Ere[83] he had made[84] earth[85] or outside and the first clumps of dirt of the inhabitable world

---

Proverbs 1–15, 413.

83. Loader notes that עַד־לֹא is perhaps "the best example of the negative formulation typical of creation hymns" especially as it is so unusual in Biblical Hebrew (Loader, Proverbs 1–9, 353). Fox points out that it is common in Syriac and similar to phrases in LBH and RH and may be an Aramaism here (Fox, Proverbs 1–9, 283). While the grammar is a little awkward, (i.e., "until not") the meaning is not nebulous, before the time when something occurred.

84. "He made" (עשה) is a common enough word for YHWH's work in creation and should not be too sharply distinguished from the more unique and theologically loaded word, ברא. See Gen 1:1 and Exod 19:11; Gen 1:16 and Ps 148:3–5 and Isa 40:26; Gen 1:21 with 1:25; 1:26 and 1:27 and both verbs in Gen 2:4a (Waltke, Proverbs 1–15, 413).

85. The series of nouns: "earth" (ארץ), "open fields" or literally "outside" (חוץ), and "first clumps of dirt" (רֹאשׁ עָפְרוֹת תֵּבֵל) point to an increasing emphasis and specification of earth or soil. Earth, "has its cosmological sense of land in contradistinction both to the heavens (cf. vv. 27–28a) and to the sea (cf. vv 28b—30)." חוץ does not take its typical meaning of "outside" or with relation to city streets (as in Prov 1:20; 5:16; 7:12; 22:13; 24:27) since none of these things were in existence, it likely refers to open fields" (Waltke, Proverbs 1–15, 413). See also Fox, Proverbs 1–9, 283. Finally, the "clumps of dirt of the inhabitable world" (וְרֹאשׁ עָפְרוֹת תֵּבֵל) begins with ראש, again used as a temporal, followed by reference to cultivatable land (Gen 2:7; 3:19), though the precise sense is unclear. See Fox, Proverbs 1–9, 284; Waltke, Proverbs 1–15, 414.

> 27 בַּהֲכִינוֹ שָׁמַיִם שָׁם אָנִי בְּחוּקוֹ חוּג עַל־פְּנֵי תְהוֹם׃
>
> In[86] his establishing the heavens, there[87] was I—In his inscribing a circle[88] upon the face of the deep,

---

86. Where Fox limits the current stanza at v. 29, and argues that the phrase, "there was I" only modifies vv. 27–28 (Fox, *Proverbs 1–9*, 284). Loader correctly argues that "there is no reason to exclude the events mentioned in v. 29, as if Wisdom were not present at these latter events or as if she were an אמון only when the last creative actions took place. Both her presence (v. 27a) and her being an אמון (v. 30a) apply to all the creative acts listed" (Loader, *Proverbs 1–9*, 354). Waltke describes vv. 27–31 as "essentially an extended sentence." Verses 27 and 30 are main clauses supported by subordinating clauses, ultimately framed by an inclusio of "there was I" in v. 27b and "I was beside him" in v. 30a (Waltke, *Proverbs 1–15*, 414). Loader provides a more sophisticated argument for the unity and interdependence of the verses: "Vv. 27–30a are bound together not only by, first, anadiplosis but, secondly, also by the repeated anaphoric use of the masculine singular suffix referring to God. Thirdly, two 'I' statements (vv. 27a and 30a) frame an extended infinitive sequence—which is also logically satisfactory since all the actions described by the infinitives are those where Wisdom was present as אמון. In the fourth place, the chiasmus in vv. 30bc–31 is further evidence for this demarcation. Fifth, the fact that ואהיה occurs twice in consecutive hemistichs (vv. 30a, 30b), makes it unlikely that the extended sentence noticed by Waltke carries on further than v. 30a. Finally, the stich division is also supported by metric considerations" (Loader, *Proverbs 1–9*, 354). The next "sextuple strophe" is held together by the six-fold repetition of ב + the infinitive construct + the 3ms pronominal suffix. See Waltke, *Proverbs 1–15*, 414.

87. The phrase "there was I" (שָׁם אָנִי) should not be translated as a simple temporal, but rather centers the object or agent on a set of events. The emphasis is upon her presence and witness of these events, not merely of her existence. See Fox, *Proverbs 1–9*, 284; Isa 48:16b.

88. The phrase "inscribing a circle upon the face of the deep" refers again to the horizon line based upon the three-tiered model of the cosmos. See Job 26:10; Loader, *Proverbs 1–9*, 355; Fox, *Proverbs 1–9*, 284). Waltke suggests that the image of בְּחוּקוֹ חוּג is an "incomplete metaphor" drawn from the image of a compass creating the horizon (Job 22:14; 26:10; Isa 40:22). As noted previously, the notion of an "incomplete metaphor" is difficult to explain when metaphors are associated with concepts rather than words. Moreover, the "compass" image only works with Job 26:10. In Job 22:14, YHWH walks on the "circle" and Isa 40:22 he places his throne upon it. These latter seem to be a blending of the "circle" with the metaphorical imagery of the רָקִיעַ from Gen 1:7.

188 WISDOM IS A WOMAN

> 28 בְּאַמְּצוֹ שְׁחָקִים מִמָּעַל בַּעֲזוֹז עִינוֹת תְּהוֹם׃
>
> In his making firm[89] the clouds above, in his strengthening[90] the fountains of the deep,
>
> 29 בְּשׂוּמוֹ לַיָּם ׀ חֻקּוֹ וּמַיִם לֹא יַעַבְרוּ־פִיו בְּחוּקוֹ מוֹסְדֵי אָרֶץ׃
>
> In his placing to the sea his limit,[91] and waters[92] cannot transgress his word, in his inscribing[93] the foundations of earth.
>
> 30 וָאֶהְיֶה אֶצְלוֹ אָמוֹן וָאֶהְיֶה שַׁעֲשֻׁעִים יוֹם ׀ יוֹם מְשַׂחֶקֶת לְפָנָיו בְּכָל־עֵת׃
>
> And I was beside him faithfully. And I was delight[94] day by day

89. Prima facie the idea of "making firm" or "fixing" of insubstantial and ever-changing clouds seems to be a paradox. "It may be that more stable cirrus clouds appeared to be arches holding up the dome of the sky" (Stadelmann, *Hebrew Conception of the World*, 88). It may also be that the clouds are merely associated with the creation and limits of the ocean as in Job 38:9 (Loader, *Proverbs 1-9*, 355; Fox, *Proverbs 1-9*, 285). Ultimately however, "'securing' the clouds in the present verse does not mean that God fixed them in place, but that he gave them the power or, we might say, the energy to remain suspended above the earth (Naḥmias)" (Fox, *Proverbs 1-9*, 285).

90. The Masoretic text here reads בַּעֲזוֹז instead of the expected ב + infinitive + 3ms pronominal suffix. This is the only of the six occurrences to break the mold and there seems to be no reason why the poet would have chosen to do so. Most commentators emend to *beʿazzezô* due to *waw* for *zayin* metathesis in agreement with the LXX. See Fox, *Proverbs 1-9*, 285; Loader, *Proverbs 1-9*, 355; Waltke, *Proverbs 1-15*, 391; Murphy, *Proverbs*, 48.

91. Murphy suggests that the reference to the sea (ים) here "may be a faint echo of the mythical battle between the Lord and Sea which is supposedly featured in other creation narratives" (Murphy, *Proverbs*, 52). These are typically based upon the association with the battle of Baal and Yam in the Baal Cycles, and are linked to the loan words לִוְיָתָן and תַּנִּין (Isa 27:1; Ps 74:14). The image metaphor of "battle" or "warrior" is completely absent in this case, however. The "setting of verbal limits" is much more in line with the parallel use in Job 38:11a. See Fox, *Proverbs 1-9*, 285. Note also the metonymy of פה ("mouth") for אמר ("word").

92. Van Leeuwen suggests that based upon "emphasis on liquids," the presence of similar lexemes for water sources, the outdoors (5:16; 8:25; cf. 1:20; 7:12) and the phrase "at all times" (5:19; 8:30) that "God's limits on the cosmic waters in chapter 8 provide a model for the limits on human sexual 'waters' (5:15-20) and on human behavior generally" (Van Leeuwen, "Book of Proverbs," 94).

93. Some argue that the foundations of the earth were not "inscribed" but "sunk" (8:25) and therefore propose emendation of *bḥwqw* ("in his inscribing") to *bḥzqw* ("in his strengthening") following the LXX, again based upon a metathesis of *zayin* and *waw*. See Fox, *Proverbs 1-9*, 285. Since the "circle of earth" is also reflected in the three-tiered cosmos the MT is retained.

94. There are only nine appearances of שַׁעֲשֻׁעִים in Tanakh. Five of these appear in Psalm 119 and each refers to the Torah of YHWH as a delight. The other two cases

> celebrating before him at all times[95]
>
> 31 מְשַׂחֶקֶת בְּתֵבֵל אַרְצוֹ וְשַׁעֲשֻׁעַי אֶת־בְּנֵי אָדָם: פ
>
> playing in [the] world[96] of his earth. And my delight [was] the sons of Adam.

appear in the prophets, both of which are metaphorical. In the first, Isa 5:7, Israel is figured as a vineyard of YHWH, and Judah is called "the planting of his delight" (נֶטַע שַׁעֲשׁוּעָיו). In *all* of these cases the plural noun appears in construct with a pronominal suffix ("my" in Psalms' and "his" in Isaiah). Only in Jer 31:20 does the word appear *without* a pronominal suffix. In this context, Ephraim is figured as a "son of preciousness" (יֶלֶד שַׁעֲשֻׁעִים). Notably in this context, Lady Wisdom provides neither pronominal suffix, nor a clarifying construct relationship. She says, "I was a delight, day by day" (וָאֶהְיֶה שַׁעֲשֻׁעִים יוֹם | יוֹם). Fox argues, cogently, that this statement must be understood with reference to *being a source of delight* to someone else (Fox, *Proverbs 1–9*, 285). Waltke argues conversely that the phrase is idiomatic and should be grouped with texts like Psalm 109:4 and 120:7 where "I am prayer" means "I am given totally to prayer." He continues by showing that 8:31b shows that it is not YHWH who is the agent, but rather *Wisdom*. Moreover, while it is easy enough to explain *why* Wisdom delights (i.e., in the creative acts of YHWH and in humanity), YHWH's delight is dependent upon the "child" metaphor and not substantiated in independent actions of Wisdom. "The extended protasis of vv. 28–29 about the LORD's effecting his firmly fixed, cosmological order can better be explained if in the apodosis Wisdom delights in creation (cf. Ps 119:24, 77, 92, 143, 174) than if the focus suddenly shifts to the LORD delighting in Wisdom" (Waltke, *Proverbs 1–15*, 421).

95. See also 5:19 with reference to delight.

96. Waltke notes that ארץ functions as a synecdoche for all of creation as "a world fit for humanity.... The structure of vv. 24–26 and 27–29 implied what is now made explicit. The catchwords ʾereṣ (vv. 26, 29) and tēbēl of (v. 26) link v. 31 with those verses" (Waltke, *Proverbs 1–9*, 422).

32 וְעַתָּה בָנִים שִׁמְעוּ־לִי וְאַשְׁרֵי דְּרָכַי יִשְׁמֹרוּ:

And now,[97] sons, listen to me,[98] and [the] happy[99] my path they will keep.

33 שִׁמְעוּ מוּסָר וַחֲכָמוּ וְאַל־תִּפְרָעוּ:

Listen [to] discipline[100] and be wise and do not let go.[101]

34 אַשְׁרֵי אָדָם שֹׁמֵעַ לִי לִשְׁקֹד עַל־דַּלְתֹתַי יוֹם ׀ יוֹם לִשְׁמֹר מְזוּזֹת פְּתָחָי:

Happy is the man listening to me, keeping vigil upon my doors day by day[102] guarding the posts of my doors.

97. The LXX completely changes these last lines. Internally it attests a number of different readings, however, at a general level it exchanges v. 32 for v. 3, omits v. 33 altogether and attests a number of different possible forms. Some scholars (i.e., Gemser, Whybray) propose to reorganize the MT upon the basis of the LXX, however, the alleged deficiencies of this pericope do not warrant the emendation. See Loader, *Proverbs 1–9*, 364. Rather, after the shift provided by the initial logical particle (וְעַתָּה) there is a close concatenation of imperatives (i.e., "listen" (שמע) in vv. 32a and 33) coupled with the macarism אשרי (vv. 32b, 34a) that are then capped with the imperative "guard" (שמר) which forms and inclusio. Overall, the introduction forms "a precise intertextuality between the two great, paired poems of chapters 7 and 8" which "further validates that Woman Wisdom personifies the sage and his teaching" (Waltke, *Proverbs 1–9*, 423).

98. Waltke argues that the repetition of "listen to me" (שִׁמְעוּ־לִי) here is an allusion to Prov 5:7 and 7:24 which "strongly suggests that to listen to Woman Wisdom and the sage come to the same thing" (Waltke, *Proverbs 1–15*, 424).

99. Fox points out that the macarism "happy!" is both grammatically and generically out of place, and that it might be here from the force of Prov 3:14 (אַשְׁרֵי אָדָם מָצָא חָכְמָה). See Fox, *Proverbs 1–9*, 290. Grammatically, however, אשרי in this case modifies אדם. It acts as the noun itself, and also appears with a conjunction. There is only one other case where אשרי appears with the conjunction: the Queen of Sheba's declaration to Solomon in 2 Chr 9:7. There are only four cases where "happy" (אשרי) and "guard" (שמר) are found in the same verse: Ps 106:3; Prov 8:32, 34; Isa 56:2.

100. מוסר ("discipline") may refer to a specific reprimand, the following collection of Wisdom sayings in Prov 10:1–31:31 (Waltke, *Proverbs 1–15*, 424) or "more generally as the prerequisite of wisdom in the sense of accepting authority of teachers" (Loader, *Proverbs 1–9*, 365). In context, the reflex of attending to correction seems the most likely.

101. The verb "neglect" (פרע) either implies מוסר as the direct object (i.e., Toy, Ringgren) and is therefore gapped, or the direct object אתו was lost via scribal error (Waltke, *Proverbs 1–15*, 391). In either case, discipline (מוסר) is in view. See Loader, *Proverbs 1–9*, 365.

102. As in 8:30, "day by day" "sets up Wisdom's vigilance at the creation as a model for the sons" (Waltke, *Proverbs 1–9*, 425).

35 כִּי מֹצְאִי (מֹצְאֵי) [מָצָא] חַיִּים וַיָּפֶק רָצוֹן מֵיְהוָה׃

Because[103] one finding[104] me has found life and he has obtained favor from YHWH.

36 וְחֹטְאִי חֹמֵס נַפְשׁוֹ כָּל־מְשַׂנְאַי אָהֲבוּ מָוֶת׃ פ

But one wronging me[105] injures his soul. All those hating me love death.

Stage One Perception

Stage one perception is framed around three elements provided by the foil of the *Strange Woman* and *Lady Wisdom* in Prov 7 and 8: characterization,

---

103. The epexegetic כי links v. 35 to the preceding verse, and also alludes to the image schema of women by reference to Prov 18:22. The subordinate clause explains *why* the one keeping watch at the doors of wisdom is happy. He has found life and obtained favor from YHWH. See Waltke, *Proverbs 1–15*, 425.

104. The *kethib* reads as qal masculine singular construct (מֹצְאֵי), "one finding life." The *qere* reads the same form as a 3ms perfect, "he has found." The difference in meaning is negligible.

105. Some commentators (i.e., Hame'iri, Delitzsch, Toy, Waltke) translate חטא more generally as "miss the mark" because it provides a better parallel to "finding" in the a colon (see *HALOT* s.v. "חטא"; cf. Isa 65:20; Job 5:24; Eccl 2:26; 7:26. Some of these references are debatable). "But this verse is decrying a more pernicious offense than just 'missing' wisdom. After all, the fool and sinner are not aiming at wisdom to start with" (Fox, *Proverbs 1–9*, 291). At the same time Fox argues that while the root for sin is "usually an ethical violation, but not always." He thinks that "Wisdom is not speaking of moral sins but describing a personal, 'emotional' relationship: love and devotion versus offensiveness and hatred. 'Offends against' is an antonym of 'finds,' because the latter here connotes uniting with a beloved person (namely, Wisdom)" (Fox, *Proverbs 1–9*, 291). However, the qal ms participle functions here as a substantive, "one wronging/sinning against me" (וְחֹטְאִי). The verb "sin" only appears in Proverbs as a qal participle being used as a substantive, as it is here (cf. Prov 11:31; 13:22; 14:21; 19:2; 20:2. There are also 3 cases of the adjectival root (חַטָּא) being used as a noun in Prov 1:10; 13:21; 23:17). Qohelet has the next most frequent occurrence of the root as a participle, and employs it likewise, as an antithetical parallel to wisdom and righteousness (Eccl 2:26; 8:12; 9:2, 18), moreover, the punishment for the "sinner" is to be captured by the unfaithful woman (Eccl 7:26). All other cases of the verb carry considerable cultic connotations, not merely of "offense," as an interpersonal category (cf. Lev 6:19; 1 Sam 14:33; Isa 1:4; 29:21; 65:20; Ezek 18:4, 20; Hab 2:10). These are persons who are morally culpable and therefore fall under judgment. By way of illustration, in English one would not call someone else an "offender" outside of a court room setting. In the same way, the participial use of חטא, is not used as a descriptor of relational enmity in general, but as a class of people who stand either explicitly or implicitly as violators of the divine covenant. This is *not* to say, that this is not "non-relational" but rather, it is an indication that Lady Wisdom continues to apply cultic terms and categories.

invitation, and house. Although there are numerous other points of comparison these three are adequate to demonstrate the disparity in outcomes between *infidelity* in relationship and covenant set out by the *Strange Woman* and the blessings attendant to fidelity to *Lady Wisdom*. All the same, Wisdom does not provide for the avoidance of death, but only for the chance at a blessed and secure length of mortal days. Finally, the purposeful ambiguity sustained by the poet in numerous elements of characterization only further highlights the role of *fidelity* in distinguishing the wise from the strange.

A Comparison of the Characterizations of the *Strange Woman* and *Lady Wisdom*

First, as in the discussion of the *Strange Woman* above, the description of the woman in Prov 7 is contiguous and consistent, with her presentation in Prov 2–6. (1) There is an emphasis upon her use of "smooth speech," (2) she employs explicit sexual terms and imagery (e.g., Prov 6; 5), (3) or sexual or relational metaphors, and (4) there are numerous lexical connections as noted above. This is important, because the *Strange Woman* is used as the antithetical threat to personified wisdom in Prov 2–4 as well as the opposite of the "wife of your youth" in Prov 5. In Prov 7, she reappears as the antithesis of Wisdom. *Fidelity*, then becomes the *crux interpretum*. Moreover, the image schema of Judges 5, casts new light on the character of the *Strange Woman*, not merely as a villain, but as an instrument of divine justice.

Where the *Strange Woman* is a flat character, *Lady Wisdom* continues to develop deeper complexity through the blending of new metaphorical dimensions. This deepening is illustrated in the poet's choice of the root אמון in 8:30. This word choice allows the three major image schemas of the chapter to jostle each other: Architecture, childhood, and constant fidelity. This portrayal of *Lady Wisdom* is in keeping with the diverse and paradoxical presentation in Prov 1–4 and points to the utter disparity between Wisdom and the *Strange Woman* who is equivalent to little more than a case study in *infidelity*.

The Strange Woman Characterized as an Instrument of Divine Justice through Allusion to Judges 5

In Prov 7:6, the paternal account employs a lexical activation of the imagined speech of Sisera's mother in Judges 5:28 as a conceptual frame for figuring the young man in the place of Sisera as an enemy of Israel. This secondary interpretive context is signaled by the formal similarity provided by the series of common lexemes between Prov 7:6 and Judg 5:28 which are then expanded by a number of close narrative allusions.

The activation of the parallel context begins with Judges 5:28a which records the imagined speech of Sisera's mother and Prov 7:6.

> בְּעַד הַחַלּוֹן נִשְׁקְפָה וַתְּיַבֵּב אֵם סִיסְרָא בְּעַד הָאֶשְׁנָב
>
> Through the window she peered and the mother of Sisera cried through the Lattice. (Judg 5:28a)
>
> כִּי בְּחַלּוֹן בֵּיתִי בְּעַד אֶשְׁנַבִּי נִשְׁקָפְתִּי
>
> For at the window of my house I looked through my lattice. (Prov 7:6)

Since four of the words (חלון, שקף, בעד, אשנב) are common between the two verses it is most likely that there is a direct textual allusion.[106] These lexemes not only serve to connect the two texts via allusion, but also cement the setting and role of the narrator.

After the initial activation there are a number of lexical, conceptual and narrative elements which paint the fate of the young man as analogous to the enemy of Israel in the hands of a foreign woman. First, the phrase "come out to call" has an echo in both narratives. Jael "came out to call" to Sisera (וַתֵּצֵא יָעֵל לִקְרַאת) (Judg 4:18) in a manner reasonably similar to that in Prov 7:15 (יָצָאתִי לִקְרָאתֶךָ). This is accompanied by the notion of "turning aside" wherein the feminine hero urges the victim to draw near for the fulfillment of his desire (cf. Judg 4:18, 22; Prov 7:15).[107]

Moreover, the declaration that "there is no man in his house" (כִּי אֵין הָאִישׁ בְּבֵיתוֹ) is eerily reminiscent of Sisera's instruction to Jael, "If a man should come and ask you and say, 'Is there a man here?' then you will say, "there is none" (אִם־אִישׁ יָבוֹא וּשְׁאֵלֵךְ וְאָמַר הֲיֵשׁ־פֹּה אִישׁ וְאָמַרְתְּ אָיִן). This confession ironically foreshadows Sisera's end and ties to another narrative similarity, with regard to the "house full of the dead." In Judges, the narrative ends with Jael, "coming out to call" to Barak in order to introduce him to the dead man in her tent (Judg 4:22). In parallel, the house of the *Strange Woman* is said to be "full of the dead" (7:26–27) with the implication that

---

106. It is possible that there is an underlying conventionalized schema for "peering through the window" but even so, the reference here shows lexical correspondence.

107. In Jael's case she literally calls for him to "turn aside" while in Proverbs it is more that the woman provides a much more specific invitation.

she is the cause of their demise. Finally, in both cases the male "victim" is receiving his just compensation at the hand of a foreign woman. It is not as Weeks proposes:

> This denial of male culpability or responsibility must necessarily be discomforting for a modern reader, but whatever social and sexual attitudes it may betray, it is intended to make a point that lies outside the sphere of male-female relationships. Turning aside requires assent, but even this is an uninformed assent, given by those who lack the ability to recognize their danger.[108]

The point really transcends "culpability" and passes into the realm of divine sovereignty and retribution. The man is a "victim" because he is a violator. The ignorance and stubbornness of the חסר־לב typecasts him for the role of the enemy of God's people. Simultaneously, the *Strange Woman* becomes a vehicle of God's judgment (Prov 23:28; Eccl 7:25, 26).[109]

The Expanded Personification of Lady Wisdom in Proverbs 8:30

First, it is important to note that there exists both continuity and discontinuity in the characterization of *Lady Wisdom* in Prov 8 and those of Prov 1–6. The lexemes applied to her and associated with her are the same or similar to all other presentations (Prov 8:1, 12, 14; 2:10; 5:1–2; 7:4). The depiction of her physical location is similar to that set forth in the opening (Prov 8:2; 1:21–22). She is described as calling out to a similar masculine plural audience (Prov 1:22; 8:4–5). She employs the metaphor of TREASURE to describe her instruction (Prov 8:10–11, 18–19, 21; 2:4; 3:14–16). She uses SEEKING AND FINDING and OBTAINING metaphor common to her previous portrayals (8:17, 22; 1:28; 2:4). Finally, she is depicted with relation to her presence and perhaps instrumentality in creation (8:22–30; 3:19–20). At the same time, the personification of *Lady Wisdom* in chapter eight is manifestly different from her previous characterizations.

First, in this address *Lady Wisdom* speaks of her own disposition toward speech (vv. 6–14) and insight for rulership (vv. 15–16) which have heretofore not been noted. Second, the *SEEKING AND FINDING* metaphor of previous iterations is brought to consummation, by her guarantee that those who "seek her will find her" (8:17). Third, Wisdom provides for the blending of WOMAN and PATH metaphors by the fact that she, *herself*, is to be found walking in the way of righteousness and simultaneously figures

---

108. Weeks, *Instruction and Imagery*, 149
109. Weeks, *Instruction and Imagery*, 146.

herself as a parent to those who follow her and then continues to address her audience in the same way as the father addresses his sons (8:21, 32). Finally, she describes herself as an אָמוֹן, a word that is alone in *Tanakh* and is one of the famous difficulties of Prov 8. The disagreement about this term is most frequently decided with reference to aptness for one image scheme or another. As such, the discussion of Prov 8:30 provides an apt segue into the paradox and diversity of *Lady Wisdom*'s characterization in this chapter.

> וָאֶהְיֶה אֶצְלוֹ אָמוֹן וָאֶהְיֶה שַׁעֲשֻׁעִים יוֹם | יוֹם מְשַׂחֶקֶת לְפָנָיו בְּכָל־עֵת׃
>
> And I was beside him faithfully. And I was delight day by day celebrating before him at all times. (Prov 8:30)

Before moving to the discussion of possible interpretations for the problem root, some consideration of the repetition of אהיה is in order. Murphy believes that there is "hardly any doubt" that the two fold repetition is an allusion to Exod 3:14.[110] While an allusion to 3:14 cannot be entirely ruled out, elements of "divine calling" or any other lexical or metaphorical element of the divine revelation to Moses are absent. Most other allusions to Torah in the first nine chapters have appeared in the context of other allusions to Torah.

With regard to the problem root אמון two of the threads of interpretation disagree about which image schema is held to be the dominant image for these verses: architect/building or child. The third option favors and adverbial reading of the root as "faithfully" or "constantly."

The first group of interpretations understand the controlling of image schema of Proverbs 8 to be that of order, construction and architecture. All of these elements are clearly set forth both lexically and metaphorically in the preceding verses. R. Hoshaya and Sa'adia believed that the word אמון

---

110. Murphy argues that the two-fold repetition of the verb אהיה, (30a & b), "recalls the mysterious revelation of Exod 3:14, where 'I am Who I am' occurs twice and 'I am' once more. However the mysterious aura surrounding these verbs is to be understood, there can be hardly any doubt that v. 30 alludes to that passage. This is worthy of note in view of the general tendency of Proverbs to avoid the verb 'to be' in favor of juxtaposition or simple comparison" (Murphy, *Proverbs*, 53). The "rarity" of היה verbs in Proverbs, is a difficult generalization to make. There are 28 appearances of היה in Proverbs in both parts of the book: Prov 1:14; 3:7–8, 22, 26–27; 4:3; 5:14, 17–18; 8:30; 12:8, 24; 13:19; 14:23, 26, 35; 22:19, 26; 23:20, 34; 24:1, 20, 28; 26:5; 29:21; 31:14. While Eccl has a relatively high percentage of appearances of היה relative to overall length of the book (15.7 percent), Proverbs (2.95 percent) fits pretty evenly with Psalms (3.99 percent), Job (4.39 percent), and Song of Solomon (3.42 percent). It is more noteworthy that the 1cs imperfect of היה + a preposition of personal association + a predicate nominative is exceedingly rare.

meant "artisan" (*Gen. Rab.* 1.2) but believed that she is to be identified with *Torah* and functions instrumentally as a blue print for creation.[111] Some modern scholarship argues that that *ămôn* should be emended to *'ommān* in order to provide for parallel with a hopeful Akkadian cognate in *ummānu* or *ummānē*, who are understood as semi-divine sages before and after the flood. "The title *ummānu* covers a broad spectrum of occupations, including scribe, scholar, master craftsman, officer."[112] Given the apparent parallels with ANE cosmogonies, coupled with the clear argumentation for God's word as structuring force in the universe (Prov 3:19) there is ample reason to consider "building" or "architecture" the primary image schema. Moreover, the mention of "inscribing a line" and "setting a cornerstone" also appears in the context of the metaphor CREATION IS CONSTRUCTION in Job.[113] However, this interpretation is complicated by the grammatical form, which would require an inexplicable loss of doubling and lengthening of the final vowel.[114] Moreover, there are a few attendant interpretive difficulties that accompany this reading. First, the proposed "co-agency" of Wisdom in creation, really is not supported by the text.[115] Second, as noted by Loader, the "building" schema does not explain the transition or extension to "child" imagery in 8:30–31.[116]

111. Fox, *Proverbs 1–9*, 286.

112. Fox, *Proverbs 1–9*, 286.

113. See Job 38:5–6. The primary image schema is one of masonry as it is employed in (1) laying a foundation (e.g., 1 Kgs 5:31; 6:37; 7:10; Ezra 3:10) and then (2) fixing something solidly (Ps 8:4). As a peripheral point of interest, the poet has decided against using the typical metaphor for "stretching out" (נטה) the heavens which is thought to refer to the process of unrolling and raising a tent (Job 9:8; Ps 18:10; 104:2; Isa 40:22; 44:24; 45:12; 51:13; Jer 10:12; 51:15; Zech 12:1). Instead, the author has capitalized upon the "fixing" of the heavens as a more rigid process. Choosing the "founding" metaphor is likely due to a desire to emphasize the *fixity* and *stability* of the divine order of creation. See Loader, *Proverbs 1–9*, 361–62.

114. Loader, *Proverbs 1–9*, 357.

115. Michael Fox places the emphasis of Prov 8 upon Wisdom's transcendent role in creation and figures wisdom almost as a Platonic form of which human wisdom is a shoddy duplicate (Fox, *Proverbs 1–9*, 346–59). Weeks rightly disagrees: "There is little sign of a mythos in chapters 1 or 9, and when matters do get to that sort of level in chapter 3, wisdom is barely personified at all. Much of what Fox is claiming, therefore, seems to be based essentially on chapter 8, which does indeed present Wisdom as in, but not of humanity and the world . . . there is no reading of 8:30, or of the chapter as a whole, that really requires us to take Wisdom as a transcendent universal, let alone as godlike, and there is nothing elsewhere in Fox's interludes that comes even close" (Weeks, *Instruction and Imagery*, 93).

116. Loader describes personified wisdom as "God's nursling, a little girl playing around on the building site" (Loader, *Proverbs 1–9*, 359). He concludes, "The idea of childlike playfulness is already present in the motifs fun and laughter. While, therefore,

The second group of interpretations center on the idea that the image schema for the passage is that of "childhood" and "parenting." R. Hoshaya (*Gen. Rab. 1.1*), Ibn Janaḥ (*Sefer Hariqmah 323.16*) and Ramaq all cite versions of this argument based upon references to Num 11:13 (Hoshaya); Lam 4:5; and Esth 2:7, 20b in which the word relates to either *being* or *raising* a child.[117] One benefit of this interpretation is that it requires no emendation of the MT. If read as a Qal infinitive, the present vocalization can mean "growing up with." Furthermore, Fox argues that Esth 2:20b "shows that the G—stem of ʾ-m-n, at least in the inf., can be intransitive and refer to the child's role as well as the guardian's. . . . It also shows that the verb in this sense can govern a preposition meaning 'with,' for ʾēṣel 'with'/'next to' is a near synonym of ʿet as a preposition of proximity (cf. the interchange of these preposition in 1 Kgs 20:36)."[118] The morphology corresponds much better than that of the previous option. Furthermore, the imagery compounds the notion of parental instruction. First, personified wisdom was YHWH's toddler, with the implication that he "brought her up" and she was his delight.[119] This imagery then is deepened first by her similar *delight* in the sons of Adam (v. 31b) and then furthermore by her address to human beings as *her* sons in 8:32. Unfortunately, this image does not erase the significant elements of the CREATION AS CONSTRUCTION metaphor, and does not provide a clear means to explain how or why this extension would take place.

The final group of interpretations do not privilege one image schema or another, although they are associated with the image schema of WISDOM AS WOMAN, in so far as they parse אָמוֹן with regard to constancy or faithfulness, which is a key concept in the dichotomy of *Lady Wisdom* and the *Strange Woman* in Prov 1–9. Lexically, these interpretations depend on

---

the translation of אמון as 'nursling' is not a *sine qua non* to arrive at the celebratory interpretation of this text, this meaning of the word (*vice versa*) suits the context best because the image of a playing child is present in its own right" (Loader, *Proverbs 1–9*, 360). Van Leeuwen contends that the theme of 'rejoicing' and 'celebration' is attested as a component of building projects. He points to Jer 30:18–19; Zech 8:5; 1 Kgs 8:62–66 as exemplars for the celebration that accompanies the completion of a building project. "This move from cosmic construction, delight, and feasting is basic to Proverbs 8 and 9:1–6, which follow a widespread ancient pattern that combines joy in building with celebration at its completion and inauguration. Indeed, this pattern is universal. In 8:21–30, we have the 'building' of the cosmos, employing verbs commonly used of human building projects" (Van Leeuwen, "Book of Proverbs," 95). While this is possible, the lexical connections needed to justify the interpretation are tenuous at best.

117. Fox, *Proverbs 1–9*, 287.
118. Fox, *Proverbs 1–9*, 287
119. Loader, *Proverbs 1–9*, 360.

reading the root from אמן with an English gloss of "be faithful." The heritage of this interpretation can find its roots in the Greek translation of "harmoniously" (ἁρμόζουσα) in LXX or *mhymnt'* ("trusted one") in the Targum. In the modern period, Plöger translates "constantly" and Ehrlich "trusted friend." Waltke makes a convincing argument for this gloss because it makes the best sense of the line and accentuation: If the second and third lines reference "day by day" and "in all times" then the best fit in context would be to expect a reference that corresponds to a temporal frame. Moreover, this reading would provide a tip of the hat to the centrality of fidelity to feminine imagery and wisdom in Prov 1–9. However, the meaning of אמון proposed by Waltke is not born out by usage in the Tanakh. In the context of "faithfulness" or "constancy" the word "is not productive in the G-Stem (it appears only in the frozen form, *'āmēn*). Moreover, the N-stem would be expected in the proposed sense."[120]

In summary, let us consider the poet's choice of diction. All three options are supported by broader image schema. All three options have viable explanations with regard to usage and syntax. However, given the context of "architect" the word אמון would be an unusual choice for the poet. The more natural choice would be some form of חרש or related root. In the context of "child" the word אמון would be an unusual choice, because any number of terms for "child" could have been more clearly applied (ילד, ינק, בת) with greater force and clarity. Finally, if the poet wished to emphasize the continuous or faithful nature of *Lady Wisdom*'s presence, we would expect a choice like תמיד, חסד, or אמונה. However, if the poet wished to choose a term that provided for resonance between all three metaphoric strata without privileging one particular image schema there is no other suitable term. Therefore, I would argue that the poet has *intended* a paradoxical blend of each of these metaphorical threads without subordination. Wisdom is a faithful woman, constant in companionship to YHWH and more ancient than the world. Her delight is in the created order and in the sons of Adam, among whom she regards the wise as her sons. Wisdom is the child and delight of YHWH, being born in the creative order which established the cosmos, she grew even as the LORD established order and meaning for the inhabitable world and for its denizens.

Lady Wisdom is the plurality of paradox and wonder who stands with the implied offer of honesty, integrity, intellectual, and social betterment, wealth, wonder, rule, antiquity, and delight. She stands in right relationship to YHWH and offers that relationship to the young man. Opposite her stands the *Strange Woman*, the petty aggregate of lying words, crooked

---

120. Fox, *Proverbs 1–9*, 286.

actions, stupidity, shame, and loss; but with the promise of a good time for the night. She stands in no relationship to YHWH and offers that relationship to the young man. The comparison is no comparison.

A Comparison of the Invitations of the *Strange Woman* and *Lady Wisdom*

Both the *Strange Woman* and *Lady Wisdom* offer invitations. These invitations are most clearly paralleled in Prov 9:4 and 16 where the precise phrase is found in the mouth of each woman (מִי־פֶתִי יָסֻר הֵנָּה חֲסַר־לֵב אָמְרָה לּוֹ:). However, this parallel invitation is merely the capstone reiteration of previous appeals. In particular, Prov 7 provides a very vivid and explicit depiction of the *Strange Woman's* invitation to the חסר־לב. Likewise, in Prov 8 the reader is privy to *Lady Wisdom's* final argument and self-presentation. In the offer of the *Strange Woman*, cultic, and erotic elements are fused in a manner similar but contrary to those of Prov 5. In Prov 7, the same image schemas are disposed to show the disastrous outcomes of marital and therefore covenant infidelity. In Prov 8, *Lady Wisdom's* Invitation is the fusion of the prophetic call which began the book (Prov 1:22) and the refrain of parental entreaty that echoes through each chapter (Prov 8:32). The comparison of the two invitations compares the long punishment of unfaithful eros versus the long blessing of attentiveness to familial, divine, and sapiential calling.

The Erotic and Devious Invitation of the Strange Woman to Infidelity

The *Strange Woman's* speech joins elements of orthodox lexicon and practice with novel metaphors which betray an apotropaic/magical understanding of the cult. Superficially it seems odd that the first words from the mouth of the *Strange Woman* are specifically cultic. Moreover, there seems to be no indication that the sacrifices are pagan. On the contrary, both the vocabulary (זִבְחֵי שְׁלָמִים) and the prescription and regulation for peace offerings are set forth in Leviticus chapters 4 and 7. Outside of the book of Proverbs, the roots involved in this construction appear in only two other context in the Writings, and both are in Chronicles.[121] This is a jarring and purposeful

---

121. The root usage for זבח and שלם is overwhelmingly localized in the Torah, but with a few occurrences in the Prophets (Exod 24:5; 29:28; Lev 3:1, 3, 6, 9; 4:10, 26, 31, 35; 7:11, 13, 15, 18, 20–21, 29, 32, 34, 37; 17:5; 19:5; 22:21; 23:19; Num 6:17–18; 7:17, 23, 29, 35, 41, 47, 53, 59, 65, 71, 77, 83, 88; 10:10; 15:8; Josh 22:23, 27; 1 Sam 10:8; 11:15; 1 Kgs 8:63; 2 Chr 30:22; 33:16; Prov 7:14). Moreover, in every case where these

imposition of cultic language into an otherwise sapiential narrative. Second, the "fulfillment of her vows" (שִׁלַּמְתִּי נְדָרָי) is equally cultic in its orientation, but the force of the mention is more difficult to determine.[122] While different vows were not only permitted but expected within the Israelite cult, there is some question of what she would have vowed and why. From the broader witness of the canon, vows were typically offered by a worshipper in exchange and contingent upon divine action or protection.[123]

While there is a sudden imposition of standard cultic terminology, the *Strange Woman* employs a novel metaphor for sacrifice that is out of sorts with that employed in the rest of Tanakh. At no place in Tanakh are sacrifices said to be "upon" (עַל) anyone. Rather, *guilt* is said to be "upon" individuals and groups.[124] God's hand, Spirit or favor may be "upon" individuals or groups.[125] Righteousness and integrity may be "upon" individuals or groups.[126] Each of these divine or abstract elements are typically figured as either a fluid or physical presence that then rests upon the party in question. The metaphorical use of "upon me" with regard to cultic acts is a mismatch of metaphor. Consider the case of Job:

> וַיְהִי כִּי הִקִּיפוּ יְמֵי הַמִּשְׁתֶּה וַיִּשְׁלַח אִיּוֹב וַיְקַדְּשֵׁם וְהִשְׁכִּים בַּבֹּקֶר וְהֶעֱלָה עֹלוֹת מִסְפַּר כֻּלָּם
>
> And so it was that when the days of the feast came round, then Job sent and sanctified them and rose early in the morning and offered burnt offerings according to the number of all of them.

---

roots appear it is as a part of the construction "peace offering" whether singular, plural, construct or absolute.

122. First, Numbers 30 legislates that the vows of women were subject to rejection by responsible males, either by the father or the husband. Only the vows of the divorced or widowed women were beyond being overturned by men (Num 30:9). As the woman in question has not only made but fulfilled vows, the question of her status with relation to her husband presents an interesting ambiguity.

123. For instance, Jacob made a vow to YHWH in exchange for providence and a safe return to his home (Gen 28:20). Jephthah vowed to sacrifice the first thing that met him in return for safety and success in battle (Judg 11:30–31).

124. Gen 27:13; 2 Sam 14:9; 2 Chr 28:13; Ezek 33:10. Guilt is understood metaphorically as a "stain," "blemish," or "dirt" that is "upon" someone and then needs to be cleansed or removed.

125. E.g., Ezra 10:12; Ps 90:17.

126. E.g., Ps 7:9

> כִּי אָמַר אִיּוֹב אוּלַי חָטְאוּ בָנַי וּבֵרֲכוּ אֱלֹהִים בִּלְבָבָם כָּכָה יַעֲשֶׂה אִיּוֹב כָּל־הַיָּמִים:
>
> Because Job said, "perhaps they my sons sinned and cursed God in their heart," so thus Job would do all the time. (Job 1:5)

Despite the fact that the motivation seems remarkably similar, note that the use of metaphor is not. Job "sanctified them" and "offered burnt offerings" but this was not in order to provide a protective charm *upon* his offspring, but to appease an offended God. The center of the activity is relationship, not a quasi-magical cultic act.

Moreover, the temporal element gives a present and apotropaic/magical element to these cultic activities. In the second half of the same colon, "*Today*, I have paid my vows" (הַיּוֹם שִׁלַּמְתִּי נְדָרָי) places accent on the present nature of the action. Not only are the "sacrifices upon" her, she has also paid her vows "today." The overall feeling is one of completed religious obligation somewhat similar to that witnessed in the Psalms.[127] In one sense, the woman is saying the right things, just not in the right way.

THE *STRANGE WOMAN*'S INVITATION IS A CONCEPTUAL BLEND OF *THIRST* AND *IDOLATRY* METAPHOR

The invitation of the *Strange Woman* revisits the metaphors of LOVE IS THIRST and IDOLATRY IS ADULTERY and therefore identifies infidelity to spouse with infidelity to YHWH.

> 18 לְכָה נִרְוֶה דֹדִים עַד־הַבֹּקֶר נִתְעַלְּסָה בָּאֳהָבִים:
>
> Come and let us drink love until the morning. Let us delight ourselves in the love.
>
> 19 כִּי אֵין הָאִישׁ בְּבֵיתוֹ הָלַךְ בְּדֶרֶךְ מֵרָחוֹק:
>
> Because the man is not in the house. He has gone in a distant road. (Prov 7:18–19)

The woman's initial invitation, (i.e., the imperative form of הלך) is unusual insofar as it retains a paragogic heh, that is first of all identical to the invitation of violent youths in Prov 1:11, but also the erotic invitation found in Song 7:12. Moreover, in verse 18 the poet chooses an unusual word for "enjoy" (עלס). Though he likely could have chosen a more conventional

---

127. See Ps 22:26; 50:14; 56:13; 61:9; 65:2; 66:13; 116:14, 18.

Hebrew word (i.e., "exult" (עלז), "rejoice" (שמח), or even "taste" (טעם), the contexts in which these words occur point to a sort of "stupid delight" or pride (20:18; 39:13).

Finally, the Masoretes note that the construction "with love" (בָּאֲהָבִים) is alone in Tanakh. With the prepositional phrase appended, this is true. However, the noun *does* appear in two contexts as a plural: once in Hos 8:9 with regard to *lovers*—again in the context of the IDOLATRY IS ADULTERY metaphor.

Additionally, the woman evokes the LOVE IS THIRST metaphor as found in Prov 5:19 and canonical parallels, but then combines this with elements of the prophetic metaphor IDOLATRY IS ADULTERY. As noted in the previous context, the metaphor of LOVE IS THIRST, is reflected in the word glossed as "let us take our fill" (רוה) and is the same as that found in Prov 5:19. Finally, the word for "love" (דודים) appears in four contexts in *Tanakh* not as a romantic vocative but with the meaning of "love" or "lust." Two of these contexts are in Ezekiel and implicated in the IDOLATRY IS ADULTERY metaphor (Ezek 16:18; 23:17) the other two are with decidedly erotic and intimate contexts (Prov 7:18; Song 5:1).[128] In most other contexts the word is modified either by pronominal suffixes or other constructs.

Finally, and obviously, the woman's proposition is explicitly in the context of adultery because it is predicated upon the subordinate clause that her "husband is away." However, the implications run much deeper, as noted by Aletti:

> The rare cloths with which the woman decorated her bed, the perfumes which she names . . . are they not presents by which a man demonstrates his love for his spouse? The myrrh, the aloe, the cinnamon, do they not express metonymically the couple's desire? (cf. for example the use of this symbol in Cant or Ps 45)? But when these symbols are used in the end, they are inverted by the "tortuous speech." Everything collapses. One can understand why Prov 1:22 expressed this situation by a reversal of moral contents (like lack of experience and hatred of knowledge) in which there was no other exit than misfortune.[129]

In the final assessment, the son's willingness to accept such an invitation, places him both figuratively and literally in enmity with YHWH.

---

128. Ginsberg, *Massorah*, 1:266.
129. Aletti, "Seduction et Parole," 139 (translation mine).

Lady Wisdom's Renewed and Redoubled Invitation to the Youth

Compared to the open, explicit, and purposeful *proposition* of the *Strange Woman*, what can be said about the *invitation* of *Lady Wisdom*? The stated audience, imperatives and voice join the prophetic entreaty of chapter 1 with the refrain of attentiveness to parental instruction while fulfilling the stated aims of the book in Prov 1:1–7.

> 5 הָבִינוּ פְתָאיִם עָרְמָה וּכְסִילִים הָבִינוּ לֵב׃
>
> Discern, simple ones, subtlety and stupid ones discern heart
>
> 6 שִׁמְעוּ כִּי־נְגִידִים אֲדַבֵּר וּמִפְתַּח שְׂפָתַי מֵישָׁרִים׃
>
> Hear, that direct things I will speak and the opening of my lips is rectitude. (Prov 8:5–6)
>
> 10 קְחוּ־מוּסָרִי וְאַל־כָּסֶף וְדַעַת מֵחָרוּץ נִבְחָר׃
>
> Take my discipline and not silver and knowledge before choice gold. (Prov 8:10)
>
> 33 שִׁמְעוּ מוּסָר וַחֲכָמוּ וְאַל־תִּפְרָעוּ׃
>
> Listen [to] discipline and be wise and do not let go.[130] (Prov 8:33)

First, her audience is not an individual "empty head" (חסר־לב) as the *Strange Woman* in Prov 7. Rather, her audience returns to who it has been since the beginning. The "simple" (פְּתָאיִם) and the "stupid" (כְּסִילִים) are again *Lady Wisdom*'s audience, with the more general implication that she is calling to those who *lack* wisdom.[131] Second, her appeal is equally familiar and novel. She calls the youths to *discern* (בין). The appeal is familiar first because the lexeme is repeated dozens of time in chapters 1–9, and more particularly because it is one of the prevalent aims of the book as listed in Prov 1:2, 6:

---

130. The verb "neglect" (פרע) either implies מוסר as the direct object (i.e., Toy, Ringgren) and is therefore gapped, or the direct object אתו was lost via scribal error (Waltke, *Proverbs 1–15*, 391). In either case, discipline (מוסר) is in view. See Loader, *Proverbs 1–9*, 365.

131. Waltke believes that these two groups are "lumped together" (cf. Waltke, *Proverbs 1–15*, 396) where Fox and Loader both see a sort of continuum presented between the mere dolt and the hardened fool (Fox, *Proverbs 1–9*, 268; Loader, *Proverbs 1–9*, 328).

> לָדַעַת חָכְמָה וּמוּסָר לְהָבִין אִמְרֵי בִינָה׃
>
> To know wisdom and discipline, to *discern* the sayings of insight, (Prov 1:2)
>
> לְהָבִין מָשָׁל וּמְלִיצָה דִּבְרֵי חֲכָמִים וְחִידֹתָם׃
>
> To discern the proverb and the mocking song, the words of the wise and their riddles. (Prov 1:6) .

It is novel, because this is the only appearance of the hiphil imperative in Prov 1–9. It is as if *Lady Wisdom* is finally appealing to the youth: *discern*. The verb "discern" (בין) combines elements of perception and understanding, and "come[s] to refer to the insight and understanding that is achieved through such observation."[132] "When the dir. obj. of *hēbîn* is an intellectual-spiritual faculty, the verb means to *acquire* or *possess* its object in a perceptive, intelligent way. Prov 29:7 says that 'the wicked man does not 'understand knowledge' [*yābîn dā ʿat*]; his failure lies not in lacking a grounding in epistemology but in lacking knowledge itself."[133] Therefore, by their observation of Wisdom, the simple are able to *discern* subtlety. Likewise, by observation the stupid may learn that they have not acted in accordance with plain sense. The aims of this discernment correspond not only to the aims of the introduction but to those values that separate the youth from the poor fellow in Prov 7.[134]

Immediately following, the next component of *Lady Wisdom*'s invitation is to *hear* (שמע). As with discernment, this imperative finds its roots in the introduction to the book (Prov 1:5, 8) but even more in the reiteration of *Lady Wisdom*'s appeal to attentiveness to YHWH's covenant in 1:33. From this verse the form becomes one of the main imperatives employed in paternal instruction (4:1, 10; 5:7, 13; 7:24). Finally, it reappears here as the capstone imperative by a threefold repetition 8:32–34. Discernment, hearing and obedience fuses values of *Torah*, parental instruction and wisdom.

Next, in verse 10, Wisdom urges the youths to "take my discipline." "Take" (לקח) "normally has the educational nuance of accepting what is true (1:5; 2:1; 24:32) or false (6:25; 7:21; 22:24–25), not of developing an independent critical faculty. Whatever you take takes you."[135] Moreover,

---

132. Fretheim, "בין," (NIDOTTE 2 653).

133. Fox, *Proverbs 1–9*, 268.

134. The acquisition of "subtlety" (עָרְמָה) is listed as one of the main goals of Proverbs in 1:4. The "lack of heart" is the defect of the חסר־לב in Prov 7.

135. Waltke, *Proverbs 1–15*, 399.

the value of "discipline" (מוסר) again is anchored in the introduction to the book as a whole (Prov 1:2–3, 7). Like discernment and hearing, the usage of discipline is a fusion of the discipline of the paternal instruction (Prov 1:8; 4:1), wisdom (Prov 4:13; 8:10) and YHWH (Prov 3:11).[136]

Wisdom, then, "has been calling." She has been calling in the voice of the sage parent, echoing the strains of covenant. Wisdom's appeal is not for a short pleasure and a long suffering like the *Strange Woman*, but rather *for attentiveness to the ongoing conversation* and a *desperate appeal for real perception*. In Prov 9, *Lady Wisdom* and the *Strange Woman* are placed in a final dichotomy. They both make the same appeal to the same audience (Prov 9:4, 16). Wisdom's appeal, situated in luxury and plenty offers all the same things that the father has promised in the previous eight chapters, the *Strange Woman* offers only stolen waters and secret bread in another man's house. The comparison is no comparison.

A Comparison of the Houses of the *Strange Woman* and *Lady Wisdom*

As noted above, the image schema of the "road" structures numerous metaphors and conceptual blends throughout the book of Proverbs. In addition to the basic metaphor LIFE IS A ROAD, there are numerous dependent and related metaphors based either upon the manner of walking (securely, stumbling) or the nature of the path (dark, twisted, bright, straight). The house of the *Strange Woman* relates to ROAD metaphor primarily as destinations that are associated with the *outcomes* and *maintenance* of paths. The abode of the *Strange Woman* is associated with wandering from righteous paths and is depicted as equivalent to death and *sheol*. The house of Wisdom is conceptually problematic. Her house is likewise depicted as a place of arrival that is the end of those who fear the LORD and maintain paths of Wisdom, however, her house is not associated with life as an abstract and enduring good. Rather, her house is depicted in terms of luxury, security, and material goods. All the same, the silent assumption is that Wisdom can provide for no eternal house, merely earthly blessing.

---

136. There are a few occurrences in which the origin of "discipline" is abstract or unclear (5:12; 6:23; 7:22; 8:33).

The House of the Strange Woman as the Destination for All Those Who Wander from Faithful Paths

As roads lead to destinations, then LIFE IS A ROAD finds extension in DEATH IS A DESTINATION. More poignantly in the case of the characterization of the *Strange Woman*, her house is not a point upon the way but a final end (5:8–14). The house of the *Strange Woman* is equivalent to death itself. For example consider Prov 2:18–19, in which wisdom/instruction is to protect the youth from the *Strange Woman*:

> 18 כִּי שָׁחָה אֶל־מָוֶת בֵּיתָהּ וְאֶל־רְפָאִים מַעְגְּלֹתֶיהָ:
>
> Because her house[137] descends to death and to the shades her tracks.
>
> 19 כָּל־בָּאֶיהָ לֹא יְשׁוּבוּן וְלֹא־יַשִּׂיגוּ אָרְחוֹת חַיִּים:
>
> All those coming to her will not return and they will not regain paths of life. (Prov 2:18–19)

---

137. It seems that the rare lexeme שׁוח has been selected by the poet to provide a sound play with 2:17b (וְאֶת־בְּרִית אֱלֹהֶיהָ שָׁכֵחָה: כִּי שָׁחָה אֶל־מָוֶת בֵּיתָהּ). "Her house" (ביתה) cannot grammatically function as the subject of the 3fs perfect verb. However, the conjectural emendation does not explain away the clear parallel in 7:27, where her house is figured in light of the metaphor DEATH IS A DESTINATION. The remaining option is to read שׁוח as a transitive verb. There are only two cases of the verb in Tanakh (Prov 2:18; Lam 3:20) and both of these appear to be intransitive/reflexive. All the same, this option is no less complicated than emendation of the text or forcing disagreement between subject and verb. Moreover, the sound play noted above also makes a neat chiasm "house" and "covenant" in the center and the verbs at the outside. This structure could also have pushed the intransitive verb into a transitive stance. The chief implication of the reading, however, is moving the woman from a passive symbol for death to an agent who is in some manner responsible in a manner similar to the "evil men" of vv. 12–15. Fox argues "MT's *byth* should be emended to *ntybth*. ... The presumed original *mwtntybth* became *mwtbuth* by partial haplography and metatheses: י-ב for ב-י. From the standpoint of both sense and grammar, it is awkward to say 'her house' [m.sg] inclines down [fem. sg.]. ... The emendation provides a fem. subject for *šaḥaḥ* and a better parallel to 'her tracks.' The image of the woman's house sinking down to the underworld is not found elsewhere, whereas, the image of paths or steps leading down to death appears in 5:5; 7:27; 14:12 and 16:25; cf. 12;28b, but the text is uncertain MT's *beytahh* may be influenced by 7:26, where the word is grammatically feasible" (Fox, *Proverbs 1–9*, 121–22). If the conjectural emendation is accepted, then the controlling metaphor for the verse is LIFE IS A ROAD and her habits are equated with death itself. Unfortunately, that does not make sense in this context or the broader context of Proverbs. The ROAD of the *Strange Woman* is not a danger because the young man will emulate her habits or manner of life, it is a danger because *it leads to her*. For this reason, "house" as destination makes more sense in context.

WISE OR STRANGE? 207

Those who are led into breaching the divine covenant through marital and therefore divine infidelity have reached their final end. There is no return. In this paragraph (7:24–27) the poet provides the final statement of this metaphor, but does so first by establishing a unique lexical connection to Torah. After the initial exhortation to heed paternal instruction, the poet returns to the road metaphor, but extends it by employing a non-standard verb choice.

> 25 אַל־יֵשְׂטְ אֶל־דְּרָכֶיהָ לִבֶּךָ אַל־תֵּתַע בִּנְתִיבוֹתֶיהָ׃
>
> Do not let your heart stray into her roads and do not turn aside into her tracks.
>
> 26 כִּי־רַבִּים חֲלָלִים הִפִּילָה וַעֲצֻמִים כָּל־הֲרֻגֶיהָ׃
>
> Because she has caused many slain to fall and strong men all she has slain.
>
> 27 דַּרְכֵי שְׁאוֹל בֵּיתָהּ יֹרְדוֹת אֶל־חַדְרֵי־מָוֶת׃ פ
>
> [The] Roads of Sheol are toward her house, descending to the chambers of death. (Prov 7:25–27)

"Do let your heart go astray" (שטה) appears in only one other context outside of Proverbs. It appears four times in Num 5:12–29 in describing the trial by ordeal for the "straying wife."[138] As such, the ROAD and DESTINATION metaphors are also being extended through a double entendre of the metaphor INFIDELITY IS WANDERING. Moreover, beyond the initial metaphor that "straying" is associated with "unfaithfulness" there is the strong legal and covenantal thrust granted from the allusion. Moreover, it is not merely the son but "his heart/mind" that is implicated in the unfaithfulness of "wandering" into her roads.[139]

Finally, by returning to the road metaphor the poet considers the depicted woman as a final destination and piles up terms for the unhappy dead. Verse 26 joins the last four cola as the conclusion to the paragraph as an epexegetic clause.[140] The lad is commanded to avoid wandering into the woman's paths, because the woman is figured quite explicitly as a killer

---

138. See Num 5:12, 19, 20, 29.

139. The second verb for "wander" (תעה) is far more standard within the *Tanakh* and Proverbs in particular (Prov 7:25; 10:17; 12:26; 14:22; 21:16).

140. Verse 26 by itself generates a referential half-meaning. Is the woman really a murderer? Verse 27 recasts those dead in light of *sheol* in a manner very similar to Prov 1:12; 2:18; 5:5–6.

of many men. She has "caused many to fall," drawing from the metaphor wherein death is equated with falling to the earth or down generally. The poet moves from the "slain" (חללים) generally to the "mighty" (אצומים). Likewise from cause to fall (הנפיל) to "kill."

While *sheol* casts long shadows over the wandering wicked as an image metaphor, the more basic image schema that underlies it is that of destination. Wandering paths lead to only one destination. The *Strange Woman*'s house is full of the dead, precisely because she "multiplies the unfaithful." Yet again, infidelity to spouse is counted as infidelity to YHWH. Breach of faith will bring one to the house of the *Strange Woman*: death itself.

The House of Lady Wisdom as a Secure but Merely Earthly Life

Contrary to the *Strange Woman*, *Lady Wisdom* has appeared to be homeless through the bulk of the first eight chapters. A significant part of the difficulty is fixing a metonymic reference that is conceptually meaningful. If LIFE IS A ROAD and the negative destination provided by the *Strange Woman* is DEATH, what destination is provided by *Lady Wisdom* as her antithesis?

Options for Identification of the House of *Lady Wisdom*

There are basically three options: Some argue that the seven pillars and "house" of wisdom are an oblique reference to textual divisions within the book of Proverbs.[141] Unfortunately, there has been an utter inability to provide any sort of consensus to what textual divisions would coincide with these seven pillars. Conversely, the reference to "Wisdom's house" may be an allegory for either the temple or the cosmos itself. Lang argues in favor of the former.[142] The strong association of Wisdom with YHWH would certainly seem to allow for such an association. There is slight lexical and canonical evidence to support of understanding Wisdom's house as the temple; though mostly because the presence of "pillars" and the manner of construction only find canonical parallels in the construction of the temple. However, if the poet *intended* to show association with the temple he could have used any number of specific references that would have fixed the temple as the intended allegorical referent. For example, the presence of "seven pillars" has no counterpart in the temple. Moreover, the manner and style of building would be difficult to describe using other terms. The lexical

---

141. Skehan, "Seven Pillars of Wisdom's House," 290–97.
142. Lang, *Wisdom*, 90–93.

associations could be coincidental. Finally, the poet's disposition toward the cult (Prov 7:14–15; 15:8; 21:3, 23) would seem to betray a wariness of identifying the home of wisdom in cult.

Some scholars identify the "house of Wisdom" with creation. For example, Van Leeuwen argues that "house building" is an image schema not only for temples, but also for the created order as a whole. As such then, the "temple building" language may be merely an extension of the metaphor of the *CREATION OF THE COSMOS AS BUILDING A HOUSE*.[143] This image schema also would be at home in Prov 8, especially given the prevalence of the three tiered cosmos image that reappears continually with regard to creation. However, if the "house of Wisdom" is creation, how are the "doors" to be understood? Moreover, the choice of "seven pillars" and the absence of any mention of other, more typical, creation imagery is difficult to explain.

In short, proposed referents for the "house of Wisdom" are close, but at the same time, deficient. I believe that the poet avoids an explicit parallel, because the core element of the image schema from the house of the *Strange Woman* (i.e., *DEATH*), cannot meaningfully map antithetically onto a target. The importance of Wisdom's house in not merely in the book of Proverbs, nor should she be reduced to temple piety, nor to a secular empiricism of nature, rather the House represents the place Wisdom's dwelling in the abstract. Her banquet represents her manner of life that is secure, blessed, and luxurious. The image schema argues that the one who remains near Wisdom's house will find her.

Death Remains the Destination

The lack of a clear image schema, while maintaining an *attached expectancy* provides for a parity between the relational and erotic appeal of the feminine, and a sort of resting place. Wisdom's house, is where Wisdom is. The temple is not precluded, nor is the realm of the created order. All the same, she provides no eternal home but rather her house exists more like a dreamlike hope. Wisdom may provide for security, luxury, and the good pleasure of YHWH, but she does not cancel death. The basic metaphors of *LIFE IS A ROAD* and *DEATH IS A DESTINATION* do not allow for extension to any antithesis of death. Despite all the benefits and allurements of the house of Wisdom, *LIFE IS A DESTINATION* cannot be mapped as antithesis because even those who whole-heartedly pursue Wisdom will come to the grave.

---

143. Van Leeuwen, *Proverbs*, 101.

She provides a remedy for untimely or unlucky death, but she does not cure death (Job 3; Eccl 3:18–21).

It is in this, then, in the quiet admission that there is no remedy for death, that *Lady Wisdom* and the *Strange Woman* do become objects of comparison. The goods offered by wisdom, can only be for the possibility of a richer, better, longer, and more comfortable mortal life. If this is called into question, the difference in the final abode erases any distinction whatever.

Conclusion for Stage One Perception: Ambiguity and Fidelity

The disparity between the *Strange Woman* and *Lady Wisdom* with regard to their characterization, invitation, and role as destination does not entirely do justice to the demonstrable similarity between these two characters. This has been stated nowhere as articulately and eloquently as in J. N. Alletti's work, "Seduction et Parole en Proverbes I—IX."[144] While Aletti's thesis is concerned mainly with how speech serves in relation to the seduction of the youth, he clarifies many of the central issues that inform the following discussion. First, Aletti demonstrates how Proverbs holds forth the reality and surety of judgment upon the wicked and protection and blessing for the righteous as an unqualified reality in formulaic fashion. The surety of this judgment is sharp and unambiguous (1:32–33; 2:21–22; 3:32–35; 4:18–19; 8:32–36).[145] Against this axis of the certainty of sapiential retribution is the purposeful ambiguity in the representation of *Lady Wisdom* and the *Strange Woman*. While Aletti explains that ambiguity is a continuous element in the presentation of certain outcomes in Prov 1–9, most of his examples are linked to feminine imagery.[146]

> Likewise, in Prov 9, *Lady Wisdom* and Lady Folly both offer the food (*lhm*) of their banquet. And if the sage requests his disciple to love his spouse (5:15), the senseless woman of Prov 9 uses the same picture (waters of the well, 9:17) to attract him towards her house. Nevertheless ambiguity is fundamentally caused by

---

144. Aletti, "Seduction et Parole," 129–44.

145. Aletti, "Seduction et Parole," 132.

146. Aletti notes the various lexical linkages noted throughout: a man can "embrace" Lady Wisdom (4:8) or the *Strange Woman* (5:20). He can grasp and cling to wisdom (3:18; 4:13) or be grasped and clung to by the *Strange Woman* (7:13). He also notes the parallels in the women in Proverbs 9. All other citations are linked to similar metaphors or lexemes in the treatment of feminine metaphor. See Aletti, "Seduction et Parole," 133–34.

> the situation of the speaker. Two persons can offer the same things; but the one wants evil and other one the good. Therefore, how can they be recognized? Here the seduction of the word can more easily slide: Does not the biggest seduction consist in inviting to evil with (almost) the same words as the one who calls to the good? Villains say to the inexperienced (1:13): "we shall fill (*ml* ·) our houses of booty," and wisdom asserts similarly (8:21): "'I bring resources to those who love me and I fill (*ml'*) their coffers." "Rejoice in the wife of your youth ... and be drunk in her breasts at all times' says the master (5:19)," and, as if in response, the adulterous woman repeats: "Come! Let us become intoxicated (*rwh*) of sensuousness (*ddym*; obvious allusion in 5:19) till morning (7:18)." The starkest example, because marked stylistically, is in Prov 9 where *Lady Wisdom* and Lady Senseless each say "Let the simple turn aside here!" (vv. 4, 15).[147]

The purposeful ambiguity, first of all, allows for what Aletti calls the "mechanism of seduction" which amounts to nothing more than the cognitive disassociation of means from ends.[148] So, for example in Prov 7, the youth is encouraged to infidelity because the "husband is away," therefore, the assumption is that consequences will be averted. Second, the early introduction (e.g., 1:10) and continuous presentation of seduction in Prov 1–9 allows for a cycle of "confusion" and "clarification" not only about what constitutes stupidity, but also what constitutes wisdom.[149] Speech acts as a frame for the experience of things and thereby generates a gap between the things themselves and the agents.

> We are not, therefore, irremediably captive to charm or violence. Since seduction comes from speech, a distance always resides between speech and execution; a distance, that is to say the possibility of thinking, resisting, and even of desisting. The idiot is precisely the one who does not know nor wants to take time to discern truth or falsehood in the speech of other people. The

---

147. Aletti, "Seduction et Parole," 133 (translation mine).

148. "The mechanism of seduction, as we have seen, consists in dissociating the end of means in a radical manner as in Prov 1:11–14 (i.e., 'Can't one become rich, blessed of God, without practicing justice? Has the righteous man necessarily the happiness which should sanction the effort?' In an adjacent manner, 'is it true that the single poor action inevitably draws one away to dishonor and death?')" (Aletti, "Seduction et Parole," 138 [translation mine]).

149. "And it is this repetition of the stylistic phenomenon of confusion and then clarification which alone allows us to understand the rapport which the text causes to exist between seduction and speech and which we shall analyse from the point of view of connotation" (Aletti, "Seduction et Parole," 133 [translation mine]).

sage denounces this haste (1:16; 6:18; 7:23) several times. Only the detailed observation of words and things, as well as patient listening to the masters (4:13), permits one to evade seduction. Seduction renders the discourse of the wise suspect. If misleading speech starts to use the same expressions as true word how can one distinguish between the two?[150]

Aletti, asserts that Wisdom is determined by a cluster of values that must be carefully discerned. Wisdom is distinct from seduction because seduction is "smooth," where the words of wisdom are a severe mercy.[151] He argues that the Wisdom differs in its source, being first transmitted from parents and ultimately finding its source in YHWH.[152] Ultimately, however, he neglects the one simple criterion that arises from the text: *fidelity*. This is ultimately the manner of discerning wisdom from folly.

Consider a different literary example by way of illustration. Xenophon reproduces a poem from the sophist poet Prodicus on lines 21-34 in *Memorabilia*.[153] Some scholars have found in this work a conceptual parallel to the "two women" of Proverbs 1-9. In Prodicus's story Herakles is presented at a crossroads in his youth when he is approached by two women. The first is a personification of *Virtue* who promises a difficult way, awarded with substance and honor. The second is a personification of *Vice* who promises a life of ease and delight; robbed from the labors and belongings of others. The pairing of *ROAD* and *WOMAN* metaphors and the antithesis of these values seem to provide a more than adequate parallel. However, the distinctions are even more telling. First, *Virtue* and *Vice* are lexically and conceptually antithetical. In Prov 1-9 *Wisdom* and *Strange* are not, rather, they show that the true axis of comparison is not in *action* (ethical or otherwise) but in *fidelity*. Second, and more important to our present purposes, *Virtue and Vice* are obvious and undefined. The reader is expected to recognize both women by association with the concepts they embody. This is precisely not the case in Prov 1-9. Wisdom amounts to an unknown quantity who is continually expanded and reframed but always antithetical to *infidelity*. While the wise and the strange may be same in their presentation, they may be differentiated by two simple questions: "Is it faithful to YHWH and people?" and "What are the probable outcomes?"

---

150. Aletti, "Seduction et Parole," 140.

151. Aletti, "Seduction et Parole," 141.

152. Aletti, "Seduction et Parole," 141. However, the words of the wise can also be "smooth" or "soft" (cf. Prov 25:15).

153. Xenophon, *Memorabilia* and *Oeconomicus*, 103-111.

Stage Two Perception: A Sufficient Beauty: The Beauty of the Person, Invitation, and Destination Provided in Jesus

Where the glorious personification of wisdom in Prov 8 reiterated the prophetic entreaty in the language of parental instruction but was unable to provide a lasting abode, Jesus provides a comparison of no comparison. Where *Lady Wisdom* is a literary personification, the use of a metaphorical source to describe an abstract metaphorical target, Jesus is the divine person who radiates the glory of the Triune God. Where *Lady Wisdom* offers an invitation to temporal blessing in the language of wisdom and Prophets, Jesus uses similar methods to make himself the invitation into the life of the Trinity. Finally, where *Lady Wisdom*'s house is a nebulous stopping point on the journey to death, Jesus transcends her house. He founds a new house in the sacrifice of his body, and thereby provides a new road, which we know, that will lead us to His Father's eternal House. In Jesus, the best hopes of wisdom are utterly overwhelmed. The partial and tentative beauty of *Lady Wisdom* is confounded by the glory of the Trinity expressed in Jesus.

Jesus is a Person Not a Personification

In considering the relationship between *Lady Wisdom* and Jesus Christ it is first needful to consider how metaphor has made a muddle of ontology. Since Proverbs is historically previous to the birth of Christ, the common line of thinking is that *Lady Wisdom* is the source category used to describe Jesus. In actuality, the opposite is true, Jesus as YHWH is ontologically *prior* to wisdom and provides the basis and substance which the personification of wisdom reflects.[154]

---

154. "However, some scholars have given this extrabiblical literature too much explanatory value in understanding the New Testament's portrayal of Christ. They argue that the exalted picture of Jesus found in the New Testament was largely the result of the early church's reflection on Lady Wisdom as a divine figure. The earliest church supposedly came to think of the human Jesus as divine because it gradually came to associate him with this first-century figure. We reject this approach for the following reasons: (1) While early church fathers, after the close of the New Testament canon, sometimes identified Jesus with the Old Testament personification of Wisdom, the New Testament itself never makes this identification. (2) Wisdom personified is a way of talking about an attribute of God, even in the intertestamental writings; but the New Testament teaches that Jesus is an actual person—namely, God's Son, who is included in the identity of God. (3) There are references to God's creation of Lady Wisdom in Jewish literature. The New Testament portrays Jesus in his deity as eternal. It should be noted that the heretic Arius argued on the basis of the creation of Sophia that Jesus was not fully God. This was rightly rejected by the church. (4) While Lady Wisdom is described as playing a "saving" role in Israel, this never involves salvation from sin. To argue that

The issue with *Lady Wisdom*, then, is not so much with regard to *metaphor* as with regard to an assumed *identity* between the literary personification, *Lady Wisdom*, and the real person of Jesus Christ. There are a number of uncomplicated difficulties related with this line of interpretation. First, since *Lady Wisdom* is to be deemed as a *personification* and therefore *metaphor* we must then be cognizant of the fact that "she" has no ontological existence. Rather she is a literary model which provides conceptual mold which is applied to guide and structure our thoughts and feelings about wisdom as an abstract concept. As metaphor, *some* qualities of woman are mapped onto the abstract category of wisdom (womanhood, relationality, gendered desire) while others are not.[155] Likewise, in the wisdom Christologies of New Testament, the *metaphor* of *Lady Wisdom* is extended, remapped, and frequently overturned. To assert that there is any sort of a precise parity between *Lady Wisdom* and Jesus Christ, first of all translates *Lady Wisdom* from the category of "metaphor" into the category of "independent person/deity" and therefore ontological realty. The superficial similarity between the ontological person of Jesus Christ and the conceptual figure of *Lady Wisdom* should not lead us into a misappropriation of metaphor.

"The constellation of ideas related to *Lady Wisdom* fails to explain the story of Jesus. At best, the background Wisdom material provided language

---

personified Wisdom deepened the New Testament's understanding of the saving role of Jesus is to read the redemptive work of Christ into the earlier Jewish literature. The redemptive work of Christ is central to the New Testament's message about Jesus; it is absent in any substantive sense in the narratives about Lady Wisdom. (5) Finally, the existence of a well—developed story line about a Sophia in Jewish literature is highly suspect. Scholars tend to read back into these writings elements taken from the gospel story that are foreign to what the Jewish authors in their own contexts intended. In the Jewish literature, there is no actual personal existence of Wisdom, no incarnation, no redemptive work, and no second coming. The constellation of ideas related to Lady Wisdom fails to explain the story of Jesus. At best, the background Wisdom material provided language to express truths about Christ, especially in his revelatory and creative functions. These Christological concepts were already assumed by the earliest church on other grounds. Our study rejects a Christology in which "Dame Wisdom" plays a leading role. Yet there is a wisdom Christology, one that finds in Jesus God's fullest revelation for the church and the world. True wisdom, rooted in the nature and life of the triune God, is revealed by Christ and the gospel. Something new and definitive is made known in Jesus; yet at the same time, this Christological wisdom is the oldest wisdom, for it is 'the wisdom of God.' All other conceptions, whether philosophical or religious, are judged by this wisdom" (Ebert, *Wisdom Christology*, loc 335).

155. "Personified Wisdom is a way of talking about an attribute of God, and reflects some important truths about God's work in the world. But Jesus, as a distinct person, along with the Father and the Spirit, is identified as God. This divine identity of the Son is grounded in multiple Old Testament themes, as well as in the events of the life of Christ" (Ebert, *Wisdom Christology*, loc 179).

to express truths about Christ, especially in his revelatory and creative functions. These Christological concepts were already assumed by the earliest church on other grounds."[156] As noted above in chapter 4, the qualities of Wisdom that we find in Christ, are actually properties of YHWH found in Wisdom. It is again, that we confuse the reflection with the source of the light. Jesus transcends the beauty of Wisdom because he is the reality which she reflects.

The Invitation of Jesus is into the Life of the Triune God

In considering the invitation which Jesus offers in Matt 11:25–30, there are two components. The first, and utterly novel, component of Jesus's invitation is that it is not merely into wisdom, or temporal salvation, but is actually a personal invitation into the shared life of the Trinity. The second component of Jesus's invitation finds its roots in a novel blend of wisdom, Torah, and Prophets that aims this invitation at *everyman*. Jesus is the substance of the divine invitation extended to the broken human race.

The Utterly New Component of Jesus's Invitation

In Matt 11:25–11:30 Jesus explains the person of the Father as Father and Creator of the Cosmos, even as he is the Son of God who has been granted divine authority to reveal the Father on earth.[157]

> 25 At that time Jesus declared, "I thank you, Father, Lord of heaven and earth, that you have hidden these things from the wise and understanding and revealed them to little children; 26 yes, Father, for such was your gracious will. 27 All things have been handed over to me by my Father, and no one knows the Son except the Father, and no one knows the Father except the Son and anyone to whom the Son chooses to reveal him. 28 Come to me, all who labor and are heavy laden, and I will give you rest. 29 Take my yoke upon you, and learn from me, for I am gentle and lowly in heart, and you will find rest for your souls. 30 For my yoke is easy, and my burden is light." (Matt 11:25–12:1, ESV)

In this is the primary departure from any invitation that can be offered by personified Wisdom. It is not an invitation to understanding, or

---

156. Ebert, *Wisdom Christology*, loc 335.
157. Swain, "Mystery of the Trinity," 28–29.

blessing, or favor. "This revelation is not a puzzle we are called to solve or a conundrum devised to confound us. It is a source of Joy: first in Jesus, then in those who come to know this revelation through Jesus . . . the mystery of the Trinity makes known the supreme life of communication that is God's life as Father, Son, and Spirit."[158] Jesus's invitation is into the very life the Triune God and the vehicle by which that invitation is delivered.

The "Old" Component of the Invitation of the LORD

Dan Ebert argues that this is the invitation provided by Jesus the sage into *His* wisdom. Matthew 11:25–30 fits into a series of contexts which are primarily concerned with *revelation and rejection*. The earlier part of Matt 11 explains how the message of Jesus had been rejected by the cities where he had ministered.[159] However, Jesus's invitation is different than the ethical blessing of the covenant held forth by personified Wisdom in Prov 8. Rather:

> It is a wisdom that, if rejected, brings awful judgment (11:22–24). It is a wisdom that requires repentance (11:20–21) and a humble, childlike faith (11:25; cf. Matt 18:3–4; 19:14). It demands that we come radically teachable. This wisdom is also dangerous because if we accept the invitation, everything must change as we leave an old life behind and begin, through Jesus, to participate in the very life of the triune God.[160]

However, the *way* Jesus offers wisdom is formally similar to that offered by *Lady Wisdom*, in so far as he *blends* sapiential and prophetic categories into a new conceptual blend. First, Jesus' appeal in Matthew 11:28 is corporate, public, and based upon an image metaphor of "movement" as invitation (i.e., the imperative, "come" is also found in Prov 9:5). Second, the imagery of the "yoke" is one that is provided from Sirach, in which the "yoke" is the fusion of the parental instruction and Torah similar to that found in Proverbs 1–9.[161] Sir 51:23–26, a poem dedicated to personified wisdom, reads:

> 23 Draw near to me, you who are uneducated, and lodge in the house of instruction. 24 Why do you say you are lacking in these things, and why do you endure such great thirst? 25 I opened

---

158. Swain, "Mystery of the Trinity," 28.
159. Ebert, *Wisdom Christology*, loc 430.
160. Ebert, *Wisdom Christology*, loc 422.
161. Ebert, *Wisdom Christology*, loc 587.

my mouth and said, acquire wisdom for yourselves without money. 26 Put your neck under her yoke, and let your souls receive instruction; it is to be found close by. (Sir 51:23–26, NRS)

Therefore, Jesus is making a fairly direct appeal to sapiential metaphor for "taking guidance and correction." However, the manner in which he extends this appeal is a radical *annulment* of the metaphor as it existed in second temple Judaism.

> If there is a literary echo here in Matthew, it is one more of contrast than of identification. Jesus is not identifying himself with the wisdom of Torah as understood by much of the tradition of his day, but rather he is identifying himself as the law's fulfillment. "Take my yoke, rather than that of Wisdom/Torah." Here is welcome relief, not the burden of a works-oriented rendering of Old Testament law, but rather the light yoke of gospel rest. It is the "burden" of Jesus (Matt 11:30) and not the "burden" of the scribes and Pharisees (Matt 23:4).[162]

Moreover, contra to the description of attaining wisdom in Sirach, which was "largely restricted to the upper classes" because it required leisure and literacy, this is a wisdom that is directed to the common man, and especially those who labor.[163] Jesus demolishes sapiential categories and invites *all people* (Prov 8:4) and presents *himself*, not Torah or parental instruction, as the substance of the invitation.

Ebert asserts that the next component of Jesus conceptual blend is the prophetic metaphor of *SALVATION IS REST* as it is found in Jer 6:16 and Isa 28:1–16 which is extended from exhortations to the Sabbath rest in Exod 33:14. Of these passages Isa 28:12–16 most highlights the LORD's invitation in the context of scoffing and rejection.

> 12 אֲשֶׁר ׀ אָמַר אֲלֵיהֶם זֹאת הַמְּנוּחָה הָנִיחוּ לֶעָיֵף וְזֹאת הַמַּרְגֵּעָה וְלֹא אָבוּא שְׁמוֹעַ׃
>
> To whom he said to them, 'This is the rest. Give rest to the weary. And this is repose,' but they would not listen.
>
> 13 וְהָיָה לָהֶם דְּבַר־יְהוָה צַו לָצָו צַו לָצָו קַו לָקָו קַו לָקָו
>
> And the word of YHWH will be to them command upon command, line upon line, line upon line

---

162. Ebert, *Wisdom Christology*, loc 587.
163. Ebert, *Wisdom Christology*, loc 587. See also Sir 38:24–25.

> זְעֵיר שָׁם זְעֵיר שָׁם לְמַעַן יֵלְכוּ וְכָשְׁלוּ אָחוֹר וְנִשְׁבָּרוּ וְנוֹקְשׁוּ וְנִלְכָּדוּ: פ
>
> A little there, a little there, in order that they will walk and they will stumble backward and be broken, and be snared, and be captured.
>
> 14 לָכֵן שִׁמְעוּ דְבַר־יְהוָה אַנְשֵׁי לָצוֹן מֹשְׁלֵי הָעָם הַזֶּה אֲשֶׁר בִּירוּשָׁלָ͏ִם:
>
> Therefore, listen to the word of YHWH, scornful men, the ones ruling this people in Jerusalem.
>
> 15 כִּי אֲמַרְתֶּם כָּרַתְנוּ בְרִית אֶת־מָוֶת
>
> Indeed you have said, 'We cut a covenant with death
>
> וְעִם־שְׁאוֹל עָשִׂינוּ חֹזֶה (שִׁיט) [שׁוֹט] שׁוֹטֵף כִּי־(עָבַר) [יַעֲבֹר] לֹא יְבוֹאֵנוּ
>
> And with Sheol we have made agreement. [The] overwhelming scourge will pass over us. It shall not come to us.
>
> כִּי שַׂמְנוּ כָזָב מַחְסֵנוּ וּבַשֶּׁקֶר נִסְתָּרְנוּ: ס
>
> Because we have set up a lie (as) our refuge and in falsehood we will be secreted.
>
> 16 לָכֵן כֹּה אָמַר אֲדֹנָי יְהוִה הִנְנִי יִסַּד בְּצִיּוֹן אָבֶן אֶבֶן בֹּחַן פִּנַּת יִקְרַת מוּסָד מוּסָּד הַמַּאֲמִין לֹא יָחִישׁ:
>
> Therefore, thus says my Lord YHWH, behold me, he has laid in Zion a stone, a tested stone, a precious cornerstone, a sure foundation. The one being faithful/trusting will not give way. (Isa 28:12–16)

So, as in Proverbs, as in Isaiah, Jesus calls to human beings as children; in the sure context of rejection, offering comfort and rest for the common man predicated not on the obligations of Torah or wise and ethical action, but upon himself as the substance and surety of the LORD's promise. He blends Wisdom, Torah, and Prophets in a single invitation: Come. Come, common man. Come, child. Come, weary. Come downtrodden. Come, last and lost and lonely. "What these background texts indicate is that Jesus is being presented as the culmination of God's WORD to his people, the word that brings rest. He is the fulfillment of the former covenant and the true Torah—Wisdom (Sirach); he is the good way (Jeremiah); he is the promised, precious cornerstone (Isaiah)."[164] If there is any question of the shattering

---

164. Ebert, *Wisdom Christology*, loc 619.

beauty of Christ as the ultimate expression of the love of our triune God, then we simply aren't paying attention.

Jesus Becomes the House of YHWH in His Incarnation in Order to Become the Way to His Father's House

There are four different metaphorical uses of *HOUSE* as a source category that are employed by Jesus and in the broader NT which are intimately related. First, the temple of YHWH is metonymically featured as "the house of YHWH" which is then rightfully Jesus's Father's House, (i.e., *TEMPLE AS HOUSE*) (cf. Luke 2:49). Second, Jesus figures the house of the temple in relation to his physical body that is to be sacrificed on the cross (cf. John 2:19–21). The title of this metaphor would read something like *PHYSICAL BODY OF CHRIST AS HOUSE*. Again building from this metaphor, the church becomes associated with the body of Christ as a new house, built up with its members, (i.e., *BODY OF CHRIST [CHURCH] AS HOUSE*) (cf. 1 Pet 2:4–7). Finally, Jesus does employ the *HOUSE IS DESTINATION* metaphor as it is used by the *Strange Woman*, but this time it bespeaks life in place of death in *THE FATHER'S HOUSE AS ETERNAL LIFE* (John 14:1–7). The New Testament turns house imagery from temple to salvation, from salvation to fellowship and from fellowship to eternal life. Jesus provides the eternal dwelling which wisdom cannot.

Jesus early indicates a special affinity with the temple as both the "house of his Father" (Luke 2:49) but also as his "own house" (Matt 21:13; Mark 11:17; Luke 19:46; John. 2:16–17). This designation is not exactly metaphorical. Though God may not have a "house" per say, if the temple belongs to anyone it belongs to the LORD. More clearly, though, Jesus identified *himself* with the temple:

> 19 Jesus answered them, "Destroy this temple, and in three days I will raise it up." 20 The Jews then said, "It has taken forty-six years to build this temple, and will you raise it up in three days?" 21 But he was speaking about the temple of his body. (John 2:19–21, ESV)

Where the "house" offered by Wisdom is a nebulous antithesis to death that represents the security and blessings available through faithful and perceptive living, Jesus identifies himself with a new temple: a new and literal dwelling of the LORD upon earth. The metaphor of *CHRIST AS HOUSE* is then extended in the New Testament, to refer believers who are "built into" Christ:

> 4 As you come to him, a living stone rejected by men but in the sight of God chosen and precious,5 you yourselves like living stones are being built up as a spiritual house, to be a holy priesthood, to offer spiritual sacrifices acceptable to God through Jesus Christ. 6 For it stands in Scripture: "Behold, I am laying in Zion a stone, a cornerstone chosen and precious, and whoever believes in him will not be put to shame." 7 So the honor is for you who believe, but for those who do not believe, "The stone that the builders rejected has become the cornerstone." (1 Pet 2:4–7, ESV)

This "house of Christ" then is founded in his death and resurrection, and built up via the lives and testimonies of believers through the Holy Spirit, rather than obedience to Torah (Heb 3:1–12). Finally, there is another usage of *HOUSE* as image schema that corresponds most directly with the usage in Prov 8. The house of wisdom, represents a blessed life figured as a destination antithetical to the "untimely death" in the house of the *Strange Woman*. However, as noted, wisdom is ultimately frustrated and fractured by the reality of death. Jesus in a similar manner, points his followers toward His Father's house.

> "Let not your hearts be troubled. Believe in God; believe also in me.2 in my Father's house are many rooms. If it were not so, would I have told you that I go to prepare a place for you? 3 And if I go and prepare a place for you, I will come again and will take you to myself, that where I am you may be also. 4 And you know the way to where I am going." 5 Thomas said to him, "Lord, we do not know where you are going. How can we know the way?" 6 Jesus said to him, "I am the way, and the truth, and the life. No one comes to the Father except through me. 7 If you had known me, you would have known my Father also. From now on you do know him and have seen him." (John 14:1–7, ESV)

In this case, the "Father's house" cannot be a representation of the temple, rather he employs this "house" as a *final destination*, that is *truly* antithetical to death. Moreover, Jesus likewise *fuses* the *PATH* and *DESTINATION* metaphors, by referencing not Torah, or parental instruction, righteous action or *Wisdom* as the way—but points to *himself as YHWH*. Moreover, the way of wisdom that is synonymous with faithful obedience to Torah and parental instruction is transcended but not displaced. Jesus himself is the *way*. His revelation is not of precepts of wise and faithful living but the final seal of his invitation. He invites believers into the eternal fellowship of YHWH. In this the frustrated house of Wisdom is overcome, and the LORD himself has provided the *WAY* via the triune life and self-revelatory will.

Conclusion

While the external presentation of the "wife of your youth," the *Strange Woman,* and *Lady Wisdom* are presented in ambiguous terms and metaphors, the essential and substantial differences are highlighted with relation to *fidelity* to the covenant. The choices held forth for the youth are that of *marital* and therefore *covenant* infidelity resulting in enmity with YHWH and destruction in Prov 7 or the vastness and transcendence of blessing via fidelity to *Lady Wisdom* in Prov 8. The juxtaposition of the character, invitation, and destinations of each of these options yields a comparison that is no comparison.

Lady Wisdom, personifying a faithful relation to the LORD, humanity and creation, is utterly superior to the *Strange Woman*. However, the person, invitation, and houses of Christ transcend those of *Lady Wisdom*, even as the creator surpasses creation. "And the world is passing away along with its desires, but whoever does the will of God abides forever" (1 John 2:17, ESV). In all, Wisdom Christology is less about Jesus conforming to those categories set forth in the personification of wisdom, but more about *Lady Wisdom* reflecting the person and actions of YHWH and the reality of Jesus's perfect humanity. Jesus, and not Wisdom, provides life and not death as a final destination for those who would faithfully love and obey him. Wisdom reflects the person and invitation of YHWH in the created order and expressed first in terms by a dynamic canonical correspondence. The beauty of creation and the OT is in turn both transcended and deepened by his coming and fulfilled in his sacrificial death.

7

Faithful Desire

Following Woman Home to God

STUDIES dedicated to the personification of Wisdom in Proverbs 1–9 have been hindered by shortcomings in the understanding of what metaphor is and how it works. Without a solid definitional and theoretical framework for metaphor, studies have tended to apply alien conceptual frameworks as *source* or *input* categories for *Lady Wisdom*. The opening chapters of this work illustrated the shortcomings in traditional linguistic and philosophic models and proffered more adequate definitions and methods from CMT and conceptual blending. In traditional models the terms "metaphor" and "analogy" are not only arbitrary but self-contradictory. The categorization of metaphor as an element of rhetoric forces the concept of metaphor into an insoluble division between pragmatics and semantics. In CMT and conceptual blending, the definition of metaphor as a conceptual mapping from source to target clarifies and dissolves this definitional conundrum.

The ultimate aim of this work has been to consider what elements of *women* and *womanhood* are highlighted in Proverbs 1–9, and how these entailments help us to approach and understand wisdom as an abstract entity. While definitional and methodological refinements improve our ability to assess the contents and function of the conceptual blend of *Lady Wisdom*, recent scholarship has suggested that there are considerable cultural pitfalls in approaching the *target* of that blend: Wisdom. Through an engagement with Ian McGilchrist and Ignatio Carbajosa, it was determined that the consideration of wisdom was not entirely possible using only the assumptions

FAITHFUL DESIRE 223

and values provided by our left-hemisphere dominated scientific culture. Theological aesthetics modeled by Balthasar and Garrett provide a more balanced framework for perception anchored in the beauty of the triune God.

The challenge of the "double gaze" of aesthetic vision yielded two stages in exegesis. The first stage considered the formal beauty of the text itself, engaging with elements of diction, allusion, metaphor, and purpose. Rather than approaching the text in order to obtain propositional claims about the text, provenance, and background; the method was more like approaching an artwork as illustrated in the *Rokeby Venus*. The text, like any great art work, exists not only as *form*, but also as *lumen*: a means of transport by considering the nature of beauty itself, expressed in the life and death of Jesus Christ. While WOMAN is the vehicle by which the LORD educates our desire and *faithfulness*, both WOMAN and WISDOM are reflections of the deeper and more absolute beauty of the Trinity expressed in the life, death, and resurrection of Jesus. The desire for and fidelity to these feminine persons beckon to a deeper longing for life and love that reside only in the life of the triune God.

The *superform* of Christ is the objective event that enables us and drives us into the experience of the beauty of our Trinitarian God. The Son, in obedience perfectly communicates the Father's character as he completes the mission for which he was sent.[1] The Spirit provides the inner light that draws all toward the Son, and then accomplishes the rapture that joins man to God.[2] The balance and harmony of the Persons encapsulate the aptness, beauty, and condescension of the Trinity's love for mankind.[3]

---

1. "Christ, being the Lord of Glory, and the unique form that measures all others, displays God's beauty as fittingness, which is exemplified in the concordance between Christ's mission and existence such that he acts in accordance with who he is (John 8:42–47)" (Garrett, *God's Beauty-In-Act*, 143).

2. "The extent to which God's transpersonal and Trinitarian work of revelation respects and perfects the creature's personality is shown by the fact that freedom is apportioned to the Holy Spirit. Precisely at the moment when he unites man with Christ, the Holy Spirit bestows freedom on him: he elevates man's restricted, creaturely freedom to the level of a liberated, mighty, divine freedom, in order then to entrust this grace-gift of freedom to the believer as a freedom truly his own and truly to be exercised by him" (Balthasar, *Seeing the Form*, 190).

3. "God's beauty, therefore, is the attunement or fittingness of the incarnate Son's actions in the Spirit to the Father's will that radiates the splendor of God's triune love. In other words, it is fitting for the Father to glorify the Son because the Son does all that the Father plans for him to do. He leaves nothing undone. The Son's obedience to the Father is not one of duty or compulsion but one of love, self-giving love that takes him to the point of death (Phil 2:8), for the Son does not desire to do his own will but the will of the Father (Matt 26:39; John 4:34; 6:38). The Father delights in the Son because

God has done the unexpected and inconceivable by communicating his Trinitarian love in and through the hideous form of the cross, the most unsightly thing humanly imaginable. By doing so, the *Gestalt Christi* radiates the splendor of God's glory as Christ is perfectly in tune with the Father's will by obeying the Father and fulfilling his mission to the world. Through the *Gestaltungs-kraft* (shaping power) of the Holy Spirit, Christ's beauty enraptures and beckons perceiving subjects by drawing them out of themselves and into God's drama of redemption.[4]

Lady Wisdom, and indeed the love of and love for a good woman, borrows of this beauty and rapture. It reflects the splendor of our loving, suffering, and risen LORD. Let us review the conclusions of the previous chapters.

Diversity and Paradox in the Presentation of Lady Wisdom and the Reality of Christ

Since the way the poet presents *Lady Wisdom* colors how we feel about not only the character but about the entity she represents, changes in personification alter the disposition of the reader.[5] The substance of chapter 4 was an exploration of the diverse and dichotomous presentation of *Lady Wisdom* in Prov 1 and 2.

In Prov 1:20–33, *Wisdom* is presented less according to the input of *WOMAN* than as a conceptual blend dominated by the inputs of *PROPHET* and *YHWH*. Feminine personification maintains personal and relational categories but in the domain of the divine, transcendent and covenantal. *Lady Wisdom* is not presented as a hypostasis or consort to YHWH, but rather a mouthpiece to reiterate the ongoing and prophetic conversation between YHWH and the people of Israel. In this initial paragraph, the personification of wisdom is to exhort obedience to the divine covenant and yields a disposition of distance, awe, and passivity in the reader. However, in Prov 2:1–11 this strong, unified, and transcendent personification is only one among a number of other basic metaphors. The force of *WOMAN* as a source category is increased. She is now an attainable familiar protector and object for the son's affections. This familiar *Lady Wisdom* begins to take on elements of characterization that evoke those of a wife. This personification elicits feelings of intimacy, desire, and active pursuit.

---

of his perfect obedience, illuminating the beauty of God's holiness and wisdom" (Garrett, *God's Beauty-In-Act*, loc 3674).

4. Garret, *God's Beauty-In-Act*, 73.

5. Lakoff and Johnson, *More Than Cool Reason*, 72–80.

The disparity between these two personifications highlight the paradox of wisdom and simultaneously urges obedience and desire as well as awe and gratitude. The life, ministry, and death of Jesus anchor this disposition in the lived reality of the triune God. The divine and prophetic appeal is characteristic of his life, and the paradox of humble divinity and beautiful sacrifice transcend all of the best hopes of Wisdom. He provides the substance for the poetic reflection.

Desire and Fidelity as Keys to the Covenant Accomplished in Christ

In Prov 5:15–23; 6:20–35 the poet meaningfully switches targets. Up until this point he has dwelt mainly upon the *WOMAN* as an input or source which is used to provide entailments for *WISDOM* as a target. In these chapters the poet uses other domains (i.e., WATER, ANIMAL, INEBRIATE, FIRE, etc.) in the metaphorical depiction of "the wife of your youth" and "the wife of your neighbor." Here, the poet showcases those elements of womanhood that are key to his use of feminine metaphor. By pairing *WATER* against *FIRE* and *BLESSING* against *THEFT* the poet highlights the fact that relational fidelity is the key element for the conceptual blend. Moreover, the poet's diction and choice of metaphor point to the lower level metaphor drawn from the prophets: *COVENANT IS MARRIAGE/ IDOLATRY IS ADULTERY*. The human dimension of marital fidelity is the substance of fidelity to YHWH. Infidelity with the *Strange Woman* is the reverse.

The resonance with prophetic metaphor accentuates the coupling of desire and covenant by blending materials from the Decalogue with the Song of Songs. Not only is fidelity to the "wife of your youth" synonymous with fidelity to YHWH, the covenant requires the sort of desire that allows fidelity. Desire cannot be the shallow, short-sided love of nothing that yields only condemnation, rather it is a longing rooted in substance that is anchored in the LORD himself.

The NT also treats fidelity in marriage as an ontic metaphor, however, it adds another dimension, that of the church. Husbands are to love their wives as Christ loved the church and wives are to submit to their husbands as the church to its LORD. Marital fidelity is a reflection of fidelity of the LORD to his church. Jesus also shows the parity between desire, fidelity and worship by employing many of these same metaphors in his discussion with the Samaritan woman at the well in John 4. By a reversal of categories Jesus offers the waters of life to this *Strange Woman*, even in spite of her own infidelity. He himself becomes the fount of forgiveness and love: the well-spring of true worship.

The Discernment of Strange from Wise and Wise from Jesus

The ambiguity that has accompanied the presentation of the *Strange Woman* and *Lady Wisdom* are resolved in Prov 7–8 via a closing appeal from both. It is now clear that the *Strange Woman* appears as a foil both to the "wife of your youth" (Prov 5) and *Lady Wisdom*. The poet's choice of diction, the activation of romantic categories, similar metaphors, and ultimately identical appeals (Prov 9) show that these women are held in parallel. However, the ambiguity is clarified specifically with regard to a simple choice, that of infidelity or fidelity. The comparison of the *Strange Woman* and *Lady Wisdom* is demonstrated to be a comparison that is no comparison with regard to their character, invitation, and their *houses* as final outcomes. The *Strange Woman* is illustrated within the narrative framework of the Jael narrative from Judges 5, by so doing the חֲסַר לֵב is cast in the role of Sisera, an enemy of God and therefore under punishment. The *Strange Woman* is therefore less a villain than a mode of divine punishment for infidelity to divine covenant.

Conversely, the characterization of *Lady Wisdom* continues only to expand both in categories of transcendence and love. Prov 8:30 shows *Lady Wisdom* to be allied with the principles of order, delight and fidelity. Faithfulness becomes the expression of desire and obedience.

The invitations of the *Strange Woman* and *Lady Wisdom* also highlight the central role of fidelity. The invitation of the *Strange Woman* exists only as an appeal to infidelity couched in the ornament of sexuality and freedom from consequences. Conversely, the offer of *Lady Wisdom* is substantially the same as her offer in Prov 1, only this time formally synonymous to the parental appeal, "Now sons, listen to me . . ." (Prov 8:32). Wisdom offers the blessings of covenant fidelity via the desire for covenant obedience. The *Strange Woman* offers only death.

Finally, both women offer a closure to the LIFE IS A ROAD metaphor by reference to the metaphor DEATH AS DESTINATION. As previously, the house of the *Strange Woman* is *Sheol*, the consummation of infidelity is the fullness of death. However, the presentation of Wisdom's house is problematic, because she cannot provide a genuine antithesis. She is able to promise the luxuriant blessings guaranteed by covenant fidelity, but her house cannot be ultimately associated with life.

With regard to the lexical and conceptual parallels between Wisdom and Strange what we discover is a chasm of comparison. In Wisdom we find woman who is both transcendent and personal. She is a companion of YHWH himself. She surpasses all worldly goods. She is delight. She is the embodiment of parental instruction: equivalent to the fullness of life itself. In the *Strange Woman*, we find the antithesis of *both*. She is neither truly personal, nor transcendent. She betrays no empathy either for her husband, or for the youth. She does not relate to either as persons, but one as resource and the other as target. Her designs for them are equivalent to the left hemisphere values of *utility* and *profit*. The men in her life are for *use*. She is the embodiment of faithlessness and folly that is nothing short of the bottomless vacuum of *self*. In place of the ever-expanding horizons of creation, rule, knowledge, order, perception, and understanding, conduct and the pursuit of righteousness there is only the decadent bed, the sheer physicality of sex, and the false promise of avoiding the consequences of infidelity. The foil is almost no foil, because it brutally illustrates that there is no comparison between the women. *Lady Wisdom* is the substance of everything. The *Strange Woman* is the false promise of substance stolen from someone else.

Finally, we review the differences between the person, invitation, and house of Jesus with those of *Lady Wisdom*. The key is that Jesus is not a characterization, but a divine person. *Lady Wisdom* is a personification that exists to exhort desire for and fidelity to the relational covenant of YHWH. As such, the elements of personification that reflect transcendence are not generative of a later Christology, but rather are reflections of the person of YHWH reflected *from* Christ. It is not that Jesus looks like Wisdom; it is that Wisdom looks like Jesus. Jesus's invitation in Matt 11:29 is issued as an appeal to a "yoke" like one offered by a wisdom teacher, but Jesus extends the invitation not merely to *learning* but to eternal life. Finally, Jesus's HOUSE is able to finally provide the possibility for the metaphor *LIFE IS A DESTINATION*. The death of Christ, ends death. Jesus through the *HOUSE* of his body, founds the *HOUSE* of his church, which will come to his Father's *HOUSE* in glory.

Woman as a metaphorical source entails desire and fidelity. Fidelity to divine covenant and human relationships then becomes the criteria for discerning wisdom. Jesus transcends these values as the creator transcends the creation. Jesus, the triune expression of love models ultimate obedience in his sacrificial death and provides a window into the *deeper* wisdom of the LORD himself in the expression of his infinitely and substantially more beautiful person.

Further Study

Due to the amount of space given to addressing problems of definition, methodology, and cultural assumptions the engagement of feminine imagery in this work was more indicative than exhaustive. Numerous excellent passages were omitted or glossed over due to space restraints. There are several profound areas of study that lie temptingly on the brink of this work. Consider for example the role of Prov 31 with relation to these blends and its purpose in framing the book as a whole. From the discussion of אשת חיל the reader is forced to reckon with the identity of Ruth as a kind of *Wisdom Woman* while simultaneously existing as a foreign woman (נכריה). Likewise, the palatial and banquet metaphors of our home-born stranger, Esther, calls out for treatment. Both of these books raise the question, "What does it *mean* to be *faithful*?" Both paint with radically different brushes and confound our cold left-hemisphere assumptions.

Second, consider the stereotype of the "disputatious wife" (אשת מדינים) who seems to exist without the categories provided by either *Lady Wisdom* and company or the *Strange Woman*. The remarkable diversity and similarity of this group of proverbial sayings presents another complication for the otherwise life or death relational experience with women in Proverbs.

Finally, while this work has capitalized mainly upon the role of metaphor in a poetic and canonical study of *Lady Wisdom*, comparative, and diachronic studies of the book could also beneficially employ both theological aesthetics and conceptual blending. Balthasar has convincingly argued that Christ is the center of creation and history. While this does not allow for salvific knowledge outside of Christ, it does grant dignity to natural knowledge. I would be curious to discover what an aesthetic approach would look like with regard to comparative materials. Many scholars have used something like a conceptual blending approach to ANE and comparative studies.[6] A clearer and more rigorous metaphorical method could clarify the relationship between different conceptual blends. For example, in Prov 8 the image schema of the "three-tiered universe" appears repeatedly. While I pursued inner-biblical references in pursuance of canonical ends, a similar methodology could be employed with regard to determining the overall force of this schema in light of comparative materials. Differences in the formulation of this imagery could be highly instructive.

---

6. E.g., Assman, *Mind of Egypt*; Brown, *Seeing the Psalms*; Keel, *Symbolism of the Biblical World*.

Rejoinder: Jesus and Lady Wisdom

As a final rejoinder, the words of Brevard Childs in the preface of his *Introduction to Old Testament as Scripture* seem entirely appropriate:

> Having experienced the demise of the Biblical Theology movement in America, the dissolution of the broad European consensus in which I was trained, and a widespread confusion regarding theological reflection in general, I began to realize that there was something fundamentally wrong with the foundations of the biblical discipline. It was not a question of improving on a source analysis, of discovering some unrecognized new genre, or of bringing a redactional layer into sharper focus. Rather, the crucial issue turned on one's whole concept of the study of the Bible itself. I am now convinced that the relation between the historical critical study of the Bible and its theological use as religious literature within a community of faith and practice needs to be completely rethought. Minor adjustments are not only inadequate, but also conceal the extent of the dry rot.[7]

In many ways, this work has endeavored to be just such a "rethinking" of the theological interpretation of scripture within the confines of the canon but bounded ultimately by faithfulness to the person of the living God, YHWH. All the same, where *Lady Wisdom* may have previously been thought lost in a sea of comparative materials, should she now be swallowed up as a mere typology of Christ? In proposing Christ as the ultimate and absolute norm for beauty is Lady Wisdom (and all of the Old Testament for that matter) simply to be swallowed by the New? There is not only justice but a real philosophical quandary in the complaint.

If Christ, as the LORD is the perfect and ultimate expression of YHWH (Heb 1:1–3), doesn't that necessarily diminish the value of everything else by comparison, in the same way that putting an infinity symbol on one side of a mathematical equation makes the finite numbers meaningless by comparison? The analogy is indeed similar, and for this reason the Old Testament has been neglected by too many Christian churches and interpreters. However, in the same way that infinity is not a numerical void, but rather is the set of all numbers, so also is the witness of Emmanuel not a dissolution but the witness of all the very real and particular workings of the LORD in creation and throughout the history not only of Israel but of his church (Heb 1:1–3). Jesus, as the absolute norm of beauty is not the *abrogation* of

---

7. Childs, *Introduction to the Old Testament*, 15.

the LORD's witness in creation and history, but the consummation of it. As spoken poignantly by Christopher Seitz:

> Even within the maturation of the first scriptural witness, Law and Prophets are not successive phases in a history of religion but belong together as a reciprocal account of God's providential work in creation, law, and historical action in Israel and the nations, including future promise, the fulfillment of God's righteous will, and new creation. The same dynamic governs the way the Old and the New now work together, a single canonical totality dynamically related and mutually informing. The New is not a phase of development that grounds the Old but rather a statement of the Old's abiding sense and final meaning, perceived now afresh within its own plain-sense deliverance and helping to interpret and ground the New's meaning and final purpose as well.[8]

Though not mentioned by Seitz, I believe that we have demonstrated that even Wisdom Literature partakes in that same dynamic reciprocity that is characteristic of the Law and the Prophets. Through the balance of allusion to Torah and conceptual metaphors shared with the Prophets, *Lady Wisdom* is a unique expression perhaps shaded by the broader ANE but uniquely, broadly, and solidly canonical.[9]

Second, there is an important differentiation between Jesus as the person and perfect expression of YHWH, and the real target of *Lady Wisdom*—the right perception of the created order. This right perception is a gift of the LORD. It is a hard won human attainment. It is learned via covenant obedience to parents and Torah. It is available universally through embodied human experience. Wisdom is a significant end in itself, though it does not

---

8. Seitz, *Goodly Fellowship of the Prophets*, loc 1009.

9. In assessing the wide diversity of possible influences upon the characterization of *Lady Wisdom*, Gerhard von Rad remarked: "But what does all this prove? Only that ideas which had their roots elsewhere came to Israel's help when she needed them, in order to be able to progress in her thinking within her own domain. For in the process of this transference of foreign ideas to the Hebrew thought-world, many of them have become completely different. What is described in Prov 8 as 'wisdom,' as world order, can be compared only with difficulty to the Egyptian concept, *Maat*. It has no divine status, nor is it a hypostatized attribute of Yahweh; it is rather, something created by Yahweh and assigned to its proper function. Although it is clearly differentiated from the whole of creation, it is an entity which belongs in the world, even if it is the first of the works of creation, the creature above all creatures. This special position accorded to wisdom *vis-à-vis* all created things, a position emphasized also in Job 28, is of great significance in our didactic poem" (Rad, *Wisdom in Israel*, 153). *Lady Wisdom* is not a foreign import to the OT but uniquely and intricately informed by it and engaged with it.

rise to the level of being equal to its creator. Partially due to the nature of this study, as a particular pursuit of feminine metaphor, the necessary reliance of wisdom on the perception of the created *nature of things* has not received its due. However, what should be clear is the perception of the embodied human experience of the created order is one of *relationship*. In the end, our conclusions are much the same as those proffered by Gerard von Rad fifty years ago in describing the personification of Wisdom in Prov 8:

> The didactic poem in Prov 8, in expounding the basic idea, does not simply surpass the old doctrine in that it is able to give expression to particular details about Yahweh's relationship to this world order. The most interesting feature of what is new is that this world order turns, as a person, towards men, wooing them and encouraging them in direct address. What is objectified here, then, is not an attribute of God but an attribute of the world, namely that mysterious attribute, by virtue of which she turns towards men to give order to their lives. Thus, Israel was faced with the same phenomenon which more or less fascinated all ancient religions, especially, of course, the nature religions, namely that of the religious provocation of man by the world. But Israel did not agree to the mythicization and deification of the first principle of the world. Her interpretation was quite a different one, because she held fast to this phenomenon within the sphere of her faith in Yahweh as creator. We can do no more than express in other words this thing which is immanent in the world and which the texts call "wisdom." Whether we render it as "primeval order" or "mysterious order" or "world reason" or as the "meaning" created in the world by God or as the "glory" reflected back from the world, in every case it is spoken of in the form of a graphic personification. But this personification is anything but a freely chosen, decorative stylistic device which the reader who is skilled in rhetoric could easily have replaced with a different one, with the sole aim of simplifying understanding. Rather, this form of speech was determined by the subject in question and could be fixed in words only in this way without incurring loss, for this primeval order addressed man.... There was, then, no choice, for the personal element was completely indispensable.[10]

Whatever we may know then of the created order is best known in right relationship. One of the keys to this relationship beyond the obvious and repeatedly stated need for the fear of YHWH, and the ultimacy of

---

10. Rad, *Wisdom in Israel*, 156–57.

Christ, is the instrumental nature of Eros. The many faceted and relational nature of the embodied creaturely experience is to arouse in us feelings of awe, wonder, intimacy, responsibility, respect, and *desire*. It may not be cold and objective, neither can it be a divine *agape* predicated on selfless commitment.[11] Rather, we learn best of wisdom by beholding the eyes of faithful love, as indeed they are typified in the "wife of your youth." It is very much as described by Peter Black in his discussion of *eros* in the *Symposium* of Plato:

> We desire what is natural to us but strangely also what is lacking in us. According to the speech that Plato puts on the lips of Aristophanes, we humans are always desiring and pursuing the whole which we are not, ever since we were cut in half by Zeus and only patched up by Apollo. This is in fact what love is, the desire for self-completion by the desired or loved object. In other words, it is because of our incompleteness that we desire, and we desire another object or person to complete us, and such a desire can be love. "The lover desires the object of his/her love and thus lacks that object, but it is the lack that explains the very phenomenon of desire." Now we can desire with a physical passion or a sensual love which is closely linked to the body, and sensual love is certainly part of eros. However, since the soul is always attempting to quench the lack, it needs to ascend from the desire of beautiful material things to complete us to the desire of spiritual things "until it ultimately comes to rest where alone it can find its complete and final satisfaction, in the contemplation of the absolutely Beautiful itself."[12]

As such *Lady Wisdom* is that search for the beautiful beyond the beautiful and she finds so much in common both with the divine and the feminine. So the metaphor WISDOM IS A WOMAN creates a conceptual blend in which our gendered longing is able to reach out to creation and beyond creation to the creator. Simultaneously the blend creates a new understanding of woman and the feminine, not as a shallow fulfillment and long punishment, but rather as the first part of infinity. We are *created*, male and female, for a relationship hinted at by wisdom, promised by Tanakh and fulfilled in Christ.

> To reach that stature and be shaped in his likeness refers not so much to literal size as to the inner person and the condition of immortality. No weakness will persist: sexual differentiation

---

11. See Black, "Broken Wings of Eros," 112–20.
12. Black, "Broken Wings of Eros," 108–9.

will, though there will be no lust or childbirth, so the female organs will be part of a new beauty arousing praises of God "for his wisdom and compassion, in that he not only created out of nothing but freed from corruption that which he created". The Body of Christ is what is meant by perfect humanity—so the gradual building up of the church is what will find fulfillment at the resurrection. When Augustine attempted a description, it is of a society in heaven, which is genuinely a body politic, at peace and bound in the closest possible harmony, where God is the goal of all longings, and we shall "see him forever, love him without satiety and praise him without weariness."[13]

In conclusion, I would ask that we frame the end of the work in the same metaphor with which we began. Womanhood is used as a source/input category for *Lady Wisdom* to highlight the key domains of relational, marital, and covenant fidelity, while allowing for the fusion of desire, obedience, and blessing. The life, death, and resurrection of Jesus is the apex of divine revelation and the point to which all creation and history lean. Every point where *Lady Wisdom* bears similarity to YHWH, or to human attempts to please YHWH, necessarily produces an image that is a reflection of the person of Jesus Christ. As Velázquez illustrated the role of aesthetic vision in the introduction, it is perhaps helpful to close the study with a similar illustration.

Christ after the Flagellation Contemplated by the Christian Soul (fig. 6), was likely completed before the *Rokeby Venus*, but provides a number of interpretive clues to the painter's means and motive. Both subjects are accompanied by winged celestial creatures as mediators. Both Cupid and the angel serve to direct attention to the central subject. However, in *Christ after the Flagellation Contemplated by the Christian Soul*, the viewer is duplicated standing both within and without the image plane.

---

13. Young, *God's Presence*, 104.

Figure 7: Diego Velázquez,
Christ after the Flagellation Contemplated by the Christian Soul,
(c. 1628–32, oil on canvas 165.1x 206.4 cm, National Gallery, London).

"The image forms a barrier between the spectator and the object of his devotion while at the same time acting as a medium by which this very barrier can be overcome."[14] This image of Christ shows a similar kind of "dynamic reciprocity" with the *Rokeby Venus*. The paintings portray two profoundly different subjects but are drawn together by common themes and metaphors. Moreover, the obscure beauty of Venus becomes radiant in the face of Christ.

> Reflections on a comparison of *Venus* with *Christ after the Flagellation* are not intended to suggest that Velázquez's *Venus* is a pagan erotic "devotional image." Yet Velázquez clearly adopted certain characteristics of the religious devotional image in his handling of the pagan theme. . . . Velázquez has adopted pictorial formulae of the devotional image and, borrowing from Titian and Rubens, even elements of its topos in the *Rokeby Venus*.

14. Prader, *Venus at Her Mirror*, 80.

This connection is clearest in the personal appeal of the image through the gaze. Finally, the mirror image of the *Rokeby Venus* as the "radiance of the light of the face of god" in the sense of Ripa, suggests an initially unsuspected allegorical path towards theocentric, if not theological, interpretation.[15]

Therefore, the *Rokeby Venus,* is not an allegory for Christ. Rather, Velázquez saw in the personification of love something human that was more than human, something mythic that required reality. So also, in the book of Proverbs we discover, not details, but ruddy shadows of the face of *Lady Wisdom*. She is not a two dimensional illusion generated by an ignorant patriarchy nor a hackneyed composite of ANE imagery glued together by the vagaries of time. Rather, she is the literary substance of a divine and *ontological* invitation to relationship: first to creation and our fellow creatures, but ultimately rooted in the person of YHWH. Even as the goddess of love smiles upon us in Velázquez's master work, so we turn to discover not "what" but "*who*" beckons to us; not "how" but "why" the God of all creation should use the metaphor of a woman to make us wise.

---

15. Prader, *Venus at Her Mirror*, 80–81.

Appendix A

Aristotle's Categories for Metaphor

FIRST, a word may be moved from a general category to a specific one (from genus to species): "'There stands my ship'; for to be at anchor is a species of standing."[1] In this case, the word "stand" is removed from the large general category "things that stand" where it is typical, and is used to describe the non-typical and specific entity, "boat."

Second, a specific word may be used to represent the general category which it represents (species to genus). Aristotle provides the example of "'Verily ten thousand noble deeds hath Odysseus wrought'; for ten thousand is a species of large number, and is here used for a large number generally."[2] In this case the specific number 10,000 stands in for large numbers in general. This conventionalized usage is recognized as an abstraction upon deliberation, but might easily be overlooked as metaphor.

Third, two words may be combined to yield a new entity, an equivocation (species to species equivocation). Aristotle provides the example, "'Drew away the life with the blade of bronze,'" and "'Cleft the water with the vessel of unyielding bronze.'" In the first of these examples "drawing away the life" imposes the image and function of carrying water in a vessel onto the alien species of the sword. Likewise, in the other example the oar of a boat is refigured not as an oar, but as a sword cleaving the water.

Fourth, a metaphor may be formed by a proportion of terms wherein one entity imposes that ratio on another (analogy or proportion). "When the second term is to the first as the fourth to the third. We may then use the fourth for the second, or the second for the fourth. Sometimes too we qualify the metaphor by adding the term to which the proper word is

---

1. Aristotle, *Poetics* 1457b5 [73].
2. Aristotle, *Poetics* 1457b5 [73].

relative. Thus the cup is to Dionysus as the shield to Ares."[3] In this case, the metaphor expresses the non-generic likeness of "symbol of power" for the two deities mentioned.

In summary then, a metaphor is first of all a mode of speech, not ontology, and therefore belongs to the realm of linguistics (i.e. semantics) as a form of polysemy or equivocation. While aptness in spoken metaphor may be a sign of genius, Aristotle deems it so because of the speaker's ability to recognize underlying *analogies*. Metaphor is not a conceptual category, but a rhetorical one which relates more with liveliness and ornament in speech and is therefore to be avoided in dialectic. *Analogy* then is the ontological component which Aristotle reserved for the dialectical discussion of perceived likenesses

---

3. Aristotle, *Poetics* 1457b6 [73].

Appendix B

Historical Survey of CMT

WHILE many appraise Cognitive Metaphor Theory (CMT) as a late twentieth century development, this is not entirely true. Olaf Jäkel demonstrates that the idea that cognition and metaphor are profoundly intertwined can be traced as far back as John Locke's *Essay Concerning Human Understanding* (1689) in which the author states:

> It may also lead us a little towards the Original of all our Notions and Knowledge, if we remark, how great a dependence our *Words* have on common sensible *Ideas;* and how those, which are made use of to stand for Actions and Notions quite removed from sense, *have their rise from thence, and from obvious sensible* Ideas *are transferred to more abstruse significations*, and made to stand for *Ideas* that come not under the cognizance of our senses.[1]

Although Locke did not use the contemporary expression "Cognitive Metaphor Theory," his explanation is an apt description of the central aims and processes of the theory.[2] Jäkel is able to find corresponding articulations of CMT in statements from notable scholars in each century hence.[3]

---

1. Locke, *Essay Concerning Human Understanding*, 403, quoted in Gibbs and Steen, *Metaphor in Cognitive Linguistics*, 11.

2. While it is just to note that Locke *did* in fact have certain affinities with CMT, it is also necessary to note that metaphor remained a "rhetorical trope" that jeopardized clear communication. "But yet if we would speak of things as they are, we must allow that all the art of rhetoric, besides order and clearness; all the artificial and figurative application of words eloquence hath invented, are for nothing else but to insinuate wrong ideas, move the passions, and thereby mislead the judgment" (Locke, *Essay Concerning Human Understanding*, 59).

3. Only a partial listing of these detailed by Jäkel includes: Johann Gottfried Herder's *Abhandlung über den Ursprung der Sprache* (1770); Johan Adam Hartung's *Ueber die*

In particular, he dwells upon the profoundly similar contributions of Hans Blumenberg from 1960–1989 and Harald Weinrich from 1958–1976. Between these two scholars they discussed and defined the role of metaphors in shaping perception, and thereby culture. Blumenberg even named conventionalized conceptual metaphors in ways very similar to Lakoff, Turner and Johnson (i.e. *TRUTH AS LIGHT. WORLD AS A LIVING BEING. WORLD AS A CLOCKWORK.* etc.).[4] Weinrich included the consideration of Internal Cognitive Models (ICM) but also defined the metaphoric image field in two parts: the *image donor* and the *image recipient*.[5] The issue is, however, not so much to distinguish rightful credit in the development of the theory, but to show that the roots of this line of thinking are not rooted in a philosophical fad, but in a movement much deeper and broader.[6]

> The central tenets of the cognitive theory of metaphor are confirmed by the fact that scholars of completely different backgrounds have reached the same or very similar results independently of each other. Thus the epistemologist Kant hits on metaphor in the course of his critical stocktaking of human understanding. Blumenberg, the historian of philosophy discovers metaphor while reconstructing the history of central scientific concepts. The linguist Weinrich resembles the cognitive researchers of metaphor most closely also as regards his own heuristics, with his theory of metaphor resulting from the philologic-linguistic observation of everyday language.[7]

Casus, ihre Bildung und Bedeutung, in der griechischen und lateinischen Sprache (1831); Benjamin Lee Whorf's "The relation of habitual thought and behavior to language" (1939); Nelson Goodman's *Languages of Art* (1968); and Hannah Arendt's *Von Leben des Geistes I: Das Denken* (1971). See Jäkel, "Kant, Blumenberg, Weinrich," 9–10.

4. Jäkel, "Kant, Blumenberg, Weinrich," 16.

5. Jäkel, "Kant, Blumenberg, Weinrich," 18–19.

6. Olaf Jäkel is somewhat critical of Lakoff and Turner as relates to cognizance of developments in continental philosophy. This criticism may or may not be justified. George Lakoff gives credit to Michael Reddy for providing the impetus for CMT via his ground-breaking article, "The conduit metaphor: A case of frame conflict in our language about language," in which in one concise example he overturned the contemporary models of metaphor as word, and instead opened the door to consider the role of metaphor in shaping perception, and perception predicating metaphor (Lakoff and Johnson, *Metaphors We Live By*, 10). Mark Johnson in his introduction to his edited work *Philosophical Perspectives on Metaphor* notes the accomplishments particularly I.A. Richards and Max Black, but also that there was recent support "especially in Continental hermeneutics" (Johnson, *Philosophical Perspectives on Metaphor*, 44).

7. Jäkel, "Kant, Blumenberg, Weinrich," 23.

One implication of this broad and independent foundation is that CMT is not a singular and unitary phenomenon. In addition to the foundational work of those listed above, seminal contributions in English have been provided by a *team* of scholars. In addition to the preliminary work by George Lakoff, Mark Johnson, and Mark Turner, important critiques and refinements have been provided by Raymond Gibbs, Gerard Steen, Joseph Grady, Zoltán Kövecses, and Gilles Fauconnier among many others.

The earliest models for Cognitive Metaphor Theory (CMT) were drawn from the discipline of mathematics. "A mapping, in the most general mathematical sense is a correspondence between two sets that assigns to each element in the first a counterpart in the second."[8] In this model an entity in a "target" domain could be systematically "mapped" onto a "source" domain.[9] Unfortunately, the model was inadequate because *mathematical mappings* do not generate new entities, cognitive metaphors, on the other hand, seem to generate new conceptual models that in turn influence the subject's perception of reality.[10] This shortcoming in the "mapping" model led to the next refinement, that of "projection," based upon the metaphor of an overhead projector. Via this image, the source domain constituted a base transparency upon which the target transparency was aligned, thereby projecting a new conceptual structure onto the lived experience of the subject. The unintended outcome of this particular heuristic, however, was that it suggested that *every* element of the source domain be expressed in the target, which was simply not the case. At present metaphorical models have

---

8. Fauconnier, *Mappings in Thought and Language*, 1n1. George Lakoff, points out that the analogy with the mathematical concept should not be overdrawn. He writes, "Mappings should not be thought of as processes, or as algorithms that mechanically take source domain inputs and produce target domain outputs. Each mapping should be seen instead as a fixed pattern of ontological correspondences across domains that may, or may not, be applied to a source domain knowledge structure or a source domain lexical item. Thus, lexical items that are conventional in the source domain are not always conventional in the target domain" (Lakoff, "Contemporary Theory of Metaphor," 210).

9. In the afterword to Lakoff and Johnson's second edition to *Metaphors We Live By*, the authors state: "This metaphor proved useful in several respects. It was precise. It specified exact, systematic correspondences. It allowed for the use of source domain inference patterns to reason about the target domain. Finally, it allowed for partial mappings. In short, it was a good first approximation" (Lakoff and Johnson, *Metaphors We Live By*, 252).

10. "For example, time doesn't necessarily have a use and isn't necessarily a resource. Many people in cultures around the world simply live their lives without being concerned about whether they are using their time efficiently. However, other cultures conceptualize time metaphorically as though it were a limited resource" (Lakoff and Johnson, *Metaphors We Live By*, 252–53).

diversified and abstracted. Grady, Johnson, and Narayanan employed computer models and considered metaphorical mapping, not from the standpoint of mathematics but rather mappings within the visual cortex of the brain.[11] "When we imagine seeing a scene, our visual cortex is active. When we imagine moving our bodies, the pre-motor cortex and motor cortex are active. In short, some of the same parts of our brains are active in imagining as in perceiving and doing."[12] The key function, therefore, in this understanding of metaphoric activation is *enactment*. While there are promising new avenues of research in neural approaches to cognitive science, two difficulties preclude more than cursory influence upon this methodology. First, while the function of mirror neurons do seem to be implicated in the processing of figurative language generally, there is still considerable doubt about the agreement between the popularized notion of mirror neurons and their actual function.[13] Second, neural function does not provide any apparatus, conceptual model or theoretical refinement that contributes significantly to the ability to recognize and understand metaphorical expressions.

11. Grady, "Foundations of Meaning"; Hiraga et al., *Cognitive Linguistics*, 155–69; Narayanan, "Embodiment in Language."
12. Lackof and Johnson, *Metaphors We Live By*, 257.
13. Hickok, *Myth of Mirror Neurons*.

Appendix C

Critiques of CMT

Cognitive Metaphor Theory (CMT) as outlined by Lackoff and Turner had a few important deficiencies and criticisms, especially in the early iterations. First, as a theory of cognition CMT is deficient. In the initial formulation of Cognitive Metaphor Theory by Lakoff and Turner it fell into disrepute for a number of scientific and linguistic inadequacies. Many scholars cited a lack of scientific rigor in the selection and identification of conceptual metaphors. The difficulty and inherently subjective nature of semantically autonomous concepts also easily gave rise to multiple and valid assessments of the same metaphor.[1] Second, most scholars were not persuaded that metaphors could be condensed to a few "basic" metaphors or semantically autonomous concepts predicated in human embodiment which were a part of a "great chain metaphor'"[2] In a similar vein, Lakoff and Johnson's introductory work, considered metaphor largely from a synchronic standpoint of a cultural insider's approach to Anglo-American metaphors. Especially as more universal appropriations of "embodiment metaphor" were forthcoming in research, many anthropologists questioned

---

1. For example, in *More Than Cool Reason,* 41–42, Lakoff and Turner provide different categorization for the basic conventional metaphors "TIME IS A DEVOURER" and "TIME IS A DESTROYER." Ultimately, the maintenance or reduction of these statements to a more basic level is difficult to falsify. See Vervaeke and Green, "Women, Fire, and Dangerous Theories," 59–80; "Metaphors in Language and Thought," 273–84.

2. "Thus we see that though there is an infinitude of potential conceptual metaphors, only a very few of these have special status as basic metaphors in our conceptual systems. It is also the case that there is an infinitude of potential metaphorical expressions at the linguistic level, but this does not imply that they are all conceptually unique. The reason is that the relatively small number of basic conceptual metaphors can be combined conceptually and expressed in an infinite variety of linguistic expressions" (Lakoff and Turner, *More Than Cool Reason,* 51).

the universal applicability of CMT.[3] Finally, there are a number of rules and axioms for "source–target mapping" which have proven problematic.[4] It is important to note, that CMT is not here employed as a theory of cognition, but rather as a definition and methodology for poetic metaphor.

3. In fairness, the role of culture in forming metaphor was much more pronounced in *More Than Cool Reason,* where they write: "General conceptual metaphors are thus not the unique creation of individual poets but are rather part of the way members of a culture have of conceptualizing their experience. Poets, as members of their cultures, naturally make use of these basic conceptual metaphors to communicate with other members, their audience" (Lakoff and Turner, *More Than Cool Reason,* 51). The cultural critique was more than likely spawned by the original consideration of ANGER AS HEATED FLUID IN A CONTAINER produced by Lakoff and Kövecses, "Cognitive Model of Anger." Kövecses in turn expanded this study in a series of articles in 1995 (see Kövecses, "'Container' Metaphor of Anger"; "Anger"). The cultural considerations in these works were not adequate to establish the conventional metaphor. For a complete consideration, both of the cultural and scientific shortcomings of CMT and a more than adequate redress of both, see Dobrovol'skij and Piirainen, *Figurative Language,* 131–35.

4. For example, the invariance principle states: "Metaphorical mappings preserve the cognitive topology (that is, the image–schema structure) of the source domain, in a way consistent with the inherent structure of the target domain." Also consider the "target–domain override" in which "the logic of the target ultimately constrains mappings from the source." Given that these axioms are supposed to be of universal application consider the metaphors: "He kicked the bucket." "He bought the farm." Or "I need to see a man about a dog." Like examples could be multiplied *ad nauseum.* Frequently, metaphorical examples do *not* preserve topology, and the "target–domain override" is merely a convenient apparatus for protecting the theory from its own weakness. See Lakoff, "Contemporary Theory of Metaphor," 215–16. One reason Lakoff appreciates neural theory is that "no theory of overrides is needed" (Lakoff and Johnson, *Metaphors We Live By,* 259).

Appendix D

Conceptual Integration Networks

Simplex Networks

SIMPLEX networks use some basic element of cultural or biological experience as a *framework* for other experiences at the simplest level. What makes the simplex network different from the others is that the organizing frame is drawn directly from experience and there is no conflict between the inputs or frames, and therefore "a simplex network does not look intuitively like a blend at all." Faucconier and Turner discuss the biological institution of "family" which organizes human experience. It is not merely the figurative usage of statements like, "He was a father to me," but more basically in the description of actual biological relationships. These relationships are mental constructions in themselves.[1] In short, a simplex network has no additional input spaces, no generic space, and no emergent structure.

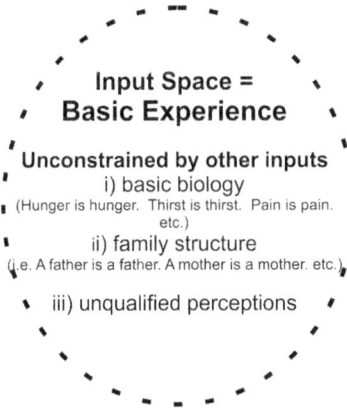

Figure 8. Simplex Network

---

1. Fauconnier and Turner, *Way We Think*, 120.

It is the most basic level in which former experiences are used to frame present perception.

Within the book of Proverbs, familial terminology can neatly be described as a simplex network. The reader understands the relationship between father, mother, and son by analogy with human experience in similar family constructions.

Mirror Networks

Mirror networks are similar to simplex networks in so far as that there are no clashes at the level of the framework itself. Elements within this frame should consistently function in paradigmatic ways, mirror networks retain the stability of the conceptual frame.[2] So for example, the statement "this lemonade is sweeter today than it was yesterday," compares today's lemonade with an imaginative construction of the same lemonade yesterday. The shifts that make the network functional happen in the *vital relations* that exist within the conceptual frame.[3] In the example above, the vital relations of *time* and *change* have been compressed in order to place yesterday's lemonade in the same frame with the present lemonade.

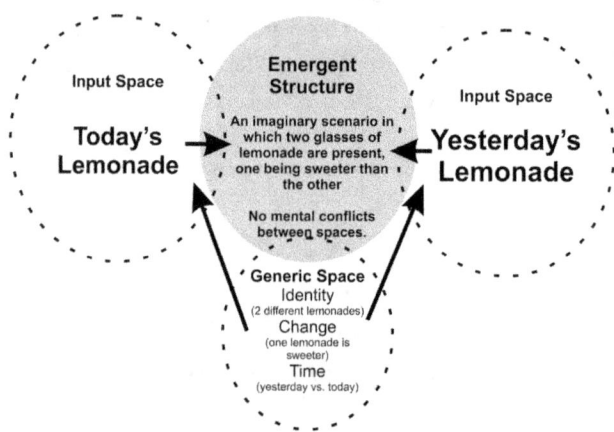

Figure 9. Mirror Network

2. Fauconnier and Turner, *Way We Think*, 122.

3. Vital relations include: Change, Identity, Time, Space, Cause–Effect, Part–Whole Representation, Role, Analogy, Disanalogy, Property, Similarity, Category, Intentionality and Uniqueness. Although there may be some question about the shades of meaning included within each these relations are helpful in discussing metaphorical function. See Fauconnier and Turner, *Way We Think*, 101.

Within the book of Proverbs an example of a mirror network function might be in the case of the repentant youth's confessions in the middle of chapter 5: "and at the end of your life you will groan, when your flesh and body are consumed, and you say, "Oh, how I hated discipline, and my heart despised reproof!" (Prov 5:11–12, NRS). In this case, the vital relations of identity, role, uniqueness, and space are maintained, but cause and effect and time are compressed within the frame of the young man's experience in order to highlight the disastrous outcomes of involvement with the *Strange Woman*.

Single Scope Networks

Single scope networks have two different cognitive frameworks and therefore two different sets of possible inputs. Our traditional formulation of metaphor is a single scope network. One input acts like the *source* domain containing the imagery and terminology that is used to describe the other input, which acts as the *target* space concept being described. What makes a single scope network different from a double scope network, is the fact that one frame (i.e. the source) is used to describe the other frame (i.e. the target). Analogy only moves in one direction and while a few elements of the comparison are drawn into sharp relief, others are compressed or omitted.[4] Ultimately the single scope network is not meant to enlighten the entire target and extending the network would lead to distortion.[5] So for example, fig. 2 (above), is an excellent example of a single scope network, in which the "sickness" space clarifies the entities and functions of the "computer" space. As such, the emergent structure of the blend is largely the transfer of the

---

4. Fauconnier and Turner, *Way We Think*, 126.

5. "Single-scope networks offer a highly visible type of conceptual clash, since the inputs have different frames. They are cases where the clash is dealt with by giving the overall organizational power of the network to only one of the input spaces, the framing input. In the typical case, the framing space has a prebuilt superb compression that is exploited to induce a compression for the focus input. Naturally, then, single-scope networks give us the feeling that 'one thing' is giving us insight into 'another thing,' with a strong asymmetry between them. This feeling of insight has three causes: The blend brings to bear inferences that are available from the framing input; it brings to bear useful compressions that already exist in the framing input; and it evokes emotions, seemingly anchored in the trustworthy framing input, that feel to us as if they are all-clarifying. As we have seen for blends in general, strong emotions emergent in the blend can induce the feeling of global insight, because the highly compressed blend remains actively connected to the entire network" (Fauconnier and Turner, *Way We Think*, 129).

"sickness" domain onto computer structure. In this case the second input does not requalify or shift any elements in the first.

Most of the sentence literature in Proverbs does not belong in this category, since every sentence contains *at least* two input spaces that frequently contain *numerous* conflicts in conceptual frame. Most elements of Proverbs that could be equated with a single scope network are implicit *basic* metaphors like LIFE IS A ROAD. In this case, "road" is used as the consistent and unqualified source which elucidates the abstract concept of "life."

Double Scope Networks

In double scope networks there are multiple and frequently *conflicting* frames which are blended to yield a novel output. The example given by Turner and Faucconier is the saying: "You are digging your own grave." On the surface the saying seems to be a simple, single scope network where the imagery and concepts of death and burial are imported onto the present situation. However, as the authors point out, only in rare cases do people dig their own graves, and usually digging the grave does *not* result in death. Here the present situation, which includes elements of "unwitting failure" are being imported and blended with what would have otherwise been deemed simply the source category.

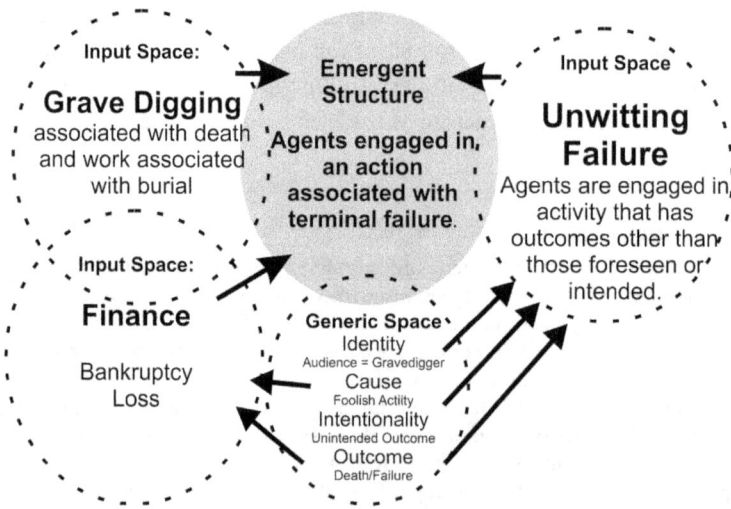

Figure 10. Double Scope Network

The person in question is *not intending* to dig their own grave by their present activity, and therefore elicits the dire warning. The blend creates a number of clashes that we generally overlook when we consider a blend. The people who dig graves do not normally do so for themselves. Digging a grave does not normally *cause* death as this saying implies. Yet by virtue of the imaginative blend of unwitting failure and grave, hearers equate the grave with death, and associate the agent's process of digging as self-destructive. This blend can then be almost infinitely combined with other elements like "finance" or "relationship" that would employ these blends to those particular target areas with similar motivation, but different ends.[6]

Within the book of Proverbs the most pertinent double scope network is personification of the abstract concept of wisdom as a woman in Prov 1–9 and 31. The use of woman as a frame to describe wisdom is unambiguous throughout, although many frames are included and therefore clash. *Lady Wisdom* calls out to relate to men in public places, and invites all men to her house (Prov 1:21; 9:4), such conduct would not be applauded in a "normal woman" or wife. In Prov 8:12ff divine qualities are attributed to *Lady Wisdom*. Simultaneously, however, very similar qualities and accolades are associated with the "Woman of Valor" in Prov 31:10ff. Source and target spaces are both conflicting and mutually informative.

---

6. Fauconnier and Turner, *Way We Think*, 131–35.

Appendix E

Fruit of Their Roads

LADY Wisdom's metaphor, "they will eat of the fruit of their roads," is a novel extension of Deuteronomic and prophetic retribution metaphors. The initial metaphorical image of Prov 1:31 is of fruit, and the basic metaphor that accompanies that image is something like, FRUIT IS CONSEQUENCE. This metaphor is perhaps as an extension of the planting metaphor generally, i.e. that what is sown will yield harvest in kind.[1] Outside of Proverbs, this metaphor is mostly in the Prophets.[2] However, in those cases the "fruit" metaphor is then extended in novel ways, first by the addition of "eating" and "satiety" elements.

The placement of "they will eat" and "they will be sated" at the extremity of the two cola of Prov 1:31 makes for beautiful syntax. However, the inclusion of both verbs also points to a conceptual metaphor that occurs in numerous contexts in the Tanakh. The initial eating metaphor likely had something to do with the promises of Israel entering the land, of divine blessing that would guarantee not only satiety, but blessing upon the production of the land.[3] The eating metaphor is extended in the direction of "apathy produced by satiety," where the ample produce and satiety of the Israelites produces not joy and gratitude, but rather indifference and faithlessness.[4]

---

1. For example, Hosea 10:13 uses the full "planting to reaping" scheme for the metaphor.

2. There are nine cases of "fruit" (ירפ) in construct relating figuratively to actions or consequences: Prov 1:31; 8:19; 11:30; 12:14; 13:2; 18:20–21; 31:16, 31. Outside of Proverbs there about the same number of cases localized in Isaiah, Jeremiah, and the book of the twelve: Isa 3:10; 10:12; Jer 6:19; 17:10; 21:14; 32:19; Amos 6:12; Mic 7:13.

3. See Ps 5:11; 81:13; Prov 22:20; Jer 7:24; Hos 4; 11:6; Mic 6:16; 2 Chr 31:10; Neh 9:25; Isa 9:19; 35:30; 65:13; etc. The notion of eating and satiety as a figure for divine blessing is also represented in the Psalms (e.g., Ps 22:27; 59:16; 78:25, 29; 81:17).

4. The conceptual metaphors of eating and consumption are most vividly developed

In a turnabout "eater becomes eaten." The whole notion of "devouring" and "being devoured" become key elements in the prophetic corpus. However, there are few if any cases where *what* is equal to the product of judgment. One near case, involves a proverbial saying provided in Ezekiel 18, where "the fathers have eaten sour grapes and the childrens' teeth are set on edge." However, this saying deals more with generational consequences. The nearest parallel to this metaphor is found in Isaiah 3:10–11.

> 10 אִמְרוּ צַדִּיק כִּי־טוֹב כִּי־פְרִי מַעַלְלֵיהֶם יֹאכֵלוּ׃
>
> Say (mp) (to the) righteous one: indeed good. Because the fruit of their deeds they will eat.
>
> 11 אוֹי לְרָשָׁע רָע כִּי־גְמוּל יָדָיו יֵעָשֶׂה לּוֹ׃
>
> Woe to the wicked: bad, because the accomplishment of his hands will be done to him.

However, our poet is not done with the changes. While he employs the "fruit" metaphor and the "eating and satiety" metaphor as expressed in Isaiah, he does not employ "fruit of their deeds" or any other conventional association. Rather the poet invents something entirely novel, "the fruit of their roads." First, this construction appears nowhere else in Tanakh. Second, while the "road" metaphor is lexically associated with the fruit metaphor, even in the passages listed (cf. Jer 17:10; 32:19; Hos 10:13), the metaphors are never mixed in this way. The *LIFE IS A ROAD* metaphor is used as another figure. Here, alone in scripture, the two metaphors are precisely blended.

---

in Deut 28–32, but also in Isa 1:19–20.

Bibliography

Albright, W. F. "The Goddess of Life and Wisdom." *AJSL* 36 (1920) 258–94.
Aletti, Jean Noel. "Seduction et Parole en Proverbes I–IX." *Vetus Testamentum* 27.2 (1977) 129–44.
Alt, A. "Zur literarische Analyse der Weisheit des Amenemope." *SVT* 3 (1955) 16–25.
Anselm of Canterbury. "Proslogion." In *The Prayers and Meditations of Saint Anselm*, translated by Benedicta Ward, 238–47. Harmondsworth: Penguin, 1973.
Aristotle. *Analytica Posteria*. Vol. 1 of *The Works of Aristotle Translated into English*. Edited by W. D. Ross. Translated by G. Mure. Oxford: Clarendon, 1910.
———. *The Complete Works of Aristotle*. Edited by Jonathan Barnes. 2 vols. Princeton, NJ: Princeton University Press, 1983.
———. *The Poetics: Translated with a Critical Text*. Translated by S. H. Butcher. London: Macmillan, 1895.
———. *Posterior Analytics* and *Topica*. Translated by Hugh Tredennick and E. S. Forster. London: Heienemann, 1960.
———. *Rhetoric*. Translated by Rhys Roberts. New York: Modern Library. 1954.
Assman, Jan. *The Mind of Egypt: History and Meaning in the Time of the Pharaohs*. New York: Metropolitan, 2002.
Augustine. *Confessions*. Translated by Garry Wills. New York: Penguin, 2006.
———. *Sermons*. Vol. 3.5 of *The Works of Saint Augustine: A Translation for the Twenty-First Century*. Edited by John Roselle. Translated by Edmund Hill. Hyde Park, NY: New City, 1992.
———. *The Trinity*. Vol. 1.5 of *The Works of Saint Augustine: A Translation for the Twenty-First Century*. Edited by John Roselle. Translated by Edmund Hill. Hyde Park, NY: New City, 1991.
Balthasar, Hans Urs von. *The Realm of Metaphysics in Antiquity*. Vol. 4 of *The Glory of the Lord: A Theological Aesthetics*. Translated by Brian McNeal, et al. San Francisco: Ignatius, 1989.
———. *Seeing the Form*. Vol. 1 of *The Glory of the Lord: A Theological Aesthetics*. Translated by Erasmo Leiva-Merkakis. San Francisco: Ignatius, 1982.
Barr, James. *Comparative Philology and the Text of the Old Testament*. Winona Lake, IN: Eisenbrauns, 1987.
Barth, Karl. *The Doctrine of Creation*. Vol. 3/2 of *Church Dogmatics*. Edited by W. Bromiley and T. Torrence. Translated by H. Knight et al. Edinburgh: T&T Clark, 1960.

———. *The Doctrine of God*. Vol. 2 of *Church Dogmatics*. Edited by G. W. Bromiley, et al. Edinburgh: T&T Clark, 1957.
Bauer-Kayatz, Christa. *Studien zu Proverbien 1–9. Wissenschaftliche Monographien zum alten und neuen Testament 22*. Neukirchen-Vluyn: Neukirchener, 1966.
Baumgartner, A. *Etudes critiques sur l'état du texte du Livre des Proverbes*. Leipzig: W. Drugulin. 1890.
Baumgartner, W. *Israelitische und altorientalische Weisheit*. Tübingen: J.C.B. Mohr, 1933.
Bautch, Richard J., and Jean-François Racine eds. *Beauty and the Bible: Toward a Hermeneutics of Biblical Aesthetics*. Atlanta: SBL, 2013.
Bentley, Jerry H. *Humanists and Holy Writ: New Testament Scholarship in the Renaissance*. Princeton, NJ: Princeton University Press, 1983.
Berg, George Olaf. *Metaphor and Comparison in the Dialogues of Plato*. Berlin: Mayer and Müller, 1903.
Berlin, Adele. *The Dynamics of Biblical Parallelism*. Bloomington, IN: Indiana University Press, 1992.
Bernat, David A. "Biblical Waṣfs beyond Song of Songs." *JSOT* 28.3 (2004) 327–49.
Bewer, Julius A. "Two Suggestions on Prov 30:31 and Zech 9:16." *JBL* 67.1 (1948) 61–62.
Bielfeldt, Dennis. "Luther, Metaphor, and Theological Language." *Modern Theology* 6.2 (1990) 121–35.
Black, Peter. "The Broken Wings of Eros: Christian Ethics and the Denial of Desire." *Theological Studies* 64 (2003)106–26.
Black, Max. *The Labyrinth of Language*. New York: Frederick A. Praeger, 1968.
———. *Language and Philosophy: Studies in Method*. Ithaca, NY: Cornell University Press, 1949.
———. *Models and Metaphors*. Ithaca, NY: Cornell University Press, 1962.
Boman, Thorleif. *Hebrew Thought Compared with Greek*. New York: Norton, 1970.
Boström, Gustav. *Proverbiastudien: Die Weisheit und das Fremd Weib in Spr 1–9*. LUA N.F. Avd. 1. Vol. 30.3. Lund: Gleerup, 1935.
Botterweck, Johannes, and Helmer Ringgren, eds. *Theological Dictionary of the Old Testament*. 14 vols. Grand Rapids: Eerdmans, 1974.
Boys-Stones, G. R. *Metaphor, Allegory and the Classical Tradition: Ancient Thought and Modern Revisions*. Oxford: Oxford University Press, 2003.
Brown, William P. *Character in Crisis: A Fresh Approach to the Wisdom Literature of the Old Testament*. Grand Rapids: Eerdmans, 1996.
———. "The Didactic Power of Metaphor in the Aphoristic Sayings of Proverbs." *JSOT* 29.2 (2005) 133–54.
———. *Seeing the Psalms: A Theology of Metaphor*. London: Westminster John Knox, 2002.
Budge, E. A. Wallis. *The Teaching of Amen-em-apt, Son of Kanekht*. London: Hopkinson, 1924.
Bultmann, Rudolph. *Glauben und Verstehen*, Vol. 2. 2nd ed. Tübingen: J.C.B. Mohr, 1958.
Bunimovits, Shelomoh, and Zvi Lederman. "The Archaeology of border Communities: renewed Excavations at Tel Beth-Shemesh." *Near Eastern Archaeology* 72.3 (2009) 114–42.
Butcher, Samuel Henry, *Aristotle's Theory of Poetry and Fine Art: With a Critical Text and Translation of Poetics*. London: Macmillan, 1895.

Cajetan, Cardinal. *The Analogy of Names.* Pittsburgh: Duquesne University Press, 1953.
Camp, Claudia V. *Wisdom and the Feminine in the Book of Proverbs.* Sheffield: Almond, 1985.
———. *Wise, Strange, and Holy: The Strange Woman and the Making of the Bible.* Sheffield: Sheffield Academic, 2000.
Carbajosa, Ignacio. *Faith the Fount of Exegesis: The Interpretation of Scripture in Light of the History of Research on the Old Testament.* San Francisco: Ignatius, 2011.
Carr, David. "Gender and the Shaping of Desire in the Song of Songs and its Interpretation." *JBL* 119.2 (2000) 233–48.
Carson, D. A. *The Gospel According to John.* Grand Rapids: Eerdmans, 1990.
Chisholm, Robert B., Jr. "'Drink Water from your own Cistern': A Literary Study of Proverbs 5:15–23." *Bibliotheca Sacra* 157.628 (2000) 397–409.
Clifford, Richard, ed. *Wisdom Literature in Mesopotamia and Israel.* Houston: SBL, 2007.
Colloque de Strasbourg. *Les sagesses du proche-orient ancient.* Paris: Presses Universitaires de France, 1963.
Collins, Billie Jean. "Pigs at the Gate: Hittite pig Sacrifice in its eastern Mediterranean Context." *Journal of Ancient Near Eastern Religions* 6 (2006) 155–88.
Copeland, Rita C., and Peter T. Struck, eds. *The Cambridge Companion to Allegory.* Cambridge: Cambridge University Press, 2010.
Crenshaw, James L. "Method in Determining Wisdom Influence upon Historical Literature." *Journal of Biblical Literature* 88.2 (1969) 129–42.
———. "A Mother's Instruction to Her Son (Proverbs 31:1–9)." *Perspectives in Religious Studies* 15.4 (1988) 9–22.
———. *Old Testament Wisdom: An Introduction.* 3rd ed. Louisville: Westminster John Knox, 2010.
———, ed. *Studies in Ancient Israelite Wisdom.* New York: KTAV, 1976.
———, ed. *Theodicy in the Old Testament.* London: SPCK/Philadelphia: Fortress, 1983.
Crüsemann, F., et al., eds. *Dem Tod nicht glauben. Sozialgeschichte der Bibel. Festschrift für Luise Schottrof zum 70. Geburtstag.* Gütersloh: Gütersloh Verlagshaus, 2006.
Dillard, Raymond B., and Tremper Longman III. *An Introduction to the Old Testament.* Grand Rapids: Zondervan, 1994
Dobrovol'skij, Dmitirj, and Elisabeth Piirainen. *Figurative Language: Cross-Cultural and Cross Linguistic Perspectives.* Amsterdam: Elsevier, 2005.
Doll, P. *Menschenschöpfung und Weltschäpfung in der alttestamentlichen Weisheit.* Stuttgarter Bibel-Studien 117. Stuttgart: Verlag Katholisches Bibelwerk, 1985.
Ebert, Daniel. *Wisdom Christology: How Jesus Became God's Wisdom for Us.* Kindle edition. Phillipsburg, NJ: P & R, 2011.
Edwards, Jonathan. *Ethical Writings.* Vol. 8. Edited by Paul Ramsey. New Haven: Yale, 1989.
Eissfeldt, Otto. *Der Maschal im Alten Testament. Eine wortgeschichtliche Untersuchung nebst einer literargeschichtlichen Untersuchung der lvm gennanten Gattungen 'Volkssprichwort' und 'Spottlied.'* BZAW 24. Giessen: Töpelmann, 1913.
Enns, Phil. "To What Does the Bible Refer? On Metaphor and Analogy." *The Conrad Grebel Review* 23.3 (2005) 63–73.
Erman, Adolf. "Das Weishetsbuch des Amen-em-ope." *OLZ* 27 (1924) 241–52.
———. "Eine ägyptische Quelle der 'Sprüche Salomos.'" *SPAW* 15 (1924) 86–93.
Exum, Cheryl. *Song of Songs.* Louisville: Westminster John Knox, 2005.

Fauconnier, Gilles. *Mappings in Thought and Language*. Cambridge, MA: Cambridge University Press, 1997.

———. *Mental Spaces: Aspects of Meaning Construction in Natural Language*. Cambridge, MA: Cambridge University Press, 1994.

Fauconnier, Gilles, and Mark Turner. *The Way We Think: Conceptual Blending and the Mind's Hidden Complexities*. New York: Basic, 2002.

Feintuch, Yossi. "Beauty in the Bible." *Jewish Bible Quarterly* 31.4 (2003) 249–51.

Fokkelman, J. P. *Reading Biblical Narrative: An Introductory Guide*. Louisville: Westminster John Knox, 1999.

Fontaine, Carole R. "The Proof of the Pudding: Proverbs and Gender in the Performance Arena." *JSOT* 29.2 (2005) 179–204.

———. *Smooth Words: Women, Proverbs, and Performance in Biblical Wisdom*. London: Sheffield Academic, 2002.

———. *Traditional Sayings in the Old Testament*. Sheffield: Almond, 1982.

———. "Wisdom traditions in the Hebrew Bible." *Dialogue* 33.1 (2000) 101–17.

Fox, Michael V. "Ideas of Wisdom in Proverbs 1–9." *JBL* 116.4 (1997) 613–33.

———. *Proverbs 1–9: A New Translation with Introduction and Commentary*. New Haven: Yale University Press, 2000.

———. *Proverbs 10–31: A New Translation with Introduction and Commentary*. New Haven: Yale University Press, 2009.

———. "Scholia to Canticles (1:4b, 2:4, 1:4ba, 4:3, 5:8, 6:12)." *Vetus Testamentum* 33.2 (1983) 199–206.

———. *The Song of Songs and the Ancient Egyptian Love Songs*. Madison, WI: University of Wisconsin Press, 1985.

Freedman, David Noel. "Proverbs 2 and 31: A Study in Structural Complementarity." In *Tehillah le-Moshe*, edited by Mordecai Cogan, et al., 47–55. Winona Lake, IN: Eisenbrauns, 1997.

Gadamer, Hans-Georg. *Truth and Method*. New York: Bloomsbury Academic, 1975.

Gammie, J. G., et al., eds., *Israelite Wisdom: Theological and Literary Essays in Honor of Samuel Terrien*. Missoula, MT: Scholars, 1978.

Garrett, Stephen. "God's Beauty-In-Act: An Artful Renewal of Human Imagining." *International Journal of Systematic Theology* 14 (2012) 459–79.

———. *God's Beauty-In-Act: Participating in God's Suffering Glory*. Kindle edition. Eugene, OR: Pickwick, 2013.

Garrone, Daniele, and Felice Israel, eds. *Storia e tradizioni di Israele: scritti in onore di J Alberto Soggin*. Brescia: Paideia Editrice, 1991.

Gemser, B. *Spüche Salomos*. HAT 16. Tübingen: J.C.B. Mohr, 1963.

Gerstenberger, E. *Wesen und Herkunft des "apodiktischen Rechts."* WMANT 20. Neukirchen-Vluyn: Neukirchener Verlag, 1965.

Gese, Helmut. *Lehre und Wirklichkeit in der alten Weisheit*. Tübingen: Mohr/Siebeck, 1958.

Gibbs, Raymond W., and Gerard J. Steen, eds. *Metaphor in Cognitive Linguistics: Selected Papers from the Fifth International Cognitive Linguistics Conference; Amsterdam, July 1997*. Amsterdam: John Benjamins, 1997.

Ginsberg, Christian, ed. *The Massorah: Compiled from Manuscripts*. 3 vols. London: Brög, 1880.

Goldingay, John. "Proverbs V and IX." *Revue Biblique* 84.1 (1977) 80–93.

Griffith, Susan Blackburn. "Unwrapping the Word: Metaphor in the Augustinian Imagination." *Studiapatristica* 18 (2013) 213–20.
Grimm, Karl. "The Form tārōnnâ Prov. i.20; viii.3." *JBL* 21 (1902) 192–96.
Grohman, M. "Fruchtbarkeit und Geburt in den Psalmen." *FAT* 53. Tübingen: Mohr/Siebeck, 2007.
Gutstein, Naphtali. "Proverbs 31:10–31: The Woman of Valor as Allegory." *Jewish Bible Quarterly* 27.1 (1999) 36–39.
Guttenplan, Samuel. *Objects of Metaphor*. Oxford: Oxford University Press, 2005.
Habel, N. C. "The Symbolism of Wisdom in Proverbs 1–9." *Interpretation* 26 (1972) 131–56.
Harris, Scott L. *Proverbs 1–9: A Study in Inner-Biblical Interpretation*. Atlanta: Scholars, 1995.
Hawkins, Tom R. "The Wife of Noble Character in Proverbs 31:10–31." *Bibliotheca Sacra* 153.609 (1996) 12–23.
Hecke, Pierre van. *Metaphor in the Hebrew Bible*. Dudley, MA: Peeters, 2005.
Heim, Knut Martin. "A Closer Look at the Pig in Proverbs xi 22." *Vetus Testamentum* 58.1 (2008) 13–27.
———. *Poetic Imagination in Proverbs: Variant Repetitions and the Nature of Poetry*. BBR Supplement 4. Winona Lake, IN: Eisenbrauns, 2013.
Hermisson, H. J. *Studien zur israelitischen Spruchweisheit*. WMANT 28. Neukirchen-Vluyn: Neukirchener Verlag, 1968.
Hesse, Mary. "Aristotle's Logic of Analogy." *Philosophical Quarterly* 15 (1965) 238–40.
———. *Models and Analogies in Science*. Notre Dame, IN: Notre Dame Press, 1966.
Hickok, Gregroy. *The Myth of Mirror Neurons: The Real Neuroscience of Communication and Cognition*. New York: Norton, 2014.
Hill, Andrew. *Haggai, Zechariah, Malachi*. Kindle ed. Westmont, IL: IVP, 2015.
Hochschild, Joshua P. *The Semantics of Analogy: Rereading Cajetan's De Nominum Analogia*. Notre Dame, IN: University of Notre Dame Press, 2010.
Holcomb, Justin, ed. *Christian Theologies of Scripture: A Comparative Introduction*. New York: New York University Press, 2006.
Holladay, William L. *Jeremiah*. Minneapolis: Fortress, 1986.
Hurowitz, Victor. "The Seventh Pillar—Reconsidering the Literary Structure and Unity of Proverbs 31." *Zeitschrift für Die Alttestamentliche Wissenschaft* 113.2 (2001) 209–18.
Imray, Kathryn. "Love Is (Strong As) Death: Reading the Song of Songs through Proverbs 1–9." *CBQ* 75.4 (2013) 649–65.
Johnson, Mark, ed. *Philosophical Perspectives on Metaphor*. Minneapolis: University of Minnesota Press, 1981.
Johnson, Mark, and George Lakoff. *Metaphors We Live By*. Chicago: University of Chicago Press, 1980.
Jones, Scott C. "Wisdom's Pedagogy: a Comparison of Proverbs vii and 4Q184." *Vetus Testamentum* 53.1 (2003) 65–80.
Joüon, Paul. "Les Temps dans Proverbes 31, 10–31 (La Femme Forte)." *Biblica* 3.3 (1922) 349–52.
Joüon, Paul, and T. Muraoka. *A Grammar of Biblical Hebrew*. Rome: Editrice Pontificio Istituto Biblico, 2008.

Kayatz, Christa. *Studien Zu Proverbien 1–9: Eine form- und motivesgeschichtliche Untersuchung unter Einbeziehung ägzptischen Vergleichsmaterials*. Assen, Netherlands: Neukirchener Verlag, 1966.
Keck, Leeander, et al., eds. *The New Interpreter's Bible*. Vol. 5. Nashville: Abingdon, 1997.
Keel, Othmar. *The Song of Songs*. Translated by Fredrick J. Gaiser. Minneapolis: Fortress, 1986.
———. *The Symbolism of the Biblical World: Ancient Near Eastern Iconography and the Book of Psalms*. Translated by Timothy Hallet. Winona Lake, IN: Eisenbrauns, 1997.
Kinzie, Mary. *A Poet's Guide to Poetry*. Chicago: University of Chicago Press, 1999.
Koch, K. "Gibt es ein Vergeltungsdogma im Alten Testament?" *ZTK* 52 (1955) 1–42. Reprinted as "Um das Prinzip der Vergeltung in Religionn und Recht des Alten Testaments." In *Wege der Forschung*, edited by K. Koch, 125. Darmstadt: Wissenschaftliche Buchgesellschaft, 1972.
Kohler, Ludwig, and Walter Baumgartner. *The Hebrew and Aramaic Lexicon of the Old Testament*. Translated by M. E. J. Richardson. Leiden: Brill, 1999.
Kövecses, Zoltán. "Anger: Its Language, Conceptualization, and Physiology in Light of Cross-Cultural Evidence." In *Language and the Cognitive Construal of the World*, edited by John Taylor and Robert MacLaury, 153–80. Berlin: de Gruyter, 1995.
———. "The 'Container' Metaphor of Anger in English, Chinese, Japanese, and Hungarian." In *From a Metaphorical Point of View*, edited by Zdravko Radman, 117–48. Berlin: de Gruyter, 1995.
———. *Metaphor: A Practical Introduction*. Oxford: Oxford University Press, 2002.
Kretzmann, Norman, and Eleonore Stump. *The Cambridge Companion to Aquinas*. Cambridge: Cambridge University Press, 1993.
Kruger, Paul A. "Promiscuity or Marriage Fidelity: A Note on Prov 5:15–18." *Journal of Northwest Semitic Languages* 13 (1987) 61–68.
Lakoff, George. *Women, Fire, and Dangerous Things: What Categories Reveal about the Mind*. Chicago: University of Chicago Press, 1987.
Lakoff, George, and Zoltán Kövecses. "The Cognitive Model of Anger inherent in American English." In *Cultural Models in Language and Thought*, edited by D. Holland and N. Quinn, 195–221. Cambridge: Cambridge University Press, 1987.
Lakoff, George, and Mark Turner. *More Than Cool Reason: A Field Guide to Poetic Metaphor*. Chicago: University of Chicago Press, 1989.
Lambdin, Thomas O. "Egyptian Loan Words in the Old Testament." *Journal of the American Oriental Society* 73.3 (1953) 145–55.
Lang, Bernhard. *Frau Weisheit: Deutung einer biblischen Gestalt*. Düsseldorf: Patmos, 1975.
———. *Wisdom and the Book of Proverbs: An Israelite Goddess Redefined*. New York: Pilgrim, 1986.
———. "Women's Work, Household, and Property in Two Mediterranean Societies: A Comparative Essay on Proverbs xxxi 10–31." *Vetus Testamentum* 54.2 (2004) 188–207.
Lavere, George. "Metaphor and Symbol in St Augustine's De Civitate Dei." In *Augustine, Second Founder of the Faith*, edited by Joseph Schnaubelt and Frederick Van Fleteren, 225–43. Collectanea Augustiniana. New York: Peter Lang, 1990.
Lewis, C. S. *An Experiment in Criticism*. Cambridge: University of Cambridge Press, 1961.

———. *God in the Dock: Essays on Theology and Ethics.* Grand Rapids: Eerdmans, 1995.

Lichtenstein, Murray H. "Chiasm and Symmetry in Proverbs 31." *CBQ* 44.2 (1982) 202–11.

Lipiński, Edward. "Juges 5:4–5 et Psaume 68:8–11." *Biblica* 48.2 (1967) 185–206.

Lloyd, G. E. R. *Aristotelian Explorations.* Cambridge: Cambridge University Press, 1996.

Loader, Alfred James. *Proverbs 1–9.* Leuven: Peeters, 2014.

Locke, John. *Essay Concerning Human Understanding.* New York: Dover, 1959.

Long, V. Phillips. *Art of Biblical History.* Grand Rapids: Zondervan, 1994.

Longman, Tremper, III. *Proverbs.* Grand Rapids: Baker Academic, 2006.

———. *Song of Songs.* Grand Rapids: Eerdmans, 2001.

Longman, Tremper, III, and Peter Enns, eds. *Dictionary of the Old Testament. Wisdom, Poetry & Writings.* Downers Grove, IL: InterVarsity, 2008.

Maasen, Sabine, and Peter Weingart. *Metaphors and the Dynamics of Knowledge.* New York: Routledge, 2000.

McCreesh, Thomas. *Biblical Sound and Sense: Poetic Sound Patterns in Proverbs 10–29.* Sheffield: JSOT, 1991.

McFague, Sallie. "Parable, Metaphor, and Theology." *JAAR* 42.4 (1974) 630–45.

McGarty, Craig, et al. *Stereotypes as Explanations: The Formation of Meaningful Beliefs about Social Groups.* Cambridge: Cambridge University Press, 2002.

McGilchrist, Ian. *The Divided Brain and the Search for Meaning: Why Are We So Unhappy?* Kindle ed. London: Yale University Press, 2012.

———. *Master and His Emissary: The Divided Brain and the Making of the Western World.* London: Yale University Press, 2009.

McGrath, Allister. *A Fine-Tuned Universe: The Quest for God in Science and Technology.* 2009 Gifford Lectures. Louisville: Westminster John Knox, 2009.

Meinhold, A. *Die Sprüche.* 2 vols. Zürcher Bibelkommentare AT 16.1/2. Zurich: Theologischer Verlag, 1991.

Meyers, Carol. *Rediscovering Eve: Ancient Israelite Women in Context.* Oxford: Oxford University Press, 2012.

Mieder, Wolfgang. *Proverbs: A Handbook.* Greenwood Folklore Handbooks. Westport, CT: Greenwood, 2004.

———, ed. *Wise Words: Essays on the Proverb.* Garland Folklore Casebooks. New York: Garland, 1994.

Miller, Patrick. "Apotropaic Imagery in Proverbs 6:20–22." *Journal of Near Eastern Studies* 29 (1970) 129–30.

Milne, A. A. *The Winnie-the-Pooh Storybook Treasury.* New York: Dutton, 2004.

Moore, R. D. "A Home for the Alien: Worldly Wisdom and Covenantal Confession in Proverbs 30:1–9." *ZAW* 106 (1994) 96–107.

Muis, J. (Jan). "Can Christian Talk About God Be Literal?" *Modern Theology* 27.4 (2011) 582–607.

Murphy, Roland E. *Proverbs.* Nashville: Thomas Nelson, 1998.

———. *The Tree of Life: An Exploration of Biblical Wisdom Literature.* New York: Doubleday, 1990.

———. "Wisdom and Eros in Proverbs 1–9." *CBQ* 50.4 (1988) 600–603.

Neusner, Jacob. *The Babylonian Talmud: A Translation and Commentary.* Peabody, MA: Hendrickson, 2006. Electronic Resource.

Nogales, Patti D. *Metaphorically Speaking.* Stanford, CA: Center for the Study of Language and Information Publications, 1999.
Noppen, J. P. van. *Metaphor: A Bibliography of Post-1970 Publications.* Amsterdam: J. Benjamins, 1985.
O'Connell, Robert H. "Proverbs 7:16-17: a Case of Fatal Deception in a 'Woman and the Window' Type-scene." *Vetus Testamentum* 41.2 (1991) 235-41.
O'Connor, Michael. *Hebrew Verse Structure.* Winona Lake, IN: Eisenbrauns, 1980.
Oesterly, W. O. E. *The Wisdom of Egypt and the Old Testament in the Light of the Newly Discovered Teachings of Amen-em-Ope.* Whitefish, MT: Kessinger, 1992.
Ortony, Andrew, ed. *Metaphor and Thought.* Cambridge: Cambridge University Press, 1993.
Packer, James I., and Sven Soderlund. *The Way of Wisdom: Essays in Honor of Bruce K. Waltke.* Grand Rapids: Zondervan, 2000.
Paul, Martin. "Die 'fremde Frau' in Sprichwörter 1–9 und die 'Geliebte' des Hohenliedes Ein beitrag zur intertexualität." *Biblische Notizen* 106 (2001) 40-46.
Paxson, James. *The Poetics of Personification.* Cambridge: Cambridge University Press, 1994.
Peels, H. G. L. "Passion or Justice? The Interpretation of beyôm nāqām in Proverbs vi 34." *Vetus Testamentum* 44.2 (1994) 270-74.
Perdue, L. G. *Wisdom and Cult. A Critical Analysis of the View of Cult in the Wisdom Literatures of Israel and the Ancient Near East.* SBL Dissertation Series 30. Missoula, MT: Scholars, 1977.
Philips, Elaine. *An Introduction to Reading Biblical Wisdom Texts.* Peabody, MA: Hendricksen, 2017.
Porter, S. E., et al, eds. *Interpretation in Honour of Michael D. Goulder.* Leiden: Brill, 1994.
Prader, Andreas. *Venus at Her Mirror.* Munich: Prestel, 2002.
Preuss, H. D. "Das Gottesbild der älteren Weisheit Israels." *SVT* 23 (1972) 116-45.
Price, Ira Maurice. "Swine in Old Testament Taboo." *JBL* 44.1-2 (1925) 154-57.
Pritchard, James B. ed., *Ancient Near Easter Texts Relating to the Old Testament with Supplement.* New Jersey: Princeton University Press, 1969.
Punter, David. *Metaphor: The New Critical Idiom.* New York: Routledge, 2007.
Rad, Gerhard von, and James D. Martin. *Wisdom in Israel.* Nashville: Abingdon, 1972.
———. *Theologie des Alten Testaments I.* Munich: Kaiser Verlag, 1957.
Ringgren, Helmer. *Word and Wisdom: Studies the the Hypostatization of Divine Qualities and Functions in the Ancient Near East.* Lund: H. Ohlssons, 1947.
Roochnik, David. *Of Art and Wisdom: Plato's Understanding of Techne.* University Park, PA: Pennsylvania State University Press, 1996.
Ross, Allen P. *Malachi Then and Now: An Expository Commentary Based on Detailed Exegetical Analysis.* Kindle ed. Wooster, OH: Weaver, 2016.
Rothstein, David. "The Book of Proverbs and Inner-biblical Exegesis at Quran: The Evidence of Proverbs 24:23-29." *Zeitschrift Für Die Alttestamentliche Wissenschaft* 119.1 (2007) 75-85.
Schnabel, Eckhard J. *Law and Wisdom from Ben Sira to Paul: A Tradition-Historical Inquiry into the Relation between Law, Wisdom, and Ethics.* Tübingen: J. C. B. Mohr, 1985.

Schottroff, Luise, and Marie-Theres Wacker, eds. *Feminist Biblical Interpretation: A Compendium of Critical Commentary on the Books of the Bible and Related Literature*. Grand Rapids: Eerdmans, 2012.
Schroer, Silvia. *Wisdom Has Built Her House: Studies on the Figure of Sophia in the Bible*. Collegeville, MN: Liturgical, 2000.
Seitz, Christopher R. *Figured Out: Typology and Providence in Christian Scripture*. Louisville: Westminster John Knox, 2001.
———. *The Goodly Fellowship of the Prophets: The Achievement of Association in Canon Formation*. Grand Rapids: Baker, 2009.
———. *Prophecy and Hermeneutics: Toward a New Introduction to the Prophets*. Grand Rapids: Baker, 2007.
Shibbles, Warren. *Essays on Metaphor*. Whitewater, WI: Language, 1972.
———. *Metaphor: An Annotated Bibliography and History*. Whitewater, WI: Language, 1971.
Shupak, Nili. "Female Imagery in Proverbs 1–9 in the Light of Egyptian Sources." *Vetus Testamentum* 61.2 (2011) 310–23.
———. *Where Can Wisdom be found? The Sage's Language in Bible and in Ancient Egyptian Literature*. Fribourg, Switzerland: Vandenhoeck & Ruprecht, 1993.
Siquans, Agnethe. "Israel braucht starke Frauen und Männer: Rut als Anwort auf Spr 31,10–31." *Biblische Zeitschrift* 56.1 (2012) 20–38.
Skehan, Patrick William. "Proverbs 5:15–19 and 6:20–24." *CBQ* 8.3 (1946) 290–97.
———. "The Seven Columns of Wisdom's House in Proverbs 1–9." *CBQ* 9.2 (1947) 190–98.
———. "Structures in Poems on Wisdom: Proverbs 8 and Sirach 24." *CBQ* 41 (1979) 365–79.
Soskice, Janet. *Metaphor and Religious Language*. Oxford: Clarendon, 1987.
Spacks, Patricia. *Boredom: The Literary History of a State of Mind*. Chicago: University of Chicago Press, 1995.
Spiegelberg, W. "Agyptische Lehnworter in der alteren griechischen Sprache." *ZVS* 41 (1907) 127–32.
Steiert, F. J. *Die Weisheit Israels—ein Fremdkörper im Alten Testament?—Eine Untersuchung zum Buch der Sprüche auf dem Hintergrund der ägzptischen Weishetslehren*. Freiburger Theologische Studien 134. Freiburg: Herder, 1990.
Stone, Timothy J. *The Compilational History of the Megilloth: Canon, Contoured Intertextuality and Meaning in the Writings*. Tübingen: Mohr/Siebeck, 2013.
Struck, Peter. *Birth of the Symbol: Ancient Readers at the Limits of Their Texts*. Princeton: Princeton University Press, 2004.
Stump, Eleonore, and Norman Kretzmann, eds. *The Cambridge Companion to Augustine*. Cambridge: Cambridge University Press, 2001.
Swain, Scott. "The Mystery of the Trinity." *Credo Magazine* 3.2 (2013) 26–33.
Szlos, M. Beth. "A Portrait of Power: A Literary-Critical Study of the Depiction of the Woman in Proverbs 31:10–31." *Union Seminary Quarterly Review* 54.1–2 (2000) 97–103.
Tan, Nancy Nam Hoon. "Where is Foreign Wisdom to be Found in Septuagint Proverbs?" *CBQ* 70.4 (2008) 699–708.
Toy, C. H. *The Book of Proverbs*. Edinburgh: T&T Clark, 1977.
Treier, Daniel J. *Proverbs and Ecclesiastes*. Kindle ed. Grand Rapids: Brazos, 2011.
Turbayne, Colin Murray. *The Myth of Metaphor*. London: Yale University Press, 1962.

Van Leeuwen, Raymond. "Building God's House: An Exploration in Wisdom." In *Way of Wisdom: Essays in Honor of Bruce K. Waltke*, edited by J. I. Packer and Sven Soderlund, 204–211. Grand Rapids: Zondervan, 2000.

———. "Liminality and Worldview in Proverbs 1–9." *Semeia* 50 (1990) 111–44.

VanGemeren, Willem, ed. *New International Dictionary of Old Testament Theology and Exegesis*. 5 vols. Grand Rapids: Zondervan, 2012.

Vanhoozer, Kevin, ed. *Dictionary for Theological Interpretation of the Bible*. Grand Rapids: Baker, 2005

Vaught, Carl G. *Metaphor, Analogy and the Place of Places: Where Religion and Philosophy Meet*. Waco, TX: Baylor University Press, 2004.

Vervaeke, J., and C. D. Green. "Metaphors in Language and Thought: Falsification and Multiple Meanings." *Metaphor and Symbolic Activity* 11 (1996) 273–84.

———. "Women, Fire, and Dangerous Theories: A Critique of Lakoff's Theory of Categorization." *Metaphor and Symbol* 12 (1997) 59–80.

Vio, Thomas De, Cardinal Cajetan. *The Analogy of Names and the Concept of Being*. Translated by Edward Bushinski & Henry Koren. Duquesne Studies: Philosophical Series 4. Pittsburgh: Duquesne University Press, 1953.

Vistotzky, Burton L. *The Midrash on Proverbs*. London: Yale University Press, 1992.

Waard, Jan de, et al. *Megilloth*. Stuttgart: Deutsche Bibelgesellschaft, 2006.

———. *Proverbs*. Stuttgart: Deutsche Bibelgesellschaft, 2008.

Waltke, Bruce K. "The Authority of Proverbs: An Exposition of Proverbs 1:2–6." *Presbyterion* 13.2 (1987) 65–78.

———. *The Book of Proverbs: Chapters 1–15*. Grand Rapids: Eerdmans, 2004.

———. *The Book of Proverbs: Chapters 15–31*. Grand Rapids: Eerdmans, 2005.

———. "The Book of Proverbs and Old Testament Theology." *Bibliotheca Sacra* 136.544 (1979) 302–17.

———. "*Lady Wisdom* as a Mediatrix: An Exposition of Proverbs 1:20–33." *Presbyterion* 14.1 (1988) 1–15.

Weeks, Stuart. *Instruction and Imagery in Proverbs 1–9*. Oxford: Oxford University Press, 2007.

Whitman, Jon. *Allegory: The Dynamics of an Ancient and Medieval Technique*. Cambridge: Harvard University Press, 1987.

Whybray, Roger N. *The Book of Proverbs: A Modern Survey*. HBI 1. Leiden: Brill, 1995.

———. "Some Literary Problems in Proverbs 1–9." *Vetus Testamentum* 16.4 (1966) 482–96.

———. *Wisdom in Proverbs: The Concept of Wisdom in Proverbs 1–9*. London: SCM, 1965.

Wolde, Ellen van. *Reframing Biblical Studies: When Language and Text Meet Culture, Cognition and Context*. Winona Lake, IN: Eisenbrauns, 2009.

Wolff, H. W., ed. *Probleme biblischer Theologie. Gerhard von Rad zum 70. Geburtstag*. Munich: Kaiser Verlag, 1971.

Wolters, Albert M. "Nature and Grace in the Interpretation of Proverbs 31:10–31." *Calvin Theological Journal* 19.2 (1984) 153–66.

———. "Proverbs 31:10–31 as Heroic Hymn: A Form-critical Analysis." *Vetus Testamentum* 38.4 (1988) 446–57.

Wright, Robert J. *Proverbs, Ecclesiastes, Song of Solomon. Ancient Christian Commentary on Scripture*. Downers Grove, IL: InterVarsity, 2005.

Xenophon. *Memorabilia and Oeconomicus*. Translated by E.C. Marchant. Cambridge: Harvard University Press, 2013.
Yee, Gale A. "'I have perfumed my bed with myrrh': The Foreign Woman ('iššâ zārâ) in Proverbs 1–9." *JSOT* 43 (1989) 53–68.
Yoder, Christine Roy. "On the Threshold of Kingship: A Study of Agur (Proverbs 30)." *Interpretation* 63.3 (2009) 254–63.
———. *Wisdom as a Woman of Substance: A Socioeconomic Reading of Proverbs 1–9 and 31:10–31*. BZAW 304. Berlin: Walter de Gruyter, 2001.
———. "The Woman of Substance ('ŠT-ḤYL): A Socioeconomic Reading of Proverbs 31:10–31." *JBL* 122.3 (2003) 427–47.
Young, Frances. *God's Presence: A Contemporary Recapitulation of Early Christianity*. Cambridge: Cambridge University Press, 2013.
Zabán, Bálint Károly. *The Pillar Function of the Speeches of Wisdom: Proverbs 1:20–33, 8:1–36; and 9:1–6 in the Structural Framework of Proverbs 1–9*. Berlin: De Gruyter, 2012.

Author Index

Aletti, J.N., 202, 210-12
Anselm of Canterbury, 61
Augustine (of Hippo), 42, 159
Albright, W.F., 11-12
Alt, A., 9
Aquinas, T., 68
Aristotle, 26-31, 33-35, 237-38
Assman, J., 228

Balthasar, H. U. Von, 22, 23, 56, 59-70, 113-15, 157-59, 223
Barth, Karl, 55-56, 157
Baumgartner, W., 8, 152
Bauer-Kayatz, C., 10, 12-13
Bentley, J., 33
Berlin, I., 46
Black, M., 26
Black, P., 232
Boström, G., 12, 136
Brown, W., 228
Budge, E.W., 7, 12
Bultmann, R., 54

Camp, C., 16-18, 19, 135-36, 176
Carbajosa, I., 50-51
Carson, D.A., 159-62
Childs, B., 229
Chisolm, R., 122, 142
Clifford, R., 136

Dobrovol'skij, D., 70-71, 73, 244
Doll, P., 10

Ebert, D., 213-18
Edwards, J., 57-58

Eissfeldt, O., 9
Erman, A., 7

Fauconnier, G., 80-82, 241, 245-49
Fontaine, C., 16
Fox, M., 14, 85, 86, 87, 89, 90, 91-92, 95, 97, 98-99, 120, 121, 122, 123, 124, 125, 126, 128, 129, 136, 137, 138, 139, 142, 143, 144, 151, 152, 153, 168, 169, 170, 172, 173, 175, 176, 177, 178, 179, 180, 181, 182, 183, 184, 185, 186, 187, 188, 189, 190, 191, 196, 197, 198, 203, 204, 206

Garrett, S., 54, 56, 57, 60, 65, 68, 223-24
Gemser, B., 143
Gerstenberger, E., 10,
Gese, H., 10, 14,
Ginsberg, A., 202
Gressman, H., 7
Grimm, K., 85
Guttenplan. S., 25-26

Habel, N.C., 136
Heim, K. M., 11
Hermisson, H.J., 8, 10
Hesse, M., 30
Hickok, G., 242
Hill, A., 132-34
Hochschild, J., 26, 29, 30
Holladay, W., 146, 147

Jäkel, O., 239-42

AUTHOR INDEX

Johnson, M., 30, 33, 71-75, 76-79, 80-82, 83, 224, 240, 241, 242, 243, 244
Joüon, P., 90

Kayatz, C., 179
Keel, O., 228
Koch, K., 9, 10
Kövecses, Z., 244

Lakoff, G., 30, 32-33, 71-75, 76-79, 83, 149, 224, 240, 241, 242, 243, 244
Lang, B., 13-14, 208
Loader, A., 76, 86, 89, 94, 95, 96-97, 98, 101, 103, 104, 105, 106, 109, 111-12, 137, 137, 139, 168, 169, 170, 171, 173, 174, 175, 176, 177, 178, 179, 180, 182, 183, 185, 186, 187, 188, 190, 196-97, 203
Locke, J., 239
Lloyd, G.E.R., 28-29, 31-32
Longman, T., 88, 106, 112

McGarty, C., 75-76
McGilchrist, I., 24, 35-52, 58-59, 61, 62-63, 69, 111, 155-56
McGrath, A., 42, 44
Meinhold, A., 9, 11, 106, 122, 143, 169, 174, 185
Milne, A.A., ix
Moore, R.D., 10
Muraoka, T., 90
Murphy, R., 8, 85, 86, 88, 89, 90, 120, 122, 123, 124, 125, 136, 151, 174, 180, 181, 182, 183, 188, 195
Murray, J.M., 25

Noppen, J.P. van, 25

Oesterly, W., 8

Peels, H.G.L., 131
Piirainen, E., 70-71, 73, 244
Plöger, J., 9, 90, 136,
Prader, A., 3-4. 234-35
Preuss, H.D., 9

Punter, D., 25

Rad, G. von, 8, 10, 14, 230-31
Ross, A., 140
Roy Yoder, C., 15-16, 136
Ringgren, H., 12, 190, 203

Schroer, S., 17
Seitz, C., 230
Shibbles, W., 33
Shupak, N., 14-15
Skehan, P., 174, 208
Soskice, J., 26
Spacks, P., 49
Stanford, W., 25
Steiert, F.J., 9
Struck, P., 34
Swain, S., 215-16

Tocqueville, A. de, 46
Toy, C.H., 89, 169, 173, 190, 191, 203
Turner, M., 245-49

Van Leeuwen, R.., 11, 96, 100, 104-5, 110, 112, 170, 171, 173, 178, 188, 197, 209
Vistotzky, B., 6

Waltke, B., 9, 85, 86, 87, 88, 90, 91, 92, 93-94, 97, 98, 120, 121, 122, 123, 124-25, 126, 127-28, 129-30, 131, 142, 143, 151, 152, 153, 154, 168, 169, 171, 172, 173, 175, 176, 177, 178, 179, 180, 181, 183, 184, 185, 186, 187, 188, 189, 190, 191, 203
Weeks, S., 18-19, 76, 92, 134, 138-39, 194, 195, 196, 204
Whybray, R., 7-9, 103
Wright, R., 6

Xenophon, 212

Young, F., 233

Zabán, K., 175,
Zimmerli, W., 10,

Scripture Index

Old Testament

Genesis — 153

1	185
1:1	186
1:7	184, 187
1:16	186
1:21	186
1:25–27	186
2:4	186
2:7	186
2:24	133
3:19	186
3:24	175
4:1	182
4:15	153
4:24	153
7:11	184
8:2	184
9:27	175
14:13	175
14:20	109
14:24	179
15:1	109
16:5	123
17:12	149
17:27	149
18:19	90
19:4	130
19:21	131
24:14	90
25:18	175
26:19	146
27:13	200
28:20	200
30:29	179
30:33	179
31:15	135, 136
32:21	131
33:15	179
34:19	185
35:2	135
35:4	135
37–50	111
38:14	94
39:8	179
41:55	129
42:23	91
42:33	179
43:8	179
43:16	179
44:28	179
43:33	182
44:34	179
49:3	182
49:17	169
50:20	111

Exodus — 138, 153

2:22	135, 136, 154
2:23	154
3:14	195
4:25	129
9:23	168
14:4	185

Exodus (continued)

14:17–18	185
18:3	135
12:43	135
18:3	136
19:11	186
20:1–7	112
20:14	151
20:15	151, 153
20:17	151–52
20:23	179
21:8	135
22:3	153
22:8	153
24:5	199
26:25	124
27:3	128
28:29	151
29:28	199
29:45	175
30:9	135
30:33	135
31:16	90
31:3	86
33:14	217
33:23	179
34: 11–16	138
34:16	138

Leviticus

3:1	199
3:3	199
3:6	199
3:9	199
4	199
4:10	199
4:26	199
4:31	199
4:35	199
6:19	205
7	199
7:11	199
7:13	199
7:15	199
7:18	199
7:20–21	199
7:29	199
7:32	199
7:34	199
7:37	199
10:1	128, 135
10:3	185
14:5	146
16:17	128
17:5	199
18:10	131
19:5	199
19:11	153
19:15	131
20:10	130, 131, 152
20:18	144
22:3	138
22:10	135
22:12–13	135
22:21	199
22:25	135
23:19	199
26:28	153

Numbers

1:51	135
3:4	135
3:10	135
3:38	135
5:12–29	207
6:17–18	199
7:17	199
7:23	199
7:29	199
7:35	199
7:41	199
7:47	199
7:53	199
7:59	199
7:65	199
7:71	199
7:77	199
7:83	199
7:88	199

SCRIPTURE INDEX 269

10:10	199	25:58	185
11:13	197	28–32	250–51
14:17	110	28:4	121
15:8	199	28:13	90
17:5	135	28:15	90
18:4	135	28:50	131
18:7	135	28:65–67	87
21:15	90	29:21	135
22:15	185	30:10	90
22:37	168	30:19–20	133
23:13	179	31:16	135
24:7	142	32:4–5	171
25:2	138	32:5	172
26:61	135	32:15	125
30	200	32:16	137
30:9	200	32:18	184
		33:12	175
		33:15	185
		33:29	109

Deuteronomy 87, 138, 161,

4:5–6	20
4:37	88
5:18	151
5:19	152, 153
5:21	151, 152
5:26	146
6	125
6:4–7	126
6:7	151
6:8	150
6:6–9	150
7:1–5	138
7:25	152
8:3	161
10:17	131
11:18–20	151
11:22	151
12:2	185
12:22	131
13:19	90
14:21	135
15:3	135
15:5	90
17:5	135
22:24	152
23:21	135
24:7	152

Joshua

6:19	181
8:5	179
14:12	179
22:23	199
22:27	199
24:20	135
24:23	135, 199

Judges 138

1:3	179
2:1–3	138
2:3	97
2:21	101
4:18	193
4:22	193
5	164, 192–94, 226
5:8	108
5:10	126, 169
5:28	193
7:18	179
9:3	90
9:19	121

Judges (continued)

10:16	135
11:27	179
11:30–31	200
16:15	179
17:2	193
18:6	124
19:12	135
19:16	185

Ruth   6, 15, 111, 228

1:15	138
2:10	135, 136
4:16	123

1 Samuel

1:14	96
1:16	126
3:7	91
6:12	169
7:3	135
9:6	185
10:8	199
11:15	199
12:17	90, 168
13:2	185
14:33	90, 191
15:13	147
16:5	179
17:9	179
19:3	170
19:5	90
22:14	185
22:23	179
24:19	179
25:35	131
26:6	179
26:14	168
26:26	168
28:1	179
29:3	179
29:6	179

2 Samuel

1:21	108
2:22	131
3:12	179
6:20	185
6:22	185
9	111–12
12:8	123
12:13	123
14:9	200
15:19	135
15:33	179
17:14	112
19:34	193
19:39	193
22:3	109
22:14	168
22:17	172
22:31	109
22:36	109
22:45–46	135
23:19	185
23:23	185

1 Kings

1:3	90
1:30	88
2	111–12
3:11	179
3:13	179
3:18	135
5:31	196
6:37	196
7:10	196
7:51	181
8:41	135
8:43	135
8:62–66	197
8:63	199
10:17	108
11:1	135, 136, 137
11:8	135, 136, 137, 138
12:24	179
13:7	179

SCRIPTURE INDEX 271

13:15	179	12:9–10	108
14:8	90	14:2	135
14:26–27	108, 181	14:7	108
17:19	123	17:5	179
18:21	110	17:17	108
18:27	126	18:1	179
20:36	179, 197	18:23	179
22:4	179	22:1	88
22:24	179	23:9	108
22:36	170	24:9	168
		26:14	108
		28:13	214
		30:22	199
		31:10	250

2 Kings

		32:5	108
3:7	179	32:27	108, 179
5:1	131	33:15	135
9:30	128	33:16	199
9:32	131, 179		
10:16	179		
14:10	185		

Ezra 15–16

18:31	179
19:24	135
19:32	108

3:10	196
9	138
10:2	135–37
10:10–11	135–37
10:12	200
10:14	135–37
10:17–18	135–37
10:44	135–37

1 Chronicles

4:9	185
4:41	88
5:18	108
11:21	185
11:25	185
15:29	128
18:17	170
21:12	130
23:28	170
29:12	179
29:28	179

Nehemiah 15–16, 137

4:10	108
9:2	135
9:25	250
11:24	170
13:25	138
13:26	135–37
13:27	135–37
13:30	135
Esther	111, 228
1:1	127
2:7	197
2:20	197
1:4	179

2 Chronicles

1:11–12	179
6:32–33	135
9:7	190
9:16	108
11:4	179

Nehemiah (continued)

1:11	127
5:11	179

Job   195–96

1:5	200–201
3	210
3:18	97
3:21	91
3:25	87
4:19	175
5:13	172
5:24	191
6:13	92
7:11	101, 126
7:13	126
9:6	184
9:8	196
9:27	126
10:1	126
10:11	183
11:6	92
11:15	131
12:13	177
12:16	92
15:19	135
15:26	108
19:4	179
19:12	169
19:15	134, 135
19:23	178
19:27	31:3
22:8	131
22:14	184, 187
22:28	169
24:15	130
26:3	92
26:7	185
26:10	187
28	230
28:11	185
28:28	176
29:7	170
31:3	135
31:35	101
31:36	126
32:21	131
34:19	131
34:34	101
38:5–6	196
38:6	185
38:9	188
38:11	188
38:16	184
39:1	122
40:19	182
41:7	108

Psalms   100, 126, 184, 195, 201, 250

2:4	100
2:6	183
3:4	109
5:11	250
6:4	96
7:9	200
7:11	109
8:4	196
11:4	128
12:7	153
14:4	168
16:8	126
16:9	175
18:3	109
18:10	196
18:8	184, 185
18:16	184, 185
18:14	168
18:28	172
18:31	109
18:36	109
18:45–46	135
19:3	99
22:6	201
22:27	250
28:7	109
33:20	109
34:4	179
35:2	109

36:7	184	90:17	200
36:10	146	104:2	196
38:11	179	104:12	168
42:2	122	104:34	126
45	202	106:3	190
45:12	127	109:2	179
47:10	109	109:4	189
49:17	179	109:11	135
50:2	127	109:21	179
50:14	201	114:4	185
50:18	130	114:6	185
52:7	128	115:9–11	109
53:5	168	116:14	201
54:5	135	116:18	201
56:13	201	119	188–89
59:9	100	119:24	189
59:12	109	119:36	907
59:16	250	119:77	189
61:9	201	119:92	189
65:2	201	119:114	109
65:11	122	119:143	189
66:13	201	119:174	189
66:20	179	120:7	189
68:27	146	127:2	105
69:9	135	128:3–4	121
71:22	101	132:4	128
72:3	185	137:4	135
74:10	96	139:13	182, 183
74:14	188	140:6	170
75:4	184	141:4	170
76:4	109	144:2	109
77:4	126	144:4	135
77:7	126	144:11	135
77:13	126	148:3–5	186
78:25	250	148:9	185
78:29	250	149:8	185
79:12	153		
80:5	96		
81:10	135		
81:12–14	101, 102		
81:13	250		
81:17	250		
84:10	109		
84:12	109		
87:3	185		
89:19	109		
90:2	183, 184, 185		
90:13	96		

Proverbs

1–9	1–5, 11–20, 22, 106, 143, 172, 197–98, 204, 210, 211, 212, 216, 222, 249
1–4	131–32, 162, 164, 192,
1	77, 82, 87, 169, 226

Proverbs (*continued*)

1:1–7	176, 203
1:2–3	205
1:2	176, 203–6
1:3	176
1:5	182, 204
1:6	203–6
1:7	176, 205
1:8	125, 204, 205
1:10	191, 211
1:11	200
1:11–14	211
1:12	207
1:13	211
1:14	195
1:15	79
1:20–33	83–89, 94–102, 106–117, 224
1:20	186
1:21	249
1:21–1:22	194
1:22	194, 199
1:23	99
1:26	101
1:28	194
1:31	180, 250
1:32–33	210
1:33	175
2	103, 105
2:1–11	84–85, 89–83, 102–6, 106–117, 224
2:1	204
2:3	168
2:4	194
2:7	109
2:8	92, 108, 109, 150
2:10	194
2:11	92, 108
2:15	176
2:16	54, 135, 136
2:17	127, 137, 150
2:18–19	206
2:18	79, 207
2:19	126
2:21	175
2:21–22	210
3–4	150
3	21, 87
3:1	92, 150
3:3	150
3:7–8	195
3:11	205
3:14–16	194
3:14	180, 190
3:15	118, 174, 179
3:16	179
3:17	176
3:18	210
3:19–20	194
3:19	196
3:20	184
3:21	92, 150
3:22	195
3:23	79
3:24–25	87
3:26	92
3:27–27	195
3:32	171
3:32–35	210
4	21
4:1	204, 205
4:3	195
4:4	124–25
4:5–9	110–11
4:5–6	54
4:5–10	118
4:5	182
4:6	92, 150
4:6–8	21
4:7	182
4:8	123, 210
4:9	126
4:10	204
4:12	79
4:13	92, 150, 205, 210
4:18–19	210
4:23	150
4:25	124, 128
5–9	159–60, 163, 164
5–6	132, 162, 192
5	6, 134, 144, 199, 226
5:1–2	194
5:2	924
5:3	127, 135, 150, 171

SCRIPTURE INDEX

5:5	79, 125, 206	7	54, 130, 134, 144, 164–66, 199, 203, 204, 211
5:5–6	207		
5:6	126		
5:7	190, 204	7:3	150
5:9–14	127	7:4	13, 194
5:10	136	7:5	135, 136
5:11–12	247	7:6–21	164–66, 166–67, 191–92, 192–202, 205, 206–8, 226
5:12	205		
5:13	204		
5:14	195	7:6	192–93
5:15	210	7:11	85
5:15–23	54, 118–20, 120–25, 131–48, 154–63, 225	7:12	94, 120, 143, 186
		7:13	210
5:16	186	7:14–15	209
5:17	135	7:14	199
5:17–18	195	7:15	101, 193
5:18–20	144	7:18–19	201–2
5:18	140, 144, 145, 155	7:18	122, 144, 202, 211
5:19	122, 126, 202, 211	7:21	204
5:20	128, 135, 136, 146	7:22–23	124, 128
5:21	124	7:22	205
5:22	124–25	7:23	79
5:23	119	7:24	190, 204
6	154	7:25–27	207–8
6:1	135	7:26–27	193–94
6:4	128	7:26	206
6:9	96	7:27	79, 92, 206
6:11	109	8	21, 164–66, 168–91, 191–92, 196, 199, 203–5, 205, 208–210, 210–21, 226, 228, 231
6:16	171		
6:20–35	118–20, 125–31, 148–54, 154–63, 225		
6:20–22	151	8:1	194
6:20	92	8:2	85, 194
6:21	150	8:3	170
6:22	79, 151	8:4	217
6:23	205	8:4–5	194
6:24–35	54	8:5–6	203
6:24–26	124	8:6–14	194
6:24	119, 136, 150	8:7	171
6:25	127, 151, 152, 155, 204	8:8	171, 172
		8:10–11	194
6:26	151	8:10	203, 205
6:27	128 149–50	8:12	194, 249
6:29	119, 126, 151, 152	8:14	194
6:30–31	151–52, 153	8:15–16	194
6:32	136, 139, 141, 151		
6:34	131		
6:35	131		

Proverbs (*continued*)

Reference	Pages
8:17	181, 194
8:18–19	194
8:18	179
8:19	180, 250
8:21	181, 194, 211
8:21–32	195
8:22–30	194
8:22	194
8:24	185
8:25	185
8:30	190, 195, 226
8:32	181, 190, 199, 226
8:32–8:36	210
8:32–34	204
8:33	203, 205
8:34	190
8:35	118
9	205, 210, 211, 226
9:3	170
9:4	164, 199, 205, 211, 249
9:5	216
9:6	199
9:13	21, 85
9:14	94, 170
9:15	211
9:16	164, 205
9:17	144, 161, 210
10:1–31:31	190
10:2	109, 181, 147
10:6	147
10:7	147
10:11	146
10:17	207
10:21	125
10:22	147
10:30	175
11:1	171
11:11	147, 170
11:16	179
11:20	171
11:26	147
11:30	180, 250
11:31	191
12:8	195
12:14	180, 250
12:22	171
12:24	195
12:26	207
12:28	79, 206
13:2	180, 250
13:6	92
13:9	126
13:19	171, 195
13:22	191
13:14	80, 146
13:20–21	181
13:21	191
13:22	181
14:10	135
14:12	80, 92, 206
14:21	191
14:22	207
14:23	195
14:26	195
14:27	80, 146
14:28	178
14:35	195
15:3	124
15:8–9	171
15:8	209
15:10	125
15:16	181
15:26	171
15:32	182
16:5	171
16:10–16	178
16:12	171
16:16	176, 182
16:17	92
16:22	146
16:25	80, 206
16:28	137
17:9	137
17:15	171
17:16	182
17:23	128
18:2	90
18:5	131
18:7	79
18:9	130
18:15	182
18:20–21	180, 250

18:22	118, 123, 191
19:2	191
19:8	182
19:10	178
19:12	178
19:14	118
19:16	125
19:19	90
20:2	191
20:10	171
20:14	182
20:16	136
20:20	126
20:23	171
20:25	79
20:27	126
20:28	92
21:3	209
21:6	79, 181
21:14	128
21:16	207
21:20	181
21:23	209
21:24	126
21:27	171
22:4	179
22:9	147
22:12	92
22:13	186
22:14	144
22:17–24:22	7–8
22:19	195
22:20	250
22:24–25	204
22:25	79
22:26	195
22:29	178
23:4	173
23:13	125
23:17–18	90
23:17	191
23:20	195
23:23	182
23:26	92
23:27	136, 144
23:28	194
23:34	195
24:1	195
24:9	171
24:11	80
24:12	92
24:20	126, 195
24:21	178
24:27	186
24:28	195
24:32	204
24:34	109
25:1–7	178
25:15	212
25:22	128
26:5	195
26:25	171
27:2	136
27:10	135
27:13	136
27:18	92, 180
27:28	92
28:7	92
28:9	171
28:20	147
28:24	130
29:4	178
29:7	204
29:14	178
29:21	195
29:25	79
29:27	171
30:5	109
30:20	130
30:31	178
31	6, 15, 143, 226, 249
31:4	178
31:10	118, 173, 249
31:14	195
31:16	180, 250
31:18	126
31:30	127, 176
31:31	180, 250

Ecclesiastes 195

2:26	191
3:18–21	210

Ecclesiastes (continued)

6:2	135, 136, 179
7:25	194
7:26	191, 194
8:12	191
9:2	191
9:18	191

Song of Songs 141–44, 153–54, 163, 195, 202, 225

1:2	144
1:4	144
2:6	123
2:8	185
4:4	108
4:5	122
4:6	185
4:8	179
4:10	144
5:1	144, 202
7:2	144
7:9	144
7:12	201
8	162
8:2	144
8:3	137
8:6	131, 151
8:6–7	144
8:7	154

Isaiah 250

1:4	191
1:7	135
1:15	96, 97, 98, 101
1:16	160
1:19–20	250–51
11:23	86
2:2	185
2:6	135
2:7	181
2:14	185
3:5	185
3:10	89, 250
3:10–11	251
3:24	127
5:7	189
5:16	180
6:2	129
6:9	96
7:20	129
8	146
8:3	97
8:6–8	146
8:21	129
9:19	250
10:1	178
10:12	250
10:32	185
11:2	191
11:2–3	88
11:23	86
12:3	160
16:9	122
17:10	137
18:21	135
21:5	108
21:9	138
22:6	108
23:8–9	185
25:2	135
25:5	135
26:15	185
26:20	128
27:1	188
27:3	92
28:1–16	217
29:12–16	217–19
28:21	134, 135, 136
28:29	92
29:5	135
29:13	113
29:21	191
30:8	178
30:10	172
30:12	97
30:14	128
30:17	185
30:26	153
31:4	185

32:14	128	61:8-9	133
33:16	175	62:8	135
33:17	127	63:3	179
34:8	131	63:4	131
35:30	250	65:7	185
36:16	179	65:12	97
37:29	97	65:13	250
37:33	108	65:20	191
39:2	181	66:4	97, 101
40:4	185		
40:12	185		
40:22	184, 187, 196		
40:23	178		
40:26	186		
41:15	185		
42:15	185		
43:4	185	1:19	96
43:12	137	2	146. 148, 162
44:3	99, 160	2:1–4:4	146
44:24	179, 196	2:13	141–42, 145–46, 160
45:3	91	2:15	168
45:12	196	2:19	97
48:1	142	2:20–26	136
48:16	187	2:21	135, 136, 137
49:5	185	2:25	136, 137
49:9	169	2:30	130
50:8	179	3	137
51:4	179	3:2	169
51:6	88	3:4	137, 168
51:13	196	3:6	97
53:2	152	3:8	97
53:3	170	3:11–12	97
54:6	132	3:13	137
54:10	185	3:22	97
54:16	130	3:23	185
54:17	179	4:14	96
55:12	185	4:18	97
56:2	190	4:21	96
56:3	135	4:24	185
56:6	135	4:30	128
57:8	179	5:6	97
57:13	126, 130	5:8	152
59:12	99	5:19	135
59:14	172	5:26	130
60:10	135	6:16	169, 217
61:1	113	6:19	250
61:2	131	6:30	180
61:5	135		

Jeremiah 95, 96, 97, 132, 136, 137, 180, 218, 250

Jeremiah (continued)

7:13	96, 97
7:24	250
8:5	97
8:12	97
8:19	135
9:1	130
9:17	128
9:23–24	180
10:12	196
11:8	97
11:11	96, 97, 98, 101
11:14	96, 97, 101
13:25	179
14:7	97
15:13	181
15:19	96
16:16	185
16:32	137
17:10	89, 250, 251
17:13	146
17:16	124
17:23	97
18:11	96
18:14	135
20:7	96
20:11	179
21:14	89, 97, 250
22:20	168
23:6	175
23:10	130
24:7	93
25:5	96
25:7	97
25:30	168
30:8	135
30:10	97
30:18–19	197
31:14	122
31:20	189
31:22	96
31:29–34	160
31:31–34	93
31:35	178
32:19	250, 259
32:33	97
32:37–41	93
33:16	175
34:17	97
35:14	97
35:17	97
38:11	181
40:4	179
41:8	91
44:3	90
46:3	108
46:9	108
46:10	131
46:27	97
46:28	138
48:11	97
48:16	97
48:34	168
49:8	97
50:16	185
51:1	130
51:15	196
51:51	135
51:53	169, 179
52:3	126

Lamentations

2:15	127
2:19	124
3:20	206
4:5	197
5:2	134, 135

Ezekiel 132

3:7	96
3:24	179
6:3	185
6:13	185
7:21	135
8:18	96, 97, 101
11:9	135
14:3–4	124
14:7	124
16:8	122

16:14–15	127	47:9	160
16:18	202		
16:25	94, 127, 169		

Daniel

16:31	137
16:32	130, 137
16:38–63	137
16:38	131
18	251
18:4	191
18:6	152
18:11	152
18:15	152
18:20	191
20:23	101
21:26	169
21:36	130
22:11	152
23:3	138
23:17	122, 202
23:24	108
23:45	131
27:3–4	127
27:10	108
27:11	127
28:7	127, 135
28:10	135
28:12	127
28:17	127
28:22	185
30:12	135
31:8	127
31:12	135
33:10	200
33:26	152
33:31	113
34:6	185
35:8	185
36:4	185
36:6	185
36:25–27	160
36:27	93, 99
37:13	99
38:4–5	108
39:9	108
39:13	185
39:29	99
44:7	135
44:9	135

11:39	135

Hosea 88, 97, 132, 136

2	146
2:15	138
2:17	138
3:1	130
4	250
4:1–2	112
4:1	91
4:6	88
4:13	185
5:6	96, 97
5:7	137
6:4–6	88
6:6	91
7:4	130
7:9	137
8:1	96
8:5	96
8:7	135
8:9	122, 202
8:12	135
10:8	185
10:13	250, 251
11:6	250
11:7	97
13:7	169
14:1	138
14:5	97

Joel

2:11	168
2:28–32	160
3:1–2	99–100
4:16	168
4:17	135
4:18	142, 185

Amos

1:2	168
5:11	96
6:12	250
9:13	185

Obadiah

1:11	134, 135
1:12	135

Micah

2:2	154
3:4	97, 98
4:1	185
6:1	185
6:16	250
7:13	89, 250

Nahum

1:5	185
2:4	108
3:10	185

Habakkuk

2:10	191
3:6	185

Zephaniah

1:8	135
3:2	138

Haggai

1:8	185

Zecheriah

7:13	97, 127
8:5	197
12:1	196
14:8	160

Malachi 134

1:2	134
1:8	131
2	141, 162
2:5	134
2:6	179
2:11–12	139–41
2:11	135
2:14–15	132–34
2:14	134
2:15	121
3:5	130
4:4	134

New Testament

Matthew

1:23	113
4:23	114
5	116
5:1	114
6:8–10	112
6:11–13	112
6:24	173
6:25–34	116
7:7	113
7:24–29	115
9:6	115
9:35	114
11:20–25	216
11:25–30	215–19
11:28	116
11:29	165–66, 227
11:30	217
16:25	117
18:3–4	216

SCRIPTURE INDEX

19:14	216	4:29	162
19:30	116	4:34	223
20:16	116	5:24	115
20:27	116	5:26	65
20:29	114	5:43–47	114
21:13	219	6:38	223
23	114	6:65	57
23:4	217	8:42–47	223
26:39	223	8:42	117
		8:58	115
		10:37	115

Mark

		13:1	117
		14:1–7	219–20
1:39	114	14:26	115
2:10	115	15	115
3:7	114	16:14	65
7:6–7	113	17:23	117
8:35	117	18:20	114
10:44	116		
11:17	219		

Acts

Luke

4:28	116

1:67–79	113		
2:49	219	## Romans	
3:4	113		
4:15	114	8:20–33	58
4:44	114	8:29–30	116
5:24	115	8:32–34	116
9:24	117	8:38	58
10:38	114		
11:9–10	113		
14:26	116		
19:46	219	## 1 Corinthians	
24:19	113		
		1:18–21	117
		6:1–3	58
		13:11–12	58

John

		## Ephesians	
1:10–11	114		
1:12–13	116		
2:16–17	219	1:5	116
2:19–21	219	1:11	116
3:14–16	115	2:8	116
3:16	117		
4	157–63, 225–26		

Ephesians (continued)

5	119
5:17–33	158–59
6:12	58

Philippians

2:8	223

Hebrews

1:1–2	22
1:1–3	229
3:1–12	220

James

2:17	116

1 Peter

2:4–7	219–20

1 John

2:17	221
4:14	159
4:20	157

www.ingramcontent.com/pod-product-compliance
Lightning Source LLC
Chambersburg PA
CBHW061433300426
44114CB00014B/1670